Cognitive Therapy
with Children and Adolescents

Cognitive Therapy with Children and Adolescents

A Casebook for Clinical Practice

Edited by

Mark A. Reinecke
Frank M. Dattilio
Arthur Freeman

Foreword by Aaron T. Beck

THE GUILFORD PRESS
New York   London

© 1996 The Guilford Press
A Division of Guilford Publications, Inc.
72 Spring Street, New York, NY 10012

Printed in the United States of America

This book is printed on acid-free paper.

Last digit is print number: 9 8 7 6 5 4 3

Library of Congress Cataloging-in-Publication Data
Cognitive therapy with children and adolescents : a casebook
   for clinical practice / edited by Mark A. Reinecke, Frank
   M. Dattilio, Arthur Freeman; Foreword by Aaron T. Beck.
       p. cm.
   Includes bibliographical references and index.
   ISBN 1-57230-022-1
   1. Cognitive therapy for children.   2. Cognitive therapy for
   teenagers.   3. Cognitive therapy for children—Case studies.
   4. Cognitive therapy for teenagers—Case studies.
   I. Reinecke, Mark A.   II. Dattilio, Frank M.   III. Freeman,
   Arthur.
   RJ505.C63C65   1996
   618.92'89142—dc20   95-36991
                                                           CIP

Contributors

Mark A. Reinecke is Assistant Professor of Child and Adolescent Psychiatry and Director of the Center for Cognitive Therapy at the University of Chicago School of Medicine. His interests include childhood depression, suicide, anxiety disorders, and cognitive mediation of adjustment to chronic pediatric illness. He is the coauthor with Arthur Freeman of *Cognitive Therapy of Suicidal Behavior* and was a Fulbright Scholar recently as visiting lecturer at the Graduate School of Psychology of National Chengchi University, Taipei, Taiwan. Dr. Reinecke has published a number of chapters and papers on the cognitive-behavioral treatment of children and adolescents and has lectured throughout the world. He completed his undergraduate and early graduate work at Stanford University and his doctoral studies at Purdue University. He received his postdoctoral training at the Center for Cognitive Therapy, University of Pennsylvania.

Frank M. Dattilio received his Ph.D. from Temple University and is a Clinical Associate in Psychiatry at the Center for Cognitive Therapy, University of Pennsylvania School of Medicine. He is in the private practice of clinical psychology in Allentown, Pennsylvania, and is a licensed psychologist, listed in the National Register of Health Service Providers in Psychology. He is also a diplomate in behavioral psychology with the American Board of Professional Psychology and serves as a full adjunct Professor of Counseling Psychology at Lehigh University in Bethlehem, Pennsylvania. He is also a visiting professor and Fulbright lecturer at several major universities worldwide.

Dr. Dattilio trained in behavior therapy through the Department of Psychiatry at Temple University School of Medicine under the direction of Joseph Wolpe, M.D., and received his postdoctoral training through the Center for Cognitive Therapy, University of Pennsylvania School of Medicine under the direction of Aaron T. Beck, M.D. He has more than 70 professional publications in the areas of anxiety disorders, behavioral problems, and marital discord and has also presented extensively throughout the United States, Canada, Europe, Africa, South America, and Mexico on the treatment of anxiety disorders and marital discord. Among his many publications, Dr. Dattilio is coauthor of *Cognitive Therapy with Couples* and coeditor of *Comprehensive Casebook of Cognitive Therapy, Cognitive-Behavioral Strategies in Crisis Intervention,* and *Integrative Cases in Marriage and Family Therapy: A Cognitive-Behavioral Approach* (in preparation). He is also on the editorial board of several professional journals.

Arthur Freeman is in private practice in Philadelphia, Pennsylvania, and is the coordinator of the program in Professional Psychology at the Philadelphia College of Osteopathic Medicine, and Visiting Professor of Medical Psychology at Shanghai Second Medical University, People's Republic of China. He is a licensed psychologist and holds a diplomate in behavioral and clinical psychology from the American Board of Professional Psychology. In the past, he has served as a senior consultant to the Center for Cognitive Therapy at the University of Pennsylvania School of Medicine.

Freeman is a widely published author and editor. His published works include *Cognitive Therapy with Couples and Groups; Cognition and Psychotherapy; Depression and the Family; Cognitive Therapy: Applications in Psychiatric and Medical Settings; The Practice of Cognitive Therapy; Comprehensive Handbook of Cognitive Therapy; Woulda, Coulda, Shoulda; Clinical Applications of Cognitive Therapy; Cognitive Therapy of Personality Disorders; Comprehensive Casebook of Cognitive Therapy; Cognitive Therapy of Suicidal Behavior: A Treatment Manual;* and *Cognitive-Behavioral Strategies in Crisis Intervention.*

He is well known nationally and internationally for his seminars and has presented at a variety of local, regional, national, and international conferences. He has lectured in 15 countries over the past 5 years.

Arthur D. Anastopoulos is Associate Professor of Psychiatry and Pediatrics at the University of Massachusetts Medical Center, where he also serves as Chief of the Attention-Deficit/Hyperactivity Disorder (ADHD) Clinic. Dr. Anastopoulos has given numerous professional presentations and has authored journal articles, book chapters, and professional texts on ADHD, parent training, child assessment, and various other clinical child psychology topics.

Serena Ashmore-Callahan is a therapist at the Child and Adolescent Anxiety Disorders Clinic and a graduate student in the doctoral training program in Clinical Psychology at Temple University. Her research interests in the area of childhood anxiety include the effects of parental cognitions and emotions on parenting behaviors.

Christine L. Bankert is a doctoral student in the School Psychology Program at Lehigh University. Her research interests include parent tutoring and disruptive behavior disorders.

Wayne A. Bowers is Assistant Professor and Director of Psychological Services in the Department of Psychiatry at the University of Iowa. He was trained in cognitive therapy at the Center for Cognitive Therapy at the University of Pennsylvania. He has presented research at national and international conferences on the use of cognitive therapy with depressed inpatients. He has published in the area of cognitive therapy with depressed inpatients and is currently studying the efficacy of computerized cognitive therapy with depressed inpatients and cognitive therapy with inpatients diagnosed with anorexia nervosa.

Kathy L. Bradley is a doctoral student in school psychology and a research scientist for the Regional Consulting Center for Adolescents with Attention-Deficit Disorders at Lehigh University. Her research interests include assessment and self-management interventions for students with ADHD, and curriculum-based assessment.

David L. DuBois is an Assistant Professor of Psychology at the University of Missouri. He received his doctorate in clinical–community psychology from the University of Illinois in 1992 and completed his predoctoral internship at the University of Chicago in the Section of Child and Adolescent Psychiatry. Dr. DuBois's research interests include longitudinal studies of risk and resiliency among school-age children and adolescents, with a focus on the role of the self system in developmental pathways to health and disorder. He is also engaged in a series of studies involving the application of understandings gained from his research to the design, implementation, and evaluation of prevention programs for children, youth, and families.

Esther Deblinger is an Associate Professor of Clinical Psychiatry and Clinical Director of the Center for Children's Support at the University of Medicine and Dentistry of New Jersey—School of Osteopathic Medicine. Her areas of expertise are child sexual abuse and posttraumatic stress disorder. She has published and presented research on these and related topics nationwide.

George J. DuPaul is an Associate Professor in the School Psychology Program at Lehigh University. He has coauthored numerous publications regarding the assessment and treatment of children with ADHD. His current research interests include the school-based assessment and treatment of ADHD.

David J. A. Edwards was born in England and studied psychology at Oxford. He moved to South Africa in 1970 and completed his postgraduate studies at Rhodes University where he has been on the faculty since 1974. He completed his clinical internship at the University of Surrey in 1978 and was postdoctoral fellow at the Center for Cognitive Therapy at the University of Pennsylvania in 1984. He teaches cognitive therapy to students in clinical psychology and has published articles and book chapters on integrative approaches to cognitive therapy, including two on the use of guided imagery. For the past 5 years, he has taught case study research methodology to postgraduates and has published two book chapters on the subject. He is also one of the editors of an introductory psychology textbook for South African students in which he has authored the chapter on personality and coauthored the chapter on altered states of consciousness.

Norman Epstein received his Ph.D. in clinical psychology from the University of California at Los Angeles in 1974. He currently is Professor in the Department of Family Studies at the University of Maryland, College Park, and maintains a part-time private practice in Rockville, Maryland. He is a licensed psychologist, a Fellow of the American Psychological Association, and a clinical member of the American Association for Marriage and Family Therapy. He has published three books, including *Cognitive-Behavioral Marital Therapy*, as well as numerous book chapters and journal articles, with an emphasis on marital and family assessment and treatment.

Ruth A. Ervin is a doctoral student in the School Psychology Program at Lehigh University. Her research interests include disruptive behavior disorders and functional analysis of classroom behavior problems with an emphasis on proactive interventions.

Kay Evans is a Clinical Nursing Specialist II in the Department of Nursing, Psychiatric Division at the University of Iowa Hospitals and Clinics. She completed undergraduate and graduate degrees in nursing at the University of Iowa College of Nursing. Ms. Evans has worked in the mental health field since 1974 at the Menninger Foundation in Topeka, Kansas, and at the University of Iowa Hospitals and Clinics in Iowa City, Iowa. One of her specialty areas is in the treatment of patients with eating disorders.

Robert D. Felner is Director of the Center for Prevention Research and Development and Professor in the Institute of Government and Public Affairs at the University of Illinois. Previously, Dr. Felner served as Director of Clinical Training both at the University of Illinois and Auburn University and on the faculty of the Department of Psychology at Yale University.

He received his doctorate in clinical psychology from the University of Rochester in 1977. Dr. Felner has published extensively in the fields of child clinical and community psychology, particularly in the area of prevention initiatives for children and families at risk. He is currently the principal investigator on a large-scale national study of school restructuring and reform as a means of enhancing the developmental outcomes of children and youth, with funding from the Carnegie Corporation, Lilly Endowment, and Kellogg Foundation.

Barbara A. Fitzgerald is an Associate Professor in the Department of Psychiatry and Behavioral Sciences at the University of Louisville School of Medicine. She received her medical degree from Vanderbilt University in Nashville and completed her postgraduate residency in psychiatry at Vanderbilt, as well. She has been the Director of the Adolescent Inpatient Psychiatric Unit at Norton Hospital in Louisville since 1983.

Maribeth Gettinger is Professor in the School Psychology Program in the Department of Educational Psychology at the University of Wisconsin–Madison. She is also the Director of Research and Training at the Waisman Center Early Childhood Program. She received her doctorate from Columbia University in 1978. Her primary research interests are in learning disabilities, early childhood education, and effective teaching practices.

Nancy G. Guerra is an Associate Professor of Psychology at the University of Illinois at Chicago and the University of Michigan. She received her doctorate in human development from Harvard University. Her major research interests are prevention of antisocial behavior and the role of cognitive factors in the development of aggression and delinquency. She is the author of *Viewpoints Violence Prevention Curriculum* and has published numerous articles about aggression and delinquency.

Laura D. Hanish is a doctoral student in clinical and developmental psychology at the University of Illinois at Chicago. Her research interests include aggression and victimization among children, gender differences in children's social behavior, and social cognition. Her clinical interests include child and family therapy and the application of treatment techniques to urban and inner-city populations.

Susan Harter is a Professor of Psychology and Head of the Developmental Psychology Program at the University of Denver. She received her Ph.D. from Yale University in 1966. She remained at Yale, holding a joint appointment as an Assistant Professor in the Psychology Department and Chief Psychologist at the Yale Child Study Center until 1973, when she moved to Denver. Her research, supported by the National Institutes of Health, has focused on the development of a theoretical model of the causes, correlates, and consequences of self-esteem. This work has resulted in the construction of a battery of self-report measures in widespread use in this country and abroad.

Ann Hope Heflin is Assistant Professor of Clinical Psychiatry at the University of Medicine and Dentistry of New Jersey—School of Osteopathic Medicine. She is a clinical psychologist at the Center for Children's Support, a program devoted to the evaluation and treatment of child sexual abuse. Her research interests are in the areas of child sexual abuse and children's peer relationships.

Masaya Ichii is a lecturer and research associate at Waseda University in Tokorozawa, Japan. During the 1992–1993 academic year, he was a Rotary Scholar at Temple University, where he studied cognitive-behavioral treatments, anxiety and stress disorders, and cross-cultural influences on psychopathology and therapeutic process.

Philip C. Kendall is Professor of Psychology, Head of the Division of Clinical Psychology, and Director of the Child and Adolescent Anxiety Disorders Clinic at Temple University. He was president of the Association for Advancement of Behavior Therapy, and his research and clinical interests lie in cognitive-behavioral assessment and treatment, especially with children and adolescents. He has lectured throughout the United States, Canada, Europe, and South America.

Susan M. Knell is a licensed clinical psychologist and currently the Director of the Diagnostic Assessment Center of the Child Guidance Center of Greater Cleveland, Ohio. Dr. Knell holds appointments at Cleveland State and Case Western Reserve Universities. She developed the cognitive-behavioral approach to play therapy, and is the author of *Cognitive-Behavioral Play Therapy* and numerous articles in the area of child clinical psychology.

Margot R. Levin is a therapist and diagnostician at the Child and Adolescent Anxiety Disorders Clinic and a doctoral student in Clinical Psychology at Temple University. Her research interests in the area of child anxiety include how mothers of anxious children handle fearful situations with their children.

Catherine Lord is Professor of Psychiatry at the University of Chicago School of Medicine and is the Director of the Developmental Disorders Clinic in the Section of Child and Adolescent Psychiatry. She received her doctorate from Harvard University in 1976. Her primary research interests include autism and pervasive developmental disorders.

David F. O'Connell is a licensed psychologist with 15 years of experience treating chemically dependent patients. He is editor/author of three books on chemical dependency, a consulting psychologist for the Caron Foundation, and is in private practice in Reading, Pennsylvania.

Henry O. Patterson is Assistant Professor of Psychology at Pennsylvania State University in Reading, Pennsylvania. He has presented numerous papers at national conferences and has conducted research and authored journal articles on cognitive development in children and adolescents.

Alan J. Ravitz is Associate Professor of Clinical Psychiatry and Pediatrics at the University of Chicago. He is currently Director of Child and Adolescent Inpatient Psychiatry at the University of Chicago, and is Medical Director at HCA–Chicago Lakeshore Hospital. He received his masters degree in pharmacology and his medical degree from Michigan State University. His research interests center on the implications of attachment theory for custody evaluations and the uses of brief psychotherapy with inpatient children and adolescents.

Lynn P. Rehm received his bachelor's degree from the University of Southern California and his master's and doctorate degrees from the University of Wisconsin–Madison. He has been on the faculties of the University of California at Los Angeles Neuropsychiatric Institute in Psychiatry, University of Pittsburgh in psychology and psychiatry, and the University of Houston, where he is currently Professor of Psychology. Dr. Rehm's primary area of interest has been depression in adults and children. He is the developer of the Self-Management Treatment Program for depression, which has been adapted for diverse adult and child populations.

Christine D. Ruma is the Coordinator of the Sexual Abuse Treatment Team and Clinical Supervisor at the Child Guidance Center of Greater Cleveland, Ohio. She specializes in individual, group, and family treatment of children who have been sexually abused. She has published in the area of cognitive-behavioral play therapy with sexually abused children.

Stephen E. Schlesinger received his Ph.D. from the State University of New York at Buffalo. He is a licensed psychologist and maintains a private practice in clinical psychology. He is an Assistant Professor in the Department of Psychiatry and Behavioral Sciences of Northwestern University Medical School. His research and publications are in the areas of addictions, and marital and family therapy.

G. Randolph Schrodt Jr. received his M.D. and completed his psychiatric residency at the University of Louisville. He is currently the Medical Director of Outpatient Services and Partial Hospitalization Program at the Norton Psychiatric Clinic in Louisville, Kentucky. He is also Associate Professor of Psychiatry and Behavioral Sciences at the University of Louisville School of Medicine. Dr. Schrodt has written and lectured extensively on various applications of cognitive-behavioral therapy in medical and psychiatric settings.

Edward S. Shapiro is the Coordinator of the School Psychology Program at Lehigh University, Bethlehem, Pennsylvania, where he has been a Professor of School Psychology since 1980. He is editor of *School Psychology Review*, the official journal of the National Association of School Psychologists, and has numerous publications in the areas of curriculum-based assessment, behavioral assessment, behavioral interventions, and self-management with persons with developmental disabilities. Dr. Shapiro has published four books, including *Academic Skills Problems: Direct Assessment and Intervention*. He recently published his newest book *Behavior Change in the Classroom: Self-Management Interventions*, co-authored with Christine L. Cole.

Robbie N. Sharp received her bachelor's and master's degrees from Northeast Louisiana University and her doctorate from Tulane University. She has been employed in public schools in New Orleans and Houston and is currently on the faculty in the Departments of Psychiatry and Behavioral Sciences and Community Medicine, Allied Health Sciences at Baylor College of Medicine, Houston. Dr. Sharp's primary area of interest has been depression and attention deficits in children and adults, and gifted and talented children and adults. She is involved in community prevention research and advocacy in mental health issues.

Stephen Shirk is the Director of the Child Study Center at the University of Denver. He received his Ph.D. in clinical psychology from the New School for Social Research and completed his clinical training at the Judge Baker Children's Center and Children's Hospital in Boston. After serving as a Supervising Psychologist at Judge Baker and Clinical Director of the Family Development Clinic at Children's Hospital, he moved to Denver in 1987, where he directs the training clinic for the Clinical Child Psychology Program. The focus of his current research is on interpersonal processes in child psychotherapy and child psychopathology.

Patrick H. Tolan is an Associate Professor in the Departments of Psychiatry and Psychology at the University of Illinois at Chicago. He is also the Director of Research at the Institute for Juvenile Research. He is coeditor of the *Handbook of Clinical Research and Practice with Adolescents*, and his research interests include the prevention and prediction of antisocial behavior.

Catherine Trapani is Associate Professor of Clinical Psychiatry in the Department of Psychiatry at the University of Chicago. She is currently the Director of a Psycho-educational Evaluation Service (ASSET) and Director of Educational Psychology Services. She received her doctorate from the University of Wisconsin–Madison. Her primary interests are in the academic and behavioral assessment and intervention of children and youth with learning disabilities and severe conduct and behavior disorders.

Laura Van Cleve is a third-year resident in the Department of Psychiatry at the University of Iowa. She is interested in the treatment of eating disorders and schizophrenia. She has experience in the inpatient treatment of children, adolescents, and adults diagnosed with anorexia nervosa.

Foreword

As I reflect on the many domains that cognitive-behavioral therapy has influenced, I feel a true sense of satisfaction with the implementation of its strategies and techniques with children and adolescents. By the time adults finally engage in treatment, they have, in many cases, suffered from unnecessary disorders—sometimes for decades. A refreshing aspect about working with children and adolescents is that one can intervene with disorders that, in many cases, can be ameliorated early in life. Children and adolescents are often quite amenable to cognitive-behavioral interventions and often respond more quickly than adults. This may be due to their ability to be flexible and to the relatively briefer duration of their behavioral or emotional difficulties.

I am extremely pleased that Drs. Reinecke, Dattilio, and Freeman have embarked on assembling a casebook to address the needs of children and adolescents. The literature is surprisingly lacking in this area, especially with regard to the presentation and analysis of case material.

The chapters selected highlight critical areas of treatment that are encountered by many mental health professionals who work with children and their families. The specific case content allows the reader to experience in an almost firsthand fashion how specific techniques and strategies are chosen and, most important, how they are implemented with difficult and sometimes challenging cases.

This text draws its content from some of the most experienced researchers and clinicians in the field. Each chapter has been edited carefully in order to provide the reader with an understanding of cognitive-behavioral theory as it is applied with children and adolescents, and well-calibrated case examples so that the therapeutic techniques may be replicated. Drs. Reinecke, Dattilio, and Freeman are all former students of mine at our center in Philadelphia. Dr. Reinecke, now at the University of Chicago School of Medicine and the Director of its Center for Cognitive Therapy, has proven himself to be an excellent researcher as well as an active practitioner in the field of child and adolescent psychology. Dr. Dattilio has continued to work with me both at the University of Pennsylvania School of Medicine and at the Beck Institute in our extramural training program. Dr. Dattilio has many years of experience working with children and adolescents and is known throughout the world for his cognitive therapy work with couples and families. Dr. Freeman, who served with me as a senior staff member at the University of Pennsylvania for 15 years, now continues training cognitive therapists worldwide. He is noted for his clear presentation style as well as his many fine publications in cognitive therapy. All three men have contributed their valuable editing experience and clinical expertise to this text. These editors are to be commended for assembling such a fine set of case examples to add to the rather lean collection of case material available in the literature regarding cognitive-behavioral interventions with children and adolescents. I am confident that readers will find this to be an illuminating volume as well as a resource for both the active practitioner and the researcher.

AARON T. BECK, M.D.
University Professor of Psychiatry
University of Pennsylvania School of Medicine

Preface

Childhood and adolescence are distinct developmental stages. Although something of a truism, this simple statement has important theoretical and clinical implications. The treatment of behavioral and emotional difficulties experienced by children requires an attention to differences in cognitive and emotional development, and to the varying social systems in which children function. The decision to compile this text, as such, grew out of two concerns. First, although cognitive therapy has developed rapidly, almost exponentially, during recent years, its application with children and adolescents has received less attention. Although a number of excellent volumes have been published providing in-depth examples of how cognitive therapy can be applied in work with clinically referred adults (Beck, Rush, Shaw, & Emery, 1979; Dattilio & Freeman, 1994; Freeman, Pretzer, Fleming, & Simon, 1990; Freeman & Dattilio, 1992; Freeman & Reinecke, 1993; Hawton, Salkovskis, Kirk, & Clark, 1989; Linehan, 1993; Persons, 1989; Scott, 1989; Scott, Williams, & Beck, 1989; Steketee, 1993), there is a lack of available literature providing careful descriptions of "hands-on" case material with children, adolescents, and their families. Second, there has been relatively little exchange between researchers and practicing clinicians exploring the development of behavioral disorders during childhood. Although our understanding of developmental psychopathology has matured during recent years, this appears to have had relatively little impact on the practice of cognitive-behavioral therapy. We continue, in many ways, to "adultomorphize" children, and to employ without modification clinical interventions that have been successfully used with adults.

With this in mind, these chapters were selected in an attempt to address disorders that are commonly confronted by mental health professionals working with children and their families. In addition, we included discussions of less frequently encountered topics that serve to expand the boundaries of contemporary cognitive therapy. Our authors had two directives in preparing their case examples—to maintain a developmental orientation, and to integrate the case examples with critical reviews of the empirical literature.

Each of these chapters incorporates an extended case example. They might be considered as single-case designs. Whereas the value of case studies remains controversial in that the generalizability and validity of findings are limited in comparison with other research methodologies (Galassi & Gersh, 1993), their utility as a teaching tool still obtains. The single-case method has proven to be one of the most useful tools for educating practitioners on the use and implementation of cognitive-behavioral techniques (Freeman & Dattilio, 1992). This may be particularly so when working with children and adolescents due to the variability of their clinical presentations, the overlap between clinical disorders observed, and the transience of symptoms so frequently observed over the course of development.

Each chapter begins with a brief review of recent citations in the literature. The format of the case studies also is uniform in an attempt to provide the reader with background information, case conceptualization, and specific inventories used in completing the clinical assessment. *Diagnostic and Statistical Manual of Mental Disorders* (4th ed.) (DSM-IV; American Psychiatric Association, 1994) diagnoses were incorporated into each case example so that readers will be better able to apply the interventions described to their own cases. When available, follow-up data on the maintenance and generalizability of therapeutic gains are included.

We hope that this compendium will provide readers with practical recommendations that are both clinically useful and conceptually parsimonious. We hope, as well, that the case studies will serve as examples of how cognitive models and interventions can be adapted to accommodate developmental differences. An integration of findings in developmental psychology and developmental psychopathology with contemporary cognitive therapy will enrich both fields.

MARK A. REINECKE
FRANK M. DATTILIO
ARTHUR FREEMAN

REFERENCES

American Psychiatric Association. (1994). *Diagnostic and statistical manual of mental disorders* (4th ed.). Washington, DC: Author.

Beck, A. T., Rush, A. J., Shaw, B. F., & Emery, G. (1979). *Cognitive therapy of depression.* New York: Guilford Press.

Dattilio, F. M., & Freeman, A. (Eds). (1994). *Cognitive-behavioral strategies in crisis intervention*. New York: Guilford Press.

Freeman, A., & Dattilio, F. M. (1992). *Comprehensive casebook of cognitive therapy*. New York: Plenum Press.

Freeman, A., Pretzer, J., Fleming, B., & Simon, K. (1990). *Clinical applications of cognitive therapy*. New York: Plenum Press.

Freeman, A., & Reinecke, M. A. (1993). *Cognitive therapy of suicidal behavior*. New York: Springer.

Galassi, J., & Gersh, T. (1993). Myths, misconceptions, and missed opportunity: Single case designs and counseling psychology. *Journal of Counseling Psychology, 40*(4), 525–531.

Hawton, K., Salkovskis, P. M., Kirk, J., & Clark, D. M. (Eds). (1989). *Cognitive behavior therapy for psychiatric problems: A practical guide*. Oxford, UK: Oxford University Press.

Linehan, M. M. (1993). *Cognitive-behavioral treatment of borderline personality disorder*. New York: Guilford Press.

Persons, J. (1989). *Cognitive therapy in practice: A case formulation approach*. New York: Norton.

Scott, J., Williams, J., & Beck, A. (1989). *Cognitive therapy in clinical practice: An illustrative casebook*. London: Routledge.

Scott, M. (1989). *A cognitive-behavioral approach to client's problems*. London: Tavistock/Routledge.

Steketee, G. S. (1993). *Treatment of obsessive–compulsive disorder*. New York: Guilford Press.

Acknowledgments

In any given text, the acknowledgments typically comprise the briefest section. This is usually due to the fact that space is limited and acknowledgments are simply regarded as less of a priority than other sections. This is unfortunate because most acknowledgments begin with the statement, "This book would not have been possible without the help and support of. . . ." As embarrassing as this is to admit, we, as seasoned editors, have also been guilty of this oversight in the past, and we have therefore decided to amend this situation with this edited text.

We therefore express our extreme gratitude first to all of the book's contributors for providing us with an excellent array of chapters. Many of the authors are experienced clinicians and researchers who have provided us with case studies depicting the typical difficulties and challenges that face practitioners. Their insights and expertise serve as the backbone for a comprehensive project such as this.

We also thank our fine secretarial staff, Ms. Luz Rosa, for her expert word-processing and coordination skills. She served as the main relay for organizing the drafts, and her skills proved to be invaluable. A great deal of thanks also is due to the fine staff of The Guilford Press, particularly Ms. Jodi Creditor for her excellent production skills, and Ms. Marian Robinson for engineering the advertising and marketing. We are also grateful to Mr. Seymour Weingarten, Editor-in-Chief, for his direction, patience, guidance, and approval of this work.

Last, we thank our spouses and families for their patience with our absences during the long hours of preparation of this volume.

MARK A. REINECKE
FRANK M. DATTILIO
ARTHUR FREEMAN

Contents

1

General Issues

Mark A. Reinecke
Frank M. Dattilio
Arthur Freeman

A report by the President's Commission on Mental Health (1978) suggests that 10% to 20% of children may require mental health services. This recommendation is in accord with recent epidemiological evidence suggesting that 15% to 22% of children experience emotional or behavioral problems that warrant treatment (Costello, 1990; Langer, Gersten, & Eisenberg, 1974; Leslie, 1974; Rutter, Tizard, Yule, Graham, & Whitmore, 1976; Zill & Schoenborn, 1990). Unfortunately, fewer than 20% of these children actually receive the treatment they desperately require. Of that group, a sizable percentage are likely to have childhood disorders that would respond to cognitive-behavioral interventions.

Morris and Kratochwill (1991) observed that the child mental health literature, unlike the adult treatment literature, is relatively young and can be traced only to the early 20th century. It was not until the late 19th century, for example, that adolescence came to be viewed as a distinct developmental period, and it was not until years later that psychotherapeutic treatments for behavioral and emotional problems experienced by children and adolescents were proposed. As noted elsewhere (Reinecke, 1993), the use of psychotherapy with children and adolescents dates to Freud's treatment of Dora, an 18-year-old girl suffering from low spirits, headaches, social withdrawal, and a nervous cough. This case is of interest in that Freud was not explicitly concerned with Dora's developmental status or the social context in which her difficulties arose. The importance of adopting a developmental perspective for conceptualizing and treating children and adolescents was not recognized until more recently (Cicchetti, 1984, 1993; Cicchetti & Richters, 1993; Dattilio, 1983; Furman, 1980;

Garber, 1984, 1992; Kendall, Lerner, & Craighead, 1984; Kimball, Nelson, & Politano, 1993; Shirk, 1988). The mental hygiene movement and the establishment of child guidance centers during the 1920s contributed to an increased concern for children's emotional development and an awareness of their mental health needs. Although child guidance programs provided clinical services to children and their families, they were not developed with the goal of supporting the empirical study of the etiology and treatment of psychopathology. The recognition of the value of adopting an objective, empirical approach for assessing, conceptualizing, and treating childhood emotional disorders also did not begin to emerge until several years later. Cognitive-behavioral therapy deserves praise, as such, for its sensitivity to the developmental issues of children and adolescents, as well as its emphasis on empirically validating the effectiveness of interventions derived from the model.

Cognitive therapy with children, as in work with adults, is founded upon the assumption that behavior is adaptive, and that there is an interaction between an individual's thoughts, feelings, and behaviors. The major thrust of cognitive-behavioral therapy is toward understanding the nature and development of an individual's behavioral repertoire and the accompanying cognitive processes. Cognitions are viewed as a body of knowledge or beliefs and a set of strategies for utilizing this information in an adaptive manner. As Kendall and Dobson (1993) state, "Cognition is not a singular or unitary concept, but is rather a general term that refers to a complex system" (p. 9). Cognitions include one's current thoughts or self-statements, as well as perceptions, appraisals, tacit beliefs or schemas, attitudes, memories, goals, standards and values, expectations, and attributions. The term "cognition" refers not only to cognitive "contents," but also to the ways information is represented in memory and the mediational or control procedures by which the information is processed or used. Cognitions, as such, may be viewed as a set of complex skills (Weimer, 1977) that incorporate problem-solving or coping strategies, communication and linguistically based knowledge, and interpersonal skills.

In practice, the fundamental assumption of cognitive therapy is that cognitions influence emotions and behavior. Moreover, individuals are believed to respond to cognitive representations of events, rather than to the events themselves. These are important assumptions in that they designate cognitive change as a prerequisite to behavioral and emotional improvement. This is not to say that cognitive factors play a causal role in the etiology of all behavioral and emotional problems. No single factor or agent appears to "cause" psychopathology in childhood. Rather, recent research suggests that behavior is multiply determined (Rutter, 1989) and that a number of factors interact in contributing to the emergence of behavioral and emotional problems. Biological, genetic, interpersonal, and environmental factors reciprocally influence one another in placing children at risk for developing behavioral and emotional difficulties. In a similar manner, there appears to be a range of interpersonal, cognitive, and social factors that serve a protective function and ameliorate these risks (Anthony & Cohler, 1987). As a consequence, some children, when exposed to stressful life events, may experience only mild distress, whereas others experience relatively severe adjustment problems. Our challenge as clinicians and researchers, as such, is to attempt to understand the ways in which cognitive, biological, and environmental factors interact in mediating the emergence of psychopathology during childhood. This task is complicated by the fact that different factors appear to be more or less important at different stages of development, and that the specific etiologic factors may differ from one form of behavioral or emotional problem to another. Although we are not suggesting that cognitive processes "cause" behavioral or emotional difficulties during childhood, evidence suggests that there are cognitive and behavioral differences between children who manifest difficulties in adaptation and those who do not (Kendall, 1991; Kendall & MacDonald, 1993). It is these cognitive and behavioral factors that become the focus of our clinical interventions.

Cognitive-behavioral therapy with children, as in work with adults, emphasizes the effects of maladaptive or dysfunctional beliefs and attitudes on current behavior. A presumption is made that a child's reaction to an event is influenced by the meanings he or she attaches to the event. That is to say, emotional and behavioral responses to events in one's day-to-day life are a function of how these events are perceived and recalled, the attributions that are made about the causes of the event, and the ways in which the events affect one's self-perceptions and the pursuit of one's goals. These cognitive processes are believed to be influenced, in turn, by underlying beliefs that individuals maintain about themselves, the world, and their futures (Guidano & Liotti, 1983; Hammen & Goodman-Brown, 1990; Ingram, 1984; Segal, 1988). These tacit beliefs or schemas are actively constructed over the course of development, and might be thought of as "lenses" or "templates" guiding the perception, processing, recollection, interpretation, and analysis of incoming information (Mahoney, 1991). When children's behavioral or emotional responses to an event are maladaptive—that is, they are inappropriate given the nature of the event, or significantly impair the children's social or academic adjustment—it is presumed that they may lack more appropriate behavioral skills, or that their beliefs (cognitive contents) or problem-solving capacities (cognitive processes) are in some way disturbed. The latter difficulties may reflect cognitive deficiencies or cognitive distortions (Kendall, 1991). "Cognitive deficiencies" refer to the lack of effective cognitive processing, as might be demonstrated by an inattentive child who approaches problems in an impulsive, nonreflective manner. "Cognitive distortions," in turn, refer to beliefs or attitudes founded on irrational or "distorted" logic, as might be manifested by a depressed teenager who systematically minimizes his or her abilities, and who selectively overlooks or dismisses support provided by others. With this in mind, cognitive therapists endeavor to assist children and adolescents by facilitating the acquisition of new behavioral skills and by providing children with experiences that will precipitate cognitive change.

The course of therapy, as such, begins with a careful assessment of factors contributing to the child's behavioral or emotional difficulties. This is followed by the introduction of interventions designed to increase behavioral competence, as well as techniques employed to correct erroneous or maladaptive cognitions (Brewin, 1988; Freeman, Pretzer, Fleming, & Simon, 1990; Zarb, 1992). An outline of a standard course of cognitive therapy is presented in Table 1.1.

Ellis (1962) and Beck (1967, 1976) are often credited with introducing the concept of "cognitive restructuring" to the clinical literature. This term refers to the use of Socratic questioning or rational disputation to modify maladaptive or "distorted" thoughts. This approach was refined by Goldfried (1979), Kendall and Hollon (1979), and Meichenbaum (1977), and has now been applied to the treatment of depression and anxiety

TABLE 1.1. Outline of a Standard Course of Cognitive-Behavioral Therapy

1. Therapist elicits information regarding the development of the specific symptom, as well as situational determinants and temporal course. Objective data (preferably from several informants) are collected regarding the nature of the presenting problem.
2. Underlying beliefs, assumptions, expectations, goals, attributions, and self-statements or automatic thoughts are identified. Patients learn to monitor negative or maladaptive thoughts.
3. Specific behavioral or interpersonal skills deficits are identified.
4. Medical and environmental factors supporting or maintaining the symptoms are identified. The latter may include stressful life events or the modeling and reinforcement of the symptoms by others in the child's life.
5. Cognitive and behavioral interventions are selected and introduced. The rationale for the interventions is reviewed with the child and his or her caregivers.
6. Homework is assigned. The patient practices the cognitive or behavioral techniques during the session. Attempts are made to ensure that the interventions are clearly understood, that each of the individuals is motivated to complete the assignment, and that they expect the interventions to be helpful. Factors that may interfere with the completion of the homework assignment are identified and addressed.
7. Effectiveness of the intervention is evaluated through objective ratings and subjective reports.

experienced by children and adolescents (Braswell & Kendall, 1988; Stark, Rouse, & Livingston, 1991; Wilkes, Belsher, Rush, Frank, & Associates, 1994; Zarb, 1992). Other cognitive interventions include exercises in social perspective taking or social problem solving, relaxation training, guided imagery, the use of coping self-statements, stress inoculation, and self-control exercises. These interventions would be employed flexibly, with their selection based on the specific needs of the individual child.

Cognitive interventions have also been proposed to remediate cognitive deficiencies. These take the form of techniques employed to facilitate the development of reflective thought, effective problem solving, and self-regulation (Barkley, 1990; Braswell & Bloomquist, 1991; Dattilio, 1981; Kazdin, 1987; Kendall & Braswell, 1993; Lochman, Burch, Curry, & Lampron, 1984).

Interventions such as cognitive restructuring and self-control therapy were initially developed for treating emotional disorders among adults, and are derived from rationalist or "realism-based" models of human functioning (Mahoney & Nezworski, 1985). These techniques must be adapted for use with children and adolescents in that children lack the social, linguistic, and cognitive sophistication to benefit from these techniques if they are introduced in an unmodified form. School-age children, for example, typically are unable to readily identify their current thoughts or to discriminate and label specific emotional states. Children appear, as well, to be less able than adults to recall emotions apart from the environmental events that generated them. The use of "dysfunctional thought records" (DTRs) and rational disputation—staples of cognitive therapy with older adolescents and adults—are, as a consequence, not feasible with this population. With this in mind, we must simplify our interventions (Stark et al., 1991) such that they are commensurate with the abilities of our patients, or assist children in developing the requisite skills so that they may benefit from these techniques.

Rationally based models of psychotherapy have been criticized in that they, in their current form, are not sensitive to developmental issues faced by children and adolescents and do not attend to the self-organizing, constructive processes of child development (Mahoney & Nezworski, 1985). The development of tacit beliefs regarding the reliability of relationships, personal security, and the stability of the family, for example, are of critical importance to children, but are rarely explored in the cognitive therapy literature. These factors are rarely incorporated into cognitive-behavioral conceptualizations of childhood emotional disorders. In a similar manner, the relationships between early attachments—working models of the self in relation to others—and interpersonal schemas (Guidano & Liotti, 1983) have received little attention. This is a potentially important oversight in that these variables may play a role in the etiology of depression during later childhood and adulthood (Hammen & Gotlib, 1992). It is possible, for example, that early attachment difficulties, or an ongoing pattern of unreliable parental support, may result in the consolidation of maladaptive, depressogenic schemas that are founded on the beliefs that it is "essential to maintain relationships" and that "relationships are inherently unstable." Finally, even a cursory review of the cognitive therapy literature reveals that the developmental tasks of adolescence—the establishment of autonomy from one's family, stabilization of self-concept, and the consolidation of an adult identity—have not received significant attention.

Nonetheless, cognitive-behavioral therapy with children and adolescents is promising in that it explicitly recognizes the importance of cognitive, behavioral, affective, and socioenvironmental variables in the etiology and maintenance of emotional disorders. Moreover, it is consistent with contemporary integrative, constructivist models of behavioral change, and maintains the objective, empirical focus that has served as the foundation of both behavioral psychotherapy and child psychiatry. These themes are reflected in the chapters that follow. As will be seen, cognitive-behavioral therapy with children is fundamentally similar, both in theory and in practice, to cognitive therapy with adults. It challenges these models, however, by requiring us to carefully attend to the interpersonal contexts in which children's beliefs and attitudes are acquired, as well as developmental factors associated with behavioral and emotional change.

REFERENCES

Anthony, E. J., & Cohler, B. J. (Eds.). (1987). *The invulnerable child.* New York: Guilford Press.

Barkley, R. A. (1990). *Attention-deficit hyperactivity disorder: A handbook for diagnosis and treatment.* New York: Guilford Press.

Beck, A. T. (1967). *Depression: Clinical, experimental, and theoretical aspects.* New York: Harper & Row.

Beck, A. T. (1976). *Cognitive therapy and the emotional disorders.* New York: New American Library.

Braswell, L., & Kendall, P. C. (1988). Cognitive-behavioral methods with children. In K. Dobson (Ed.), *Handbook of cognitive-behavioral therapies* (pp. 167–213). New York: Guilford Press.

Braswell, L., & Bloomquist, M. L. (1991). *Cognitive-behavioral therapy with ADHD children: Child, family, and school interventions.* New York: Guilford Press.

Brewin, C. (1988). *Cognitive foundations of clinical psychology.* Hillsdale, NJ: Erlbaum.

Cicchetti, D. (1984). The emergence of developmental psychopathology. *Child Development, 55*(1), 1–7.

Cicchetti, D. (1993). Developmental psychopathology: Reactions, reflections, projections. *Developmental Review, 13*(4), 471–502.

Cicchetti, D., & Richters, J. (1993). Developmental considerations in the investigation of conduct disorder. *Development and Psychopathology, 5*(1–2), 331–344.

Costello, E. (1990). Child psychiatric epidemiology: Implications for clinical research and practice. In B. Lahey & A. Kazdin (Eds.), *Advances in clinical child psychology* (Vol. 13, pp. 53–90). New York: Plenum Press.

Dattilio, F. M. (1981, Winter). The Carkhuff Systematic Human Relations training model in a short-term treatment program for adolescent offenders. *Adolescence, 16*(64), 865–869.

Dattilio, F. M. (1983). The use of operant techniques and parental control in the treatment of pediatric headache complaints: Case report. *Pennsylvania Journal of Counseling, 1*(2), 55–58.

Ellis, A. (1962). *Reason and emotion in psychotherapy.* New York: Lyle Stuart.

Freeman, A., Pretzer, J., Fleming, B., & Simon, K. (1990). *Clinical applications of cognitive therapy.* New York: Plenum Press.

Furman, W. (1980). Promoting social development: Developmental implications for treatment. In B. Lahey & A. Kazdin (Eds.), *Advances in clinical child psychology* (Vol. 3, pp. 1–40). New York: Plenum Press.

Garber, J. (1984). Classification of childhood psychopathology: A developmental perspective. *Child Development, 55*(1), 30–48.

Garber, J. (1992). Cognitive models of depression: A developmental perspective. *Psychological Inquiry, 3*(3), 235–240.

Goldfried, M. (1979). Anxiety reduction through cognitive-behavioral intervention. In P. Kendall & S. Hollon (Eds.), *Cognitive-behavioral interventions: Theory, research, and procedures* (pp. 117–152). New York: Academic Press.

Guidano, V. F., & Liotti, G. (1983). *Cognitive processes and emotional disorders.* New York: Guilford Press.

Hammen, C., & Goodman-Brown, T. (1990). Self-schemas and vulnerability to specific life stress in children at risk for depression. *Cognitive Therapy and Research, 14*, 215–227.

Hammen, C., & Gotlib, I. (1992). *Psychological aspects of depression: Toward a cognitive–interpersonal integration.* Chichester: Wiley.

Ingram, R. (1984). Toward an information processing analysis of depression. *Cognitive Therapy and Research, 8*, 443–447.

Kazdin, A. (1987). Treatment of antisocial behavior in children: Current status and future directions. *Psychological Bulletin, 102*, 187–203.

Kendall, P. (Ed.). (1991). *Child and adolescent therapy: Cognitive-behavioral procedures.* New York: Guilford Press.

Kendall, P., & Braswell, L. (1993). *Cognitive-behavioral therapy for impulsive children* (2nd ed.). New York: Guilford Press.

Kendall, P., & Dobson, K. (1993). On the nature of cognition and its role in psychopathology. In K. Dobson & P. Kendall (Eds.), *Psychopathology and cognition* (pp. 3–17). San Diego: Academic Press.

Kendall, P., & Hollon, S. (1979). Cognitive-behavioral interventions: Overview and current status. In P. Kendall & S. Hollon (Eds.), *Cognitive-behavioral interventions: Theory, research, and procedures* (pp. 1–13). New York: Academic Press.

Kendall, P., Lerner, R., & Craighead, W. (1984). Human development and intervention in childhood psychopathology. *Child Development, 55*, 71–82.

Kendall, P., & MacDonald, J. (1993). Cognition in the psychopathology of youth and implications for treatment. In K. Dobson & P. Kendall (Eds.), *Psychopathology and cognition* (pp. 387–427). San Diego: Academic Press.

Kimball, W., Nelson, W., & Politano, P. (1993). The role of developmental variables in cognitive-behavioral interventions with children. In A. Finch, W. Nelson, & E. Ott (Eds.), *Cognitive-behavioral procedures with children and adolescents: A practical guide* (pp. 25–66). Boston: Allyn & Bacon.

Langer, T., Gersten, J., & Eisenberg, J. (1974). Approaches to measurement and definition in epidemiology of behavior disorders: Ethnic background and child behavior. *International Journal of Health Services, 4*, 483–501.

Leslie, S. (1974). Psychiatric disorder in young adolescents of an industrial town. *British Journal of Psychiatry, 125*, 113–124.

Lochman, J., Burch, P., Curry, J., & Lampron, L. (1984). Treatment and generalization effects of cognitive-behavioral and goal-setting interventions with aggressive boys. *Journal of Consulting and Clinical Psychology, 52*, 915–916.

Mahoney, M. (1991). *Human change processes*. New York: Basic Books.

Mahoney, M., & Nezworski, M. (1985). Cognitive-behavioral approaches to children's problems. *Journal of Abnormal Child Psychology, 13*(3), 467–476.

Meichenbaum, D. (1977). *Cognitive-behavior modification: An integrative approach*. New York: Plenum Press.

Morris, R., & Kratochwill, T. (1991). Introductory comments. In T. Kratochwill & R. Morris (Eds.), *The practice of child therapy* (2nd ed., pp. 3–5). New York: Pergamon Press.

President's Commission on Mental Health. (1978). *Report to the President* (Vol. 1). Washington, DC: U.S. Government Printing Office.

Reinecke, M. (1993). Outpatient treatment of mild psychopathology. In P. Tolan & B. Cohler (Eds.), *Handbook of clinical research and practice with adolescents* (pp. 387–410). New York: Wiley-Interscience.

Rutter, M. (1989). Pathways from childhood to adult life. *Journal of Child Psychology and Psychiatry, 30*, 23–51.

Rutter, M., Tizard, J., Yule, W., Graham, P., & Whitmore, K. (1976). Research report: Isle of Wight studies, 1964–1974. *Psychological Medicine, 6*, 313–332.

Segal, Z. (1988). Appraisal of the self-schema construct in cognitive models of depression. *Psychological Bulletin, 103*(2), 147–162.

Shirk, S. (Ed.). (1988). *Cognitive development and child psychotherapy*. New York: Plenum Press.

Stark, K., Rouse, L., & Livingston, R. (1991). Treatment of depression during childhood and adolescence. Cognitive-behavioral procedures for the family. In P. Kendall (Ed.), *Child and adolescent therapy: Cognitive-behavioral procedures* (pp. 165–208). New York: Guilford Press.

Weimer, W. (1977). A conceptual framework for cognitive psychology: Motor theories of mind. In R. Shaw & J. Bransford (Eds.) *Perceiving, acting, and knowing* (pp. 267–311). Hillsdale, NJ: Erlbaum.

Wilkes, T. C. R., Belsher, G., Rush, A. J., Frank, E., & Associates. (1994). *Cognitive therapy for depressed adolescents*. New York: Guilford Press.

Zarb, J. (1992). *Cognitive-behavioral assessment and therapy with adolescents*. New York: Brunner/Mazel.

Zill, N., & Schoenborn, C. (1990). *Developmental learning and emotional problems: Health of our nation's children, United States, 1988* (Advance data from *Vital and Health Statistics*, No. 190). Hyattsville, MD: National Center for Health Statistics.

2

Case Study Research

The Cornerstone
of Theory and Practice

David J. A. Edwards

The case study has played a central role in clinical psychology
—Kazdin (1981, p. 183)

The individual case study, or situation analysis is the bedrock of scientific investigation.
—Bromley (1986, p. ix)

THE CASE STUDY AND CONTEMPORARY
RESEARCH PARADIGMS

The case study method is a fundamental tool in social science (Eckstein, 1975; Mitchell, 1983; Yin, 1984), and has proven particularly valuable within the fields of clinical and developmental psychology (Bolgar, 1965; Bromley, 1986; Edwards, 1990a, 1991; Kazdin, 1981; Kratochwill, Mott, & Dodson, 1984). In the field of psychotherapy, careful and systematic observation and description of individual cases has been the cornerstone on which the development of scientific knowledge has been built (Strupp, 1981). This began with Freud's pioneering development of psychoanalytic theory, which proceeded in conjunction with detailed description and discussion of case material (Bolgar, 1965). Careful description and analysis of cases has also played an important role in the behavior therapy literature (Eysenck, 1976; Hersen & Last, 1985).

In cognitive therapy, however, as in much contemporary research, the steps whereby theory is developed in dialogue with case material have largely been implicit, and little formal case study research appears in the journals. In practice, however, the systematic analysis of individual cases has played a fundamental role in the development of cognitive therapy. Beck's (1967, 1976) pioneering work, for example, is based on careful clinical observation, and case vignettes are routinely used to illustrate specific points in these and other classic presentations of the theory and practice of cognitive therapy (Beck & Emery, 1985; Beck, Rush, Shaw, & Emery, 1979; Freeman, Pretzer, Fleming, & Simon, 1990; Freeman, Simon, Beutler, & Arkowitz, 1989; Hawton, Salkovskis, Kirk, & Clark, 1989). These are more than useful devices for communicating ideas to readers; they point to the central role of work with individual cases in the development of clinical knowledge.

The paucity of case study research stems from the nature of (ruling) ascendent, accepted paradigms of research methodology during recent years. Historically, the ruling metatheory in science, modeled on physics, has been that any event (or dependent variable) is a mathematical function of a discrete set of predictor (independent) variables. Within this model, the task of research on any phenomenon was seen to be the identification and measurement of its key predictors and the mathematical functions that link them. This paradigm, which may be unsuited to many branches of meaningful psychological theory (Polkinghorne, 1986), supported the focus on quantitative, multivariate research methodologies and resulted in the virtual eclipse of the naturalistic, ecological, case study approach (Kiesler, 1981). Even in sociology, where case study research had an established reputation in the first half of the century, advances in computer technology in the 1950s brought a decisive shift toward quantitative methods and a decline in respect for and use of case studies. Among the social sciences, it was only in anthropology that the method continued to flourish (Mitchell, 1983).

Any research process involves a set of systematic and rigorous procedures for answering a specific question. These include observation, description, classification, experimentation, and interpretation (Gelfand, Jenson, & Drew, 1988). When these procedures are carried out on a large number of subjects, as is the case with much quantitative research, there is often little in-depth information about each subject, and only specific variables are measured. Case studies offer the advantage that resources can be used for a much more thorough investigation of each individual, yielding a complex set of psychologically rich, qualitative information that provides an in-depth understanding. This option will appeal to researchers doing small-scale studies with limited resources, who would prefer to examine psychological phenomena in qualitative depth but do not have the time or resources to work with large samples.

Case study research is a method in its own right that is complementary to methods using groups of subjects and, when carried out rigorously (a process that may or may not involve the inclusion of an experimental component), yields valid scientific knowledge. Unfortunately, the use of case studies has often been dismissed as "preexperimental" and too fundamentally unreliable to yield valid knowledge. As a result, it is often overlooked in research method courses, and quantitative group comparison has been presented as the *only* form of research (Hayes, 1981). This has resulted in alienation of practitioners of clinical psychology from experimental research (Barlow, 1981; Polkinghorne, 1986; Safran, Greenberg, & Rice, 1988).

Over at least the past decade, however, there has been a new appreciation of the value of the case study. Thus Kratochwill et al. (1984, p. 55) write, "Increasingly, researchers . . . are recognizing the importance of case study and single case investigations for the development of a knowledge base . . . that is unobtainable through traditional large-N–between-group-designs in therapy research." It is the purpose of this chapter to outline the basic principles through which systematic in-depth description and analysis of individual cases contribute to the development of clinical theory and practice. When these principles are understood, readers will see that it is not an exaggeration to claim that this method is not simply "a somewhat useful secondary tool for the serious work of scientific hypothesis testing" (Mahrer, 1988, p. 697), but it has a central place in the development of systematic and valid scientific knowledge.

PRINCIPLES OF THE CASE STUDY RESEARCH METHOD

Developing Case Law or Grounded Theory

The first step in case study research is to develop in-depth, accurate descriptions of particular cases. In a clinical setting, this may be based on interviews with the client and sometimes with other informants, as well as the use of self-report questionnaires and psychological tests (Kratochwill et al., 1984). Once a client has been in therapy for several sessions, further material is gathered that can contribute to a more detailed and extensive understanding.

The second step is to achieve a conceptualization of the case material in behavioral and psychological terms that will be of practical value. This requires the availability of relevant constructs and the accurate application of these constructs to new cases. Case conceptualization in cognitive therapy, for example, frequently draws on the following constructs to furnish an understanding of the presenting problem (Dattilio & Freeman, 1994; Freeman et al., 1990; Hawton, 1989; Persons, Curtis, & Silberschatz, 1991; Young, 1990; Young & Lindemann, 1992):

1. *Predisposing factors* in the form of dysfunctional assumptions or maladaptive schemas that have usually developed in response to adverse personal circumstances.
2. *Precipitating factors*, in the form of one or more upsetting recent events, such as a failure in a project or a relationship breakdown.
3. *Maintaining factors* in the form of cognitive distortions that shape clients' perceptions of everyday events to make them consistent with the negative assumptions and schemas, and self-defeating behaviors that elicit responses from others that confirm the dysfunctional assumptions and schemas.

The value of these constructs has been clinically proven, and each new case that can be usefully conceptualized within this existing theory provides further evidence for the generality and practical validity of the theory. This testing and retesting against new cases is the third step in theory development. The case study method is sometimes inappropriately criticized because it is claimed that there is a danger of inappropriately generalizing from one case. Thus Gelfand et al. (1988, p. 323) write that case studies "usually only describe one subject, or at most, a few (such as a family). The information thus may not apply to other individuals or situations different from those studied." However, the methodology of case study research depends upon working with *series of cases*, even though a particular investigator may only work in depth with a single case. When an observation is made from one case, it is at best a hypothesis. When it is repeatedly confirmed in other cases, it becomes a general principle. Once a general principle becomes established, the limitations of the application of that principle need to be identified. This is achieved by an active search for cases in which the generalization does not hold, and by attempts to identify criteria that distinguish between cases in which the principle holds and others in which it does not (Bromley, 1986; Henwood & Pidgeon, 1993; Strauss & Corbin, 1990).

Bromley (1986, p. 2) likens this process to the establishment of case law in jurisprudence, which "provides rules, generalizations and categories which gradually systematize the knowledge (facts and theories) gained from the intensive study of individual cases. Case-law (theory, in effect) emerges through a process of conceptual refinement as successive cases are considered in relation to each other." This process is quite different from the mathematico-deductive model of the positivist research paradigm. It provides, rather, a framework for practical understanding, the embodiment of what Dilthey sought when he envisaged a science of understanding (*Verstehen*) rather than one of explanation (*Erklarung*; Kruger, 1988). Sociologists refer to this process as the building of "grounded theory"

(Glaser & Strauss, 1967; Strauss & Corbin, 1990). This is a phrase that may appeal to clinicians who wish to develop a working theory that accords with their everyday practical experience.

Therapists are uniquely placed to play a key role in this process as applied scientists (Edwards, 1990a; Kiesler, 1981). They have privileged access to data relevant to a range of questions related not only to psychological disorders but also to important cultural and existential questions. The development of this type of knowledge also depends on the skills routinely exercised by clinicians: establishing a collaborative relationship with a client, interviewing empathetically, asking sensitive and well-chosen questions, and organizing interview data into coherent synoptic forms that accurately reflect the psychological dimensions of the material without distortion or bias. These are not only clinical skills, but they are also research skills. Furthermore, this process has all the characteristics of the scientific exploration of a new phenomenon. Moreover, clinical decisions are made by applying or extending existing knowledge in the same way as is done in any area of formal research (Hayes, 1981). Finally, clinicians often enjoy an infrastructure provided by supervision, peer discussion, case conferences, congresses, and publications that supports an ongoing critical approach and accountability.

From Description to Theory Testing: A Continuum

Two phases in the advancement of knowledge can be distinguished: (1) a phase of discovery followed by (2) a phase of verification. Case studies play a role in both phases, and a continuum from description to theory testing can be employed to locate any individual case study (Eckstein, 1975; Edwards, 1991). At the descriptive pole, the context is largely that of discovery; at the theory-testing pole, it is largely that of verification. In recent decades, explication of the research process has focused largely on the context of verification, so that the context of discovery has been overlooked (Giorgi, 1986b; Henwood & Pidgeon, 1993). Yet, as Bolgar (1965, p. 31) pointed out 30 years ago in her discussion of case study method, "Experimentation is mainly concerned with proof and rarely leads to discovery. . . . In the rigid attention to hypothesis testing the researcher often overlooks unexpected outcomes which might be discoveries. On the other hand . . . the case study method is the ideal way to generate hunches, hypotheses and important discoveries." Twenty years later, Giorgi (1985, 1986a), responding to the continuing imbalance in the way the research process was being conceived, called for the restoration of descriptive science as the cornerstone of the process of discovery, without which the elaborate machinery of verification is meaningless.

Because any case study research depends on accurate in-depth descriptions of particular cases, it respects the descriptive phase as an essential feature of the research process. Such description may be the sole aim of an *exploratory–descriptive case study*. When clinicians encounter some new clinical phenomenon, the first step in exploration of it is to prepare an articulated description of the individual case. There is a minimum of interpretation. This stage honors Husserl's dictum, "Back to the things themselves" (Kruger, 1988, p. 28). A descriptive case synopsis, which furnishes an accessible working summary of interview material stripped of redundancy and coherently organized, is a good means of achieving this. Whereas case synopses can be written objectively in a detached style, they can also be written more vividly, using the subject's own words in a way that invites the reader into an empathic response to the experience of the subject being studied (Fischer & Wertz, 1979; Wertz, 1985). As Shapiro (1986, pp. 172–173) points out, "As investigators we are embedded in our cultural and historical situation. We are both subject and object of and in this human realm. . . . In this very involvement there is possible a direct access to understanding and to a form of verification inherent in the lived relation between the object of knowledge and its investigator." The inclusion of therapist–client dialogue is a practical way in which case study writing can benefit from this kind of direct access to experience.

As soon as we describe, we use language and concepts that commit us to at least the beginnings of theory because we rely on constructs familiar to the users of the language we employ. As we deepen our understanding, we draw on progressively more technical language because we need to make fine distinctions and to refer to relationships between constructs that are not allowed for in the language of everyday discourse. These first steps in theory construction are taken in the *descriptive–dialogic case study*. This stage requires that the case under discussion be taken in conjunction with other related cases so that the adequacy of particular constructs, distinctions, and principles can be informally examined.

The value of the case study is not confined to the context of discovery. A series of well-described cases can form the basis for the development of theory (grounded theory or case law) and for the subsequent rigorous testing of points of theory (Bromley, 1986; Eckstein, 1975). Bromley (1986, p. 286) writes,

> The intensive, largely retrospective study of individual cases can be as rigorous and informative as the extensive, prospective study of samples of people, whether in surveys or experiments. One can generalize from individual cases, and many important real-life human problems cannot be studied effectively, or at all, by experimental methods of enquiry.

The rigorous extension and testing of existing theory is undertaken in a *theoretical–heuristic case study*. Here the cases studied must furnish a means of testing specific principles, generalizations, or hypotheses. In *crucial* or *test case studies*, which can be undertaken once theory is well developed and operationalized, a case must be carefully chosen that can furnish the data that can provide a crucial test of a particular theoretical proposition (Eckstein, 1975).

EXPERIMENTS WITHIN CASE STUDIES: TIME SERIES ANALYSIS

Principles of Time Series Analysis

Although many case studies are not experimental in character because they use in-depth descriptions of naturally occurring phenomena as their data, an experimental component can be incorporated. In practice, once a clinical intervention is implemented, an experiment is under way because the clinician will draw conclusions from the response of the client to the intervention. In some cases, it is valuable to make the experimental aspect of a case study more formal by identifying specific variables for quantitative measurement and taking repeated measures over the course of the therapy. This enables the data to be treated by a single-case experimental design or time series analysis (Hayes, 1981; Kratochwill et al., 1984). Measurements are divided across three or more phases: baseline, intervention, and follow-up. Beames, Sanders, and Bor (1992), for example, studied the cognitive-behavioral treatment of headaches in two children. They measured headache frequency and a number of specific behaviors of the children and the parents. These variables were measured on a regular basis throughout a baseline pretreatment period, during a structured nine-session treatment, and at follow-up, 6 months after the end of the treatment.

The intervention phase may be broken into subphases. In a reversal design, the intervention is implemented and withdrawn and then reinstated as a means of examining its relationship to a particular target behavior. This is particularly appropriate for assessing the effect of environmental interventions such as reinforcement contingencies. The method was used by Morrow, Burke, and Buell (1985) to investigate the effects of self-monitoring on the attention paid to academic tasks of two adolescents with mental retardation and schizophrenia. During self-monitoring, attention to the task and number of arithmetic problems solved increased, but when self-monitoring stopped, there was a decline toward baseline levels. A longitudinal design with a controlled reversal can provide strong evidence that an intervention (in this case, the self-monitoring) is causally related to a behavior (in this case, attention to task and number of problems solved).

In a multiple-baseline design, the intervention includes two or more components that are introduced serially. This allows for the impact on the target behaviors of the different components to be assessed. For example, Ollendick, Hagopian, and Huntzinger (1991) investigated the effect of a two-phase intervention with two girls, aged 8 and 10, who had separation anxiety disorder. Both girls habitually slept in their parents' beds, and the intervention focused on training them to sleep in their own beds. The first phase of 8 weeks involved a comprehensive anxiety-management intervention that included self-instructional training and relaxation. In the second phase, reinforcement for sleeping in their own beds was added to the anxiety management. In both cases the anxiety management alone had little impact on getting the girls to sleep in their own beds, but the addition of the reinforcement resulted in a marked increase. The intervention was continued until each girl had slept in her own bed continuously for 3 weeks. This required 10 weeks in the second phase for one girl and 12 weeks for the other. Follow-up at 1 year in one case and 2 years in the other indicated that the problem had not returned.

The multiple-baseline strategy enables the effect of specific components of an intervention to be examined. In the Ollendick et al. (1991) study, it can be concluded that the anxiety-management training, although very comprehensive, was not sufficient by itself to alter the problem behavior. The addition of the contingency management was needed to bring about change.

Dismantling Complex Interventions: Ethical and Theoretical Issues

When a multifaceted intervention has been successful, the question arises as to whether some aspects of the intervention were more important than others. However, the implications of this question are quite different when asked from the perspective of case study methodology rather than from that of the multivariate research paradigm. In the multivariate paradigm, a dependent variable (in this case, which bed the girl slept in) is understood to be influenced by a set of discrete independent variables (the child's skills in anxiety management, and reinforcement contingencies). Each of these independent variables is supposed to contribute to the dependent variable to a different degree. It should be possible, therefore, to dismantle a multifaceted intervention into its component parts so that the relative contribution of each can be determined. This approach is often employed in group comparison designs in which different treatment components are given to randomized groups. Strupp (1988) has criticized such approaches as misguided, and Masters, Burish, Hollon, and Rimm (1987, p. 545) have pointed out the potential harm that can be done by focusing on group testing of standardized treatment programs: "Unfortunately the individualization of a behavior therapy regimen is an advantage that has not been fully developed in psychological research. That is, to ensure standardization, the rigors of experimental design require that no differences exist between separate applications of a single intervention." This does violence to the nature of actual clinical practice, in which the choice of specific intervention strategies is based on a three-stage process: The *case conceptualization* is used as a basis for identifying general *strategies* of intervention, and these in turn are implemented using specific *techniques or tactics* (Freeman et al., 1990; Beck & Emery, 1985; Persons, 1989). Thus, interventions are individually tailored to the complex of problems presented by particular clients and are not linked to disorders or symptoms in a simplistic or mechanical manner. Case study methodology provides a more flexible approach because it does not subscribe to the same mechanistic assumptions and permits a more subtle qualitative evaluation of case material.

In the Ollendick et al. (1991) separation anxiety study, the authors questioned whether contingency management procedures alone would have been sufficient to alleviate the anxiety. They suggested that a crossover design might be employed to investigate this question. This would involve taking new cases and introducing the reinforcement first, followed by the anxiety management procedures. Although this suggestion retains the case study approach, it does not incorporate the use of case conceptualization into planning the research. Consider the question: "How would a child suffering from separation anxiety disorder respond to contingency management, having been thoroughly trained in coping skills, and how would the same child respond to contingency management without that training?" It is easy to see that the contingency management is likely to potentiate the effects of the anxiety-management skills by motivating children to confront the anxiety more firmly, something they have been equipped to do through the anxiety-management training. Conversely, we might anticipate at least three outcomes if contingency management were applied without anxiety-management training: either (1) existing coping skills that had fallen into disuse would be mobilized (this would occur only in those children who had developed the skills already), or (2) children might spontaneously discover new coping skills to enable them to face and overcome the anxiety (which might happen in some resourceful children), or (3) they would experience heightened conflict over the desire to sleep in the parents' bed and the demand that they sleep on their own, which could result in feelings of guilt, self-critical thinking, lowered self-esteem, and reduced self-efficacy, with a resultant increase in emotional distress.

In light of this, it would hardly be ethical to implement the type of design suggested by Ollendick et al. (1991) given the real possibility of increasing the distress of an already distressed child (one of Ollendick's subjects also met the criteria for major depression).

A multiple-baseline design allows for the effects of different components to be evaluated in a single case. If the selection and timing of interventions is thoroughly informed by the assessment and case conceptualization, and not dictated in a mechanistic manner, it provides a valuable means of evaluating the impact of specific tactics. From this perspective, it would not be appropriate to randomly select children with separation anxiety disorder for treatment with contingency management without first providing them with anxiety-management skills. However, in a specific case, where a child had shown evidence of having good coping skills that had fallen into disuse, it might be appropriate to begin with contingency management as a means of motivating the child to exercise these existing skills.

A longitudinal design would therefore be enhanced by integration of qualitative analysis. Integrated into the clinical process of case conceptualization and intervention planning, it could play a valuable role in improving the quality of case studies in cognitive therapy and enhancing our ability to draw conclusions from case material, particularly in the area of evaluating the efficacy of specific interventions.

VALIDITY IN THE CASE STUDY RESEARCH PROCESS

Case study research has its own methodological traps. The process and the pitfalls need to be thoroughly understood if it is not to become a vehicle for baseless speculation, a process that has brought it into disrepute in the past. Strupp (1981, pp. 217–218) summarizes some of the dangers, based on difficulties encountered in the development of psychoanalysis. These include

> total commitment to a single theoretical and technical model; enshrinement of theoretical formulations as dogma; imperviousness to research progress in neighboring fields; rigid indoctrination of trainees; failure to inspire students to become critical and independent thinkers; failure to teach students abiding respect for empirical data and rival hypotheses; insufficient attention to clinical realities. . . .

The philosophical orientation of the tradition of cognitive therapy provides much protection against the worst abuses because it has tended to be open-minded, empirically focused, integrative, and respectful of the rules of scientific discourse. Nevertheless, researchers are advised to pay specific attention to the specific steps that must be taken to protect the validity of knowledge gained from case studies, which will be discussed here.

If a case study is to contribute to the development of scientific knowledge, it needs to follow a series of stages. The satisfactory completion of each stage serves as a sound basis for the execution of the next. At each stage, there are various threats to validity that must be encountered and addressed. The stages of a typical clinical case study are examined here. In the stage of "data collection," the researcher must guard against biasing the data by asking leading questions, setting up a situation with subtle demand characteristics, or only seeking or recording selected information (Gelfand et al., 1988). Where appropriate, information from one source (e.g., interview) can be cross-checked against information from another source (e.g., observation). These problems of validity are, of course, common to quantitative research methods.

The second stage is called "data reduction." The raw data, which may include interview transcripts, self-reports, objective test results, and observational records usually become too voluminous to be of practical use, and the researcher must prepare a synoptic summary in which the main themes are presented, irrelevant material omitted, and repetitious material removed. Here, there is the risk that researchers will select material for the synopsis that favors a specific point of view. Ideally, tape recordings of interview and test material, as well as case synopses, should be available for evaluation by independent judges, although this process may be too laborious to execute in many settings.

At the third stage, "case conceptualization," validity depends on the careful use of evidence and the quality of argument. In integrating the case material within existing theoretical constructs, the researcher needs to present evidence for the identification of particular processes within a case. For example, researchers need to be able to demonstrate the appropriateness of their classification scheme for identifying predisposing, precipitating, or maintaining factors or for identifying specific types of cognitive distortion or self-defeating behavior. The development of a treatment or intervention plan can also be regarded as part of the case conceptualization because, where there is a well-developed case law, the appropriate intervention should follow from the case analysis. At this stage, support for the validity of the conceptualization can be provided by having independent judges who are familiar with the case law evaluate the conclusions drawn (Persons et al., 1991). In a professional clinical setting, the process of regular supervision and case conference presentation provides a structure that supports this process.

The fourth stage is "outcome evaluation," which involves the collection and examination of data that will enable an evaluation to be made of the effectiveness of the intervention, and speaks to the issue of "internal validity" (which concerns the validity of claims about causal relationships). Such claims can more safely be made in experimental studies in which variables that might confound the observations can be controlled. This can be accomplished through careful sample selection, or through the use of comparison groups or subject matching. It is often claimed that, given the many possible competing explanations for a positive therapy outcome (e.g., extra therapy factors, spontaneous remission, nonspecific therapy factors), the effectiveness of a particular intervention can never be shown in a single case. However, the data from a well-conducted case study can provide the basis for an evaluation of various competing explanations for therapy outcome. Kratochwill et al. (1984) identify 12 factors that can lend support to the conclusion that positive outcome was related to a specific intervention. These include situations in which the problem is chronic rather than acute, therapeutic change is immediate and large, and outcome is assessed by a series of repeated measurements. Some of these factors can be enhanced by incorporating longitudinal observations into the study. Evidence is enhanced if the effect can be demonstrated in further cases, especially if they are unlike the original case in important respects.

An additional factor not mentioned by Kratochwill et al. is that qualitative data often provide evidence that a process of change has been set in motion by the therapy that can be expected on theoretical grounds to be therapeutic. For example, there is abundant evidence from at least three decades of published case studies that the training of the mother in parenting skills can increase compliance and reduce disruptive behavior in a child. If, in a study of the treatment of a noncompliant child, evidence was available that the mother had systematically improved relevant parenting skills, this would support a conclusion that the intervention contributed to the child's improved behavior. Similarly, Edwards and Bailey (1991) treated a retarded girl for pica (consumption of inedible objects) using a discrimination-training program in which candy was used as a reward. The problem behavior decreased in frequency and on one occasion the mother reported her daughter said, "I must not eat these things or *Mlungukazi* [the therapist] will not give me candy." This suggests that she had developed her own self-instructions, a process known to enhance self-control. It also suggested that her enhanced self-control was a result of the therapeutic intervention.

The final stage is "theory development." Well-conducted clinical case studies allow for the testing of existing generalizations and hypotheses as well as for the proposal of new conceptual distinctions, generalizations, or hypotheses. To ensure validity here, claims must be based upon evidence from the case material. Links between theoretical constructs or between the theory and the data, need to be logically argued and internally coherent. As already suggested, validity is established by carefully considering alternative explanations and actively searching for cases that enable competing theories to be evaluated against each other. "External validity," which refers to the generalizability of principles, is less of a problem in case study research based on case law than in experimental research (Kiesler, 1981; Taylor & Bogdan, 1984; Yin, 1984). This is because case studies usually employ qualitative methods that stay close to the everyday details of clients' lives, whereas in experimental research the generalization of conclusions is put at risk because variables are strictly controlled and personal experience is filtered through indirect measurements and operational definitions.

THE CASE STUDY IN COGNITIVE THERAPY

In this section, case studies from the literature on cognitive therapy, mostly with children, are examined in order to illustrate how case study research contributes to the development of knowledge. Because case study methodology has generally not been recognized as contributing to scientific knowledge, the literature on cognitive therapy does not contain a large public database of well-described case studies that meet each of the formal requirements that have been described above. Instead, a great deal of this literature is in the form of case law relating to the treatment of specific disorders (e.g., Beck, Rush, Shaw, & Emery, 1979; Beck & Emery, 1985; Freeman et al., 1990; Hawton et al., 1989; Hersen & Bellack, 1985a). In addition, behavior therapy and cognitive therapy have been the subject of a series of case study collections (e.g., Dattilio & Freeman, 1994; Emery, Hollon, & Bedrosian, 1981; Eysenck, 1976; Freeman & Dattilio, 1992; Hawton et al., 1989; Hersen & Last, 1985; Lazarus, 1985; Scott, Williams, & Beck, 1989) to which the present volume is a valuable addition. Although the case studies included in these works are seldom presented as formal contributions to the clinical research literature, they often include many or all of the stages of a clinical case study. In addition, many of the concerns regarding validity are addressed, especially when the cases have originated in research clinics where they have been thoroughly supervised and discussed.

Multiple-Case Study of Obsessive–Compulsive Disorder

The first study to be described is a theoretical–heuristic study of obsessive–compulsive disorder (Salkovskis, 1985). Although it addresses the treatment of an adult, it is included because it serves as an excellent model of rigorous theory development using multiple cases. A detailed model of the underlying emotional, cognitive, and behavioral processes in the disorder was presented, based on the existing literature and tested against material from 16 new cases. The model incorporates the major features found in obsessive–compulsive disorder: ego-dystonic cognitive intrusions in the form of disturbing thoughts or images triggered by contact with certain people or objects believed to be harmful or contaminating; convincing automatic thoughts on the theme of being responsible for harming others; dysfunctional assumptions, such as "thinking of doing it is the same as doing it," that enhance feelings of guilt; and phobic-like avoidance of trigger situations or compulsive thoughts or behaviors that serve to neutralize the intrusion and are reinforced by the anxiety reduction they produce. The model contains specific predictions that could be tested against new cases, and Salkovskis actively searched for cases that failed to meet these predictions. He describes such a case: that of a girl whose compulsion to arrange objects in neat lines was not associated with thoughts of responsibility for harm, as the model predicts. This is, in effect, a crucial case study because it rigorously asks whether the theory is consistent with the case material. Analysis of the case led to an extension of the model by specifying circumstances under which a behavior that was initially neutralizing could develop into a self-maintained habit.

With such a body of case law, any therapist treating a case of obsessive–compulsive disorder is in a position to contribute to the scientific process. A working case study would be one that accords with the model and is, in effect, an exercise in applied science. Investigating and solving the problems posed by a new case using existing theory further demonstrate the practical value of the theory and add to its external validity. It is therefore, in the language of research methodology, a true "clinical replication." Cases that do not fit the model call for a reexamination of specific propositions and may lead to further conceptual differentiation and development.

Cognitive Therapy with Children: General Case Law

Typically, case law is presented at a general level and with much less rigor. Two papers by DiGiuseppe (1981, 1989) are good examples of such informal presentations of general principles of case law on cognitive therapy with children. He addresses the question of the extent to which the general principles of cognitive therapy with adults can be applied to children and to what extent they need to be modified or extended. He argues that his case material demonstrates that a number of principles established for cognitive therapy with adults also apply to cognitive therapy with children. Here are some examples:

1. The treatment plan must be derived from a careful case conceptualization based on appropriate valid information about the child's behavior, cognitions, and emotions.
2. Children's problem-solving skills, self-instructions, cognitive distortions, and idiosyncratic personal meanings can be assessed and addressed.
3. Children's limited schemas regarding their own emotions can be modified by teaching them procedures such as rating emotions on subjective scales and teaching them about the different types of emotions through role play and Socratic dialogue.

In what is, in effect, an extension of adult case law, DiGiuseppe (1981) outlines factors that require special attention with children. These factors illustrate the relation between case studies and theoretical principles:

1. An assessment of the family is essential so that the therapist can assess whether the source of the problem lies largely with the child or with other family members. Just because the child is brought for therapy does not mean that individual therapy with the child is the treatment of choice.
2. If a child's dysfunctional behavior (e.g., yelling at others when thwarted) is regularly displayed by other family members, it will be impossible to change it. DiGiuseppe's (1981) statement, "I have never successfully changed a child's behavior when significant family members behave similarly" (p. 61), is an informal claim that this principle is derived from a series of his own cases. Of course, for research purposes it would be valuable if detailed studies of some of these cases were presented in order to provide evidence for the theory that the modeling by the family member is a stronger determinant of the child's behavior than the therapeutic intervention. However, a statement such as this is an invitation to researchers to test the principle against new cases and to examine in more depth the psychological processes involved.
3. It is important to form a collaborative relationship with the child on mutually agreed goals. Therapy cannot be initiated if the child has been coerced into therapy and does not perceive any advantages of engaging in it. Of course, this principle applies to adults as well, but it is less often that adults are brought to therapy by more powerful family members.
4. In order to establish rapport, the therapist must be scrupulously honest and should avoid excessive reliance on questioning, especially at first.

5. In young children, cognitive restructuring can successfully be taught through the use of dolls and puppets. This is supported by a case vignette of 6-year-old Paula, who learned the self-instruction, "My Daddy loves me, and I will see him next week" to help her deal with sadness at the end of his weekly visits.

The process of case-law development is also illustrated by DiGiuseppe's (1981) comparison of the merits of two cognitive restructuring strategies for distorted cognitions. These were based on Ellis's distinction between "empirical disputing" (examining and testing the evidence), and "elegant disputing" (challenging an underlying assumption such as, "I have to be approved of by others, and it is terrible when I am not"). DiGiuseppe (1981) concludes the discussion of the treatment of socially isolated, 8-year-old Linda as follows:

> No experimental evidence exists to prove which of these strategies or combination thereof is most successful. My own clinical experience suggests it is best to start with the simpler strategies, problem-solving and inelegant disputing, even though the remaining strategy, elegant disputing, may be more prophylactic. The first two strategies usually provided more rapid symptom relief. The third, challenging basic philosophical assumptions, is difficult with children because of their less developed reasoning ability. (p. 64)

He acknowledges that no group-comparison studies have been reported comparing elegant disputing with problem solving and reality testing. However, there is a body of relevant evidence from the material of individual cases, which, in accordance with the principles of case study methodology, DiGiuseppe goes on to discuss. His experience suggests that inelegant disputing produces more rapid symptom relief—a claim that he has examined in a number of cases. Material from four cases, including Linda's, is discussed, of which three support the value of problem solving and empirical testing. In the fourth, a 10-year-old boy was depressed because he believed his stepfather did not care about him. Empirical testing showed that this belief was accurate, and the boy remained somewhat depressed. Relief was only obtained when he identified and gave up the belief that he could only be happy if his stepfather cared for him much more than he actually did. It is evident that this last case differed from the first three in that empirical testing failed to invalidate the dysfunctional assumption that was contributing to the depression. It is precisely because of the risk of this happening that Ellis regards empirical testing as inelegant. To make a rigid ideological rule, as Ellis does, is not in accord, however, with the case study approach. The advantages and disadvantages of each need to be examined in practice in a series of cases in order for valid and refined case law to be developed, which will provide a reliable guide to identifying the types of situation to which each type of strategy is most suited.

DiGiuseppe's presentations of case law are informal in that he does not use case material systematically to argue for the validity of the general principles he describes. However most of the principles are supported by case vignettes, and there is an implicit claim that the generalizations are derived from many cases and could be tested against new ones. A more rigorous account of case law could be given if our research paradigms had supported the development of a good public database of case studies. Nevertheless, this presentation provides an excellent starting point for new case study research in which fresh cases are used to confirm, test, and refine general principles.

Adolescent Depression: A Case Vignette

Braswell and Kendall (1988) describe a case vignette in their discussion of the extension to children and adolescents of case law developed for cognitive therapy with adults. Like DiGiuseppe, they summarize some of the principles that are applicable to children and adolescents and illustrate their own experience of applying these principles by presenting the case of Sharon, a suicidal 15-year-old girl who displayed several vegetative signs of depression. Sharon was very perfectionistic, as were her parents, and this perfectionism became a focus in the therapy. Even though her parents were willing to moderate their demands on her, she was at first unwilling to challenge her perfectionism because she viewed it as a valuable asset. However, she was willing to review with the therapist those situations in which her perfectionism worked in her favor and those in which it worked against her. As a result, she experimented with relaxing her standards in some areas and maintaining them in others. She gained insight into the manner in which she had acquired her perfectionistic beliefs and recognized that she could now assume the choice of whether, and in what contexts, to continue it.

Although the authors do not intend this brief report to be a rigorous case study, the vignette contributes to cognitive therapy case law in a number of ways. First, although the links between the perfectionism and the depression are not identified, the report is used as the basis for the hypothesis that perfectionism can be an important therapy issue for depressive adolescents, just as it can be for adults. Second, it documents the successful use of a number of standard cognitive therapy interventions with an adolescent: self-monitoring, recognition of the way mood responds to specific automatic thoughts and behavior, and behavioral experiments to evaluate perfectionistic rules. Third, it documents the solution to a familiar problem for cognitive therapists: how to engender the collaboration of a client who is unwilling to examine self-defeating behavior and cognitions. This was achieved by means of two well-established cognitive therapeutic strategies: (1) reviewing the advantages and disadvantages of a particular behavior, and (2) pointing out that the behavior originally became a habit as a result of social learning that took place outside of awareness, but that it is now possible to take active steps to change the habit and exercise self-control.

In terms of the continuum described earlier, this is a descriptive–dialogic study in that components of the therapy are documented sufficiently to enable them to be used to support the claim that aspects of existing case law are applicable to adolescents. No claim is made that this is an outcome study. The girl was given antidepressants as well as cognitive therapy, and not enough material is presented to link cognitive change to therapeutic change. However, current case law in cognitive therapy suggests that medications relieve the cognitive-biasing effect of depressed mood, but may not alter underlying depressogenic assumptions and schemas. The limited data from this case are consistent with this perspective and suggest that there would have been little or no modification of her perfectionistic beliefs without the cognitive interventions.

Childhood Depression: A Clinical Case Study

The second case of depression is a detailed clinical study of the 22-session therapy of Bill, a 10-year-old boy suffering from major depression and separation anxiety disorder (Reinecke, 1992). A thorough assessment was based on interviews with Bill, with his parents, and, by phone, with his teacher. His mother completed a children's personality inventory, and his teacher completed several behavioral rating scales. Bill exhibited depressed mood, suicidal ideations, anxiety, and hopelessness. There were no serious problems at home or with his schoolwork. The roots of his depression were certain cognitions about himself and his peers that severely affected his peer relationships at school. His teacher perceived him to be critical and uncompromising in his attitudes toward his peers. Probably as a compensation (Young, 1990), he had developed an arrogant, positive self-schema that he was smarter than everyone else. As a result, he was intolerant of others' shortcomings, bragged about his own achievements, and insisted on dictating the rules of games. This led to his becoming socially isolated and often involved in fights. This created a self-defeating cycle that had the effect of reinforcing three key cognitions: (1) that he was "repellent" to other children, (2) that other children were rejecting and malicious, and (3) the compensatory belief that he was better than other people. In addition to this, he sought revenge on other children for rejecting him, which reinforced his aggressive behavior. The resultant rejection and loneliness brought on a depressed mood that increased his social withdrawal and self-critical thinking, which in turn fed into the downward spiral of depression (Freeman et al., 1990) as he felt more and more hopeless about changing the situation.

The case study documents how a number of problems were addressed. First, Bill found it hard to accept that he had a problem and did not want to talk to the therapist. The therapist used drawing as a means of initiating a relationship with him. He spoke empathetically about Bill's drawings, which focused directly or indirectly on his perceptions of himself and his problems with his peers, and he invited him to tell stories related to them. Through this, Bill began to feel understood and to feel safe enough to talk about his problems. This documents the application of a well-established principle of adult cognitive therapy—that the therapist needs to establish an empathic relationship in which the client is motivated to work collaboratively—and shows how methods used widely in child psychotherapy can be appropriated into cognitive therapy to achieve this.

Second, a range of standard cognitive therapy interventions including Socratic questioning, guided discovery, rational responding, and behavioral coaching and rehearsal, were employed to break the cycles of self-defeating cognition and behavior. These interventions helped him to identify and restructure dichotomous thinking ("People are either good or bad"); to recognize that a person can experience two different emotions simultaneously; to become more tolerant of his own mistakes; to develop his capacity for social perspective taking and thus to recognize how his arrogant, demanding behavior alienated other children; and finally, to acquire adaptive social behaviors.

Third, Reinecke showed how work with children's drawings can provide valuable information about dysfunctional cognitions as well as bring about cognitive change. In working with a story of "the invisible man" derived from a drawing, he was able to prompt Bill to generate alternative perspectives and more adaptive solutions to problems about which "the invisible man" felt hopeless. Evidence of Bill's feeling more optimistic as a result of becoming aware of new options was provided by his comments at the end of the session that he would think about this for next time and that he had liked the session, although he had not expected to. He also showed how insights gained from the work with "the invisible man" proved valuable in conceptualizing and working with Bill's problems at school.

Fourth, Reinecke briefly documents the role of meetings with the parents. These meetings enabled him to discover and address the origins of some of Bill's beliefs. His father complained frequently, was a perfectionist, and felt frustrated that his applications to medical school had been repeatedly rejected. Familial interactions thus provided a model of maladaptive thoughts and behaviors that had reinforced Bill's negative schemas and self-defeating thoughts and behaviors. A second feature of the work with the parents was to promote their support and encouragement of Bill's engaging in enjoyable social activities.

This study is descriptive–dialogic in style because it illustrates the use of cognitive therapy with childhood depression and serves as a vehicle for exploring theoretical issues and general principles. However the quality of the material lends itself to a more disciplined theoretical–heuristic case presentation in that it provides support for several theoretical conclusions, only some of which are made explicit. For example, Reinecke documents (1) the applicability of standard cognitive therapy case-conceptualization procedures to a case of childhood depression, (2) the successful use of a range of standard cognitive therapy techniques with a child, and (3) the value of working with drawing and storytelling.

In addition, evidence regarding the effectiveness of the interventions could have been more systematically presented. At termination, Bill had not been in a fight for 6 weeks, he criticized peers less often, he rarely withdrew or became inappropriately angry, he was less perfectionistic, and he had no suicidal ideations. Informal evidence is provided that there was a systematic and observable relationship between the interventions and the therapeutic outcome. For example, it is reasonable to conclude that without the drawing and storytelling, Bill might not have engaged in the therapy process at all. Some evidence is included regarding the relationship between the process of training Bill in perspective taking, social skills, and problem solving and changes in his peer relationships. For example, "the dramatic decline in the frequency of Bill's fighting as thoughts underlying his feelings of anger were examined" (p. 155) is evidence for a causal connection in terms of the criteria set out by Kratochwill et al. (1984) in the earlier discussion of "internal validity." This aspect of the study could have been strengthened by more detailed accounts of the relation between therapeutic interventions and changes in Bill's negative mood; in target behaviors, such as the fighting; and in dysfunctional cognitions, such as beliefs about his peers' maliciousness. If this were the main aim of the study, then a formal time series analysis with carefully quantified measures would have been of value. However, as I have argued elsewhere, relatively informal data at a coarse level of measurement can be quite adequate for this purpose, provided it is valid (Edwards & Bailey, 1991).

Reinecke remarks that the reliability and validity of the use of drawing and storytelling as a means of cognitive assessment have yet to be demonstrated. This is unduly apologetic since, as already pointed out, the case material itself provides evidence to support its validity both for assessment and treatment. In addition, there is already a basis in published case studies to construct a basic case law. For example, DiGiuseppe (1981, 1989) provides evidence for the value of integrating the use of dolls and puppets into cognitive therapy with children. With adults, there is evidence for the value of guided imagery in furnishing information about and bringing about changes in schemas (Edwards, 1990b). For children, there is an extensive literature on the role of play and fantasy in the development and modification of their cognitive and emotional schemas (J. L. Singer, 1973; D. G. Singer & J. L. Singer, 1990). The use of play therapy as a means of identifying dysfunctional cognitions and bringing about cognitive change has been documented and discussed by Harter (1977) in the context of cognitive developmental theory. She used a series of case vignettes to show how dichotomous thinking and difficulties with recognizing and accepting ambivalent feelings could be identified and modified by play therapy. Storytelling was also used by Klingman (1992) in the treatment of a 4-year-old Israeli child who refused to wear a gas mask during air-raid emergencies in the Gulf War. Treatment included biblioguidance (a story about a bear who was confused and anxious about the war and did not want to wear a gas mask), structured play in which the child trained a bear to wear a gas mask, and parent-administered positive reinforcement. Kendall's *Coping Cat Workbook* (see Chapter 8) is another application of this principle.

Childhood Depression: A Rigorous Theoretical–Heuristic Study

A rigorous case study of the assessment and cognitive-behavioral treatment of an 11-year-old depressed boy is presented by Frame and Jackson (1985). Ben was brought for treatment by his mother following his threat to jump out of a car. He had previously expressed on several occasions the wish that he were dead. Assessment was based on reports by his mother of a range of symptoms suggesting a diagnosis of depression, Ben's responses on a depression inventory, behavioral observations at school, and a role-play task to assess interpersonal behavior and clinical interviews. The case conceptualization, which is in behavior therapy terms, is fully in accord with standard cognitive therapy case law and is summarized here. A precipitating event (Ben's not being selected for the school safety patrol) had initiated a series of responses that fed into a downward spiral of depression (Freeman et al., 1990). Lacking the skills and experience to express his disappointment, he withdrew socially from peers and at home. His father spent little time at home and sometimes became intoxicated by alcohol and was very irritable. The family seemed to be quite disengaged socially. As a result, there was little support for Ben to speak about his feelings, and he spent much of his time alone in his room. In a classic self-defeating cycle, his mood-syntonic automatic thoughts about his worth as a playmate led to withdrawn behavior which, together with his consistently sad demeanor, alienated his peers. This, in turn, reinforced his cognitive distortions and loneliness and resulted in the loss of all satisfaction or pleasure from relationships. Another self-defeating cycle developed around his schoolwork: Ben was vulnerable to negative cognitions about failure even when he achieved consistently at school. As the depression developed, additional negative automatic thoughts about being unable to complete his work or do it correctly were exacerbated by, and contributed to, diminished concentration and procrastination. These negative thoughts served to reinforce his cognitive distortions. As the spiral continued, Ben experienced increasing distress and became more and more hopeless about ever being happy. This led to the suicidal ideations, which were reinforced by positive attention from his mother and sister and eventually led to the suicide threat.

Interventions were designed to alter specific behaviors that contributed to Ben's various self-defeating cycles maintaining his depression. Behavioral targets were to (1) increase time spent on tasks at school, (2) increase the number of social approaches Ben would receive and initiate on the school playground, (3) decrease the time he spent alone in his room and the frequency of suicidal talk, and (4) increase the positive attention he would receive from his mother and sister. Many of the interventions involved active cognitive retraining and included training in the following: (1) breaking tasks down into small steps and pacing himself with positive self-instructions (this was effective in increasing the time he spent focused on class work), (2) responding positively when another child initiated an interaction, (3) initiating interactions himself and rehearsing positive thoughts about his social competence, and (4) assertiveness and expression of his feelings and needs. The interventions were implemented in eight 30-minute sessions at the rate of twice a week. At the end of treatment, there had been major changes on all the behavioral criteria and no evidence of depressed mood. At a follow-up 15 months later, there was no evidence of recurrence of the depression, and Ben was cheerfully involved socially and was a member of a soccer team.

For several reasons, this study is an excellent demonstration of the value to the research process of good case study writing. First, a great deal of attention was paid to establishing the validity of the behavioral description and analysis by gathering relevant information from a range of sources. Second, the case conceptualization is thoroughly grounded in the data that was gathered. Third, the conceptualization and treatment are consistent with the cognitive therapy formulation of depression. It was designed to increase the amount of pleasurable and rewarding activities Ben would engage in and disrupted cycles of self-defeating behaviors and cognitive distortions. Moreover, it included training in cognitive restructuring and the use of positive self-instructions. Finally, changes in study and interpersonal behavior were specifically linked to changes in his cognitions about his competence and likability.

The inclusion of dialogue from therapy sessions not only provides the reader with insights into the nature of the interventions, but also a check that the interventions were consonant with their descriptions. Finally, the following objective evidence was provided for the effectiveness of the treatment:

1. The child had become steadily more and more depressed over a period of 2 months, to the point of becoming suicidal. The response to treatment was therefore relatively rapid.
2. There is an implicit, multiple-baseline methodology: Specific target behaviors changed only when the intervention that targeted them was implemented. There is thus clear evidence that the behaviors responded to the interventions.
3. In addition to measures of depression, outcome was assessed in terms of objective evidence that there was a systematic change over time in behaviors known to contribute to depression.

The study provides support for the validity of the clinical constructs of cognitive therapy as genuine grounded theory and shows that the processes identified in adults can be identified in children. There is a coherent account of a process of therapeutic change that was in accordance with the therapist's intentions, and that would, on theoretical grounds, be expected to alleviate the depression. In light of this, Frame and Jackson's remark that it is impossible to be certain that improvement was not due to spontaneous remission is unduly cautious. Spontaneous remission means that the condition remits without there being an intervention that might be expected to alleviate it. What is appropriate is to be alert to the fact that some extratherapy factor might have played a role in the improvement. It would be useful to examine the evidence for the effects of any extratherapy factors identified relative to the effect of the intervention. Although it is impossible to be certain, research is not about certainty. Rather, it is about building up a body of evidence that supports or undermines particular conclusions more or less strongly. Within this context, this study provides excellent support for widely recognized principles of cognitive-behavioral conceptualization and treatment and is a good example of a theoretical–heuristic case study.

CONCLUSION

The general framework of case study research methodology set out here, and the analyses of case studies within that framework, should provide a basis for an appreciation of the scientific basis of clinical knowledge. It is my hope that this will enable readers to recognize and evaluate the extent to which the case studies in this volume contribute, implicitly or explicitly, to the presentation and development of grounded clinical theory. It is also intended to guide clinicians who would like to work more systematically with their ongoing cases in such a way that they will be in a position to present detailed and rigorous case descriptions for peer discussion or publication. In the long term, this could lead to the development of a much needed universal database for the development and extension of clinical theory. In this way, a greater number of clinicians could contribute to the research process as scientist-practitioners. Cognitive therapy has a tradition of commonsense pragmatism. The case study method is very much in accord with this approach, and if its place in the research process can be honored, the future development of cognitive therapy can only be enhanced.

ACKNOWLEDGMENTS

This chapter is based on a paper presented at the World Congress of Cognitive Therapy, Oxford, England, in June 1989. Preparation of this chapter was supported by grants from the National Programme in Research Methodology of the Human Sciences Research Council, from the Center for Science Development, and from the Joint Research Committee of Rhodes University.

REFERENCES

Barlow, D. H. (1981). On the relation of clinical research to clinical practice: Current issues, new directions. *Journal of Consulting and Clinical Psychology, 49*, 147–155.

Beames, L., Sanders, M., & Bor, W. (1992). Cognitive-behavioral treatment of children's headaches. *Behavioral Psychotherapy, 20*, 167–180.

Beck, A. T. (1967). *Depression: Clinical, experimental, and theoretical aspects.* New York: Harper & Row.

Beck, A. T. (1976). *Cognitive therapy and the emotional disorders.* New York: New American Library.

Beck, A. T., & Emery, G. (1985). *Anxiety disorders and phobias: A cognitive perspective.* New York: Basic Books.

Beck, A. T., Rush, A. J., Shaw, B. F., & Emery, G. (1979). *Cognitive therapy of depression.* New York: Guilford Press.

Bolgar, H. (1965). The case study method. In B. B. Wolman (Ed.), *Handbook of clinical psychology* (pp. 28–39). New York: McGraw-Hill.

Braswell, L., & Kendall, P. C. (1988). Cognitive-behavioral methods with children. In K. S. Dobson (Ed.), *Handbook of cognitive-behavioral therapies* (pp. 167–213). New York: Guilford Press.

Bromley, D. B. (1986). *The case-study method in psychology and related disciplines*. Chichester, UK: Wiley.

Dattilio, F. M., & Freeman, A. (Eds.). (1994). *Cognitive-behavioral strategies in crisis intervention*. New York: Guilford Press.

DiGiuseppe, R. (1981). Cognitive therapy with children. In G. Emery, S. D. Hollon, & R. C. Bedrosian (Eds.), *New directions in cognitive therapy* (pp. 50–67). New York: Guilford Press.

DiGiuseppe, R. (1989). Cognitive therapy with children. In A. Freeman, K. M. Simon, L. Beutler, & H. Arkowitz (Eds.), *Comprehensive handbook of cognitive therapy* (pp. 515–534). New York: Plenum Press.

Eckstein, H. (1975). Case study and theory in political science. In F. I. Greenstein & N. W. Polsby (Eds.), *Handbook of political science: Vol. 7. Strategies of enquiry* (pp. 79–137). Reading, MA: Addison-Wesley.

Edwards, D. J. A. (1990a). Research and reality: How clinical theory and practice are actually developed—Case study method in cognitive-behavior therapy. In J. Mouton & D. Joubert (Eds.), *Knowledge and method in the human sciences* (pp. 359–374). Pretoria, South Africa: Human Sciences Research Council.

Edwards, D. J. A. (1990b). Cognitive therapy and the restructuring of early memories through guided imagery. *Journal of Cognitive Psychotherapy: An International Quarterly, 4*, 33–50.

Edwards, D. J. A. (1991). Duquesne phenomenological research method as a special class of case study research method. In R. van Vuuren (Ed.), *Dialogue beyond polemics* (pp. 53–70). Pretoria, South Africa: Human Sciences Research Council.

Edwards, D. J. A., & Bailey, G. (1991). Treatment of multiple behavioural problems in a retarded township child: A case study. *South African Journal of Psychology, 21*, 26–31.

Emery, G., Hollon, S. D., & Bedrosian, R. C. (Eds.). (1981). *New directions in cognitive therapy*. New York: Guilford Press.

Eysenck, H. J. (Ed.). (1976). *Case studies in behavior therapy*. London: Routledge & Kegan Paul.

Fischer, C. T., & Wertz, F. J. (1979). Empirical phenomenological analyses of being criminally victimized. In A. Giorgi, R. Knowles, & D. L. Smith (Eds.), *Duquesne studies in phenomenological psychology* (Vol. 3, pp. 135–158). Pittsburgh: Duquesne University Press.

Frame, C. L. & Jackson, J. L. (1985). Childhood depression. In M. Hersen & C. G. Last (Eds.), *Behavior therapy casebook* (pp. 258–270). New York: Springer.

Freeman, A., & Dattilio, F. M. (1992). *Comprehensive casebook of cognitive therapy*. New York: Plenum Press.

Freeman, A., Pretzer, J. Fleming, B., & Simon, K. M. (1990). *Clinical applications of cognitive therapy*. New York: Plenum Press.

Freeman, A., Simon, K., Beutler, L. E., & Arkowitz, H. (1989). *Comprehensive handbook of cognitive therapy*. New York: Plenum Press.

Gelfand, D. M., Jenson, W. R., & Drew, C. J. (1988). *Understanding child behavior disorders: An introduction to child psychopathology*. Fort Worth, TX: Holt, Rinehart & Winston.

Giorgi, A. (1985). *Phenomenology and psychological research*. Pittsburgh: Duquesne University Press.

Giorgi, A. (1986a). Theoretical justification for the use of descriptions in psychological research. In P. D. Ashworth, A. Giorgi, & A. J. J. de Koning (Eds.), *Qualitative research in psychology: Proceedings of the International Association for Qualitative Research in Social Science* (pp. 3–93). Pittsburgh: Duquesne University Press.

Giorgi, A. (1986b). The "context of discovery/context of verification" distinction and descriptive human science. *Journal of Phenomenological Psychology, 17*, 151–166.

Glaser, B. G., & Strauss, A. L. (1967). *The discovery of grounded theory*. London: Weidenfeld & Nicolson.

Harter, S. (1977). A cognitive-developmental approach to children's expression of conflicting feelings and a technique to facilitate such expression in play therapy. *Journal of Consulting and Clinical Psychology, 43*, 417–432.

Hawton, K. (1989). Sexual dysfunctions. In K. Hawton, P. M. Salkovskis, J. Kirk, & D. M. Clark (Eds.), *Cognitive behavior therapy for psychiatric problems: A practical guide* (pp. 370–405). Oxford, UK: Oxford University Press.

Hawton, K., Salkovskis, P. M., Kirk, J., & Clark, D. M. (Eds.). (1989). *Cognitive behavior therapy for psychiatric problems: A practical guide*. Oxford, UK: Oxford University Press.

Hayes, S. C. (1981). Single case experimental design and empirical clinical practice. *Journal of Consulting and Clinical Psychology, 49*, 193–211.

Henwood, K. L., & Pidgeon, N. F. (1993). Qualitative research and psychological theorizing. In M. Hammersley (Ed.), *Social research: Philosophy, politics and practice* (pp. 14–32). London: Sage.

Hersen, M., & Bellack, A. S. (Eds.). (1985). *Handbook of clinical behavior therapy with adults*. New York: Plenum Press.

Hersen, M., & Last, C. G. (Eds.). (1985). *Behavior therapy casebook*. New York: Springer.

Kazdin, A. E. (1981). Drawing valid inferences from case studies. *Journal of Consulting and Clinical Psychology, 49*, 183–192.

Kiesler, D. J. (1981). Empirical clinical psychology: Myth or reality? *Journal of Consulting and Clinical Psychology, 49*, 212–215.

Klingman, A. (1992). Parent implemented crisis intervention. *Journal of Child Psychiatry, 21*, 70–75.

Kratochwill, T. R., Mott, S. E., & Dodson, C. L. (1984). Case study and single-case research in clinical and applied psychology. In A. S. Bellack & M. Hersen (Eds.), *Research methods in clinical psychology* (pp. 55–99). New York: Pergamon.

Kruger, D. (1988). *An introduction to phenomenological psychology* (2nd ed.). Cape Town, South Africa: Juta.

Lazarus, A. A. (Ed.). (1985). *Casebook of multimodal therapy*. New York: Guilford Press.

Masters, J. C., Burish, T. G., Hollon, S. D. & Rimm, D. C. (1987). *Behavior therapy: Techniques and empirical findings* (3rd ed.). San Diego: Harcourt Brace Jovanovich.

Mahrer, A. R. (1988). Discovery-oriented psychotherapy research: Rationale and aims. *American Psychologist, 43,* 694–702.

Mitchell, J. C. (1983). Case and situation analysis. *Sociological Review, 31*(2), 187–211.

Morrow, L. W., Burke, J. G., & Buell, B. J. (1985). Effects of a self-recording procedure on the attending to task behavior and academic productivity of adolescents with multiple handicaps. *Mental Retardation, 23,* 137–141.

Ollendick, T. H., Hagopian, L. P. & Huntzinger, R. M. (1991). Cognitive behavior therapy with night time fearful children. *Journal of Behavior Therapy and Experimental Psychiatry, 22,* 113–121.

Persons, J. B. (1989). *Cognitive therapy in practice: A case formulation approach*. New York: Norton.

Persons, J., Curtis, J. T., & Silberschatz, G. (1991). Psychodynamic and cognitive-behavioral formulations of a single case. *Psychotherapy, 28,* 608–617.

Polkinghorne, D. E. (1986). Conceptual validity in a nontheoretical human science. *Journal of Phenomenological Psychology, 17,* 129–150.

Reinecke, M. (1992). Childhood depression. In A. Freeman & F. Dattilio (Eds.), *Comprehensive casebook of cognitive therapy* (pp. 147–158). New York: Plenum Press.

Safran, J., Greenberg, L. S., & Rice, L. (1988). Integrative psychotherapy research and practice: Modeling the change process. *Psychotherapy, 25,* 1–17.

Salkovskis, P. M. (1985). Obsessional–compulsive problems: A cognitive-behavioral analysis. *Behaviour Research and Therapy, 23*(5), 571–583.

Scott, J., Williams, J. M. G., & Beck, A. T. (Eds.). (1989). *Cognitive therapy in clinical practice: An illustrative casebook*. London: Routledge & Kegan Paul.

Shapiro, K. J. (1986). Verification: Validity or understanding. *Journal of Phenomenological Psychology, 17,* 167–179.

Singer, J. L. (1973). *The child's world of make-believe*. New York: Academic Press.

Singer, D. G., & Singer, J. L. (1990). *The house of make-believe: Children's play and the developing imagination*. Cambridge, MA: Harvard University Press.

Strauss, A., & Corbin, J. (1990). *Basics of qualitative research: Grounded theory procedures and techniques*. Newbury Park: Sage.

Strupp, H. H. (1981). Clinical research, practice, and the crisis of confidence. *Journal of Consulting and Clinical Psychology, 49,* 216–219.

Strupp, H. H. (1988). What is therapeutic change? *Journal of Cognitive Psychotherapy, 2,* 75–82.

Taylor, S. J., & Bogdan, R. (1984). *Introduction to qualitative research methods: The search for meanings* (2nd ed.). New York: Wiley.

Wertz, F. J. (1985). Method and findings in a phenomenological psychological study of a complex life-event: Being criminally victimized. In A. Giorgi (Ed.), *Phenomenology and psychological research* (pp. 155–216). Pittsburgh: Duquesne University Press.

Yin, R. K. (1984). *Case study research: Design and methods.* Beverly Hills: Sage.

Young, J. E. (1990). *Schema-focused cognitive therapy for personality disorders and difficult patients.* Sarasota, FL: Professional Resource Exchange.

Young, J. E., & Lindemann, M. D. (1992). An integrative schema-focused model for personality disorders. *Journal of Cognitive Psychotherapy, 6,* 11–24.

3

Treatment of Attention-Deficit/ Hyperactivity Disorder

Ruth A. Ervin
Christine L. Bankert
George J. DuPaul

Attention-deficit/hyperactivity disorder (ADHD; American Psychiatric Association, 1994) involves the display of above-average levels of inattention, impulsivity, and overactivity.[1] This is a disorder of early onset (i.e., symptoms usually are present prior to age 7) and symptoms are displayed across most home, school, and community settings. ADHD affects approximately 3% to 5% of school-aged children in the United States, with boys outnumbering girls at about a 3:1 to 5:1 ratio (Barkley, 1990). The disorder tends to be chronic, and 50% or more of children with ADHD will continue to evidence significant symptomatology into adolescence and adulthood (Barkley, Fischer, Edelbrock, & Smallish, 1990; Gittelman, Mannuzza, Shenker, & Bonagura, 1985; Weiss & Hechtman, 1993). In addition, children with this disorder are at higher than average risk for problematic educational, behavioral, and social–emotional outcomes (Barkley et al., 1990; Weiss & Hechtman, 1993).

The most common forms of treatment for ADHD include the prescription of psychostimulant medications and the implementation of behavioral interventions based on operant conditioning principles (Barkley, 1990; Matson, 1993). The most effective psychostimulant medications for this disorder include methylphenidate (Ritalin), dextroamphetamine (Dexedrine), and pemoline (Cylert). These drugs have been found to enhance the attention span, impulse control, academic productivity, social relationships, and compliance with authority-figure commands of about 70% to 80% of children with ADHD receiving medication (DuPaul & Barkley, 1990; Pelham, 1993). In similar fashion, behavioral interventions that include token reinforcement, response cost, negative reprimands, and time-out from positive reinforcement have been found to reduce symptoms of ADHD while enhancing behavior control and academic performance for a majority of children receiving treatment (Barkley, 1990; Pfiffner & O'Leary, 1993; Rapport, 1987). The latter interventions have been successful across home and school settings.

Despite the salutary effects of stimulant medication, behavioral intervention, and/or their combination, these treatments are limited in several important ways. First, both treatment modalities can be associated with side effects. For example, stimulant medication can lead to insomnia, appetite reduction, and dysphoric mood among some children (Barkley, McMurray, Edelbrock, & Robbins, 1990). Second, some parents and teachers find these treatments unacceptable due to philosophical and/or logistic concerns. Third, these treatments do not "cure" ADHD in the sense of completely normalizing children's behavior, thus implicating a need for additional intervention. Finally, and most important, the effects of stimulants and behavioral interventions rarely generalize to settings and times where treatment is absent (Pelham & Murphy, 1986). Specifically, stimulant medication effects typically dissipate about 4 hours after ingestion. In similar fashion, symptomatic changes evidenced in a setting in which a behavioral intervention has been implemented rarely are found in other settings or at later times when the intervention is not being used.

The limitations of existing treatments for ADHD, particularly the lack of generalization of effects, have promoted the search for additional interventions that may promote greater maintenance of behavioral change over time and across settings. Cognitive-behavioral interventions have been among the most prominently studied treatments designed to increase the probability of achieving durable behavioral change (Braswell & Bloomquist, 1991; Kendall & Braswell, 1993). Therefore, the purpose of the present chapter is to provide some brief background regarding the results of empirical studies examining the efficacy of cognitive-behavioral interventions for ADHD. The use of a specific form of cognitive-behavioral intervention (i.e., self-management) will be explicated in the context of a case study. Readers interested in a more comprehensive review of these interventions for children with ADHD should refer to Abikoff (1985), Braswell and Bloomquist (1991), and/or Kendall and Braswell (1993).

OVERVIEW OF COGNITIVE-BEHAVIORAL
INTERVENTIONS

Cognitive-behavioral interventions have been conceptualized into two approaches, those that are cognitive based (i.e., self-instruction and social problem solving), and those that are contingency based (i.e., self-monitoring, self-evaluation, self-reinforcement, and correspondence training; Shapiro & Cole, 1994). These interventions have been investigated in isolation and in combination with other treatments (e.g., stimulant medication), as will be discussed.

Cognitive-Based Interventions

Self-Instruction Training

Luria (1961) and others have theorized that children learn to control their own behavior by gradually internalizing the commands and directives of adults (i.e., by developing self-guiding speech); that is, self-control is regulated by covert speech. Unfortunately, children with ADHD are less compliant with parental directives (Barkley, Karlsson, & Pollard, 1985) and exhibit less mature patterns of self-speech (Berk & Potts, 1991) than do normal children. In fact, the results of Berk and Potts suggest that symptoms of ADHD may be related to a delay in the development of self-directed speech. These findings imply that it may be beneficial to teach children with this disorder to talk to themselves to improve their ability to control their behavior.

A variety of self-instructional programs have been used with various populations and tasks, but most applications follow the cognitive modeling, self-verbalization, and strategy training techniques developed by Meichenbaum and Goodman (1971). The goal of self-instruction training is to teach the child verbal behavior or self-talk that eventually will be internalized and will help guide his or her nonverbal actions. In children with ADHD, self-instructional training typically is directed toward regulating impulsivity and inattention. Usually the procedure is as follows: (1) Self-statements are modeled by the instructor verbally, (2) the child performs the same task with guidance from the instructor, (3) the child performs the task while instructing him- or herself out loud, (4) the child performs the task while whispering the instructions, and (5) the child performs the task while guiding his or her behavior with private speech (Hinshaw & Erhardt, 1991).

Research on self-instruction procedures with students with ADHD has been characterized by equivocal results and poor generalization of outcomes. These results may be due to methodological weaknesses, such as the use of outcome measures that are irrelevant to home and school demands (i.e., the Matching Familiar Figures Test) and brief training periods (Abikoff, 1985; Kendall & Braswell, 1993). Researchers have suggested that without behavioral components (i.e., contingencies or reinforcement), the use of self-instruction procedures for children with ADHD cannot be advocated (e.g., Hinshaw & Erhardt, 1991). Indeed, improvement occurs most consistently when self-reinforcement for accurate verbalizations is provided along with self-instructional training. In successful programs, it may be the reinforcement that results in improvement more so than the self-instructions (Pfiffner & Barkley, 1990).

Social Problem-Solving Training

Many authors have proposed that it is necessary to teach children with ADHD how to solve problems in a systematic fashion (e.g., Braswell & Bloomquist, 1991; Kendall & Braswell, 1993). The rationale for such training is that children with this disorder do not take the time to consider alternative solutions to their problems due to their poor impulse control. A plethora of empirical investigations have found these children to display quick and inaccurate responses across tasks and situations in laboratory and "real-world" settings (for a review, see Barkley, 1994). Therefore, training is directed to engage children with ADHD to follow a series of cognitive steps prior to making a response in a problematic social situation (Braswell & Bloomquist, 1991; Kendall & Braswell, 1993). It is important to note that the putative problem-solving deficit associated with ADHD differs from cognitive difficulties associated with other forms of psychopathology. For example, problem-solving training for depressed children is directed at rigidity of thinking and feelings of hopelessness that are not found among children with ADHD (Stark, Rouse, & Livingston, 1991).

Social problem-solving training involves teaching the child to (1) recognize the existence of a problem, (2) generate alternative problem solutions, (3) evaluate the consequences of different alternatives, (4) select an alternative to try, and (5) review the outcome of the selected alternative (Abikoff, 1985; Braswell & Bloomquist, 1991). Role-playing and modeling techniques often are used during training. Other types of cognitive techniques that also may be used in conjunction with this type of training are attribution retraining and stress inoculation procedures (Braswell & Bloomquist, 1991).

Reviews of the literature on the outcomes of social problem-solving training with children with ADHD have been somewhat disappointing (e.g., Abikoff, 1985). There is little evidence that using this type of cognitive technique alone results in improved behavior, regardless of whether the children are taking stimulant medication or not (e.g., Abikoff, 1985). Children with ADHD can learn social problem-solving skills, but often do not use the techniques in situations other than the actual training setting. Cognitive training with children with ADHD may be more effective when the focus is on a few specific situations, such as with attribution retraining or stress inoculation training (Hinshaw & Erhardt, 1991). Studies of interventions that include stress inoculation training in particular have produced promising results (e.g., Hinshaw, Henker, & Whalen, 1984).

Contingency-Based Interventions

Self-Monitoring

Douglas (1980) has postulated that ADHD symptoms may be related to a variety of cognitive deficits, including a lack of awareness of one's own behavior; that is, children with ADHD do not attend to their own behavior and its consequences (Barkley, 1990). Therefore, it may be helpful to train children with this disorder to monitor their own behavior as, at least, an initial step toward the development of self-control (Braswell & Bloomquist, 1991).

Self-monitoring procedures are characterized by teaching children to observe specific aspects of their behavior and to make objective recordings of the behavior. Children record the occurrence of behavior without prompting from others, but with the aid of external cueing mechanisms (e.g., an audiotaped signal). Through this process, an active awareness of the occurrence of targeted behaviors is maintained, which might increase the self-regulatory capacity of the child (Braswell & Bloomquist, 1991). Self-monitoring has been successfully applied to various target behaviors, such as academic performance (e.g., Lalli & Shapiro, 1990) and classroom behavior (e.g., Hallahan, Lloyd, Kneedler, & Marshall, 1982).

For students without ADHD, the self-observing and self-recording that is part of self-monitoring may result in positive reactive effects, without the use of backup reinforcers for improvements in behavior. For example, Harris (1986) found that self-monitoring of attention or work productivity improved attention-to-task and work completion of children with learning disabilities. Few studies have been conducted with students with ADHD, but given the nature of this disorder, it is assumed that reinforcers may be an important and necessary component to add to a self-monitoring procedure. For students with ADHD, it is generally accepted that self-monitoring alone will produce only weak improvement in behavior, but this intervention may be used effectively as part of more comprehensive treatment procedures, such as self-evaluation and self-reinforcement programs (e.g., Braswell & Bloomquist, 1991; Rhode, Morgan, & Young, 1983; Turkewitz, O'Leary, & Ironsmith, 1975).

Self-Evaluation and Self-Reinforcement

The impulsive and inattentive behaviors comprising ADHD purportedly result in a "seeming absence of accurate reflection over recently committed behavioral transgressions or over critical omissions in response style" (Hinshaw & Erhardt, 1991, pp. 111–112). Furthermore, children with this disorder are unlikely to carefully evaluate their task performance or to check the quality of their work (Barkley, 1990; Douglas, 1980). In similar fashion, such children presumably are less likely than their peers to engage in positive statements about their performance. Thus, task performance and social behavior may be enhanced by training children with ADHD to carefully evaluate their behavior and to reward themselves when they reach specified quality standards.

Self-management procedures with an emphasis on self-evaluation and self-reinforcement have been developed to shift responsibility from teachers to students in the monitoring of student behavior (Shapiro & Cole, 1994). Rhode et al. (1983) developed procedures wherein both teacher and student evaluations of the latter's behavior are based on a criterion that is preestablished. Students and teachers rate the behavior on a scale from 0 to 5 to indicate the degree to which student behavior was appropriate. Students earn points for appropriate behavior and for matching their self-evaluation closely to the teacher's evaluation. Gradually, the frequency of teacher ratings of student behavior is faded in order to promote maintenance and to increase student independence from the self-evaluation and self-reinforcement procedures. In addition, procedures are included that target generalization of these self-management skills to other settings.

Empirical support for the utility of self-management procedures has been demonstrated with elementary students with behavior disorders in a resource room setting (Rhode et al., 1983); with adolescents with behavior disorders in junior and senior high school settings (Smith, Young, West, Morgan, & Rhode, 1988; Young, Smith, West, & Morgan, 1987); and with adolescents identified as mildly handicapped, through the use of peer evaluations (Smith, Young, Nelson, & West, 1992). In general, these procedures have been found effective in producing, maintaining, and generalizing behavior change in students with behavior disorders (Rhode et al., 1983; Smith et al., 1988; Smith et al., 1992; Young et al., 1987).

For children with ADHD, who display many behavior problems not unlike those of students with behavior disorders, these procedures may have promise. Although research on the use of self-evaluation and self-reinforcement procedures for students with ADHD has been scant, preliminary findings have been positive (Hinshaw et al., 1984; Barkley, Copeland, & Sivage, 1980). Barkley and colleagues examined the effects of a multicomponent self-management package on the classroom behavior of children with ADHD. Children were instructed to evaluate their behavior with respect to posted classroom rules whenever a tone was sounded during independent seat work and in an experimental classroom. If their self-evaluations matched those of an independent observer, they received tokens exchangeable for backup reinforcers. Results indicated that on-task behavior improved during seat work, but these effects did not generalize to the general classroom setting.

In another study, Hinshaw and colleagues (1984) implemented a self-management program to enhance peer interactions of children with ADHD. Problem-solving and self-control skills for dealing with verbal taunting and provocation were taught to children with ADHD. The self-management procedure was effective in an analogue setting but these results did not generalize to a natural setting. Problems with maintenance and generalization of behavior change are not unique to children with ADHD. In general, it has been suggested that to achieve maintenance or generalization of effects, it is important to implement procedures that directly target these effects over time and across settings (Shapiro & Cole, 1994).

Correspondence Training

Correspondence training is a procedure that is aimed at increasing the correspondence between what a person verbally says he or she will do and his or her actual behavior (Paniagua, 1992). It has been demonstrated that changes in nonverbal behavior can be produced indirectly by programming reinforcement contingent on a relationship between two events: a verbalization of target (nonverbal) behavior and the actual occurrence of behavior (Risley & Hart, 1968). The verbalization can be made about past behavior ("do–report") or about future behavior ("report–do"), and reinforcement is provided contingent on the correspondence between verbal and nonverbal behavior (Paniagua, 1992). In the "do–report" technique, a child is taught to accurately report his or her past behavior, whereas in the "report–do" technique, a child is taught to behave consistently with predictions of future behavior.

Given the current conceptualization of ADHD as a problem of poor impulse control and deficient self-regulation of behavior (Barkley, 1994), correspondence training has been suggested as one method of teaching children to "control their own (nonverbal) behavior through the reinforcement of socially accepted verbal–nonverbal relationships" (Paniagua, 1992, p. 228). Correspondence training was first suggested for the management of children with ADHD by Abikoff and Gittelman (1985) and recently has been investigated with this population (Paniagua, 1987, 1990, 1992; Paniagua, Pumariega, & Black, 1988). Preliminary findings indicate that correspondence training was effective in producing substantial decreases in levels of hyperactivity for two children (ages 6 and 9 years) in a clinical setting (Paniagua et al., 1988). Paniagua (1992) provides a summary of five cases that illustrate the use of correspondence training for children with ADHD. In comparison with other cognitive-behavioral therapies that use verbal strategies (i.e., self-instruction), correspondence training has been described as a procedure that requires far less time for both the therapist and the child (Paniagua, 1992).

Despite the positive findings from preliminary research, some limitations associated with the use of correspondence training warrant discussion. The research that has been conducted thus far has been in clinical settings, and these results may not generalize to less controlled settings (e.g., school). In addition, in cases that involve immediate control of nonverbal behavior (e.g., severe aggression or self-endangering behaviors), the gradual shaping over time of appropriate verbal–nonverbal behavior correspondence may be impractical (Paniagua, 1992). Finally, receptive and expressive language skills are needed in order for correspondence training to be an effective intervention.

Cognitive-Behavioral Therapy
Combined with Other Interventions

Given the multifaceted nature of ADHD, treatment strategies typically are combined in an effort to ameliorate multiple-target behaviors across settings (Barkley, 1990). The assumption is that the effects of a combination of interventions will be superior to those associated with any single therapeutic modality. In particular, the combination of stimulant medication and cognitive-behavioral interventions would appear to be a complementary treatment package because the use of medication may increase the probability of children enacting therapeutic strategies (Horn, Chatoor, & Conners, 1983). Purportedly, cognitive-behavioral strategies would induce cognitive and behavioral improvement beyond that which occurs with medication alone, thus reducing the continued need for pharmacotherapy over time.

Several empirical studies have examined the separate and combined effects of cognitive (self-instruction) training and stimulant medication on the cognitions, behaviors, and academic performance of children with ADHD (see Abikoff, 1985, for a review). Most studies have found that the treatment combination is not superior to the effects of psychostimulants alone, especially with regard to behavior ratings (e.g., Abikoff &

Gittelman, 1985) and cognitive test performance (e.g., Cohen, Sullivan, Minde, Novak, & Helwig, 1981). Alternatively, cognitive training plus stimulant medication may lead to enhanced effects on academic performance, particularly if academic behaviors are included as training targets (e.g., Cameron & Robinson, 1980). The combination of self-evaluation procedures with methylphenidate has been found to be superior to either treatment in isolation in ameliorating negative social behaviors of children with ADHD (Hinshaw et al., 1984). In addition, positive social behaviors were found to significantly increase in frequency when this treatment combination was used.

Studies examining the combination of cognitive-behavioral strategies and stimulant medication have been limited by several factors (Abikoff, 1985). First, medication-induced behavioral change may be so strong that the effects of treatment combinations are limited by a ceiling effect. Second, some of the measures used to detect change (e.g., Matching Familiar Figures Test) suffer from limited validity and/or reliability. Third, the length of training has ranged from as little as 2 weeks to as many as 16 weeks, thereby introducing a significant variable moderating differential outcomes across studies. Despite these methodological limitations, it appears that the most promising treatment combination is reinforced self-evaluation plus stimulant medication with minimal support for the use of self-instructional paradigms.

CASE DESCRIPTION

Joe L., a 9-year-old third-grade student, was referred to the school-based child diagnostic team (i.e., school principal, school psychologist, special education teacher, school nurse, guidance counselor) by his teacher for problems paying attention in class, difficulties following directions, inconsistently completing his assigned seat work, and poor accuracy of academic products. Given these referring concerns, the diagnostic team conducted an assessment for the presence of ADHD through the use of a behavioral assessment approach wherein multiple methods of data collection were utilized across informants and settings (DuPaul, 1992; DuPaul & Stoner, 1994). Under this paradigm, there is an emphasis on obtaining reliable information concerning child behavior from parents, teachers, and direct observations of behavior (DuPaul, 1992).

Information was gathered to determine whether Joe (1) exhibited a signficant number of behavioral symptoms of ADHD according to parent and teacher reports, (2) exhibited ADHD symptoms at a frequency that was significantly greater than children of the same gender and mental age, (3) began exhibiting significant ADHD-related behavior prior to the age of 7 and for a duration of 6 months or longer, (4) had other deficits (e.g., learning disabilities) or factors that could account for the display of ADHD symptoms, and (5) had any associated disorders (e.g., oppositional defiant disorder, overanxious disorder).

Initial Assessment

Initial assessment began with screening through teacher and parent ratings of ADHD symptoms. For the sake of efficiency, the ADHD Rating Scale (DuPaul, 1991), a 4-point Likert scale consisting of rating the 14 symptoms of ADHD from the revised third edition of the *Diagnostic and Statistical Manual of Mental Disorders* (DSM-III-R; American Psychiatric Association, 1987) was completed by Joe's teacher and by his mother. On the ADHD Rating Scale, Joe received high ratings on 12 of 14 symptoms of ADHD from his teacher and on all 14 symptoms of ADHD from his mother. Joe's total score on both parent and teacher ratings placed him more than one standard deviation above the mean for boys his age. These scores indicated the need for further evaluation.

At the second stage of the evaluation, many methods were utilized to gather more specific information concerning Joe's history and present functioning. These methods included broadband rating scales, teacher and parent interviews, review of archival data, direct observation of behavior across settings, and collection of academic performance data.

First, Joe's mother was asked to complete the Child Behavior Checklist (Achenbach, 1991) and his teacher was asked to complete the Teacher Report Form of the Child Behavior Checklist (Achenbach, 1991). On the Attention Problems Factor of the Child Behavior Checklist, Joe received parent and teacher ratings above the 93rd percentile (i.e., *T* score greater than 65), which provided further support for the presence of problems in the areas of inattention, impulsivity, and overactivity. In addition to significant ratings on the Attention Problems Factor, maternal ratings placed Joe above the 93rd percentile on the Aggressive Behavior Factor of the Child Behavior Checklist. Behaviors that were reported to occur frequently on the Aggressive Behavior Factor included arguing, disobedience at home, stubbornness, mood changes, and temper tantrums. Teacher ratings, however, fell into the normal range on the Aggressive Behavior Factor, which indicated that these problems were not as problematic in school as they were at home. This finding is not surprising, given that oppositional behaviors that often are seen at an early age at home generally are not displayed in the school setting until later childhood (Barkley, 1990). All other subscales on parent and teacher ratings on the Child Behavior Checklist fell into the normal range.

Next, various members of the diagnostic team conducted parent and teacher interviews. The parent interview was conducted as a means of gathering historical information concerning Joe's developmental history related to behavior problems and his current functioning across a variety of areas. According to the maternal report, Joe's birth history and achievement of developmental milestones were relatively normal. Joe's mother reported no family history of emotional or learning problems, but she did report that his father had had difficulty paying attention in school.

With regard to Joe's history of problems with inattention–hyperactivity, his mother was asked to respond to questions about DSM-IV criteria for disruptive behavior disorders as well as affective and anxiety disorders. She reported that Joe exhibited all 18 of the symptoms of ADHD, which is beyond the clinical cutoff criteria for this disorder. Joe's mother reported that her son's problems with ADHD symptoms had been apparent as early as infancy. In addition, Joe was reported to exhibit several defiant behaviors (i.e., losing his temper, arguing, breaking rules, blaming others, refusing to do as told) at home. These problems placed Joe at significant risk for the development of oppositional defiant disorder, although he did not yet meet criteria for this disorder. No signficant symptoms of conduct disorder, depression, overanxious disorder, or separation anxiety disorder were reported.

Following the parent interview, the diagnostic team met with Joe's teacher, Mrs. Teri, to discuss the presence of ADHD symptoms in school and how he currently behaved in the classroom. Mrs. Teri reported that Joe had difficulty paying attention during instruction, following directions, and completing work accurately and in a timely manner. In addition, Joe was reported to constantly engage in inappropriate activities (e.g., playing with his pencil, making silly noises, talking with other students, getting out of his seat) that disrupted the classroom and often required teacher time that took away from the instruction of other students. When asked about which situations were most problematic, Mrs. Teri reported that Joe seemed to display more problems during teacher-led group instruction and independent seat work, but that he was manageable when she conducted small-group instruction during reading class. In addition, she reported that when he was engaged in a task that he enjoyed or that was of high interest to him, such as science or computers, he was more attentive. Academically, Joe was reported to demonstrate that he had the ability to do the work but that his performance was inconsistent. On some days he completed his work and did so accurately, but on other days his work was incomplete, sloppy, and incorrect. Previous interventions that had been somewhat successful, according to Mrs. Teri, included frequently stating the classroom rules or seat-work instructions, telling Joe that he would lose recess time if his work was not complete, and offering incentives for behavior. These interventions, however, were reported to be time consuming and not always effective.

Next, Joe's school records were reviewed. Joe's former teachers had made comments on his report cards that supported the presence of attention problems (e.g., "frequently talks out of turn," "difficulty following directions," and "is extremely energetic") prior to the age of 7 years.

Finally, direct observations of Joe's classroom behavior were conducted on several occasions by the school psychologist. Joe's behavior during independent seat work in math class and teacher-led reading instruction was found to be most problematic. The school psychologist observed Joe with an interval recording system in which his behavior was coded as either off-task or on-task every 15 seconds for a 20-minute period. During math, Joe was observed to be engaged in off-task behaviors (e.g., looking away from the teacher or fiddling with objects in his desk) for an average of 58% of the intervals observed. During reading instruction, Joe was observed to be engaged in off-task behaviors for an average of 36% of the intervals observed. Across his other major academic subject areas, Joe's levels of off-task behavior were much lower, with an average of 13% of the intervals observed across language arts, computer class, and social studies.

Diagnosis and Behavioral Conceptualization

Diagnostically, Joe met DSM-IV criteria for ADHD based on parent and teacher ratings, interviews, and direct observations of behavior. The presence of comorbid disorders (e.g., conduct disorder, major depression, overanxious disorder, learning disability) was ruled out through the information gathered during assessment, but it should be noted that Joe appeared to be at risk for the development of oppositional defiant disorder based on maternal report. Given the assessment information available, Joe's difficulties might be conceptualized as follows:

Presence of ADHD

- Inattention
- Poor impulse control
- Deficiencies in self-regulation of behavior

Behavior problems in the classroom

- Difficulty following general classroom rules and instructions
- Disruptive behavior during reading and math instruction (e.g., talking out, out of seat, making noises)

Academic problems in the classroom

- Incomplete independent seat work in math and reading
- Inaccurate independent seat work in math
- Poor performance on timed tests

Joe's problems in the classroom appeared to be related to his poor impulse control and deficiencies in self-regulation of his behavior. Although Joe's behavior was manageable under situations in which his teacher could provide instruction and immediate feedback on his behavior (i.e., small-group instruction), these interventions were difficult to implement on a long-term basis in a classroom setting. In addition, situations of delayed or infrequent teacher feedback (i.e., group instruction, seat work) appeared to exacerbate his display of problem behaviors.

Under classroom situations in which Joe was required to manage his own behavior, he encountered the most difficulty. First, he appeared unaware of his disruptive actions (i.e., poor self-monitoring) unless reprimanded by Mrs. Teri. Second, even when his inappropriate behavior was brought to his attention, Joe interpreted these actions as much less severe than Mrs. Teri. For instance, he made self-evaluative statements such as "I wasn't talking that loud" or "I got most of my work done," which were disparate with Mrs. Teri's appraisal of his behavior. Finally, he rarely, if ever, made positive statements about his classroom performance (i.e., lack of self-reinforcement). In fact, he was highly likely to make negative self-statements ("Boy, I really screwed up this time") after being reprimanded by Mrs. Teri. This information led school personnel to consider the implementation of a cognitive-behavioral intervention that involved the use of self-monitoring, self-evaluation, and self-reinforcement components.

Course of Treatment

A self-evaluation and self-reinforcement program was used, similar to that described by Rhode et al. (1983). Baseline data were collected on Joe's performance during Phase I of the intervention. Mrs. Teri, Joe's teacher, identified three behaviors or rules that Joe needed to improve on and three academic performance goals (see Figure 3.1). Mrs. Teri began rating Joe at the end of math class, based on a scale of 0–5 for the set of behavioral goals and also for the academic goals (see Table 3.1). Joe was unaware of these ratings at the time. Ratings were collected for 5 days.

In Phase II of the intervention (Token Reinforcement/Feedback), Mrs. Teri explained the scale and informed Joe that he would be rated on the three behavior goals and the three academic goals during math class (for a highest possible score of 10), and that his ratings could be exchanged for points to earn rewards (e.g., computer time, access to educational games). Brief verbal explanations for ratings also were given at the end of the period. The purpose of this phase was to allow Joe to learn how the rating scale applied to the targeted behaviors. When the data suggested that Joe understood the procedure (i.e., Joe's behavior improved), the next phase was implemented.

SELF-EVALUATION CARD

Name: Joe L.   **Date**: 3/15
Behavior

	1st Rating Poor				Excellent			
1. *Follows rules*	0	1	2	3	<u>4</u>	5	POINTS	<u>4</u>
							BONUS	<u>1</u>
2. *Stays in seat*							TOTAL	<u>5</u>
3. *Works quietly*	2nd Rating Poor				Excellent			
	0	1	2	<u>3</u>	4	5	POINTS	<u>3</u>
							BONUS	<u>1</u>
							TOTAL	<u>4</u>
	3rd Rating Poor				Excellent			
	0	1	2	3	<u>4</u>	5	POINTS	<u>4</u>
							BONUS	<u>0</u>
							TOTAL	<u>4</u>

SELF-EVALUATION CARD

Name: Joe L.   **Date**: 3/15
Academics

	1st Rating Poor				Excellent			
1. *Completes work*	0	1	2	<u>3</u>	4	5	POINTS	<u>3</u>
							BONUS	<u>1</u>
2. *Accurate work*							TOTAL	<u>4</u>
3. *Participates*	2nd Rating Poor				Excellent			
	0	1	2	3	<u>4</u>	5	POINTS	<u>4</u>
							BONUS	<u>0</u>
							TOTAL	<u>4</u>
	3rd Rating Poor				Excellent			
	0	1	2	3	<u>4</u>	5	POINTS	<u>4</u>
							BONUS	<u>1</u>
							TOTAL	<u>5</u>

FIGURE 3.1. Sample self-monitoring cards for rating Joe's behavior (top of figure) and academic performance (bottom of figure).

During Phase III of the intervention (Matching), Joe was given the self-evaluation card (see Figure 3.1) to tape on his desk, and the scale was reviewed. He was told to circle a rating of his behavior on the card after every 15 minutes (as indicated by an audiotaped cue). At the same time, the teacher indicated her rating on a similar card at her desk. At the end of math class, the ratings were compared and exchanged for points in the following manner: If Joe and Mrs. Teri matched ratings exactly, Joe earned

TABLE 3.1. Self-Evaluation Rating Scale

5 = *Excellent*—Followed all classroom rules entire interval; work 100% correct. No warnings to get back on-task required.

4 = *Very Good*—Minor infraction of rules (e.g., talk-out or out-of-seat occurrence), but followed rules rest of interval; worked almost entire interval; work at least 90% correct. One reminder allowed if student quickly returned to work.

3 = *Average*—Did not follow rules for the entire time, but no serious offenses. Followed rules approximately 80% of the time. Two reminders allowed from teacher.

2 = *Below Average*—Broke one or more rules to the extent that behavior was not acceptable (e.g., aggressive, noisy, talking) but followed rules part of the time. Work approximately 60% to 80% correct.

1 = *Poor*—Broke one or more rules almost entire period or engaged in higher degree of inappropriate behavior most of the time. May have been separated from the group up to half of the period because of inappropriate behavior. Work between 0% and 60% accurate.

0 = *Totally Unacceptable*—Broke one or more rules entire interval. Student may have required separation from the group. Did not work at all or work all incorrect.

Note. Based on information from Rhode, Morgan, and Young (1983).

that number of points plus a bonus point. If the ratings were within 1 point, Joe received the number of points that he awarded himself. Finally, if there was more than a 1-point discrepancy, no points were earned. Points could be exchanged at the end of the class period for rewards. Important aspects of this phase were Joe's explanation of why he rated himself as he did and the teacher's explanation of her rating.

Finally, Phase IV (Fading) was implemented after Joe consistently matched Mrs. Teri's rating for a week. The matching procedure was gradually faded so that it occurred on a less frequent basis; first every 30 minutes, then once at the end of the class period, then three times a week, two times a week, once a week, and every other week. Joe's ratings remained at a higher level than during baseline, even after fading procedures were implemented (see Figure 3.2). If Joe had begun earning fewer points as teacher matches were faded, then the frequency of matching would have been increased to a previously successful level. For example, if teacher ratings began to decrease as the frequency of matchings were faded to twice per week, then the matching frequency would be increased to three or four times per week until Joe was once again successful.

To determine whether Joe could learn to improve his behavior and academic performance in another subject area, the intervention was subsequently applied during Joe's reading class. The implementation occurred while Joe was in the Fading phase in his math class. Joe was asked to rate himself on the same behavior and academic goals, and to match ratings with his teacher at the same frequency as during math class. In reading class, Joe's behavior worsened slightly when faded to a lower frequency, and matchings had to be conducted more frequently for a week until his behavior improved.

Summary of Case Outcome

The quality of Joe's behavior control and academic performance improved measurably, according to Mrs. Teri's ratings, following the implementa-

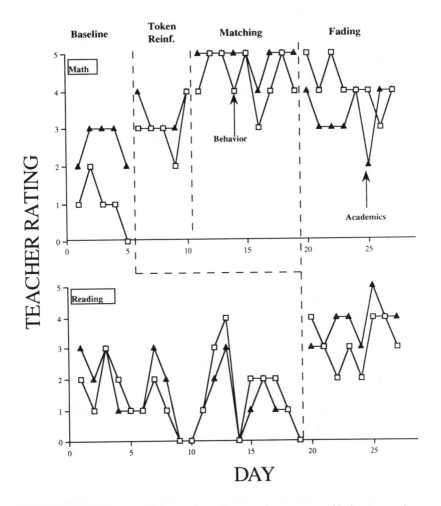

FIGURE 3.2. Points earned by Joe based on teacher ratings of behavior and academic performance in math and reading class. Open squares represent behavior and closed triangles indicate academic performance.

tion of self-evaluation procedures. He was able to maintain a high level of performance in the absence of teacher feedback across two classroom settings. Thus, the effects of the intervention were maintained over time and generalized across settings.

It is important to note that although this intervention was applied in a school setting, there is no reason why a similar treatment protocol could not be developed for use by parents or other caretakers. In fact, without parental participation, it is unlikely that behavioral effects obtained at school will generalize to the home setting. There are at least two ways that parental participation in this self-management program could be promoted. First, a home–school communication program could be developed wherein self-evaluation ratings are brought home on a daily basis and the identified child receives backup reinforcement at home for appropriate school performance. This would increase the variety and, hence, the potency of available reinforcers, as well as promote frequent communication between school and home. A second method to foster parental participation would be to design a similar parent–child matching program at home. Important behaviors at home (e.g., following directives, getting along with siblings) could be targeted with periodic, independent ratings conducted by the child and one of his or her parents. As with the school-based program, parental ratings could be gradually faded using random matching challenges.

Some of the treatment characteristics that appeared to contribute to a successful outcome are as follows:

1. Reinforcement was provided not only for behavioral change but also for matching the evaluation of an external observer (i.e., the teacher). This presumably promoted the internalization of evaluation criteria used by others in the environment.
2. Teacher feedback was gradually faded as opposed to being withdrawn abruptly. The pace of this fading procedure was determined by the degree to which Joe maintained a high level of behavior control. In similar fashion, self-evaluation programming was gradually introduced across settings once success had been attained in the original class period.
3. In contrast to some forms of cognitive-behavioral intervention (e.g., social problem solving), this intervention lends itself to implementation in the setting of interest. It has been well documented that interventions for ADHD should be implemented as close as possible to the point of performance rather than in separate training settings (Barkley, 1990).

Although this treatment led to a successful outcome in Joe's case, it is worthwhile to consider factors that may diminish the likelihood of achieving positive results. First, self-evaluation procedures that include multiple goals applied across more than one setting may not be as effective for younger students with ADHD (i.e., those under the age of 8 years). It is possible that simpler versions of this procedure could be used successfully with younger children. A second factor that may minimize success is a failure to employ specific criteria for the evaluation system. Ambiguities in the evaluation criteria increase the probability of teacher–student disagreements about ratings. Third, students may attempt to increase their chances of earning points by consistently giving themselves midpoint ratings (e.g., a score of 3 on a 5-point scale). Given that many teachers are reluctant to use ratings at either extreme, the students may maximize their point earnings by using the midpoint, because the odds are that they will at least keep the points they gave themselves, even when they do not match the teacher exactly. If a student appears to have adopted this strategy, the teacher should be encouraged to use extreme ratings when applicable. Also, the student would be informed that he or she would have to match the teacher ratings exactly in order to earn any points.

DISCUSSION

Cognitive-behavioral interventions have been designed to improve self-regulation of behavior and increase the probability of achieving durable behavior change (Braswell & Bloomquist, 1991; Kendall & Braswell, 1993). For children with ADHD who have particular difficulties in the areas of impulse control and self-regulation of behavior, cognitive-behavioral strategies have shown promise in preliminary investigations. This chapter has provided an overview of several cognitive- and contingency-based strategies that have been suggested for use with students identified as having ADHD, as well as a case example to illustrate how one procedure might be implemented in a school setting. Throughout this chapter, several special considerations for the use of cognitive-behavioral interventions for children with ADHD warrant further discussion.

In general, cognitive-behavioral interventions are most effective when combined with behavioral contingencies in the natural environment (Braswell & Bloomquist, 1991; Hinshaw & Erhardt, 1991; Paniagua, 1992). The case description provides an illustration of the use of reinforcement contingencies (i.e., token reinforcement/feedback) within the context of a self-management intervention (i.e., self-evaluation and self-reinforcement) for children with ADHD. In the case description, Joe received reinforcement contingent on his classroom behavior as well as for matching his self-evaluation to that of an external observer (i.e., the teacher). The use of behavioral components provided increased external control over Joe's behavior, which was gradually faded in the hope that Joe would internalize the evaluation criteria used by others in his environment. A similar protocol could be adapted for use in home and community settings. Thus, the use of cognitive-behavioral strategies (i.e., self-instruction, self-evaluation, self-observation) coupled with external contingencies (i.e., reinforcement) can be an effective means of fading an externally based system.

In addition to the need for external contingencies, the use of cognitive-behavioral interventions for children with ADHD should focus on specific training that matches desired performance as close as possible (Hinshaw & Erhardt, 1991). Some forms of cognitive-behavioral intervention (e.g., social problem solving) are designed to teach a generalized set of problem-solving skills with the hope that they will be utilized across settings and situations. Children with ADHD often learn these problem-solving skills but do not employ them in situations other than those in which they are trained (Hinshaw & Erhardt, 1991). Therefore, it is recommended that the cognitive-behavioral intervention procedures chosen for use with children who have ADHD address specific problem behaviors and skills.

Although cognitive-behavioral interventions have been designed to increase the probability of achieving durable behavioral change (Braswell & Bloomquist, 1991; Kendall & Braswell, 1993), this has not been the case for students with ADHD. As is true for other treatments for ADHD (Pelham & Murphy, 1986), the effects of interventions rarely generalize to times and settings in which the treatment is absent. For example, in the case description, Joe's behavior did not improve in the second setting (i.e., reading class) until the procedure was implemented in that situation. Similar programming must be implemented by parents in order for behavior change to occur at home. Thus, specific procedures designed to enhance generalization of behavior change across time and settings are needed in order for cognitive-behavioral techniques to result in lasting change (Shapiro & Cole, 1994).

The case description illustrates how one form of cognitive-behavioral intervention (i.e., self-evaluation, self-reinforcement) might be successfully applied to a child with ADHD in a classroom setting. Given the idiosyncratic response to treatment for children with ADHD, the selection of intervention strategies must be done on an individual basis. It is important to find a match between the attributional style of the child and the intervention (Kendall & Braswell, 1993). For example, Kendall and Braswell postulate that children who attribute improvements in behavior control to their own effort are more likely to respond positively to cognitive-behavioral interventions than those youngsters who attribute behavior change to external forces (e.g., luck, efforts of adults). In support of this contention, Reid and Borkowski (1987) found that the combination of a self-control intervention and attribution training resulted in clearer and more consistent gains for children with ADHD than a sample that received the self-control intervention in isolation. As Hinshaw and Erhardt (1991) point out, there are several limitations to Reid and Borkowski's findings (e.g., use of a nonclinical sample); however, their results highlight the need to consider attributional style when designing cognitive-behavioral interventions for children with this disorder.

Several other factors implicate the need for individualizing treatment. For younger children, it is important that they have the language skills and cognitive abilities to understand the intervention that is selected (Paniagua, 1992). In addition, children's response to treatments must be monitored on an individual basis and changes made accordingly. The case description provides one example of how the effects of an intervention might be monitored through graphing procedures. Finally, many children with ADHD will require intervention procedures to be applied across home, school, and community settings. The decision as to which settings to include in treatment will be based, in part, on the severity of the child's symptoms and the pervasiveness of difficulties across environments. Certainly, as pointed out earlier, the self-evaluation program discussed in the case study could be adapted easily for use in settings other than the classroom (e.g., the home).

Given the limited results that have been obtained for cognitive-behavioral interventions, especially those examining self-instructional training, Abikoff (1985) and others have questioned the overall efficacy of this approach for meeting the needs of children with ADHD. One of the most important factors accounting for these disappointing results is that many cognitive-behavioral interventions designed for ADHD have been based on a faulty premise. Specifically, it has been presumed that children with this disorder lack the cognitive strategies necessary for completing tasks and interacting with others in a reflective, attentive fashion. Thus, training such children in the use of cognitive strategies to address these putative deficits should be effective. Unfortunately, this assumption has not been supported in the empirical literature (Abikoff, 1985).

Barkley (1994) has proposed a theory of ADHD that has important implications for the design and implementation of cognitive-behavioral strategies. He posits that ADHD represents an impairment in response inhibition such that an individual afflicted with the disorder is less likely than normal peers to (1) separate affective from informational components of messages from the environment, (2) use hindsight and foresight in controlling behavior, (3) use internal speech as a guide for ongoing behavior, and (4) analyze and synthesize aspects of the environment to create novel stimuli. As such, treatment must focus first on encouraging the individual to delay responding so that the presence or absence of the above deficits in the individual's repertoire can be determined. Second, direct training of these putative deficits must take place *in the settings and at the time* that the problems occur (i.e., in classroom and home rather than in a clinic therapy room). Thus, professionals must train parents, teachers, and, possibly, peers to act as cognitive therapists. Finally, contingencies must be used to encourage the child to delay responding to the environment and to apply the cognitive strategies addressing the problems outlined earlier. This theory of ADHD should serve as a guide for the design of the next generation of cognitive-behavioral interventions for this disorder.

SUMMARY

This chapter has provided an overview and case illustration of the use of cognitive-behavioral interventions for children with ADHD. In comparison to strictly cognitive-based interventions (i.e., self-instruction, social problem-solving training), contingency-based interventions (i.e., correspondence training, self-evaluation, self-reinforcement) have been found to have more efficacy in the treatment of children with ADHD. For these children, cognitive-behavioral interventions that emphasize the fading of external contingencies such as those procedures illustrated in the case example are promising. Nonetheless, given the multifaceted nature of ADHD, cognitive-behavioral interventions must be considered in combination with other treatment modalities in an effort to ameliorate the multiple problem behaviors exhibited by these children.

NOTE

1. The fourth edition of the *Diagnostic and Statistical Manual of Mental Disorders* (DSM-IV; American Psychiatric Association, 1994) lists three subtypes of ADHD, including combined type, predominantly inattentive type, and predominantly impulsive–hyperactive type. Given the relative recency of the latter two types of ADHD, this chapter reviews treatment strategies for children with combined type ADHD because most of the research literature is relevant to this group, and this type of ADHD is the most prevalent.

REFERENCES

Abikoff, H. (1985). Efficacy of cognitive training interventions in hyperactive children: A critical review. *Clinical Psychology Review, 5*, 479–512.
Abikoff, H., & Gittelman, R. (1985). Hyperactive children treated with stimulants: Is cognitive training a useful adjunct? *Archives of General Psychiatry, 42*, 953–961.

Achenbach, T. M. (1991). *Manual for the Child Behavior Checklist and Revised Child Behavior Profile*. Burlington, VT: T. M. Achenbach.

American Psychiatric Association. (1987). *Diagnostic and statistical manual of mental disorders* (3rd ed., rev.). Washington, DC: Author.

American Psychiatric Association. (1994). *Diagnostic and statistical manual of mental disorders* (4th ed.). Washington, DC: Author.

Barkley, R. A. (1990). *Attention-deficit hyperactivity disorder: A handbook for diagnosis and treatment*. New York: Guilford Press.

Barkley, R. A. (1994). Impaired delayed responding: A unified theory of attention-deficit hyperactivity disorder. In D. K. Routh (Ed.), *Disruptive behavior disorders in childhood: Essays honoring Herbert C. Quay* (pp. 11–58). New York: Plenum Press.

Barkley, R. A., Copeland, A. P., & Sivage, C. (1980). A self-control classroom for hyperactive children. *Journal of Autism and Developmental Disorders, 10*, 75–89.

Barkley, R. A., Fischer, M., Edelbrock, C. S., & Smallish, L. (1990). The adolescent outcome of hyperactive children diagnosed by research criteria: I. An 8 year prospective follow-up study. *Journal of the American Academy of Child and Adolescent Psychiatry, 29*, 546–557.

Barkley, R. A., Karlsson, J., & Pollard, S. (1985). Effects of age on the mother–child interactions of hyperactive children. *Journal of Abnormal Child Psychology, 13*, 631–638.

Barkley, R. A., McMurray, M. B., Edelbrock, C. S., & Robbins, K. (1990). The side effects of Ritalin in ADHD children: A systematic placebo-controlled evaluation of two doses. *Pediatrics, 86*, 184–192.

Berk, L. E., & Potts, M. K. (1991). Development and functional significance of private speech among attention-deficit hyperactivity disorder and normal boys. *Journal of Abnormal Child Psychology, 19*, 357–377.

Braswell, L., & Bloomquist, M. L. (1991). *Cognitive-behavioral therapy with ADHD children: Child, family, and school interventions*. New York: Guilford Press.

Cameron, M. I., & Robinson, V. M. J. (1980). Effects of cognitive training on academic and on-task behavior of hyperactive children. *Journal of Abnormal Child Psychology, 8*, 405–420.

Cohen, N. J., Sullivan, J., Minde, K., Novak, C., & Helwig, C. (1981). Evaluation of the relative effectiveness of methylphenidate and cognitive behavior modification in the treatment of kindergarten-aged hyperactive children. *Journal of Abnormal Child Psychology, 9*, 43–54.

Douglas, V. I. (1980). Treatment and training approaches to hyperactivity: Establishing internal or external control. In C. K. Whalen & B. Henker (Eds.), *Hyperactive children: The social ecology of identification and treatment* (pp. 283–317). New York: Academic Press.

DuPaul, G. J. (1991). Parent and teacher ratings of ADHD symptoms: Psychometric properties in a community-based sample. *Journal of Clinical Child Psychology, 20*, 245–253.

DuPaul, G. J. (1992). How to assess attention-deficit hyperactivity disorder within school settings. *School Psychology Quarterly, 7*, 60–74.

DuPaul, G. J., & Barkley, R. A. (1990). Medication therapy. In R. A. Barkley, *Attention-deficit hyperactivity disorder: A handbook for diagnosis and treatment* (pp. 573–612). New York: Guilford Press.

DuPaul, G. J., & Stoner, G. (1994). *ADHD in the schools: Assessment and intervention strategies*. New York: Guilford Press.

Gittelman, R., Mannuzza, S., Shenker, R., & Bonagura, N. (1985). Hyperactive boys almost grown up. *Archives of General Psychiatry, 42,* 937–947.

Hallahan, D. P., Lloyd, J. W., Kneedler, R. D., & Marshall, K. J. (1982). A comparison of the effects of self- versus teacher-assessment of on-task behavior. *Behavior Therapy, 12,* 715–723.

Harris, K. (1986). Self-monitoring of attentional behavior versus self-monitoring of productivity: Effects on on-task behavior and academic response rate among learning disabled children. *Journal of Applied Behavior Analysis, 19,* 417–423.

Hinshaw, S. P., & Erhardt, D. (1991). Attention-deficit hyperactivity disorder. In P. C. Kendall (Ed.), *Child and adolescent behavior therapy: Cognitive-behavioral procedures* (pp. 98–130). New York: Guilford Press.

Hinshaw, S. P., Henker, B., & Whalen, C. K. (1984). Self-control in hyperactive boys in anger-inducing situations: Effects of cognitive-behavioral training and of methylphenidate. *Journal of Abnormal Child Psychology, 12,* 55–77.

Horn, W. F., Chatoor, I., & Conners, C. K. (1983). Additive effects of Dexedrine and self-control training: A multiple assessment. *Behavior Modification, 7,* 383–402.

Kendall, P. C., & Braswell, L. (1993). *Cognitive-behavioral therapy for impulsive children* (2nd ed.). New York: Guilford Press.

Lalli, E. P., & Shapiro, E. S. (1990). The effects of self-monitoring and contingent reward on sight word acquisition. *Education and Treatment of Exceptional Children, 12,* 129–141.

Luria, A. R. (1961). *The role of speech in the regulation of normal and abnormal behavior*. New York: Liveright.

Matson, J. L. (Ed.). (1993). *Handbook of hyperactivity in children*. Boston: Allyn & Bacon.

Meichenbaum, D. H., & Goodman, J. (1971). Training impulsive children to talk to themselves: A means of developing self-control. *Journal of Abnormal Psychology, 77,* 115–126.

Paniagua, F. A. (1987). Management of hyperactive children through correspondence training: A preliminary study. *Behavioral Residential Treatment, 2,* 1–23.

Paniagua, F. A. (1990). A procedural analysis of correspondence training techniques. *Behavior Analyst, 13,* 107–119.

Paniagua, F. A. (1992). Verbal–nonverbal correspondence training with ADHD children. *Behavior Modification, 16,* 226–252.

Paniagua, F. A., Pumariega, A. J., & Black, S. A. (1988). Clinical effects of correspondence training in the management of hyperactive children. *Behavioral Residential Treatment, 3,* 20–40.

Pelham, W. E. Jr. (1993). Pharmacotherapy for children with attention-deficit hyperactivity disorder. *School Psychology Review, 22,* 199–227.

Pelham, W. E. Jr., & Murphy, H. A. (1986). Attention deficit and conduct disorders. In M. Hersen (Ed.), *Pharmacological and behavioral treatment: An integrative approach* (pp. 108–148). New York: Wiley.

Pfiffner, L. J. & Barkley, R. A. (1990). Educational placement and classroom management. In R. A. Barkley, *Attention-deficit hyperactivity disorder: A handbook for diagnosis and treatment* (pp. 498–539). New York: Guilford Press.

Pfiffner, L. J., & O'Leary, S. G. (1993). School-based psychological treatments. In J. L. Matson (Ed.), *Handbook of hyperactivity in children* (pp. 234–255). Boston: Allyn & Bacon.

Rapport, M. D. (1987). Attention-deficit hyperactivity disorder. In M. Hersen & V. B. VanHasselt (Eds.), *Behavior therapy with children and adolescents* (pp. 325–361). New York: Wiley.

Reid, M. K., & Borkowski, J. G. (1987). Causal attributions of hyperactive children: Implications for teaching strategies and self-control. *Journal of Educational Psychology, 79,* 296–307.

Rhode, G., Morgan, D. P., & Young, K. R. (1983). Generalization and maintenance of treatment gains of behaviorally handicapped students from resource rooms to regular classrooms using self-evaluation procedures. *Journal of Applied Behavior Analysis, 16,* 171–188.

Risley, T. R., & Hart, B. (1968). Developing correspondence between the non-verbal and verbal behavior of preschool children. *Journal of Applied Behavior Analysis, 1,* 267–281.

Shapiro, E. S., & Cole, C. L. (1994). *Behavior change in the classroom: Self-management interventions.* New York: Guilford Press.

Smith, D. J., Young, K. R., Nelson, J. R., & West, R. P. (1992). The effect of a self-management procedure on the classroom and academic behavior of students with mild handicaps. *School Psychology Review, 21,* 59–72.

Smith, D. J., Young, K. R., West, R. P., Morgan, D. P., & Rhode, G. (1988). Reducing the disruptive behavior of junior high students: A classroom self-management procedure. *Behavioral Disorders, 13,* 231–239.

Stark, K. D., Rouse, L. W., & Livingston, R. (1991). Treatment of depression during childhood and adolescence: Cognitive-behavioral procedures for the individual and family. In P.C. Kendall (Ed.), *Child and adolescent therapy: Cognitive-behavioral procedures* (pp. 165–208). New York: Guilford Press.

Turkewitz, H., O'Leary, K. D., & Ironsmith, M. (1975). Generalization and maintenance of appropriate behavior through self-control. *Journal of Consulting and Clinical Psychology, 43,* 577–583.

Weiss, G., & Hechtman, L. T. (1993). *Hyperactive children grown up* (2nd ed.): *ADHD in children, adolescents, and adults.* New York: Guilford Press.

Young, K. R., Smith, D. J., West, R. P., & Morgan, D. P. (1987). A peer-mediated program for teaching self-management strategies to adolescents. *Programming for Adolescents with Behavioral Disorders, 3,* 34–47.

4

Treatment of Oppositional Defiant Disorder

Laura D. Hanish
Patrick H. Tolan
Nancy G. Guerra

Although noncompliant, oppositional behavior may be considered normative, particularly among preschoolers, a subset of children exhibit oppositionality of such frequency or intensity as to warrant a diagnosis of oppositional defiant disorder. As defined by the fourth edition of the *Diagnostic and Statistical Manual of Mental Disorders* (DSM-IV), oppositional defiant disorder is "a recurrent pattern of negativistic, defiant, disobedient, and hostile behavior toward authority figures" (American Psychiatric Association, 1994, p. 91). To meet criteria for diagnosis with oppositional defiant disorder, a child must exhibit a minimum of four of the following behaviors during a period of at least 6 months: lose his or her temper, argue with adults, refuse to comply with adult requests or rules, deliberately annoy people, blame others, become easily annoyed by others, be angry and resentful, or be spiteful or vindictive. Furthermore, oppositional defiant disorder is only diagnosed when these behaviors occur more frequently than is typical among children of equal age and developmental level and when the behaviors impair social, academic, or occupational functioning. Oppositional defiant disorder should not be diagnosed, however, if the criteria for conduct disorder are also met or if the oppositional behaviors are exhibited solely during the course of a mood or psychotic disorder (American Psychiatric Association, 1994).

Current prevalence estimates for oppositional defiant disorder range from 2% to 16% of the population (American Psychiatric Association, 1994), making this childhood disorder fairly common. Furthermore, oppositional defiant disorder typically emerges during early childhood, with the behaviors that characterize this disorder (e.g., defiance, hostility, arguing) usually becoming evident by age 6 (Frick et al., 1993). Because the defiant, hostile behaviors that characterize oppositional defiant disorder can intensify and evolve into more severe antisocial behaviors, the early identification and treatment of this disorder may be effective in preventing the development of conduct disorder (Tolan & Loeber, 1992). In this chapter, diagnostic considerations are discussed along with mechanisms of influence and treatment of oppositional defiant disorder. Furthermore, the role of cognitive-behavioral therapy in treatment is reviewed and an illustrative case example is provided.

DIAGNOSTIC CONSIDERATIONS

Two issues are relevant in diagnosing oppositional defiant disorder: differentiating it from normal oppositional behavior and differentiating it from other disorders, particularly disruptive disorders (Kruesi & Tolan, in press). Because oppositional defiant disorder frequently emerges during the preschool period, when oppositional and defiant behaviors are particularly common among children, it is important to distinguish oppositional defiant disorder from age-normal defiance and oppositionality. This distinction is primarily based on the severity of the behaviors. In contrast to normal development in which oppositional behaviors peak in early childhood and decrease over time, oppositional behaviors that characterize oppositional defiant disorder continue and worsen with age (Campbell, 1990). This fact highlights the importance of evaluating the severity, situational variability, and intensity of the behavior prior to making a diagnosis. As Loeber, Lahey, and Thomas (1991) recommend, the diagnosis of oppositional defiant disorder should be considered only if the oppositionality and defiance occur at an abnormal frequency or intensity, or if the behaviors continue over time (beyond preschool years). If behavior problems that characterize conduct disorder are also evident, but not at a level to meet criteria for the diagnosis of conduct disorder, then an oppositional defiant disorder diagnosis remains a viable option.

The second diagnostic task is to differentiate oppositional defiant disorder from other externalizing behavior disorders, such as conduct disorder and attention-deficit/hyperactivity disorder. Oppositional defiant disorder may co-occur with attention-deficit/hyperactivity disorder, resulting in a poorer prognosis (Hinshaw, Lahey, & Hart, 1993) and requiring a modification of the treatment regimen. Although oppositional defiant disorder and conduct disorder are developmentally related disorders, they also require different treatments (Frick et al., 1993; Kruesi &

Tolan, in press; Lahey, Loeber, Quay, Frick, & Grimm, 1992; Loeber, et al., 1991).

The development of defiance, hostility, and other oppositional symptoms in early childhood sometimes foreshadows the development of more severe antisocial behaviors, such that the symptoms of oppositional defiant disorder may come to co-occur with the symptoms of conduct disorder. In a number of cases, more serious delinquent behaviors, such as physical aggression, lying, and stealing, begin to appear at approximately age 7 (Frick et al., 1993). Although not all children with oppositional defiant disorder come to exhibit the more extreme destructive behaviors that are characteristic of conduct disorder, most children who are diagnosed with conduct disorder before puberty also meet criteria for a diagnosis of oppositional defiant disorder (Frick et al., 1993; Lahey et al., 1992; Loeber et al., 1991). As a consequence, oppositional defiant disorder cannot be diagnosed when the child also meets the criteria for conduct disorder (American Psychiatric Association, 1994). This differential diagnosis has important implications for case conceptualization and treatment planning. Since conduct disorder often is accompanied by the presence of slightly different etiological factors, more disturbance, a more perilous course, and poorer prognosis, intervention planning differs (see Lahey et al., 1992, or Loeber et al., 1991).

Externalizing behavior problems often co-occur with internalizing behavior problems, further complicating the diagnostic process (see Hinshaw et al., 1993). Accurate diagnosis is essential because the presence of anxious or depressive symptoms often indicates different treatment procedures. It may be necessary to target the internalizing symptoms rather than, or in addition to, the externalizing symptoms. For instance, externalizing symptoms may abate following successful treatment of depressive symptoms (Puig-Antich, 1982).

COGNITIVE-BEHAVIORAL MECHANISMS

In addition to an accurate diagnosis, it is important to identify factors influencing the development of oppositional defiant disorder in order to most effectively plan treatment. Although it has been argued by some (e.g., Achenbach, 1993) that the symptoms characterizing oppositional defiant disorder and conduct disorder differ only with regard to the degree of severity of behavioral disturbance, a closer examination of the mechanisms underlying these disorders reveals additional factors that may be useful in differentiating them.

One factor that discriminates oppositional defiant disorder and conduct disorder, for example, is that conduct disorder, unlike oppositional defiant disorder, involves disregard and disrespect for the basic rights of others (American Psychiatric Association, 1994). Children with conduct disorder are often characterized as having little, if any, concern about the impact of their behaviors on others. Although children with oppositional defiant disorder express opposition to parents' and other authority figures' discipline and expectations, they do not inherently devalue others as conduct disordered children do. Recasting this in cognitive terms, conduct disordered children appear to think little about the consequences of their actions and display diminished moral reasoning skills, whereas children with oppositional defiant disorder demonstrate poor problem-solving skills and attempt to use opposition to coerce particular behaviors from significant others (e.g., parents). This distinction is supported by a body of research highlighting the relations between various aspects of social cognition and serious aggression (Crick & Dodge, 1994; Guerra, Huesmann, & Hanish, 1995; Kazdin, Esveldt-Dawson, French, & Unis, 1987). Thus, it should be useful to consider the cognitive foundations of each disorder and how the beliefs, attitudes, expectations, and attributions of children with conduct disorder and those with oppositional defiant disorder differ. Unfortunately, most cognitive-behavioral research to date has focused on delinquent children or children with conduct disorder. Few studies have examined the cognitive underpinnings of oppositional defiant disorder and how they differ from those of conduct disorder. This may be due, in part, to the fact that oppositional defiant disorder typically emerges in children during the preschool and early elementary years when cognitions may be less stable and consequently, more difficult to reliably measure (Huesmann, Guerra, Miller, & Zelli, 1992).

Many studies investigating the development of oppositional defiant disorder have focused on the role of the family (Frick et al., 1993; Lahey et al., 1992; Patterson, Reid, & Dishion, 1992; Tolan & Loeber, 1992). For example, Kruesi and Tolan (in press) identify three parent characteristics that appear to increase risk for oppositional defiant disorder and should be considered in formulating treatment plans: (1) parental psychopathology, (2) ineffective parenting practices, and (3) marital disruption.

Parental psychopathology, particularly antisocial personality disorder, has consistently distinguished children with oppositional defiant disorder from clinic controls (Faraone, Biederman, Keenan, & Tsuang, 1991; Frick et al., 1992; Schachar & Wachsmuth 1990). Other forms of parental psychopathology, such as substance abuse and depression, have also been linked with child noncompliance (Forehand & Brody, 1985; Frick et al., 1992). However, the relation between parental antisocial personality disorder and child oppositional defiant disorder is so strong that it accounts for much of the variance in correlations between oppositional defiant disorder and substance abuse (Frick et al., 1992), as well as between oppositional defiant disorder and other variables, such as teenage motherhood (Christ et al., 1990). Furthermore, although antisocial personality disorder in the parent often predicts oppositional and defiant behavior in the child, it also can be a necessary focus of intervention, because parental psychopathology can interfere with attempts to change parents' child behavior management practices.

Certain parenting practices, such as coercive family interactions, tend to be associated with the oppositional, defiant, and hostile behaviors that are characteristic of oppositional defiant disorder (Patterson, 1976). Several specific family interaction patterns have been found to differentiate oppositional and nonoppositional children. For example, parents of noncompliant children tend to reinforce oppositional behavior and ignore or punish positive social behaviors (Patterson, 1976). They also have been found to be more critical than parents of compliant children (Robinson & Eyberg, 1981). In addition, parents of oppositional children tend to make directives without allowing their children to respond to them (Peed, Roberts, & Forehand, 1977). They issue more directives, particularly demanding directives that are designed to stop or inhibit behavior (Green, Forehand, & McMahon, 1979), and they make statements that are threatening, nagging, hostile, and humiliating (Delfini, Bernal, & Rosen, 1976). They also tend to impose more restrictive rules (Green et al., 1979). In some cases, oppositional behavior may be due to inconsistent discipline stemming from parental fears and anxiety about imposing limits or sanctions (Tolan, 1989). Our clinical experience is that many of these parents have difficulty imposing any discipline due to their own experience as abused or neglected children (Tolan, 1991). Thus, oppositional behavior in children appears to have clear ties to critical, conflicted, inconsistent, punitive, or coercive family interactions.

Finally, as some have suggested, when child behavior problems occur, marital problems also are common (Framo, 1975). In fact, evidence indicates that marital discord predicts noncompliant, disruptive behavior in children (see Emery, 1982; Forehand & Brody, 1985; Forehand, Brody, & Smith, 1986; Johnson & Lobitz, 1974). This relation appears to be stronger when the parents express hostility overtly than when they express general dissatisfaction, and it is more pronounced for boys than for girls (Emery & O'Leary, 1982; Porter & O'Leary, 1980). The relation between marital distress and child oppositional behavior can be an important one and should be considered in treatment planning.

With these considerations in mind, it is important to assess the cognitive underpinnings of parents' behavior and plan family treatment accordingly. A number of parenting behaviors can be linked to parental beliefs and attitudes. It appears that parents' beliefs can have considerable impact on the developing child's behavior through a variety of direct and indirect means. Parents' beliefs tend, for example, to guide their choice of socialization strategies, which play a key role in determining whether a child exhibits socially competent or deviant behavior (Rubin, Mills, & Krasnor, 1989; Sigel, 1985). Because the family provides the primary context for children's social–cognitive development, parents' cognitions and their resulting behavior appear to play an important role in maintaining a child's defiance. This is particularly true for young children (and thus is the case for many children who are diagnosed with oppositional defiant disorder) who have limited social–cognitive abilities and difficulty with internal regulation of their behavior.

Because parents' beliefs play an important role in determining their own, and ultimately their children's behavior, it is important to understand how they covary with parental psychopathology, coercive and inconsistent parenting, and marital discord, and how they may affect the child. For instance, a parent with antisocial personality disorder, through modeling and direct reinforcement, transmits his or her belief that it is acceptable to defy authority to the child. Over time, as the child internalizes this belief, he or she also begins to oppose the parent. Alternatively, beliefs about the potential negative consequences of discipline, or contradictory beliefs (between parents) about the correct way to discipline, may lead to inconsistent and ineffective disciplinary practices. As a result, the child's defiance is intermittently reinforced and becomes more frequent. These parental beliefs can differentially impact the development and the maintenance of disruptive and oppositional behavior, and their presence and contributory role should be carefully assessed.

The nature of the transaction between parental beliefs, parenting behaviors, and child behaviors is complex. Moreover, the influences of these parental risk factors are not necessarily independent; parental antisocial personality disorder, marital distress, and inconsistent parenting may co-occur (e.g., Frick, Lahey, Hartdagen, & Hynd, 1989). When a child is exposed to multiple risk factors, he or she is at risk for a more negative outcome. Although the prognostic indicators for children with oppositional defiant disorder have not been fully specified, some evidence suggests that children who have more severely disrupted family and interpersonal environments are at greater risk for developing more antisocial behavior problems, such as those that are indicative of conduct disorder (Lahey et al., 1992). Furthermore, children who have comorbid disorders also experience more negative outcomes (see Hinshaw et al., 1993). Thus, the interaction of these cognitive and behavioral factors should be carefully considered when treating a child with oppositional defiant disorder.

Changing parental beliefs is important both for modifying parental behavior and for changing the child's cognitions. This improves long-term prognosis for the parents and the child. The therapist may treat the child's disruptive behavior by changing environmental (i.e., family) circumstances *and* by helping the child to develop and internalize more positive, prosocial cognitions about his or her behavior. One important effect of this treatment strategy is to prevent the development of many of the cognitive biases that may be linked with conduct disorder. What remains unclear, and therefore must be assessed on a case-by-case basis, is which cognitive and behavioral factors are necessary and sufficient to produce oppositional defiant disorder. Assessing relevant beliefs and behaviors, however, determines the frame for intervention.

TREATMENT

As noted, the symptoms of oppositional defiant disorder often become apparent when children are at preschool or early elementary-school age. Our clinical experience suggests that these oppositional, disruptive behaviors may persist over time and can become more severe as the child grows older. Nevertheless, the behavior of young children is largely governed by external sanctions that are imposed by parents. Children, especially young children, often have difficulty exercising self-control and inhibiting impulsive behavior. Thus, treatments that focus solely on the child should be expected to have limited impact. Rather, appropriate treatment of oppositional defiant disorder is dependent on working with the child's family. As we have seen, parental characteristics are particularly important influences on the development of oppositional behavior. Thus, treatment should involve training parents in appropriate management skills, as well as modifying parental beliefs about behavior management.

To date, parent management training, which focuses on increasing positive behavior and decreasing negative behavior in the child by teaching parents social learning principles and behavior-management skills, is the best tested treatment for oppositional defiant disorder (as distinguished from other disruptive disorders). In comparisons to other treatments (e.g., family therapy, attention–placebo) and no-treatment controls, parent management training has consistently resulted in better outcomes, typically improving both parenting skills and child compliance (Eisenstadt, Eyberg, McNeil, Newcomb, & Funderburk, 1993; Patterson, Chamberlain, & Reid, 1982; Peed et al., 1977; Webster-Stratton, Hollinsworth, & Kolpacoff, 1989; Webster-Stratton, Kolpacoff, & Hollinsworth, 1988).

The effectiveness of such training is dependent on modifying parental beliefs about behavior management (Wahler & Dumas, 1989). Consequently, behavior-management training must be introduced and implemented with extensive education, counseling, and consideration of parents' concerns about the methods. The coordination of the behavior management methods with existing parental beliefs and attitudes toward such methods requires careful consideration. In fact, assessing and addressing parental reactions to the proper behavior-management programs can be as critical as ensuring that methods are learned and used.

A key intervention strategy, then, is to assess parental characteristics that relate to the child's oppositional behavior. If the parent exhibits psychopathology, other than antisocial personality disorder, appropriate treatment is a prerequisite to acceptance and use of the behavior management techniques. If an antisocial personality is evident, then cognitive-behavioral problem-solving techniques and contingency-based behavior management of the parent are needed (Kruesi & Tolan, in press). Treatment of the child's noncompliance and disruption can be facilitated, for example, by training parents in social skills for dealing with teachers, coworkers, and the child, and by providing the parent with rewards for appropriate behavior management. If the primary parental problem is marital conflict, then education, contracting, or problem-solving and communication skills may need to be provided to obtain consistency of behavior management and separation of parenting from marital disputes (cognitive approaches to marital therapy are discussed by Epstein and Schlesinger in Chapter 14 of this volume). Alternatively, if a parent experiences difficulty applying appropriate discipline due to his or her own childhood experiences, then the intervention needs to focus on changing self-attributions and distinguishing between good discipline and abuse or unjustified constraints (Tolan, 1991). In each case, the prior or concurrent focus on parental cognitions is a necessary addition to traditional parent training. As the parents' conflict and ineffective beliefs are addressed, the needed behavior management of the child will ensue. With the development of adequate parenting, in most cases, the oppositional behavior will diminish (Webster-Stratton et al., 1989). These methods are illustrated by the following case example.

CASE EXAMPLE

Presenting Problem

John L., a 6-year-old male, was brought to the child psychiatry clinic by his mother, Ms. L., following a conference with his teacher. John was beginning the first grade after a tumultuous year in kindergarten. Apparently, this year had started with a continuation of the troubles that had disrupted his kindergarten class. Although he frequently fought with other children and was rarely on-task during schoolwork, the primary concerns were that he swore at the teacher, refused to follow directives, exhibited tantrums, and refused to cooperate during group activities. He was described by his teacher as "hell on wheels" and "without discipline."

During the initial session, Ms. L. spoke slowly and softly and immediately asked for help with her son. She appeared timid and anxious. She mentioned that school officials thought her son might be hyperactive and need medication. She was reluctant, however, to include medication in the treatment program because she thought this was "blaming him" for her shortcomings as a parent. She stated that she thought she was not a good parent for a boy because she had no brothers. To her, John was just an energetic boy who had a hard life and needed support. As we talked about her parenting, she stated that she tried to avoid stifling his autonomy and that she had tried to support him because she thought he had low self-esteem. She expressed hesitation in disciplining him for fear that this might make him feel negatively about himself. Moreover, she believed that his teacher was "too interested in having children sit down and behave" when she should be interested in "developing their minds."

Family History

John was the only child of a 24-year-old mother. His parents had been separated since he was 4 years of age, and his father had been imprisoned during the past year for drug trafficking. The marriage had apparently been prompted by the pregnancy, and, in retrospect, Ms. L. saw it as a tragic mistake. She recognized that their marriage was motivated by her desire to get out from under her parents' control. She described her parents as harsh, intrusive, and uncompromising. She reportedly found her husband attractive because he was not intimidated by her parents and because he "seemed to represent everything they were not." She saw the marriage as a way to shore up her self-image as a weak person who could not stand up for herself. Soon after the marriage, however, the couple began to fight regularly. They argued about his drug use, the amount of time his friends spent at the apartment, and her desire for a less risky lifestyle. Reportedly, physical confrontations were common components of their marital disputes. Although not revealed initially, she later reported that her parents had been physically abusive with her.

Behavioral Observations

John was small in size for his age and very active throughout our initial meetings. Although he explored and handled every toy in the office very quickly, he stopped to examine each one and asked questions about them. When left to his own interests, he began constructing aggressive fantasies involving fights between toy soldiers. As the session progressed, he moved from fantasy play to board games. During these games, he appeared to enjoy the attention and companionship, but experienced difficulty negotiating rules. He would frequently cheat or make up fanciful rules that gave him special powers, therefore permitting him to win. When confronted he would, at first, start acting up and try to create a distraction. At other times, he responded to such confrontations by refusing to continue or by offering to let the therapist also change the rules.

John stated that he was the "smartest one" in his class and never got into trouble. He added that he always got along well with his mother. Despite such lies, he had a charming interpersonal style and evidenced some genuine interest in being liked by his therapist. In fact, it seemed that this was more important to him than would be appropriate and that his attachment occurred too quickly. He seemed to compete with his mother for therapeutic attention. During the course of treatment, he often tried to get his mother to leave the office, and when his insistence did not work, he would resort to tantrums. At one point, for example, he started screaming as loud as he could to drown out what she was saying. He wanted his mother and the therapist to stop talking so he could play a game with the therapist.

John appeared to meet criteria for oppositional defiant disorder. He did not, however, meet criteria for any other Axis I disorders. Also, it was clear that adult attention mattered greatly to him. His defiant behavior seemed to be directly tied to obtaining attention from his mother and others and to controlling interpersonal interactions. Such behavior often emerged when John was faced with frustration.

Course of Treatment

At first, therapy sessions were divided between time with John and time with Ms. L. The initial goals were to evaluate John's ability to control his impulses, respond to limits, and express his needs directly, and to assess Ms. L.'s behavior-management style, skills level, and beliefs about herself and her parenting that interfered with discipline. Assessment of John's behavior indicated that although he was socially immature, had few frustration-coping skills, and showed some resistance to rules and limit setting, he had the ability to respond to limits and to control himself. Assessment of Ms. L.'s behavior indicated that she was unwilling to engage in limit setting or rule development because she believed that this constituted taking out her frustrations on her child. With this in mind, a shift was instituted to spend more of the session focused on her feelings and beliefs.

As Ms. L. discussed her beliefs, she confided her deep fear that she would be acting like her parents if she disciplined him. She admitted that

John enraged her and that it took everything she had to control herself and avoid hurting him. At one point, she became upset with him and locked herself in the closet to avoid abusing him. She consequently felt terribly guilty because she believed that she was acting abusively toward John, just as her parents had acted toward her. She blamed them for much of her discontent and troubles in life. Because she had built what esteem she had on how she differed from them, these episodes were very disturbing to her.

It appeared, as such, that Ms. L.'s belief that disciplining John was abusive and her fear of acting like her parents were impeding progress. Sessions with Ms. L. focused extensively on her feelings when she was disciplining John; her worries and other thoughts; and the rules, expectations, standards, or moral principles that guided her behavior. It became clear that Ms. L., by not consistently disciplining John, was attempting to control her fears that she may abuse him, that he may reject her, and that she would be a failure as a parent. Ms. L. indicated that she felt caught between the desire to help John grow up successfully and the fears that he would reject her for doing so and that she would become a "petty tyrant" like her parents. She described John as her "only real companion" and stated that he had been her hope for vindicating what she saw as a loveless childhood and a failed marriage.

We began to examine the implications of these beliefs and to discuss qualifications and elaborations that she had not previously considered. She was encouraged, for example, to distinguish feelings of frustration from feelings of hatred. She came to realize that abuse and anger were not the basis of discipline and to understand how failure to discipline could harm a child. She also began to see how consistent, rational discipline was a gesture of love and concern. She discovered that she, unlike her parents, was concerned deeply about how such discipline affected her child. Thus, by definition, she was different and her child had the benefit of a better parent than she had had. This led to a sense of control or personal efficacy that she had not previously entertained. She also learned to distinguish between what John needed from her and the friendship orientation she had toward him. As part of that, she planned to socialize with her friends, expanded her social support network, and confided more in an adult friend. Ms. L. also began to encourage her son to play with neighborhood children. Finally, she read a number of articles on child development, and through discussion of them, became aware of her child's cognitive and emotional need for developmentally appropriate rules and discipline. Each shift was gradual, with most areas revisited several times. When John would have a particularly bad week she would revert to old, dysfunctional cognitions.

Following these shifts in beliefs, Ms. L. was able to implement, monitor, and, with the therapist, develop a point system for John that rewarded compliance with her directives: having a day without swearing and bringing home a good report from the teacher. Later, she added responsibilities such as having John make his bed and help with dishes. The sessions moved accordingly to focus more on the technical aspects of the behavior-management system and away from her motivating cognitions. Improvements were noted at this time. For instance, Ms. L. could now direct John to leave the office when she needed him to do so, and he would comply. She was also more affectionate and reassuring to him, but not by letting him break the rules.

Although John's behavior had improved in school by this time, Ms. L. also scheduled a conference with the teacher. After rehearsing with the therapist, she proposed a monitoring system of notes between the teacher and herself, explained her rules-and-rewards system to the teacher, and proposed developing a classroom behavior-management program to assist her son in learning to follow rules and behaving appropriately. The teacher worked with her to coordinate a reward system. After this meeting, John's behavior improved quickly. Although still more resistant than the average child, he was able to respond to "second warnings," to bring his behavior under control, and to focus on classroom tasks. His play in games during therapy sessions became increasingly realistic, and he learned to abide by rules. Ms. L. became more self-assured overall. In addition to her growing comfort with managing her son, she finalized her divorce and began to pursue a college education. About this time, she said that her time and finances were getting even tighter than before, and she thought they could stop the sessions. We scheduled two follow-up sessions at 1 month intervals. John's progress had been maintained at 1 month posttreatment, and so the second session was made optional. A phone conversation at that point indicated that his school achievement had improved and that his behavior at school and at home was no longer problematic. Ms. L. requested suggestions for several new issues related to normal developmental progressions (e.g., wanting to have a friend over to play). At 6-month follow-up, he had finished the school year successfully and was enjoying his summer.

DISCUSSION

In the aforementioned case, although several risk factors potentially played a role in the development of the child's oppositional defiant behavior, one factor significantly influenced both the development and maintenance of this behavior: the lack of consistent discipline due to maladaptive beliefs, expectations, and schemas in the mother. She believed that discipline would be harmful to her child and thus harmful to her relationship with him. The mother's beliefs about discipline played an integral role in treatment, because they directly impeded implementation of more positive parenting behaviors. Thus, an intervention approach utilizing both cognitive and behavioral change mechanisms focused on the parent was necessary and effective in treating the child's oppositional behavior.

In summary, effective treatment of oppositional defiant disorder is dependent upon identifying, evaluating, and modifying each of the relevant cognitive, behavioral, and environmental factors that contribute to the disruptive behavior. Most often these take the form of parental cognitions and behavior rather than the child's own cognitions, due to young children's limited cognitive development and their resulting inability to regulate their behavior internally. Modifying the parents' behaviors and cognitions that are naturally influencing the child's development may not only decrease oppositional behavior, but may also prevent the formation of antagonistic, hostile beliefs that may eventually contribute to the development of more aggressive and antisocial behaviors.

Although this parent-focused approach is effective in treating oppositional defiant disorder in young children, it may be somewhat limited in treating older oppositional children. As noted previously, although oppositionality typically emerges in early childhood, these symptoms may persist and worsen with age. Thus, symptoms of oppositional defiant disorder may be evident in older children and adolescents. These children may benefit from a combined treatment approach in which both parent management training and problem-solving skills training components are included. In this way, the older child's increased cognitive abilities and autonomy are taken into account. Similarly, when treating children who are more severely disturbed (e.g., with conduct disorder), such a dual-focus treatment approach (parent management training combined with problem-solving skills training) may also increase effectiveness (see Kazdin et al., 1987).

To date, existing research on the effectiveness of cognitive-behavioral therapy for oppositional defiant disorder is limited to treatment of existing syndromes, rather than prevention of the development of this disorder. However, prevention of oppositional defiant disorder is important because decreasing the incidence of oppositional defiant disorder may concomitantly result in decreasing the incidence of conduct disorder. Although this topic has yet to be examined, existing literature on the prevention of conduct disorder, as well as literature explaining the correlates and causes of oppositional and disruptive behavior, can inform researchers interested in preventing oppositional defiant disorder. In particular, prevention programs that target parental cognitions and behaviors, as well as the multisystemic variables that are contributing to these cognitions and behaviors, may be effective. In fact, conduct disorder prevention programs that take such an ecological approach seem to be the most promising interventions against the development of antisocial behavior (see Miller, 1994). Given the frequently observed developmental progression from oppositional defiant disorder to conduct disorder, research into the prevention of oppositional and disruptive behavior seems warranted. In addition, continued examination of the etiology, cognitive correlates, and prognosis of oppositional defiant disorder and the application of these concepts to treatment should improve future intervention and prevention strategies.

REFERENCES

Achenbach, T. M. (1993). Taxonomy and comorbidity of conduct problems: Evidence from empirically based approaches. *Development and Psychopathology, 5*, 51–64.

American Psychiatric Association. (1994). *Diagnostic and statistical manual of mental disorders* (4th ed.). Washington, DC: Author.

Campbell, S. B. (1990). *Behavior problems in preschool children.* New York: Guilford Press.

Christ, M. A. G., Lahey, B. B., Frick, P. J., Russo, M. F., McBurnett, K., Loeber, R., Stouthamer-Loeber, M., & Green, S. (1990). Serious conduct problems in the children of adolescent mothers: Disentangling confounded correlations. *Journal of Consulting and Clinical Psychology, 58*, 840–844.

Crick, N. R., & Dodge, K. R. (1994). A review and reformulation of social information-processing mechanisms in children's social adjustment. *Psychological Bulletin, 115*, 74–101.

Delfini, L. F., Bernal, M. E., & Rosen, P. M. (1976). Comparison of deviant and normal boys in home settings. In E. J. Mash, L. A. Hamerlynck, & L. C. Handy (Eds.), *Behavior modification and families* (pp. 228–248). New York: Brunner/Mazel.

Eisenstadt, T. H., Eyberg, S., McNeil, C. B., Newcomb, K., & Funderburk, B. (1993). Parent–child interaction therapy with behavior problem children: Relative effectiveness of two stages and overall treatment outcome. *Journal of Clinical Child Psychology, 22*, 42–51.

Emery, R. E. (1982). Interparental conflict and the children of discord and divorce. *Psychological Bulletin, 92*, 310–330.

Emery, R. E., & O'Leary, K. D. (1982). Children's perceptions of marital discord and behavior problems of boys and girls. *Journal of Abnormal Child Psychology, 10*, 11–24.

Faraone, S. V., Biederman, J., Keenan, K., & Tsuang, M. T. (1991). Separation of DSM-III attention deficit disorder and conduct disorder: Evidence from a family genetic study of American child psychiatry patients. *Psychological Medicine, 21*, 109–121.

Forehand, R., & Brody, G. (1985). The association between parental personal/ marital adjustment and parent–child interactions in a clinic sample. *Behaviour Research and Therapy, 2*, 211–212.

Forehand, R., Brody, G., & Smith, K. (1986). Contributions of child behavior and marital dissatisfaction to maternal perceptions of child maladjustment. *Behaviour Research and Therapy, 24*, 43–48.

Framo, J. L. (1975). Personal reflections of a therapist. *Journal of Marriage and Family Counseling, 1*, 15–28.

Frick, P. J., Lahey, B. B., Hartdagen, S., & Hynd, G. W. (1989). Conduct problems in boys: Relations to maternal personality, marital satisfaction, and socioeconomic status. *Journal of Clinical Child Psychology, 18*, 114–120.

Frick, P. J., Lahey, B. B., Loeber, R., Stouthamer-Loeber, M., Christ, M. A. G., & Hanson, K. (1992). Familial risk factors to oppositional defiant disorder and conduct disorder: Parental psychopathology and maternal parenting. *Journal of Consulting and Clinical Psychology, 60*, 49–55.

Frick, P. J., Van Horn, Y., Lahey, B. B., Christ, M. A. G., Loeber, R., Hart, E. A., Tannenbaum, L., & Hanson, K. (1993). Oppositional defiant disorder and conduct disorder: A meta-analytic review of factor analyses and cross-validation in a clinic sample. *Clinical Psychology Review, 13*, 319–340.

Green, K. D., Forehand, R., & McMahon, R. J. (1979). Parental manipulation of compliance and noncompliance in normal and deviant children. *Behavior Modification, 3*, 245–266.

Guerra, N. G., Huesmann, L. R., & Hanish, L. (1995). The role of normative beliefs in children's social behavior. In N. Eisenberg (Ed.), *Review of personality and social psychology: Social development* (Vol. 15, pp. 140–158). Thousand Oaks, CA: Sage.

Hinshaw, S. P., Lahey, B. B., & Hart, E. L. (1993). Issues of taxonomy and comorbidity in the development of conduct disorder. *Development and Psychopathology, 5*, 31–49.

Huesmann, L. R., Guerra, N. G., Miller, L. S., & Zelli, A. (1992). The role of social norms in the development of aggressive behavior. In A. Fraczek & H. Zumkley (Eds.), *Socialization and aggression* (pp. 139–152). New York/ Heidelberg: Springer-Verlag.

Johnson, S. M., & Lobitz, G. K. (1974). The personal and marital adjustment of parents as related to observed child deviance and parenting behaviors. *Journal of Abnormal Child Psychology, 2*, 193–207.

Kazdin, A. E., Esveldt-Dawson, K., French, N. H., & Unis, A. S. (1987). Effects of parent management training and problem-solving skills training combined in the treatment of antisocial child behavior. *Journal of the American Academy of Child and Adolescent Psychiatry, 26*, 416–424.

Kruesi, M. J. P., & Tolan, P. H. (in press). *Disruptive behavior.* In J. Noshpitz (Ed.), *Basic handbook of child psychiatry.*

Lahey, B. B., Loeber, R., Quay, H. C., Frick, P. J., & Grimm, J. (1992). Oppositional defiant and conduct disorders: Issues to be resolved for DSM-IV. *Journal of the American Academy of Child and Adolescent Psychiatry, 31*, 539–546.

Loeber, R., Lahey, B. B., & Thomas, C. (1991). Diagnostic Conundrum of oppositional defiant disorder and conduct disorder. *Journal of Abnormal Psychology, 100*, 379–390.

Miller, L. S. (1994). Preventive interventions for conduct disorders: A review. *Disruptive Disorders, 3*, 405–420.

Patterson, G. R. (1976). The aggressive child: Victim and architect of a coercive system. In E. J. Mash, L. A. Hamerlynck, & L. C. Handy (Eds.), *Behavior modification and families* (pp. 267–316). New York: Brunner/Mazel.

Patterson, G. R., Chamberlain, P., & Reid, J. B. (1982). A comparative evaluation of a parent training program. *Behavior Therapy, 13*, 638–650.

Patterson, G. R., Reid, J. B., & Dishion, T. J. (1992). *Antisocial boys: A social interactional approach* (Vol. 4). Eugene, OR: Castalia.

Peed, S., Roberts, M., & Forehand, R. (1977). Evaluation of the effectiveness of a standardized parent training program in altering the interaction of mothers and their noncompliant children. *Behavior Modification, 3*, 323–350.

Porter, B., & O'Leary, D. (1980). Marital discord and childhood behavior problems. *Journal of Abnormal Child Psychology, 8*, 287–295.

Puig-Antich, J. (1982). Major depression and conduct disorder in prepuberty. *Journal of the American Academy of Child Psychiatry, 21*, 118–128.

Robinson, E. A., & Eyberg, S. M. (1981). The dyadic parent–child interaction coding system: Standardization and validation. *Journal of Consulting and Clinical Psychology, 49*, 245–250.

Rubin, K. H., Mills, R. S. L., & Krasnor, L. (1989). Parental beliefs and children's social competence. In B. Schneider, G. Atilli, J. Nadel, & R. Weissberg (Eds.), *Social competence in developmental perspective* (pp. 313–331). Dordrecht, The Netherlands: Kluwer.

Schachar, R., & Wachsmuth, R. (1990). Oppositional disorder in children: A validation study comparing conduct disorder, oppositional disorder, and normal control children. *Journal of Child Psychology and Psychiatry, 31*, 1089–1102.

Sigel, I. E. (Ed.). 1985. *Parental belief systems: The psychological consequences for children.* Hillsdale, NJ: Erlbaum.

Tolan, P. H. (1989). Guidelines and pitfalls: Applying structural–strategic approaches in a multiple level perspective. *Journal of Psychotherapy and the Family, 6*, 151–156.

Tolan, P. H. (1991). The impact of therapist outcome conception on child and adolescent family therapy. *Journal of Family Psychotherapy, 1*(4), 61–78.

Tolan, P. H., & Loeber, R. (1992). Antisocial behavior. In P. H. Tolan & B. J. Cohler (Eds.), *Handbook of clinical research and practice with adolescents* (pp. 307–331). New York: Wiley.

Wahler, R. G., & Dumas, J. E. (1989). Attentional problems in dysfunctional mother–child interactions: An interbehavioral model. *Psychological Bulletin, 105*, 116–130.

Webster-Stratton, C., Hollinsworth, T., & Kolpacoff, M. (1989). The long-term effectiveness and clinical significance of three cost-effective training programs for families with conduct-problem children. *Journal of Consulting and Clinical Psychology, 57*, 550–553.

Webster-Stratton, C., Kolpacoff, M., & Hollinsworth, T. (1988). Self-adminis-
tered videotape therapy for families with conduct-problem children: Comparison with two cost-effective treatments and a control group. *Journal of
Consulting and Clinical Psychology, 56*, 558–566.

SUGGESTED READINGS

Frick, P. J., Van Horn, Y., Lahey, B. B., Christ, M. A. G., Loeber, R., Hart, E. A.,
Tannenbaum, L., & Hanson, K. (1993). Oppositional defiant disorder and
conduct disorder: A meta-analytic review of factor analyses and cross-
validation in a clinic sample. *Clinical Psychology Review, 13*, 319–340.
Patterson, G. R. (1982). *Coercive family process.* Eugene, OR: Castalia.
Tolan, P. H., & Loeber, R. (1992). Antisocial behavior. In P. H. Tolan & B. J.
Cohler (Eds.), *Handbook of clinical research and practice with adolescents*
(pp. 307–331). New York: Wiley.
Webster-Stratton, C. (1991). Annotation: Strategies for helping families with
conduct disordered children. *Journal of Child Psychology and Psychiatry,
32*, 1047–1062.

5

Recovery Maintenance and Relapse Prevention with Chemically Dependent Adolescents

David F. O'Connell
Henry O. Patterson

O ver the last two decades, cognitive therapy has attracted a considerable following. New therapy approaches and techniques are continually being developed and introduced to the clinical world, and many, although carefully conceived and clearly articulated, only achieve the status of therapeutic fads, because they do not ultimately stand the tests of empirical and clinical efficacy. Cognitive therapy clearly is neither a fad nor a passing therapeutic fancy. The proliferation of research and clinical evidence supporting cognitive therapy increasingly supports its use in a wide range of clinical settings and with a broad spectrum of disorders and dysfunctions.

A review of the growing literature on cognitive therapy, however, shows some gaps. Since the techniques were developed with adults, most of the literature deals with the treatment of various adult disorders and dysfunctions. With growing evidence of effectiveness, therapists have recently begun to adapt the methods for use with adolescents and children, especially targeting depression and anxiety. Ironically, cognitive therapist have given little attention to arguably the most common problem of childhood and adolescence—substance abuse. Only recently (e.g., Beck, Wright, & Newman, 1992; Beck, Wright, Newman, & Liese, 1993) have cognitive therapists focused attention on substance abuse in adults. The purpose of this chapter is to fill this void and to demonstrate how cognitive therapy can be used with adolescents in the treatment of substance abuse, with an emphasis on relapse prevention, a central concern in the treatment literature.

After a brief review of the literature on the use of cognitive therapy with adolescents, we compare cognitive therapy with traditional addiction treatment programs, offer some practical suggestions on using cognitive therapy with this population, and conclude with a case study from outpatient therapy sessions with a recovering 16-year-old male.

REVIEW OF LITERATURE ON COGNITIVE THERAPY WITH ADOLESCENTS

Compared with the fairly extensive clinical and empirical literature on the techniques and outcome of cognitive therapy with adults, relatively little literature exists for adolescents. We first examine the limited literature on cognitive therapy with adolescent substance abusers, then summarize the much more extensive work with adolescent depression and anxiety, focusing on the therapeutic implications for substance abusers.

The major conclusion following a search of the literature on relapse prevention with substance-abusing adolescents is that cognitive therapy essentially has been ignored as a treatment. For example, in the National Institute on Drug Abuse monograph *Adolescent Drug Abuse: Analyses of Treatment Research* (Rahdert & Grabowski, 1988), there is no mention of any type of cognitive therapy. Additionally, clinically oriented works such as *Practical Approaches in Treating Adolescent Chemical Dependency* (Henry, 1989), which specifically target adolescent substance abuse, focus on traditional individual and family therapies without even mentioning cognitive approaches.

Although oblique, the only reference to cognitive therapy techniques found in the substance abuse literature was in a major review of the research on the effectiveness of adolescent drug abuse treatment in reducing relapse. After reviewing studies of treatment effectiveness, none of which involved cognitive therapy, Catalano, Hawkins, Wells, Miller, and Brewer (1990) concluded that "few carefully controlled studies have demonstrated the superiority of any particular therapeutic approach in maintaining abstinence after treatment" (p. 1088). Considering the relative influence of pretreatment, treatment, and posttreatment factors in predicting relapse, they concluded that even though few studies have been done with adolescents, "If posttreatment factors are as important for adolescents as they are for adults . . . , addressing posttreatment factors in treatment *and* in aftercare may be critical to long-term program success" (p. 1129).

Emphasizing that much more research needs to be done with addicted adolescents before firm conclusions can be drawn about what should be done in posttreatment, Catalano et al. (1990) speculated that techniques used with delinquent youth might also be used with substance abusing adolescents. They note that Garrett (1985), who did a meta-analysis of residential programs for delinquent youth, found that "a cognitive-behavioral approach, a relatively recent development, seems to be more successful than any other" (p. 304). Specifically, because two of the predictors of relapse are posttreatment drug cravings and inability to find non-drug-using social contacts, Catalano et al. concluded that "behavioral and cognitive skills training to reduce cravings and increase social skills may reduce relapse" (p. 1130). This conclusion is bolstered by the findings of Freedman, Rosenthal, Donahoe, Schlundt, and McFall (1978) and Little and Kendall (1979) that cognitive and behavioral skill deficits are contributing factors to adolescent substance abuse and delinquency.

Although reporting no research using cognitive therapy for relapse prevention with adolescent substance abusers, the Catalano et al. (1990) review suggests that approaches that involve a cognitive component should be tried, and that carefully controlled studies need to be conducted to verify the efficacy of these newer approaches. Given the high relapse rates observed in adolescent treatment programs (35% to 85%), the need for new, more effective treatment techniques is paramount.

Since we could locate no studies using cognitive therapy specifically with adolescent substance abusers, we undertook a review of the broader literature on child and adolescent therapy with the hope of finding evidence of the use and efficacy of cognitive therapy that might have implications for the treatment of substance abuse in adolescents.

To our surprise, the major finding in our review of the recent literature on therapy with children and adolescents was much the same as with the literature on substance abuse—cognitive therapy is not yet widely studied. As would be expected from the literature with adults, the approach mostly has been used for anxiety, depression, and delinquent behavior.

The first point is illustrated by a recent tome by Tolan and Cohler (1993), the *Handbook of Clinical Research and Practice with Adolescents*. Cognitive therapy is given little attention as a treatment for any type of adolescent disorder or dysfunction. Likewise, there is no mention of cognitive therapy in Schaefer's (1988) *Innovative Interventions in Child and Adolescent Therapy*.

Although not yet the method of choice, clearly there is an emerging literature on the use of cognitive therapy with adolescents—mostly as part of a broader behavioral approach. Work by Kendall (1991, 1992) and Braswell and Bloomquist (1991) demonstrate the use of cognitive-behavioral therapy with children and adolescents for problems such as depression, anxiety, attention-deficit/hyperactivity disorder (ADHD), and anger and aggression.

Several recent empirical studies have found positive treatment outcomes: Stark (1990) with depressed children; Lewinsohn, Clarke, Hops, and Andrews (1990) and Clarke et al. (1992) with depressed adolescents; Kearney and Silverman (1990) with a severe adolescent obsessive–compulsive disorder; Hunter and Santos (1990) with adolescent sexual offenders; Larson (1990) with delinquent adolescents; and Teichman (1992) with an acting-out adolescent male.

Reviewing the literature of another major form of cognitive therapy, Ellis's rational–emotive therapy (RET), the first evidence of an application to the treatment of children and adolescents was a book by Bernard and Joyce (1984). Although there is no mention of using RET with substance abusing or addicted adolescents, nor admission that empirical research has demonstrated RET procedures to be effective with children, Bernard and Joyce conclude that "RET is an extremely important and viable counseling and therapeutic approach that is being used both preventatively or as a therapeutic intervention with both primary and secondary level children" (p. 37).

This brief review of literature on treatment of substance abuse in adolescents and on cognitive therapy techniques involving other problems with children and adolescents suggests the following two conclusions:

1. Although various forms of cognitive therapy used with adults have been tailored to the treatment of a variety of adolescent and childhood disorders and problems, the treatment of substance abuse, and more specifically relapse prevention, has been overlooked.
2. Because a number of therapists (e.g., Beck et al., 1992; Beck et al., 1993; Oei & Jackson, 1982; and Monti, Abrams, Kadden, & Cooney, 1989) have used cognitive therapy successfully with adult substance abusers, and because research, albeit limited, has generally supported positive outcomes from the use of cognitive therapy with adolescent depression, anxiety, ADHD, obsessive–compulsive disorder, sexual offenders, and delinquency, it is reasonable to assume that cognitive therapy would also be effective in treating adolescent substance abusers.

In the absence of extensively tested clinical directives for applying cognitive therapy to the problem of adolescent chemical dependency, we have relied on our own clinical judgment in selecting and utilizing those existing cognitive techniques we have found useful with adult addicts. In fact, we have found cognitive therapy approaches to be easily adapted to the adolescent population, and we believe this a testament to the flexibility and universality of cognitive therapy. In the remainder of this chapter, we describe our experience and give an example of how we have used cognitive therapy to prevent relapse and to maintain recovery in adolescent substance abusers.

APPLYING COGNITIVE THERAPY
TO THE TREATMENT OF ADDICTIONS

Based on a review of the treatment literature, it appears that cognitive therapeutic approaches to addiction treatments are underutilized in the substance dependence field. Typically, traditional treatment for chemical dependency occurs first on an inpatient basis. This type of treatment focuses on the identification and expression of feelings that are held to be repressed, suppressed, or anesthetized by the use of psychoactive substances. Along with this focus, which usually occurs in a group context, is an emphasis on the identification and lowering of defenses that block the patient's capacity to deal with troubling feelings and to develop a more intimate relationship with self and others. Traditional chemical dependency treatment for adolescents also relies heavily on psychoeducational interventions and programs. Most programs have a strong didactic component to teach patients about the process of addiction. Many of these psychoeducational approaches are consonant with the cognitive model of treatment. Educational interventions are designed to modify the perceptions, attitudes, and beliefs of chemically dependent patients. Typically, the patient is exposed to information on the psychological, physiological, and spiritual effects of addictive use of psychoactive substances. From a physiological perspective, they learn how the various psychoactive agents produce neurophysiological and neuropsychological impairment and lead to decreased adaptive functioning. From the psychological perspective, patients learn how drugs of abuse affect the thinking and perceiving processes, distort values, and modify painful feeling states. From the spiritual perspective, which is generally based on the Alcoholics Anonymous (AA), Narcotics Anonymous (NA), and other 12-step philosophies, the patient sees how the process of addiction alienates a person from him- or herself, others, and his or her higher power or sense of transcendence.

Although not typically acknowledged, 12-step programs appear to rely on approaches designed to modify the cognitions and perceptions of patients. Common aphorisms such as "There's nothing so bad that a drink won't make it worse," "Bring your body [to the meeting] and your mind will come," "First things first," "One day at a time," "Poor me, poor me, pour me a drink," all have obvious cognitive components to them. Twelve-step approaches to addictions treatment also emphasize a daily program of recovery and encourage adherents to read awareness expanding, attitude modifying, and meditative and contemplative literature on a regular basis. Implicit in the 12-step approaches to treatment are cognitive therapy techniques such as rational restructuring, reframing, countering, perceptual shifting, shame attacking, turning adversity to advantage, and exaggeration.

This rather extensive, although often implicit, cognitive focus in traditional chemical dependency treatment makes formal cognitive therapy, in our opinion, a natural treatment of choice for recovery maintenance and relapse prevention. Patients are drawn to this type of therapy and it often potentiates the existing recovery mechanisms. A psychologist or other cognitive psychotherapist typically comes in contact with an adolescent patient after he or she has already completed a 28-day inpatient program. The patient also probably has been exposed to AA and NA and may be participating in a daily program, although he or she may vary in level of commitment to 12-step activities. The cognitive therapist is unlikely to see an adolescent patient for the primary treatment of chemical dependency on a strictly outpatient basis, so cognitive therapy will likely be used in concert with other approaches to addiction treatment. Cognitive therapy is recommended, however, as the primary approach to relapse prevention.

Practical Suggestions for Clinical Management of Patients

Based on our experience treating adolescents with cognitive therapy, we offer the following advice and suggestions:

• Don't dispute the disease model of addictions. Most adolescent patients coming to treatment with a cognitive therapist have been taught that addiction is a genetically transmitted, physical disease with psychological, social, and spiritual manifestations. Patients exposed to the "medical model" of addiction will have an even more rigidly restricted view of addictive disorders and may view them as entirely physical in their origin and manifestation. The cognitive model can be used effectively with the disease model. It is usually nonproductive to attempt to change the patient's model of addiction or to dispute the utility of the medical or disease model; such discussions can confuse the patient and alienate the addictions treatment community within which the therapist operates. Rather, we suggest the concept of utilization; that is, we suggest the therapist become thoroughly familiar with the disease/medical model of addiction and build on existing cognitive techniques and ideas present in these approaches.

• Don't avoid or downplay spirituality. Many therapists are uncomfortable with or unaccustomed to dealing directly with spiritual issues with patients. However, chemically dependent patients, especially 12-step participants, view spirituality as an important area for focus in therapeutic sessions. For example, many patients use the therapeutic alliance for fourth and fifth-step work. According to the 12-step philosophy, a "spiritual awakening" is the basis for recovery from addictive diseases. The components of a spiritual experience can be operationalized, however, into cognitive-behavioral terms. Whatever the exact nature of a spiritual awakening, it has direct effects on the perceptions, attitudes, beliefs, and behaviors of patients who undergo it, and in many ways it can be viewed as a cognitive and perceptual shift in a person's relationship with self and the environment. For example, one 19-year-old patient was able to reframe the pain and struggle of her addiction as a rite of passage to spiritual maturity and as an opportunity for growth and development. In general, cognitive therapy can assist the patient in achieving a sense of freedom and love that is at the very heart of the spiritual experience. The spiritual awakening rarely occurs suddenly or abruptly; it is rather a gradual, cumulative process that unfolds as the patient matures in recovery. Once the spiritual experience is operationalized within a cognitive framework, the therapist can proceed with this aspect of the patient's treatment as with any other issue brought up in therapy.

• Be aware of the phase of recovery. The developmental model of recovery (Brown, 1985) depicts the recovery process as a developmental phenomenon. As in other areas of human development, over time the patient gradually acquires abilities and capacities and therapeutic work is accomplished. In practical terms, patients in initial stages of recovery look and act very different from patients who are drug free for a significant period of time (6 months or more), and cognitive interventions should be geared toward the style of functioning of the patient in his or her stage of recovery process. For example, patients in early phases of recovery typically are plagued by cravings and urges to use psychoactive chemicals, and the therapist may need to provide the patient with cognitive and behavioral approaches to cope with these impulses. Patients in the middle phase of recovery generally do not suffer from conscious urges to use drugs, but have difficulty dealing with the management of emotions—particularly hostility and anger—and need assistance dealing with life in a drug-free fashion. Patients in this phase also may begin questioning whether they are chemically dependent and whether they can use substances in a controlled fashion. In the later phase of recovery, patients appear to the therapist more and more like their non-substance-dependent clientele. Neurotic conflicts, personality problems, adjustment issues, and interpersonal difficulties all come to the foreground after the patient has gained a significant amount of time in abstinence from psychoactive drug use. Here the therapist can shift the focus of therapy to psychological issues that predate the addiction and may be blocking the patient's personal development.

• Avoid extensive "homework." In our experience, adolescent patients equate therapeutic homework with schoolwork and show an aversion to it and often do not complete it. We have found that focusing on the patient's lack of completion of homework assignments as resistance in the therapeutic process is not productive. Typically, the adolescent patient may be involved in daily NA or AA meetings and also concurrent traditional outpatient addictions therapy. This leaves little time for homework assignments. As an alternative, we suggest expanding the therapeutic hour to 1½ hours and allowing the patient to read brief, summarized literature on cognitive therapy, and if written techniques are to be utilized (e.g., the triple-column technique, see Burns [1989]) that they be performed with the therapist's assistance within the therapeutic session.

• Be active and challenging. Perhaps because of the cognitive development of the adolescent patient, specifically the development of "metacognition," we have found that adolescent patients enjoy the polemics and debate that can be involved in cognitive therapy. We suggest a very active, challenging, and, when appropriate, confrontational style for the therapist, so as to engage the often passive and at times taciturn adolescent in the treatment process. At the same time, it is important to be mindful of the cognitive limitations of some adolescents. Many have not fully developed Jean Piaget's stage of formal operational thought, and are not capable of highly abstract thinking about their own mental processes or the external world. Adolescent egocentrism is often a hindrance to objective self-reflection. The therapist should keep sessions as structured and concrete as possible, frequently checking to see if the patient fully grasps the concepts being discussed.

• Anticipate several relapses. Relapse rates for adolescent chemically dependent patients remain very high (Henry, 1989; Catalano et al., 1990), often over 90% following discharge from a 28-day inpatient program. Therapists should expect that their adolescent patients will relapse one or several times in the course of therapy. Therapits should also expect that they will be manipulated and lied to. Often the patient will seem to be doing very well in therapy and "look good," all the while he or she is abusing substances outside of the therapeutic environment. Random urinalysis is often helpful in dealing with the issue of relapse, and we suggest it be utilized along with the cognitive approach.

• Dual diagnosis. Previous research (O'Connell, 1989, 1990; Pierce, 1991; Bukstein, Brent, & Kaminer, 1989) has shown that chemically dependent patients are a heterogenous population, with a large proportion of patients showing a concurrent Axis I or Axis II diagnosis. Often the therapist has at least two diagnoses with which to contend, significantly complicating treatment. Again, we feel that the cognitive approach emerges as the treatment of choice for this population because cognitive therapy has been found to be effective for a wide spectrum of emotional and behavioral disorders with adolescents, as discussed earlier.

OVERVIEW OF TREATMENT

Initial work with chemically dependent adolescents involves educating the patient about the cognitive model of treatment and operationalizing their problems in cognitive terms (Beck et al., 1992). The general approach to conceptualizing problems in cognitive terms has been portrayed in many excellent books (e.g., Burns's *The Feeling Good Handbook* [1989]) and will not be repeated here. In general, clients are taught that their thoughts, beliefs, or schemata are responsible for negative emotions and behaviors. The therapist tells the patient that the bulk of therapy will be focusing on those thoughts and beliefs that are causing problems for the patient and may result in a relapse to active addiction or other emotional difficulties in the recovery process.

In addition to this general discussion of the cognitive model, several important points developed by Marlatt and Gordon (1985) should be included. First of all, the adolescent patient is told that recovery can be understood as a journey, and, like any journey, it involves continual discovery, dealing with novel situations, improvising when things do not go well, and learning new and useful ways to cope with problems along the way. Cognitive therapy provides a map for the journey and also the skills necessary to negotiate the journey in the most effective way. It is useful to tell young patients that recovery from substance dependence usually proceeds along unremarkably until the adolescent encounters what is termed a *high-risk* situation. This could be anything that threatens the adolescent, such as an awkward, stressful social situation or an internal affective state, such as extreme anger, anxiety, or depression. When an adolescent encounters a high-risk situation, the chances for picking up a drink or a drug increase significantly. The patient is then told that handling high risk situations in an adaptive way is the key to ongoing recovery and relapse prevention, and that how he or she perceives, interprets, and understands a high-risk situation can directly affect the outcome.

Here, the idea of automatic thoughts and cognitive distortions can be introduced. We have found that an explanation of common cognitive distortions in addictions is useful in conceptualizing the patient's problems. For each of the following distortions identified by Marlatt and

Gordon (1985), we offer patients common examples associated with the relapse process.

• *Overgeneralization.* With this cognitive error the patient seems to be saying, "If it happened in this situation, it's going to happen in any situation that is even remotely like it." For example, the patient has one slip by taking a drag on a marijuana cigarette and uses this as evidence that he or she is not "working a recovery program" and will not be able to avoid slips again.

• *Selective abstraction.* Similar to overgeneralization, with this error the patient measures him- or herself in terms of failure or mistakes. When committing this distortion, the patient focuses excessively on a negative situation to the exclusion of all previous positive experiences. For example, a patient with 6 months of continuous sobriety became obsessed with the idea that he had inhaled some nitrous oxide with a friend at a party. He was seized with the idea that all of his treatment and efforts at recovery were in vain.

• *Excessive responsibility.* With this error, the patient assumes more responsibility than he or she actually has for a relapse or other problem in his or her life. In the case of a relapse, patients may feel that they lack willpower, are constitutionally defective, or just do not have what it takes to remain abstinent. Patients making this error see themselves as the sole cause of their problems without giving consideration to the many other causes or variables that affect any given behavior or situation.

• *Assumption of temporal causality.* This cognitive error is the temporal equivalent to overgeneralization. The patient seems to be saying, "It was true in the past and its always going to be true." With this error, a slip is viewed as "the beginning of the end," and all future attempts at coping and staying sober are seen as abortive.

• *Self-reference.* Here, patients show egocentric thinking, a common cognitive trait associated with adolescence, and feel that the world is watching them and is overly concerned with their problems. As in excessive responsibility, patients see themselves as the cause of their problems and anticipate that others are blaming them and looking down on them. Patients who are unable to stay sober often suffer extreme guilt and shame due to this distortion.

• *Catastrophizing.* With this error, patients anticipate the worst happening. In our experience, it is probably the most common cognitive error. One patient was convinced that after he had one beer or snort he would turn into a homeless drug addict, roaming from crack house to crack house, finally ending up on the streets dying from exposure to the elements.

• *Dichotomous thinking.* This is black-and-white thinking. For example, patients committing this error may see themselves either as actively pursuing recovery and doing everything they can to stay sober or as being irresponsible and "not working a program." They approach their sobriety with an either/or mentality.

Describing common cognitive distortions in addictive thinking, along with concrete examples from the patients' lives, is highly effective in helping adolescents to understand the cognitive model and apply appropriate cognitive interventions.

In initial therapeutic sessions, patients should be apprised of the "abstinence violation effect" (AVE). This is an effect, described by Marlatt and Gordon (1985), that can occur when the adolescent patient picks up a drink or a drug. It has two components: (1) a cognitive attribution as to the perceived cause of the relapse, and (2) an affective reaction to this attribution. Typically, patients experience this response when they see themselves as the cause of a lapse and feel an overwhelming sense of guilt, shame, or other negative affect. Patients experience the AVE when they attribute a lapse to internal, stable, and global factors that are viewed as uncontrollable (e.g., having the gene for alcoholism, lacking willpower, being mentally deficient). The AVE can be decreased in intensity by assisting the patient to see that a lapse can be caused by external, unstable, changeable factors such as acquired coping skills level. The patient is then told that learning cognitive coping skills can decrease the probability of a full blown relapse when a slip occurs.

Another useful concept to consider is the "biphasic response." Typically, the adolescent does not consider both the long- and short-term effects of a drug when deciding whether to again use substances. Most patients show what is termed "positive outcome expectancies" when they pick up a drink or a drug. What they forget is that only the short-term or initial phase of the drug effect is positive. This is followed by a negative phase when the drug begins to wear off and the patient experiences physical discomfort, followed by emotional discomfort from feelings such as guilt and anxiety. In the cognitive approach to treatment, patients are encouraged to anticipate the biphasic response and to consider both the positive and negative immediate consequences of picking up a drink or a drug and also the delayed consequences, positive or negative, that can come from drug or alcohol use.

Emery (1988) has developed a structured program, Dependency Free, that can also be quite useful in the initial stages of treatment with chemically dependent adolescents. One of the useful components of Dependency Free includes the concept of "psychological reversal," a psychological state that renders the patient highly vulnerable to relapse. At such a time, patients become more concerned with seeking *pleasure* than gaining long-term results and focusing on *happiness*. Pleasure provides an immediate escape, and the person does not have to work for it; pleasure experiences are acquired. Happiness, on the other hand, involves letting go. It is a deeper, more subtle, more powerful experience and is the hallmark of psychological maturity. Happiness comes spontaneously and automatically when one stops fighting life and moves toward accepting everything life has to offer. Dropping one's need to be important is integral to creating happiness. It is achieved when one becomes involved in life in the *here and now*. Pleasure can come from the use of drugs or alcohol, but happiness can never be derived from substances.

As in RET approaches to therapy, several dysfunctional beliefs are identified for the patient in Dependency Free. We typically offer these to patients to help them dissolve the following beliefs and substitute more rational ones: "I need others' approval to prove I am worthy"; "I need to achieve to prove that I am good enough"; "I need to be in control to avoid feeling helpless"; "I am powerless to get what I want."

Substance abusing adolescent patients typically harbor one or more of these beliefs. A good deal of exploration and active direction by the therapist may be necessary to draw out these beliefs. Once they are brought to the surface, the therapist can employ the full spectrum of cognitive interventions to challenge them and supplant them with more rational assumptions.

Using a similar approach, in his book *Healing the Addictive Mind*, Jampolsky (1991) lists 13 core beliefs of the addictive thought system, followed by 13 beliefs that serve as the rational counterpart. He sees chemically dependent patients as developing a thought system based on fear and a past or future orientation that robs them of love and serenity. In Jampolsky's approach to therapy, the addictive core beliefs are to be supplanted by a rational, love-based thought system. For example, the irrational belief that "the past and the future are real and need to be constantly evaluated and worried about," is countered with the belief that "only the present is real, the past is over, and the future is not yet here." The belief that "other people are responsible for how I feel; the situation is the determiner of my experience," is replaced with, "I am responsible for the world I see, and I choose the feelings that I experience; I decide upon the goal I will achieve." The view that "I need something or someone outside of myself to make me complete and happy," is countered with, "I am complete right now."

Finally, it is important for cognitive therapists to keep in mind that patients typically view the recovery process as a spiritual as well as psychological growth process. But the emphasis on rationality of beliefs provides an interesting and useful mix with the more traditional intuitive focus on love and spirituality. In practical application, we have found them to be more useful with late adolescents who have typically developed higher levels of abstraction, self-insight, and a more articulated sense of self.

CASE REPORT

The following case is typical of the clinical scenario a cognitive therapist might encounter. Justin is a 16-year-old male who presents with a concurrent Axis I diagnosis and comes from a family in which the father is an active alcoholic. Since age 12, he has had a history of alcohol, cannabis, and inhalant dependence, and has been through two previous inpatient stays at a midsized, freestanding, specialized inpatient treatment center for chemically dependent adolescents. Previously, he was diagnosed with conduct disorder, undifferentiated type. Justin is repeating the 10th grade in high school and was active in athletics, but he discontinued his involvement as his addiction progressed. The patient was evaluated previously as part of a routine evaluation when he was admitted to treatment.

Clinically, Justin presents as a somewhat anxious but open and affable young man. Around adults he is polite and endearing. He is rather talkative and likes to discuss topics such as politics and religion, but around his age-mates it is a different story. He becomes more defiant and critical and enjoys being the focus of attention. Justin was referred for cognitive therapy because of his inability to stay sober for more than a few months. He enjoyed his previous inpatient stays and NA/AA meetings, but he had difficulty with outpatient therapy. He could not stay out of trouble and became bored with standard outpatient addictions therapy because he had "heard it all before."

The case portrays a rather tight focus on specific problems generated by the patient and those cognitive interventions drawn from the larger pool of cognitive techniques that we have found particularly useful in dealing with recovery and relapse in chemically dependent teenagers. Several cognitive techniques are illustrated, along with some sample therapeutic dialogue. However, as indicated earlier, all of the cognitive approaches and techniques developed over the past two decades can be applied to chemical dependency treatment (Freeman, Simon, Beutler, & Arkowitz, 1989).

Initial Assessment

Justin was administered the Drug Taking Confidence Questionnaire (DTCQ), developed by Annis and Martin (1985; see also Annis & Davis, 1988). This is a 50-item, self-report questionnaire designed to assess Bandura's concept of self-efficacy in relation to the patient's perceived ability to cope effectively with drugs/alcohol. Eight subscores are obtained, five for personal states (unpleasant emotions, physical discomfort, pleasant emotions, testing personal control, urges and temptations to use), and three for situations involving other people (conflict with others, social pressure to use, and pleasant times with others). The subscores are obtained by the patient's response to 50 statements in which he rates himself as zero (*Not at All Confident*) to 100 (*Very Confident*) in the ability to resist the urge to use alcohol or drugs. There are two versions of the DTCQ: one for alcohol only, and another for all other drugs. The eight subscales generate eight separate confidence levels that can then be graphed on a confidence profile. Figure 5.1 shows Justin's DTCQ confidence profile. The results reveal his lowest confidence scores to be in two areas: social pressure and unpleasant emotions. On the social pressure subscore, Justin rated himself as low in confidence in his ability to refuse drugs when they were offered to him, if he were socializing with friends and they suggested that the group use drugs, or if he were with a group of friends who were using drugs. With regard to unpleasant emotions, Justin rated himself as low in confidence in his capacity to resist drug use if he were depressed, bored, lonely, anxious, angry, or confused.

We have organized this case report around these two problem areas. Each section includes clinical comments and transcripts of actual therapeutic sessions that illustrate the various cognitive interventions we have found useful with adolescent addicts. Many presentations on cognitive therapeutic techniques use a one-technique-at-a-time case excerpt method to illustrate the technique. This approach can be quite artificial. Therapy

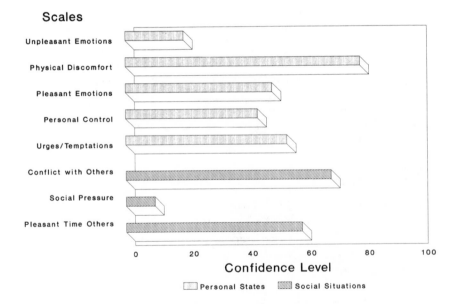

FIGURE 5.1. DTCQ Profile for Justin.

rarely proceeds in a compartmentalized, structured, point-by-point fashion—one technique after the next. Many cognitive techniques are similar and can be used at any given choice point in the therapeutic process; thus, the case excerpts illustrate our style of cognitive therapy and each session transcript illustrates a number of cognitive interventions.

Social Pressure: Fourth Session

THERAPIST: Looking at your relapse profile and based on your discussions thus far, you seem to have lots of concerns about social pressures to use drugs and alcohol again.

JUSTIN: Yeah, I'm really okay at meetings and in school for the most part, or hanging out with recovering friends. It's when I go to parties, especially if some of the cooler people at school are there and especially if they're smoking pot or drinking.

THERAPIST: So what happens when you go to one of these parties?

JUSTIN: Well, it actually starts before I get there. I start thinking about who's going to be there and how they're going to treat me.

THERAPIST: So you've gotten pretty good at this. You start upsetting yourself even before you get there.

JUSTIN: Well, yeah. But I don't do this on purpose.

THERAPIST: You mean you don't do it consciously with a goal in mind of making yourself nervous, but you've gotten quite good at it.

JUSTIN: Okay, yeah it's automatic.

THERAPIST: All right, so you're tense and now you've walked into the party. Now what happens?

JUSTIN: Well, I see several of the cooler dudes and I start thinking, well, you know, they know I've been through a rehab and here comes "reformed Jus." Here's "Mr. Recovery" or something. I feel I start making them nervous.

THERAPIST: And how do you know all this?

JUSTIN: I don't know, I can just tell.

THERAPIST: You can read their minds?

JUSTIN: Well, of course not. They just act differently toward me.

THERAPIST: So there's an appropriate, specific way to act toward you.

JUSTIN: I don't know, they just seem different when I'm there.

THERAPIST: So you're causing them to act different.

JUSTIN: Maybe.

THERAPIST: Wow, you must have a lot of power over these fellows! How cool can they be?! Sounds to me like you don't have a whole hell of a lot of information in this situation so your mind begins making stuff up and you project it on to these people. Some of this is psychological, you know. Our brains don't like incomplete or vague information that is not readily understandable, and our minds go about the process of making sense out of situations. This is all right, but we all have distorted thinking, and this can take a neutral or positive situation and make it negative. You're just beginning to become aware of the ways you do this. So far I see you *mind reading* and *personalizing*. (*Proceeds to discuss these distortions and to help the patient identify examples in other situations.*) Remember we talked before about rational counters. You've got a lot of distorted thinking in these social pressure situations. Part of an effective way of dealing with it is to identify you're thinking errors. The other part is to develop a rational counter to you're automatic negative thought. Now remember the principle here is that when you argue against an irrational thought repeatedly, that thought becomes progressively weaker over time. These thoughts have a grip on you now, but they won't always. (*Therapist and Justin work together to come up with a list of counters to offset irrational automatic thinking Justin experiences in high-pressure social situations.*) So let's write some of these down.

1. These people are more concerned with getting high than with my social status.
2. They don't know what they are doing, but *I do.*
3. There's no evidence that they think I'm a wimp. Maybe they're just curious.
4. Just because I feel nervous and I have thought of using doesn't mean I *have to.*
5. Well let's say I take a toke and blow my sobriety. Will these people be there for me to help me?

JUSTIN: (*Practices the counters subvocally.*)

In this therapeutic exchange a number of cognitive techniques were utilized: reframing, examining the evidence, listing cognitive distortions, challenging labels, and rational countering. The therapist also took the opportunity to provide information to the patient to raise his level of self-awareness and to help him understand how his mind works.

Because social pressure situations figured so prominently in Justin's history of relapse, considerable time in therapy was spent in addressing it. This focus on social pressure continues in the next excerpt.

Social Pressure: Sixth Session

THERAPIST: One of the things that I've noticed about you, Justin, is that you've gotten *so good* at putting others' opinions of you before your own and worrying about how they think! I want you to teach me how to do that.

JUSTIN: What?!

THERAPIST: No really, I really want you to teach me how to do that. I think I have the opposite problem. I'm not concerned enough with how people view me or think of me. I want you to be my teacher. I want you to teach me how to become preoccupied with how other people view me.

JUSTIN: But I don't do this on purpose, I—

THERAPIST: I didn't say you did it on purpose, I'm just saying you're good at it, and I want you to teach me. Okay, you be my trainer, you be my coach. What's step number 1? When I walk into a party and I see drug abusing, "cool" people there, what's the first thing I should do to get myself worked up?

JUSTIN: (*Laughs.*) Well, I don't know. I feel a little silly. Well, let me see, first you look around the room and see who's there.

THERAPIST: To find the coolest people?

JUSTIN: Yeah, you know, to sort of find your place.

THERAPIST: Okay, and then what?

JUSTIN: Well, then I guess you start talking to yourself and say things like, "Oh God, there's Steve, I know he's going to ask me about the rehab."

THERAPIST: Good, great. So I start to monologue with myself. Telling myself exactly what's going to happen before it starts.

JUSTIN: Yeah, that's right.

THERAPIST: So what do I do when I actually go up and start talking with these people?

JUSTIN: Uh, pretend you're not nervous.

THERAPIST: Okay, so now I introduce tension by pretending I don't feel a certain way.

JUSTIN: Yeah, I guess that's what I do.

THERAPIST: And then what? (*Continues eliciting a step-by-step process of how Justin creates the problem of social pressure to use drugs.*) Well, I'm really starting to get the knack of this, but I just realized you have to teach me your underlying beliefs and assumptions. I've got some ideas on them. How about, "One should be more concerned with others' opinions than one's own," and "It's terrible not to be in complete emotional control in social situations"? How about, "Being a recovering person is an insurmountable, everlasting, social handicap"? You see, you have to teach me these beliefs which are behind your problem here.

JUSTIN: You know I never really thought of this like that. There is so much involved.

In this exchange the therapist relies on a cognitive intervention developed by McMullin (1986), a variation of a paradoxical technique entitled Teach Thyself. This technique allows the therapist to dramatically illustrate the components of the patient's problem in social situations, including assumptions, behavioral sequence, and distorted thinking. In addition to being a powerful cognitive intervention, it can be a lot of fun for both the therapist and patient.

Unpleasant Emotions: Eleventh Session

THERAPIST: You have a really low level of confidence dealing with unpleasant emotions based on your test [DTCQ].

JUSTIN: Yeah, I know. That is really tough for me. Like when I get depressed or when I get really angry, especially, I just say, "Screw it." I guess I'm pretty moody. And then if I do pick up a drug or drink, it makes it even worse because then I figure, "What the hell, I may as well keep going."

THERAPIST: Yeah, I've heard recovering patients say that one of the worst things is to have a head full of AA and a belly full of booze.

JUSTIN: Yeah, I know what they mean. And once that happens, I'm gone, and things get worse.

THERAPIST: The weird thing about relapsing is that at the time you make the decision to use, you act as if there's not going to be any negative consequences. You forget about the biphasic drug response and stay focused exclusively on a positive outcome.

JUSTIN: Yeah, you know it happens so quickly.

THERAPIST: Yes, drugs are very predictable and very reliable, both in the positive and negative effects.

JUSTIN: But at the time it just seems to come over so quickly. It's like I don't even think, it's just automatic.

THERAPIST: Yes, well that's where the therapy comes in—to help you keep your thinking, your perceptions, and your behavior from being so automatic. Now, when you get into these negative moods, I want you to focus on what you're telling yourself, what self-talk you're engaging in. Remember you can't have an emotion without also having a thought and perception of the feeling and the situation you are involved in. Since you go through so many moods, this is going to be important. So when you realize what you're telling yourself, I want you to pick out the negative thoughts and then the distortions, and I want you to ask what evidence you have for the particular thought. Then I want you to do your countering. Above all, I want you to *do* something in these situations. Remember to be action oriented. We talked about psychological reversal. You've got to keep moving in these situations. I've found that getting out of a situation by leaving it or doing something physical, like taking a brisk walk, is really helpful in dealing with moods. I get a lot of them myself. (*Discusses how the physiology affects moods and how to use meditation to normalize mood and reduce anxiety and depression.*) Remember, moods come and go, so detach from them. Thousands of thoughts go through your mind everyday, and you might go through a dozen or more moods. So what? Why should you be concerned? Your job is to keep moving, to keep growing, and enjoy yourself.

Later in the same session:

JUSTIN: What's really hard for me is dealing with my Dad, you know, his drinking. Seeing him come home drunk really pisses me off. He's just a mess. He just ruins everything at home. I can't talk to him, he's so moody. At times he jumps on me and screams at me for no reason. It's like everything at home revolves around how drunk he is.

THERAPIST: Yeah, this could be a difficult situation, and along with your anger, I also sense a lot of hurt, seeing your father so dysfunctional.

JUSTIN: (*Tears welling up in his eyes*) I never thought of it as hurt, but it really does hurt and there's nothing I can do for him.

THERAPIST: Well, I imagine you're feeling all sorts of feelings, perhaps shame, anger, hurt, sadness, frustration. Maybe the anger is the easiest one for you to deal with. This can be a tough situation, having all of these feelings at one time. It's obviously overwhelming for you. Now let's look at what you tell yourself during these situations. When your father comes home drunk, what kind of self-talk do you have?

JUSTIN: Well, let me see. I say to myself, "What the hell is wrong with him, can't he see what he is doing and what it's doing to us? Why can't he get his act together? He acts like he knows everything and doesn't have a problem."

THERAPIST: I hear a lot of shoulds here. That he should be aware of his problems, that he should be able to stop drinking, that he should be in control of himself. It's very understandable how you would think this. But let's look at addiction. Consider your own experiences getting sober. You've had to go through a lot of hard knocks until you really got any significant clean time. Your Dad's in the same boat. But it may not always be this way. You've changed and you have all sorts of beliefs about your Dad that may not be realistic, and we'll deal with these, but what about you? What do you say to yourself in these situations?

JUSTIN: Well, I guess I just feel like, "I can't handle this." I can't stand it, and then I leave, and then I pick up.

THERAPIST: Well, getting out of there may be good sometimes, but it seems to me you rush right to chemicals. There seems to be a belief here that you can't experience a feeling and let it run its course. This is a time when you are reversed. You need to accept the situation and that you can't do anything right away to change your father, and then you need to let the feelings take their course, and then you need to do what we're doing here: Slow down, look at your thinking errors, stand back from the situation. You feel compelled to pick up a drug because you feel you don't have any options, but, as you're learning, this is clearly not the case.

In this session, the therapist took the opportunity to teach the patient about needs and feelings and how to deal with them. Helping an adolescent patient deal with an actively alcoholic parent is always difficult. There has been a considerable focus on the children of alcoholics syndrome over the past decade, and we feel it can be effectively addressed through cognitive interventions.

SUMMARY AND CONCLUSIONS

We have found cognitive therapy to be an important and effective primary component of recovery maintenance and relapse prevention with chemically dependent adolescents, a finding consistent with the extant literature on effectiveness of cognitive therapy with adults and adolescents suffering from a variety of disorders. Moreover, we believe that it can be used in a complementary fashion with other educational, medical, social, and psychological approaches to addictions treatment, as opposed to a sole approach.

Cognitive therapists who treat adolescent, chemically dependent patients should possess a knowledge of the process of relapse and, in particular, cognitive relapse determinants. A knowledge of both the disease model and the developmental model of addiction is also strongly recommended.

In considering future research and directions for treatment, it is clear that empirical outcome research must be done on the effectiveness of cognitive-behavioral strategies with substance abusing adolescents, in particular, the issue of how to most effectively fuse these strategies with not only traditional approaches such as the 12-step program, but also newer, nontraditional approaches such as meditation. Cognitive-behavioral therapists have long recognized the utility of meditation and relaxation exercises as an adjunct to cognitive therapy (e.g., Freeman & Dattilio, 1992; Kendall, 1991; Meichenbaum, 1977). Of all the methods of meditation available, transcendental meditation (TM) appears to have the most potential (see O'Connell, 1989, 1991, 1994; O'Connell & Alexander, 1994; Eppley, Abrams, & Shear, 1989; Orme-Johnson & Farrow, 1976; Chalmers, Clements, Schenklun, & Weinless, 1987, 1989, 1990). To our knowledge, no comprehensive outcome study has combined TM with cognitive-behavioral strategies; we believe such a combination would be well worth studying.

In summary, in this chapter we have reviewed the literature on cognitive approaches to the treatment of adolescent addictions and other types of disorders, compared cognitive therapy with traditional treatment programs for addicted adolescents, provided some practical suggestions on using cognitive therapy with adolescents, and illustrated their use in relapse prevention with a typical case. It is our opinion that cognitive therapeutic approaches should be standard components in both inpatient and outpatient treatment for chemical dependency with both adolescents and adults. Armed with the knowledge and skills of cognitive-behavioral therapy, addiction treatment professionals can become much more vital, potent agents of change in the lives of chemically dependent patients.

REFERENCES

Annis, H., & Davis, C. (1988). Self efficacy and the prevention of alcoholic relapse: Initial findings from a treatment trial. In T. Baker & D. Cannon (Eds.), *Addictive disorders: Psychological research on assessment and treatment* (pp. 88–112). New York: Praeger.

Annis, H., & Martin, G. (1985). *Inventory of drug taking situations*. Ontario: Addiction Research Foundation of Ontario.

Beck, A. T., Wright, F. D., & Newman, C. F. (1992). Cocaine abuse. In A. Freeman & F. M. Dattilio (Eds.), *Comprehensive casebook of cognitive therapy* (pp. 185–192). New York: Plenum Press.

Beck, A. T., Wright, F. D., Newman, C. F., & Liese, B. S. (1993). *Cognitive therapy of substance abuse.* New York: Guilford Press.

Bernard, M. E., & Joyce, M. R. (1984). *Rational–emotive therapy with children and adolescents: Theory, treatment strategies, preventative methods.* New York: Wiley.

Braswell, L., & Bloomquist, M. L. (1991). *Cognitive-behavioral therapy with ADHD children: Child, family, and school interventions.* New York: Guilford Press.

Brown, S. (1985). *Treating the alcoholic: A developmental perspective.* New York: Wiley.

Bukstein, O. G., Brent, D. A., & Kaminer, Y. (1989). Comorbidity of substance abuse and other psychiatric disorders in adolescents. *American Journal of Psychiatry, 146*(9), 1131–1141.

Burns, D. D. (1989). *The feeling good handbook: Using the new mood therapy in everyday life.* New York: Morrow.

Catalano, R. F., Hawkins, J. D., Wells, E. A., Miller, J., & Brewer, D. (1990). Evaluation of the effectiveness of adolescent drug abuse treatment, assessment of risks for relapse, and promising approaches for relapse prevention. *International Journal of the Addictions, 25*(9A & 10A), 1085–1140.

Chalmers, R., Clements, G., Schenklun, H., & Weinless, M. (Eds.). (1987). *Scientific research on Maharishi's transcendental mediation and TM-Sidhi programme* (Vol. 2). Vlodrop, The Netherlands: MIU Press.

Chalmers, R., Clements, G., Schenklun, H., & Weinless, M. (Eds.). (1989). *Scientific research on Maharishi's transcendental mediation and TM-Sidhi programme* (Vols. 3–4). Vlodrop, The Netherlands: MIU Press.

Chalmers, R., Clements, G., Schenklun, H., & Weinless, M. (Eds.). (1990). *Scientific research on Maharishi's transcendental mediation and TM-Sidhi programme* (Vol. 5). Vlodrop, The Netherlands: MIU Press.

Clarke, G., Hops, H., Lewinsohn, P. M., Andrews, J., Seeley, J. R., & Williams, J. (1992). Cognitive-behavioral group treatment of adolescent depression: Prediction of outcome. *Behavior Therapy, 23*(3), 341–354.

Emery, G. (1988). *Dependency free: Rapid cognitive therapy of substance abuse.* Santa Monica, CA: Association for Advanced Training in the Behavioral Sciences.

Eppley, K., Abrams, A., & Shear, J. (1989). Differential effects of relaxation techniques on trait anxiety: A meta-analysis. *Journal of Clinical Psychology, 45,* 957–974.

Freedman, B. J., Rosenthal, L, Donahoe, C. P., Schlundt, D. G., & McFall, R. M. (1978). A social-behavioral analysis of skill deficits in delinquent and nondelinquent adolescent boys. *Journal of Consulting and Clinical Psychology, 46,* 1448–1462.

Freeman, A., & Dattilio, F. M. (Eds.). (1992). *Comprehensive casebook of cognitive therapy.* New York: Plenum Press.

Freeman, A., Simon, K. M., Beutler, L. E., & Arkowitz, H. (1989). *The comprehensive handbook of cognitive therapy.* New York: Plenum Press.

Garrett, C. J. (1985). Effects of residential treatment on adjudicated delinquents:
A meta-analysis. *Journal of Research in Crime and Delinquency, 22,* 287–308.

Henry, P. B. (1989). *Practical approaches in treating adolescent chemical dependency: A guide to clinical assessment and intervention.* New York: Haworth
Press.

Hunter, J. A. Jr., & Santos, D. R. (1990). The use of specialized cognitive-
behavioral therapies in the treatment of adolescent sexual offenders. *International Journal of Offender Therapy and Comparative Criminology, 34*(3),
239–247.

Jampolsky, L. (1991). *Healing the addictive mind.* Berkeley, CA: Celestial Arts.

Kendall, P. C. (Ed.). (1991). *Child and adolescent therapy: Cognitive-behavioral
procedures.* New York: Guilford Press.

Kendall, P. C. (1992). *Anxiety disorders in youth: Cognitive-behavioral interventions.* Boston: Allyn & Bacon.

Kearney, C. A., & Silverman, W. K. (1990). Treatment of an adolescent with
obsessive–compulsive disorder by alternating response prevention and cognitive therapy: An empirical analysis. *Journal of Behavior Therapy and
Experimental Psychiatry, 21*(1), 39–47.

Larson, J. D. (1990). Cognitive-behavioral group therapy with delinquent adolescents: A cooperative approach with the juvenile court. *Journal of Offender
Rehabilitation 16*(1/2), 47–64.

Little, V. L., & Kendall, P. C. (1979). Cognitive-behavioral interventions with
delinquents: Problem-solving, role-taking, and self-control. In P. C. Kendall
& S. D. Hollon (Eds.), *Cognitive-behavioral interventions: Theory, research,
and procedures* (pp. 81–115). New York: Academic Press.

Lewinsohn, P. M., Clarke, G. N., Hops, H., & Andrews, J. (1990). Cognitive-
behavioral treatment for depressed adolescents. *Behavior Therapy, 21*(4),
385–401.

Marlatt, G. A., & Gordon, J. R. (Eds.). (1985). *Relapse prevention: Maintenance
strategies in the treatment of addictive behaviors.* New York: Guilford Press.

McMullin, R. (1986). *Handbook of cognitive therapy techniques.* New York:
Norton.

Meichenbaum, D. (1977). *Cognitive-behavior modification: An integrative approach.* New York: Plenum Press.

Monti, P. M., Abrams, D. B., Kadden, R. M., & Cooney, N. L. (1989). *Treating
alcohol dependence: A coping skills training guide.* New York: Guilford Press.

O'Connell, D. F. (1989). Treating the high risk adolescent: A survey of effective
programs and interventions. In P. B. Henry (Ed.), *Practical approaches in
treating adolescent chemical dependency: A guide to clinical assessment and
intervention* (pp. 49–69). New York: Haworth Press.

O'Connell, D. F. (Ed.). (1990). *Managing the dually diagnosed patient: Current
issues and clinical approaches.* New York: Haworth Press.

O'Connell, D. F. (1991). The use of Transcendental Meditation in relapse prevention counseling. *Alcoholism Treatment Quarterly, 8*(1), 53–68.

O'Connell, D. F., & Alexander, C. (Eds.). (1994). *Self-recovery: Treating addictions using transcendental meditation and Maharishi Ayur-ved.* New York: Haworth Press.

Oei, T., & Jackson, P. (1982). Social skills and cognitive-behavioral approaches to the treatment of problem drinking. *Journal of Studies on Alcohol, 43,* 532–546.

Orme-Johnson, D. W., & Farrow, J. T. (Eds). (1976). *Scientific research on the transcendental meditation, collected papers* (Vol. 1). Vlodrop, The Netherlands: MIU Press.

Pierce, T. (1991). Dual disordered adolescents: A special population. *Journal of Adolescent Chemical Dependency, 1*(3), 11–28.

Rahdert, E. R., & Grabowski, J. (1988). *Adolescent drug abuse: Analysis of treatment research* (National Institute on Drug Abuse Research Monograph 77, U.S. DHHS Publication No. (ADM)88–1523). Washington, DC: U.S. Government Printing Office.

Schaefer, C. E. (1988). *Innovative interventions in child and adolescent therapy.* New York: Wiley.

Stark, K. D. (1990). *Childhood depression: School-based intervention.* New York: Guilford Press.

Teichman, Y. (1992). Family treatment with an acting-out adolescent. In A. Freeman & F. M. Dattilio (Eds.), *Comprehensive casebook of cognitive therapy* (pp. 331–346). New York: Plenum Press.

Tolan, P. H., & Cohler, B. J. (1993). *Handbook of clinical research and practice with adolescents.* New York: Wiley.

6

Strategies for Childhood Depression

Lynn P. Rehm
Robbie N. Sharp

DEPRESSION IN CHILDREN AND ADOLESCENTS

The existence of depression in children and adolescents was debated for many years (Kashani et al., 1981). Some authorities argued that depression required an adult set of psychic structures and the disorder did not appear until the later years of adolescence, at the earliest. The current consensus is that depression before school age may exist, although it is rare, but depression in school-age children and adolescents is no longer questioned. Diagnostic criteria have historically been another area of disagreement in the study of child and adolescent depression. It was argued that depression in young people takes forms different from the adult disorder. As an example, it was argued that depression in children was often "masked" by other "manifest" symptomatic disorders of childhood. Also different sets of criteria have been proposed for different types of childhood displays of depression at different developmental eras. Current usage, since the advent of the third edition of the *Diagnostic and Statistical Manual of Mental Disorders* (DSM-III; American Psychiatric Association, 1980), is that depression in children and adolescents can be diagnosed by the same criteria as adult depression. In some instances, different indices may be used for scoring the same symptom (e.g., sleep disturbances in children may include nightmares rather than the insomnia or hypersomnia seen in adults). Although agreement seems to have been reached on criteria, other diagnostic problems are apparent. Depression in children and adolescents appears to be less stable across time than in adults (Lefkowitz & Burton, 1979), and it overlaps significantly with other diagnostic categories. Comorbidity is a complex problem that affects our understanding of the etiology and course of the disorder and has important implications for the development of treatment programs (Clarkin & Kendall, 1992).

The problems in obtaining good epidemiological data on the prevalence and incidence of depression in children and adolescents have been made even more difficult by these conceptual and empirical diagnostic problems. Available studies suggest a very high incidence of depressive symptoms in the general population of children and adolescents as assessed by depression inventories, and a significant percentage who meet formal diagnostic criteria by clinical interview (Angold, 1988; Fleming & Offord, 1990). For example, the classic Isle of Wight study (Rutter, Tizard, & Whitmore, 1970) found that 13% of grade-school children and 40% of adolescents described depressed feelings in an interview. When definite diagnostic criteria were applied, the rate of clinical depression was found to be 1.5 per 1,000 in grade-school children and 17.5 per 1,000 in adolescents. Recent data from a U.S. study (Lewinsohn, Hops, Roberts, Seeley, & Andrews, 1993) indicated a much higher rate of depression. In a large Oregon high school sample, 20% of adolescents met criteria for a current or past episode of major depression. Although these data range considerably in their estimates, depression in children and adolescents is a significant mental health problem that may be increasing in prevalence. Efforts to treat the problem have been proportionately meager.

MODELS OF DEPRESSION

Efforts at psychological treatment of children are based on a number of different models of depression. For the most part, these models are adaptations from the adult depression literature. Intervention strategies derived from the models for application with adults are then translated down for application to children and adolescents. This process of adaptation carries some dangers. Whereas it may be feasible to use adult criteria to define the symptomatic expressions of a disorder of depression in young people, doing so ignores the developmental status of the child. Many of the models posit skills deficits or deviant cognitive structures in adult repertoires, but the organization of behavior, cognition, and emotion in young people may differ greatly at different developmental stages from that of adults. Child psychopathologists have argued that we should study abnormal behavior in children in the context of models of normal development. Child psychopathology should be seen as failure to meet developmental milestones or to acquire specific skills in dealing with the tasks of normal development. Some research on childhood depression starts from the perspective of looking at the developmental variables, such as attachment behavior or language acquisition, that are related to depression in children (e.g., Cicchetti & Schneider-Rosen, 1984). By and large, however, the developmental perspective has not been incorporated very extensively in the child depression treatment literature.

Another issue concerning the use of adult models of depression for application with children and adolescents is the idea that the disorder resides within the person. A general criticism of the DSM approach to diagnosis in childhood and adolescent disorders is the presumption that the child is disordered independent of his or her environment. Depression in children can be viewed in the context of a family, school, and peer environment. The child's behavior and adaptation is often very much a function of the environment's influences. Children are responsive to the labeling, modeling, prompting, rewarding, and punishing influences of their environments. There is some recognition in the adult depression literature that depression can be seen as an interpersonal phenomenon (e.g., Gotlib & Colby, 1987). Even interpersonal models of adult depression may not adapt well to the interpersonal environment of children, in which the differentials in power and influence between the depressed person and significant others in their environment may be much greater. As we review current models of depression and their application to children, we will attempt to comment on the developmental and environmental differences that may need to receive further attention in child and adolescent treatment.

Each of the models that we will discuss can be thought of as employing a different metaphor for conceptualizing depression. Each model postulates a way of viewing depression that draws an analogy with some other psychological construct within a larger theoretical network. "Modeling" involves making simplifying assumptions and proceeding "as if" the complexity of phenomena of depression can be seen as resulting from a much simpler core mechanism. These metaphors derive from a number of basic theories or paradigms in psychology. The metaphors we will discuss are (1) the reinforcement metaphor, (2) the social skills deficit metaphor, (3) the helplessness/hopelessness metaphor, (4) the cognitive distortion metaphor, (5) the self-management metaphor, and (6) the parenting metaphor.

Reinforcement Metaphor

The reinforcement metaphor is most closely associated with the behavioral theory of depression of Lewinsohn (1974), who posits that the behavior of depression can be viewed in terms of the constructs of extinction or ratio strain, and their effects on behavior. Depression is seen as the result of a loss or lack of response-contingent positive reinforcement.

Under such reinforcement conditions, repertoires of behavior are insufficiently rewarded and behavior deteriorates in frequency, intensity, and quality. From this perspective, the individual who has lost a significant person in his or her life has suffered the loss of a major source or reinforcement and life satisfaction. Behavior that was organized around the interactions with that person are no longer rewarding and the individual sinks into depression. An environment that is stressful and merely lacking in support from others can similarly lead to the deterioration of behavior that we call "depression," because of the low rates of contingent reinforcement available.

Lewinsohn describes three ways in which a loss or lack of response-contingent reinforcement can result: (1) environmental change, as exemplified by the loss of a significant person, or lack of support from such a person; (2) lack of social skills that would be required to have rewarding and satisfying social relationships; and (3) inability to experience available reinforcement, most often because of interfering anxiety. In the early development of Lewinsohn's approach to therapy, each possible deficiency led to a different therapy strategy. Environmental loss or lack of reinforcement was countered by strategies for increasing reinforced behaviors, such as scheduling reinforcing activities. Lack of social skills was matched by the appropriate skills training. Interfering anxiety was countered by relaxation training and desensitization. In the more recent versions of the program, each of these elements has been added together in a sequential, psychoeducational course to counteract the various components of depression consistent with this metaphor. Cognitive restructuring has been added as another approach to increasing availability of perceived reinforcement and decreasing perceived punishment.

Lewinsohn's behavioral approach to therapy has been translated into a program for adolescents (Clarke, Lewinsohn, & Hops, 1991; Lewinsohn, Rohde, Hops, & Clarke, 1991). Leader manuals and workbooks for both adolescent and parent versions of the program cover the following topics: mood monitoring, social skills, increasing pleasant activities, relaxation, constructive thinking, communication, negotiation and problem solving, and maintaining gains. As with the adult version of the program, the adolescent program is an eclectic combination of behavioral, cognitive, and interpersonal therapy components. Although the adult program has been extensively evaluated (e.g., Brown & Lewinsohn, 1984), to date there has not been a published study of the adolescent version.

In modifying the adult Control Your Depression program for adolescents, the teaching aspects of this psychoeducational approach were emphasized. Content was simplified, lectures and homework were reduced, and group activities and role playing were added as teaching tools. Content was modified, for example, by developing pleasant event lists suitable for use by adolescents in determining their potential reinforcers. The environment is taken into account in the sense that a parallel program for parents enlists their support and cooperation in the adolescent program. The parent program stresses communications and problem solving.

Social Skills Deficit Metaphor

The idea that depression can be seen as the result of deficits in social skills is inherent in several models. It is part of Lewinsohn's behavioral reinforcement model in that skills deficits may lead to inadequate reinforcement. In the adult literature on depression, marriage communication skills are stressed as a component of unsatisfactory relationships and imbalance in power between spouses (Beach & O'Leary, 1986). In other approaches, assertiveness skills are seen as necessary for achieving life goals (Hersen, Bellack, Himmelhoch, & Thase, 1984). Nezu, Nezu, and Perri (1989) argued that problem-solving skills are implicated in causing depression and that depressed persons show deficits in their abilities to solve problems.

In the child and adolescent literature, there have been several case studies published describing the use of social skills training, usually assertion skills, with depressed young people (Bornstein, Bellack, & Hersen, 1977; Frame, Matson, Sonis, Filakov, & Kazdin, 1972; Matson et al., 1980). Social skills and problem-solving components are included in Lewinsohn's adolescent depression program, and several studies have compared social skills training with other approaches in between-group design studies. Stark, Reynolds, and Kaslow (1987), for example, compared social skills treatment to a self-management approach for mildly depressed junior high school students. Both groups did better than a no-treatment control.

Most of these approaches attempt to adjust teaching approaches to the children's developmental level and they may use problem situations drawn from the clinical experiences of working with children. Largely, however, the nature of the skills taught is the same as that taught to adults. Eye contact, voice quality, direct requests, and so on, are assumed to be qualities of social skills equally applicable to children and adults. Little attempt has been made in this literature to verify the validity of the skills taught in the life situations faced by children and adolescents. The results of recent studies of the social behavior of depressed young people could be instructive to the social skills treatment approaches. For example, Adams and Adams (1991) found that depressed adolescents were indeed more likely to make poor problem-solving choices, such as seeing intoxication as a solution to dealing with a breakup with a boy- or girlfriend. Problem-solving training might well be enhanced by awareness of particularly risky or inappropriate problem-solving responses. Larson, Raffaelli,

Richards, Ham, and Jewell (1990) found that depressed children were more socially isolated, generally supporting the skills deficit idea, but that they more often wanted to be alone when with their families, suggesting that family conflict might be important. Family conflict alone may not be an issue of the child's skills deficit.

Helplessness/Hopelessness Metaphor

Seligman's work (1975) on learned helplessness began with an animal model that was used as an analog for the development of depression. In essence, experience with uncontrollable aversive events were found to lead to an overgeneralized sense that one could not control important outcomes in life, a state of helplessness. A revision of the model (Abramson, Seligman, & Teasdale, 1978) incorporated an attribution metaphor from social psychology. Depression-prone people were seen as having a tendency to make internal, stable, and global attributions for the causes of negative events; that is, when something bad happens, the depression-prone people assume that they are responsible and that the reason they are to blame is constant over time and globally applicable to most things they do. For positive events, the depression-prone person makes the opposite kind of attribution: external, unstable, and specific. The positive event is attributed to something outside the person that is unlikely to occur again, and is specific to this event. The depression-prone person takes blame for bad events and never takes credit for good events. This negative attributional style leads to taking blame for important negative events and contributes to helplessness in avoiding such events in the future. In the most recent version of the development of this metaphor (Abramson, Metalsky, & Alloy, 1989; Alloy, Abramson, Metalsky, & Hartlage, 1988; Alloy, Clements, & Kolden, 1985), helplessness is seen as leading to hopelessness about the future, which is posited as a bridge to depression.

No specific therapy approach has been developed using this metaphor, but Seligman (1981) argued that four general strategies are consistent with this conceptualization of depression: (1) *environmental enrichment*, in which a change in the environment allows the person to experience greater control of outcomes to regain a sense of efficacy; (2) *personal control training*, in which the person learns new skills (such as social skills) to be more realistically effective in controlling outcomes in his or her life; (3) *resignation training*, in which the person is aided in giving up an unrealistic goal that he or she was unable to achieve and about which he or she felt helpless; and (4) *attribution retraining*, in which the person is taught to realistically take less blame for negative events and more credit for positive events.

The work that has been done with social skills training with depressed children would be considered consistent with the second of these strategies. The Stark et al. (1987) self-control therapy has an attribution retraining module in it. In a different context, Dweck (1975) has used attribution retraining in a school setting to change attributions about schoolwork failure. She trained students to make internal but unstable attributions for failure rather than internal and stable attributions, that is, attributions to insufficient effort rather than to low ability because the former is changeable. Meta-analytic review of the literature supports the predictions from the attributional revision of the theory that depressed children and adolescents make more internal, stable, and global attributions for negative events and more external, unstable, and specific attributions for positive events (Gladstone & Kaslow, in press). There is little developmental research, however, on the development of consistent styles of attribution as they relate to depression, nor on conditions that might lead to the development of depressive styles. The research leaves open the issue of when developmentally corrective training in attributional style would be effective.

Cognitive Distortion Metaphor

Beck's (1976) cognitive model of depression is based on the metaphor of cognitive distortion. The model assumes that depressive people make negative interpretations of life events because they employ biased, negative schemas as interpretive filters for understanding events. The depressive person selectively attends to negative information, arbitrarily assumes blame for negative events, magnifies the negative, minimizes the positive, attaches negative labels to events, and then reacts emotionally to the label rather than the event. Depression itself is viewed as a cognitive phenomenon involving the cognitive triad of negative view of self, negative view of the world, and negative view of the future.

Cognitive therapy (Beck, Rush, Shaw, & Emery, 1979) consists of helping persons to be aware of the interpretations or *automatic thoughts* they are having in specific situations that lead to negative feelings. Homework is assigned to identify automatic thoughts and the therapist then collaboratively helps the patient to examine the thoughts rationally and test them empirically in other situations. The examination of automatic thoughts leads to the uncovering of *underlying assumptions* that are the basis for the thoughts. For example, the automatic thought, "His differing opinion shows he doesn't respect me," might result from the underlying assumptions, "I must always be correct in my views, because people will not respect me if I make mistakes." A variation on the cognitive theory has been offered by Nolen-Hoeksema, who suggests that it is a depressive ruminative style that leads to depression (Nolen-Hoeksema, Girgus, & Seligman, 1992); that is, the depression-prone person is more likely to attend to and focus narrowly on negative events for longer periods of time, which results in depression.

Applying the theory to children raises questions about the cognitive capacities of children at various stages of development and the stability of cognitive structures that might be involved in depressive thinking. To fit Beck's model, to experience depression would imply a well-developed sense of self and a time perspective for the future. There is some research suggesting that the depressed self-image of adults may result from parental rejection and control via such methods as derision, negative evaluation, and withdrawal of affection (Crook, Raskin, & Eliot, 1981). To apply the model to children, researchers would need to take into account developmental level and possibly the source of negative schemas about self, world, and future as conveyed by the family and other environmental influences. Although a few case studies have been reported, to date, there have been no published group design studies of the application of cognitive therapy to children or adolescents. A new book by Wilkes, Belsher, Rush, Frank, and Associates (1994) on cognitive therapy for depressed adolescents may spur research interest.

Self-Management Metaphor

The self-management metaphor derives from an analogy between the behavior of depressed individuals as contrasted with behavior exemplifying self-control. Self-control involves the person's efforts at attaining long-term goals in the face of external contingencies adverse to the goal (e.g., losing weight despite the presence of tempting foods). Depressed persons are seen as having problems in organizing behavior toward long-range goals. Rehm (1977) suggested that the behavior of depressed individuals may be seen as a series of deficits in the self-monitoring, self-evaluation, and self-reinforcement stages of self-control as conceptualized in Kanfer's (1970) model of self-control. Depressed persons or persons prone to depression were posited as doing the following: (1) attending selectively to negative events to the relative exclusion of positive events; (2) attending selectively to the immediate, as opposed to the delayed, consequences of behavior; (3) setting stringent self-evaluative standards for their behavior; (4) making negative attributions for the causes of events; (5) administering to themselves insufficient reward to motivate effective behavior; and (6) administering to themselves excessive punishment, thus further decreasing effective behavior. Evidence is generally supportive of these views in the behavior of depressed adults (Rehm, 1988) and the model has been employed as the basis for a structured, group-format, psycho-educational therapy program for depression (Rehm, 1984).

There is some evidence that similar deficits are seen in depressed children (e.g., Cole & Rehm, 1986; Kaslow, Rehm, & Siegel, 1984). The therapy program has been adapted for upper elementary school children by Stark and for high school children by Reynolds. Stark et al. (1987), as reviewed earlier, compared a child's version of a problem-solving therapy approach to a modified version of the self-control therapy program for depression. Materials were modified for age-appropriate teaching with cartoons and role-play illustrations of principles. A parallel parent program involved parents in their children's assignments and encouraged change in their behavior consistent with improving the child's self-management behavior and, thus, the child's depression. Reynolds and Coats (1986) compared a version of the self-management therapy program to relaxation training and a waiting-list control with 30 high school aged subjects. Both of the active treatments decreased depression and anxiety and increased academic self-image in contrast to the waiting-list control. Another trial of self-management therapy by Rehm, Sharp, and Mehta (1994) will be described later.

As with the other programs adapted from adult therapies, self-management therapy has not taken into account developmental issues in the acquisition of self-control skills. Skills taught, however, do seem to be within the developmental repertoire of the early and late adolescents with whom the program has been used.

Interpersonal/Parental Metaphor

The interpersonal metaphor makes the assumption that depression is due to a disruption in interpersonal relationships. The concept is similar to some of the social skills approaches to depression, but does not necessarily assume that the depressed person's skills deficits are responsible for the etiology or maintenance of the depression. Rather, the interpersonal situation itself is seen as the source of the depression. Two specific approaches fall under this rubric: interpersonal therapy and parent training. Interpersonal therapy (Klerman, Weissman, Rounsaville, & Chevron, 1984) is based on a more psychodynamic conception of disruption of important interpersonal relationships. Therapy involves identifying the most problematic relationship in the person's life and counseling to repair or adjust to the disruption. A number of studies have evaluated the approach with adults. No studies have been published using this approach with children or adolescents; however, a new book on the approach with adolescents (Mufson, Moreau, Weissman, & Klerman, 1993) should encourage further investigation of the approach.

The second approach acknowledges the research showing a fairly strong relationship between depression in parents and depression and other psychopathology in their children (e.g., Forehand, McCombs, & Brody, 1987; Forehand et al., 1988). Many paths of influence may affect children's moods when parents are depressed. Modeling of depressive behavior and outlook, labeling of the child's behavior in negative terms, setting negative reinforcement contingencies, and the stress of living with a depressed parent, may all contribute to the effect of parental depression on children. This approach views the child's depression as a product of the social environment, which is largely determined by the parents. Based on this conceptualization, therapy attempts to modify the way in which the parents deal with the child via parenting training, or through treating the parental depression directly as a means of indirectly treating the child. Studies of parent training for externalizing problems of children have shown some positive effects of training on parents' psychopathology and marital satisfaction (Forehand, Greist, Wells, & McMahon, 1982; Forehand, Wells, & Greist, 1980). Rotheram-Borus, Piacentini, Miller, Graae, and Castro-Blanco (1994) present an example of skills training in the context of family therapy (e.g., teaching the family better group problem-solving skills) in a treatment program for hospitalized adolescent suicide attempters. Family therapy is also a treatment option for interrelated depressions. Implications for treating depression are that the family system should be considered and treated in its various aspects.

PSYCHOEDUCATIONAL APPROACHES
AND PREVENTION

Approaches to intervention for depression in children and adolescents need to be considered in the context of preventing adult depression. Childhood loss and early depression are risk factors for depression in adulthood. Several of the approaches that have been studied have been applied in a preventive context. Primary prevention would consist of intervention for all children, or for all children with some risk factor, such as depression in a parent. Secondary prevention involves early intervention in children who show some initial symptoms or proneness to the disorder. Tertiary prevention involves treatment approaches for cases of depression that aim at prevention of future episodes. Treatments that are oriented toward teaching skills that are hypothesized to be deficient in people who become depressed may be used for all three modes of prevention. Psychoeducational approaches are well suited for application with children and adolescents. Schools become the logical venue for offering the preventive services. Several of the programs reviewed earlier were applied within school systems.

Lewinsohn's psychoeducational approach for adolescents is designed for a classroom presentation (Clarke et al., 1991) and the parents' parallel program is designed to involve groups of parents (Lewinsohn et al., 1991). Two programs combining cognitive behavioral approaches have focused on school applications. Kahn, Jenson, and Kehle (1988) reported on a school-based intervention study that screened 1,293 sixth, seventh, and eighth graders in a middle school system to identify children with clinically significant depressive symptoms. A version of Lewinsohn's coping with depression course was compared with a relaxation treatment, and a self-modeling (of nondepressive behaviors) condition in contrast to a waiting-list control. Active treatments were superior to waiting list at posttest and 1-month follow-up. Butler and Mietzitis (1980) describe a methodology for intervening with child and adolescent depression in school systems. This emphasis is on methods teachers may use in the classroom to modify depressive behaviors of individual children. In many cases, group exercises are recommended. Butler, Mietzitis, Friedman, and Cole (1980) assessed components of this program in a study that compared a role-play–social skills approach to cognitive restructuring and to attention–placebo and no-treatment control conditions. Both active treatment programs were superior to controls, with some indications of greatest improvement in the role-play condition.

Reynolds and Coats (1986) compared self-management therapy versus relaxation and waiting-list control with 36 moderately depressed high school students. Both active therapies were found to be effective at posttest and 5-week follow-up. Stark et al.'s (1987) school-based approach studied symptomatic fourth, fifth, and sixth graders in a comparison of self-management and problem-solving approaches to a waiting-list condition. Again, active treatments were superior. Stark, Brookman, and Frazier (1990) described the application of this program to a large school system and proposed guidelines for choosing treatment components to match student needs. Components involving parents and school personnel were included. Efforts were made to make the program developmentally sensitive. Our attempt to further assess the self-management components of Stark's (1990) program will be described in the following section.

School Intervention with the Self-Management Program

Given the high incidence of depression in adolescence and its correlation with adolescent suicides (Spirito, Brown, Overholzer, & Fritz, 1989), research on prevention and intervention in childhood depression becomes very important. As educational agencies are being mandated to provide services that previously were the purview of parents, a short-term, school-based program that would benefit children with, or at-risk for, depression is desirable. We evaluated the cognitive-behavioral program developed by Stark (1990) and based on Rehm's (1977) self-control model, for use in a large urban, multicultural school setting to teach children to recognize and to remediate their depression with a cost-effective, short-format intervention program. Concurrent intervention with parents was planned to educate them about dealing with their children's depression. The focus on children's depression was to alleviate depressive symptoms and to teach other skills that might be expected to prevent or lessen future depressive episodes.

Five depression groups were formed at four volunteering elementary schools. Children who participated were fourth and fifth graders nominated by their teachers, counselors, or principals, and whose parents returned the informed consents. Selections were based on the guidelines that we supplied describing the behavior of depressed children. One elementary school chose to offer the program to all fifth graders, and the resulting two groups were composed of those children whose parents agreed to participation. In total, there were 60 children in the groups, with 45 completing both pre and post measures. Of the children, 53% were boys and 68% of the sample were fifth graders. The ethnic makeup was 36% white, 21% black, 26% Hispanic, 15% Asian, and 2% other.

Group therapists were school psychology interns, graduate counseling psychology students, and graduate clinical psychology students. Interviews of the children were conducted by the group leaders. All students were trained by us in the program and interviews, and they were supervised weekly to monitor for problems.

Children were asked to complete a set of four questionnaires pre- and postintervention: the Children's Depression Inventory (Kovacs, 1983), the Matson Evaluation of Social Skills in Youth (Matson, Rotatori, & Helsel, 1983), the Children's Attributional Style Questionnaire (Seligman et al., 1984), and the Children's Perceived Self-Control Scale (Humphrey, 1982). In addition, the children's satisfaction with the groups was assessed by an evaluation form completed by them at the completion of the group. The Kiddie Schedule for Affective Disorders and Schizophrenia diagnostic interview (K-SADS; Orvaschel & Puig-Antich, 1987) was administered to a subset of the children (those meeting the cutoff score of 13 items on the Children's Depression Inventory).

Parental participation was limited. Although parent meetings were scheduled and the parents were invited by the principal and sent reminder notes, only one evening meeting was well attended. Few parental questionnaires were returned.

The intervention program represents a means of remediating depressive symptoms in children and possibly preventing more serious depression in the future. The program is psychoeducational in nature. Through cartoon materials, stories, paper-and-pencil exercises, and role playing, children learn to recognize mood changes and the behaviors and thoughts that influence their moods. They learn to monitor their moods, to assess causes and consequences of their behavior, to set realistic goals for themselves, and to motivate themselves effectively toward those goals. The rationale is that teaching effective self-control skills modifies negative behavior and thinking patterns, which are both symptoms of depression and risk factors for future depression. The format of the program was to provide an outline of strategies and some activities that the group leaders chose to present.

Across all the subjects, mean decreases in depression were minimal. However, for the 17 depressed children (those scoring 13 or more on the CDI), there were significant decreases in depression. For these subjects, the mean pretest CDI score was 20.6 and the mean posttest score was 8.4 ($F = 12.00, p < .001$). The depressed children also made significant gains on the Matson Evaluation of Social Skills with Youngsters for the appropriate social skills factors, and on the Children's Attributional Style Questionnaire for the overall-difference score and the negative situation score. Treatment effects were not demonstated on the Children's Perceived Self-Control Scale.

It is feasible and desirable to conduct depression intervention groups in the school setting. The content of the intervention must be appropriate for the ages and interests of the children. The children must be interested and personally involved in the material and examples provided. Both schools and parents need to be involved and may need further information describing what they could do to complement the intervention programs. Based on the positive response by schools, parents, children, and group leaders and anecdotal information from counselors and teachers that positive changes were noted in participating children, we feel that depression intervention programs can be effective with children and should be continued in the schools. Long-term prevention is the ultimate goal of such programs.

CASE STUDY

The following case study demonstrates a variety of techniques applied to the various aspects of the depression in a preadolescent male. In this case, the child psychologist worked with the school, the parent, and the child to implement interventions to facilitate change at school, at home, and individually.

Jack was 9 years old when he was first referred by his elementary school counselor because he cried daily when his mother tried to leave him at school. An attractive, middle-class, white child, he had previously made good grades and had few adjustment problems. This particular year, however, Jack's life had been complicated by the discovery of his father's sexual abuse of both his older sister and a child neighbor, his father's trial, and his father's subsequent prison term. The extended family was split with tension and blame: The neighbor was in treatment for the consequences of the sexual abuse, and the sister was placed in foster care after giving birth and then giving the baby up for adoption.

When the father was incarcerated, the family's home had to be sold along with most of their belongings. His mother had always worked, although she made a limited wage in a small publishing company. Jack and his mother moved to a small apartment in the neighborhood. Jack's mother was frightened at all the changes she was called on to make and relied heavily on Jack for support and company. By the time school started, they were spending all their time together; he would go to work with her and play or read quietly, or be entertained by the other workers. When they went home, they played together and slept in the same bed.

Jack had regressed to "baby talk" when stressed and constantly looked to his mother for support when he spoke. While crying at school, he described his fear of losing his mother. He was fearful that something horrible would happen to her, that he would not be able to intervene, and that he would then be alone in the world. He cried openly at the beginning of each school day, then quietly at his desk the rest of the day. His mother was frequently reduced to tears herself, and the school counselor spent much time soothing her.

Jack described much sadness and greatly missed his father during the first few months he was away. He sent his father letters and cards every day, often at his mother's urging. His mother was experiencing very mixed feelings—love for the man she had been married to for 15 years; horror that he could be so different from what she had ever thought; blame for the daughter; guilt for not having known or intervening earlier; and finally, incredible stress at trying to maintain financial support for herself and her son. Jack showed a loss of appetite and complained of stomachaches almost every day. He slept and ate very little and experienced many illnesses that winter. His grades plummeted. His only solace was in his counselor's office.

At this point, the school counselor referred the family to one of us (R.N.S.) for evaluation and treatment. Through clinical interviews with the child, parent, and school counselor and responses to the K-SADS and Child Behavior Checklists (Achenbach & Edelbrock, 1979) completed by the parent and school, criteria meeting the diagnosis of depression were determined. To chart progress, Jack was questioned at the beginning of each individual session about his feelings, moods, and behaviors.

A contract was made to decrease Jack's crying behavior by shortening the separation time between his mother's dropping him off at school and his moving into the school environment. The school counselor would meet him at the car, greet his mother, tell Jack that they were going to have a good day, and escort him to her office to check in (before she took him to class). If Jack started to cry, he was allowed to come into the counselor's office to get himself together and then return to class to try again. If his mother called during the day, her calls were routed to the counselor, who reassured her and promised to meet Jack after school and keep him with her until the mother arrived. In 1 week, the crying had decreased, although the number of Jack's visits to the counselor's office was fairly disruptive to the educational day. In the next step, the goal was to decrease Jack's dependence on his mother and his counselor as the main sources of reinforcement. He was presented with copies of his mother's business card, her picture, a pass to the counselor, and the therapist's card and was told that he could use them if he had to do so. He was encouraged to try staying in class as long as he could. As he extended his time in the classroom, contingencies were set for Jack's having a good hour, a good half day, and then a good day, his reward being a visit to the counselor's office. This took about 2 months to accomplish on a regular schedule. Jack's mother's calls decreased as she heard more positive stories of Jack's behavior during the day. Occasionally, perhaps when Jack's father called or there was action on the civil lawsuit against Jack's mother, Jack and his mother seemed to have bad days. Without changes to the contingency schedule, Jack's behavior quickly came into line. By the end of the semester, the counselor had convinced Jack's mother to leave him in an afterschool program where he was quite successful.

Outpatient therapy focused on developing Jack's problem-solving skills. He was taught what to do if he was feeling sad or bad about himself, and how to calm himself with deep breathing exercises and visualizations of his mother sitting at her desk working. Cognitive restructuring techniques were introduced to incorporate negative perceptions of his father, positive perceptions of himself as a competent person, and positive perceptions of his mother as a dependable caretaker. Jack drew pictures and created games that allowed him to play out some of the solutions. His mother worked with the therapist on supportive parenting education, which included information about development and maturation, setting boundaries, disciplining in nonphysical and less harsh ways, and negotiation of privileges. Family therapy was not attempted because Jack's mother felt that she had to appear strong and did not feel that she wanted to address her concerns except on an individual and parental level.

A contract was drawn between Jack, his mother, and the therapist about Jack's moving to his own bedroom. Each night he was to stay longer in his own bedroom. Because his bedroom had become a place to store things, the room was cleared, and Jack and his mother decorated the bedroom. They selected and purchased a dog, which they both agreed made them feel safer. The dog would go to bed with Jack, but, on most mornings, both Jack and the dog were in his mother's room. This habit was difficult to change, probably because the mother said having him near her at night was as comforting and important to her as having Jack demonstrate the independence of moving to his own bedroom consistently.

Six months after her husband's incarceration began, Jack's mother decided to sue for divorce. There was an increase in Jack's anxiety as his father tried to involve him in the negotiations. After a short period of questioning her right to separate Jack from his father, his mother filed her divorce and custody case and stopped insisting that Jack write or call his father on a regular basis. Immediately Jack stopped communicating with his father. Although he was experiencing sadness for his father, he knew something about why he was in prison, felt badly about the behaviors, and only talked about his father around his birthday and the end-of-the-year holidays.

Jack's depression appeared to be alleviated by the end of the school year. His appetite and sleeping habits had improved, he was no longer crying or isolating himself from other children, and his energy level returned to normal. A Child Behavior Checklist completed by his counselor showed no significantly elevated scales. As Jack's mother gained self-sufficiency and confidence, so did Jack. He was teaching his dog tricks and learning songs to sing in the talent show at school. His visits to the school counselor were rare, and his grades returned to the honor roll. He won trophies at the end-of-school field day. He spent the summer in full-day YMCA camp and did very well. Some of his anxiety returned when the next school year resumed; however, the counselor immediately reinstated his contingency schedule and his behaviors quickly came under control. Follow-up has been accomplished only by occasional calls from Jack's mother. She feels that his behavior is within acceptable limits; however, some of her calls verify age-appropriateness of some of his actions.

CONCLUSIONS

In the past few years, more research is being directed toward understanding, diagnosing, and treating depression in children and adolescents. This work has arisen from various theoretical orientations and adapted adult conceptions of depression to assessment and treatment of depression in children. There still remains the task of incorporating recognition of normal developmental sequences into the conceptualization of the disorder in children and the matching of treatment strategies to the different maturity levels of children and adolescents.

Education of those who are frequently in positions of evaluation of children (e.g., parents, teachers, psychologists, and pediatricians) needs to include an awareness of depression signs and symptoms, both subtle and obvious; developmental expectations; and the possible need for treatment that may be indicated. With the national move to provide more mental health services within the school environment, clearly defined cognitive-behavioral programs are ideal for provision of these services. Prevention and early intervention efforts can be incorporated into the ongoing parenting and classroom management of the child at risk for depression or showing signs of onset. Although several studies have shown the efficacy of school-based models of intervention, there should be efforts to evaluate the preventative effects of such programs through long-term follow-up of experimental and control children. Intervention for depression in the schools holds promise for primary, secondary, and tertiary prevention of depression in later adulthood.

REFERENCES

Abramson, L. Y., Metalsky, G. I., & Alloy, L. B. (1989). Hopelessness depression: A theory-based subtype of depression. *Psychological Review, 96,* 358–372.

Abramson, L. Y., Seligman, M. E. P., & Teasdale, J. (1978). Learned helplessness in humans: Critique and reformulation. *Journal of Abnormal Psychology, 87,* 49–74.

Achenbach, T. M., & Edelbrock, C. S. (1979). The child behavior profile: II. Boys age 6–11. *Journal of Consulting and Clinical Psychology, 47,* 223–233.

Adams, M., & Adams, J. (1991). Life events, depression, and perceived problem solving alternatives in adolescents. *Journal of Child Psychology and Psychiatry, 32,* 811–820.

Alloy, L. B., Abramson, L. Y., Metalsky, G. I., Hartlage, S. (1988). The hopelessness theory of depression: Attributional aspects. *British Journal of Clinical Psychology, 27,* 5–21.

Alloy, L. B., Clements, C., & Kolden, G. (1985). The cognitive diathesis–stress theories of depression: Therapeutic implications. In S. Reiss & R. R. Bootzin (Eds.), *Theoretical issues in behavior therapy* (pp. 379–410). Orlando, FL: Academic Press.

American Psychiatric Association. (1980). *Diagnostic and statistical manual of mental disorders* (3rd ed.). Washington, DC: Author.

Angold, A. (1988). Childhood and adolescent depression: I. Epidemiological and aetiological aspects. *British Journal of Psychiatry, 152,* 601–617.

Beach, S. R. H., & O'Leary, K. D. (1986). The treatment of depression occurring in the context of marital discord. *Behavior Therapy, 17,* 43–49.

Beck, A. T. (1976). *Cognitive therapy and the emotional disorders.* New York: International Universities Press.

Beck, A. T., Rush, A. J., Shaw, B. F., & Emery, G. (1979). *Cognitive therapy of depression.* New York: Guilford Press.

Bornstein, M. R., Bellack, A. S., & Hersen., M. (1977). Social skills training for unassertive children: A multiple baseline analysis. *Journal of Applied Behavior Analysis, 10,* 183–195.

Brown, R. A., & Lewinsohn, P. M. (1984). A psychoeducational approach to the treatment of depression: Comparison of group, individual, and minimal contact procedures. *Journal of Consulting and Clinical Psychology, 52,* 774–783.

Butler, L., & Mietzitis, S. (1980). *Releasing children from depression: A handbook for elementary teachers and consultants.* Ontario: OISE Press.

Butler, L., Mietzitiz, S., Friedman, R., & Cole, E. (1980). The effect of two school-based intervention programs on depressive symptoms in preadolescents. *American Educational Research Journal, 17,* 111–119.

Cicchetti, D., & Schneider-Rosen, K. (Eds.). (1984). *Childhood depression.* San Francisco: Jossey-Bass.

Clarke, G., Lewinsohn, P. M., & Hops, H. (1991). *Adolescent coping with depression course: Leader's manual for adolescent groups.* Eugene, OR: Castalia.

Clarkin, J. F., & Kendall, P. C. (1992). Comorbidity and treatment planning: Summary and future directions. Special Section: Comorbidity and treatment implications. *Journal of Consulting and Clinical Psychology, 60,* 904–908.

Cole, D. A., & Rehm, L. P. (1986). Family interaction patterns and childhood depression. *Journal of Abnormal Child Psychology, 14,* 297–314.

Crook, T., Raskin, A., & Eliot, J. (1981). Parent–child relationships and adult depression. *Child Development, 52,* 950–957.

Dweck, C. S. (1975). The role of expectations and attributions in the alleviation of learned helplessness in children. *Journal of Personalty and Social Psychology, 31,* 674–685.

Fleming, J. E., & Offord, D. R. (1990). Epidemiology of childhood depressive disorders: A critical review. *Journal of the American Academy of Child and Adolescent Psychiatry, 29,* 571–580.

Forehand, R., Brody, G., Slotkin, J., Fauber, R., McCombs, A., & Long, N. (1988). Young adolescent and maternal depression: Assessment, interrelations, and family predictors. *Journal of Consulting and Clinical Psychology, 56,* 422–426.

Forehand, R., Greist, D. L., Wells, K., & McMahon, R. J. (1982). Side effects of parent counseling on marital satisfaction. *Journal of Counseling Psychology, 29,* 104–107.

Forehand, R., McCombs, A., & Brody, G. H. (1987). The relationship between parental depressive mood states and child functioning. *Advances in Behaviour Research and Therapy, 9,* 1–20.

Forehand, R., Wells, K., & Greist, D. L. (1980). An examination of the social validity of a parent training program. *Behavior Therapy, 11,* 488–502.

Frame, C., Matson, J. L., Sonis, W. A., Filakov, M. J., & Kazdin, A. E. (1982). Behavioral treatment of depression in a prepubertal child. *Journal of Behavior Therapy and Experimental Psychiatry, 3,* 239–243.

Gladstone, T. R. G., & Kaslow, N. J. (in press). Depression and attributions in children and adolescents: A meta-analytic review. *Journal of Abnormal Child Psychology.*

Gotlib, I. H., & Colby, C. A. (1987). *Treatment of depression: An interpersonal systems approach.* New York: Pergamon Press.

Hersen, M., Bellack, A. S., Himmelhoch, J. M., & Thase, M. E. (1984). Effects of social skills training, amitriptyline, and psychotherapy on unipolar depressed women. *Behavior Therapy, 15,* 21–40.

Humphrey, L. L. (1982). Children's and teacher's perspectives on children's self-control: The development of two rating scales. *Journal of Consulting and Clinical Psychology, 50,* 624–633.

Kahn, J. S., Jenson, W. R., & Kehle, T. J. (1988, November) *Assessment and treatment of depression among early adolescents.* Paper presented at the meeting of the Association for Advancement of Behavior Therapy, New York, NY.

Kanfer, F. H. (1970). Self-regulation: Research, issues and speculation. In C. Neuringer & J. L. Michael (Eds.), *Behavior modification in clinical psychology* (pp.178–220). New York: Appleton-Century-Crofts.

Kashani, J. H., Husain, A., Shekim, W. O., Hodges, K. K., Cytryn, L., & McKnew, D. H. (1981). Current perspectives on childhood depression: An overview. *American Journal of Psychiatry, 138*(2), 143–153.

Kaslow, N. J., Rehm, L. P., & Siegel, A. W. (1984). Social–cognitive and cognitive correlates of depression in children. *Journal of Abnormal Child Psychology, 12,* 605–620.

Klerman, G. L., Weissman, M. M., Rounsaville, B. J., & Chevron, E. S. (1984). *Interpersonal psychotherapy for depression.* New York: Basic Books.

Kovacs, M. (1983). *The Children's Depression Inventory: A self-rated depression scale for school-aged youngsters.* Unpublished manuscript, University of Pittsburgh.

Larson, R. W., Raffaelli, M., Richards, M. H., Ham, M., & Jewell, L. (1990). Ecology of depression in late childhood and early adolescence: A profile of daily states and activities. *Journal of Abnormal Psychology, 99,* 92–102.

Lefkowitz, M. M., & Burton, N. (1978). Childhood depression: A critique of the concept. *Psychological Bulletin, 85,* 716–726.

Lewinsohn, P. M. (1974). A behavioral approach to depression. In R. M. Friedman & M. M. Katz (Eds.), *The psychology of depression: Contemporary theory and research* (pp. 157–185). New York: Wiley.

Lewinsohn, P. M., Hops, H., Roberts, R. E., Seeley, J. R., & Andrews, J. A. (1993). Adolescent psychopathology: I. Prevalence and incidence of depression and other DSM-III-R disorders in high school students. *Journal of Abnormal Psychology, 101,* 133–144.

Lewinsohn, P. M., Rohde, P., Hops, H., & Clarke, G. (1991). *Adolescent coping with depression course: Leader's manual for parent groups.* Eugene, OR: Castalia.

Matson, J. L., Esvelt-Dawson, K., Andrasik, F., Ollendik, T. H., Petti, T. A., & Hersen, M. (1980). Observation and generalization effects of social skills training and emotionally disturbed children. *Behavior Therapy, 11*, 522–531.

Matson, J. L., Rotatori, A. F., & Helsel, W. J. (1983). Development of a rating scale to measure social skills in children: The Matson Evaluation of Social Skills with Youngsters (MESSY). *Behaviour Research and Therapy, 41*, 335–340.

Mufson, L., Moreau, D., Weissman, M. M., & Klerman, G. L. (1993). *Interpersonal psychotherapy for depressed adolescents.* New York: Guilford Press.

Nezu, A. M., Nezu, C. M., & Perri, M. G. (1989). *Problem-solving therapy for depression: Theory, research and clinical guidelines.* New York: Wiley.

Nolen-Hoeksema, S., Girgus, J. S., & Seligman, M. E. P. (1992). Predictors and consequences of depressive symptoms in children: A 5-year longitudinal study. *Journal of Abnormal Psychology, 101*, 405–422.

Orvaschel, H., & Puig-Antich, J. (1987). *Schedule for Affective Disorders and Schizophrenia for School-Age Children—Epidemiologic Version (Kiddie SADS-E).* Pittsburgh: Western Psychiatric Institute and Clinic.

Rehm, L. P. (1977). A self-control model of depression. *Behavior Therapy, 8*, 787–804.

Rehm, L. P. (1984). Self-management therapy for depression. *Advances in Behaviour Therapy and Research, 6*, 83–98.

Rehm, L. P. (1988). Self-management and cognitive processes in depression. In L. B. Alloy (Ed.), *Cognitive processes in depression* (pp. 143–176). New York: Guilford Press.

Rehm, L. P., Sharp, R. N., & Mehta, P. (1994). *A school-based trial of self-management therapy for depression in the 4th and 5th grades.* Unpublished data, University of Houston.

Reynolds, W. M., & Coats, K. I. (1986). A comparison of cognitive-behavior therapy and relaxation training for the treatment of depression in adolescents. *Journal of Consulting and Clinical Psychology, 8*, 18–21.

Rotheram-Borus, M. J., Piacentini, J., Miller, S., Graae, F., & Castro-Blanco, D. (1994). Brief cognitve-behavioral treatment for adolescent suicide attempters and their families. *Journal of the American Academy of Child and Adolescent Psychiatry, 33*, 508–517.

Rutter, M, Tizard, J., & Whitmore, K. (1970). *Education, health and behavior.* New York: Wiley.

Seligman, M. E. P. (1975). *Helplessness: On depression, development, and death.* New York: W. H. Freeman.

Seligman, M. E. P. (1981). A learned helplessness point of view. In L. P. Rehm (Ed.), *Behavior therapy for depression: Present status and future directions* (pp. 123–141). New York: Academic Press.

Seligman, M. E. P., Peterson, C., Kaslow, N. J., Tannenbaum, R. L., Alloy, L. B., & Abramson, L. Y. (1984). Attributional style and depressive symptoms among children. *Journal of Abnormal Psychology, 93*, 235–238.

Spirito, A., Brown, L., Overholser, J., & Fritz, G. (1989). Attempted suicide in adolescence: A review and critique of the literature. *Clinical Psychology Review, 9*, 335–363.

Stark, K. D. (1990). *Childhood depression: School-based intervention*. New York: Guilford Press.

Stark, K. D., Bookman, C. S., & Frazier, R. (1980). A comprehensive school-based treatment program for depressed children. *School Psychology Quarterly, 5*, 111–140.

Stark, K. D., Reynolds, W. M., & Kaslow, N. J. (1987). A comparison of the relative efficacy of self-control therapy and a behavioral problem-solving therapy for depression in children. *Journal of Abnormal Child Psychology, 15*, 91–113.

Wilkes, T. C. R., Belsher, G., Rush, A. J., Frank, E., & Associates. (1994). *Cognitive therapy for depressed adolescents*. New York: Guilford Press.

7

The Quadripartite Model of Social Competence

Theory and Applications to Clinical Intervention

David L. DuBois
Robert D. Felner

During the last several decades, the field of clinical psychology has shifted from a predominant focus on pathology and disorder to one in which issues relating to positive mental health and adaptation are also major concerns. This new era has been ushered in on the assumption that focusing on existing client strengths and/or promoting the development of positive mental health (and related skills and capacities) can be as important as the assessment and remediation of disorder for achieving desired outcomes in treatment. The increased focus on issues of health and competence has nowhere been more noticeable or salient than in the literature addressing the mental health needs of children and adolescents. Greater attention to concerns relating to positive mental health and adaptation for these developing populations has been fueled by the understanding that acquisition of age-appropriate competencies is critical not only for successful adaptation during the child or adolescent's current stage of development (Achenbach, 1986; Garber, 1984), but also as the necessary foundation for the acquisition of more advanced competencies and abilities required for successful negotiation of later stages of development (Sroufe & Rutter, 1984).

With this shift toward increased attention to issues of positive mental health, concepts such as resiliency, protective factors, coping, life skills, social skills, mastery, hardiness, empowerment, self-esteem, and social competence have all become popular terms in the lexicon of clinical psychology. The introduction of these concepts and the bodies of research with which they are each associated has enabled us to learn much about the conditions and factors that contribute to relatively better or poorer mental health outcomes, including those of children and adolescents (e.g., Gullota, Adams, & Montemayor, 1990). However, systematic efforts to differentiate among these constructs and to articulate the interrelationships and interdependencies they may have with each other in shaping the adaptive outcomes of youth have been sorely lacking (Felner, Lease, & Phillips, 1990). For example, although "social competence" has emerged as an umbrella term that is often used to encompass many, if not all of the concepts listed above, there has been little effort to forge a systemic framework for organizing the multiple dimensions and components of skills and abilities that are reflected in this use of the term. As a result, in much of the extant literature there is no assurance that any two researchers or clinicians are referring to the same thing when the term "social competence" is used. Nor has there been a clear elaboration of the elements of social competence that are central to the definition of the construct versus those that are related only in a peripheral or indirect manner. Finally, although a focus on competence enhancement is consistent with developmental views on cognitive-behavioral skill acquisition and learning (e.g., Cohen & Schleser, 1984; Kendall, Lerner, & Craighead, 1984), this perspective has, for the most part, not been incorporated into relevant models of clinical intervention for children. Consequently, cognitive-behavioral approaches to treatment remain pathology focused, with an emphasis on such constructs as "behavioral skills deficits" and, within the cognitive realm, "cognitive distortions," "dysfunctional attitudes and beliefs," and "biased perceptions." By contrast, the model to be presented here was developed from a competence-focused perspective and is derived primarily on the basis of theoretical and empirical work concerned with nonclinical populations (e.g., youth whose environmental circumstances place them at risk for disorder, but who are not presently demonstrating dysfunction). Thus, our hope is that the model will provide a useful extension of existing approaches to cognitive-behavioral intervention with children that have been derived largely on the basis of clinical work with disordered populations.

QUADRIPARTITE MODEL OF SOCIAL COMPETENCE

In this chapter, we consider the quadripartite model of social competence recently proposed by Felner et al. (1990). In keeping with the concerns noted above, one primary aim of the model is to provide a more systematic conceptualization of social competence and its constituent elements than has been reflected in prior work concerned with this topic. As shown in Figure 7.1, the model proposes four superordinate sets of skills, abilities, and capacities that constitute "core" elements of social competence. These skill sets include (1) cognitive skills and abilities, (2) behavioral skills, (3) emotional competencies, and (4) motivational and expectancy sets.

Another major feature of the model is derived from definitions of social competence that have emphasized the significance of person–environment transactions for understanding social competence and its adaptive implications (e.g., Zigler & Trickett, 1978). This aspect of the model is concerned with the degree of "fit" between the content and form of the behaviors that occur and the characteristics of the contexts in which adaptive success is sought. As will be discussed, an important implication of this view is that cultural and ecological regularities of developmental contexts must be taken into account when judging the competence or adequacy of a particular child or adolescent's social behavior. The reader will note that this aspect of the model is consistent with the assumption made in cognitive therapy that beliefs or attitudes are adaptive or functional within the context in which they are originally learned/acquired. However, as was noted to be the case earlier with regard to a focus on

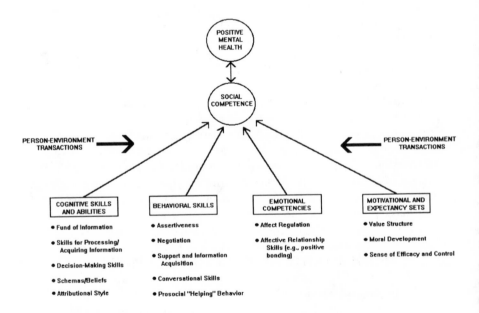

FIGURE 7.1. The Quadripartite Model of Social Competence.

competence, existing treatment models and research efforts reflect only limited attention to this issue. By contrast, we will argue that attention to contextual considerations relating to person–environment fit and setting-to-setting congruency is of critical importance in social competence enhancement efforts.

A final major feature of the model pertains to the relationship between social competence and positive mental health. Specifically, social competence and positive mental health are viewed as distinct constructs or conditions, although each is understood to have important consequences for the other. By contrast, prior conceptualizations of social competence have tended to blur the two constructs, such that characteristics viewed as core criteria for denoting the presence of positive mental health (e.g., self-esteem) have also been regarded as elements of social competence.

Skills, Capacities, and Abilities

A vast array of competencies and abilities that may have bearing on the adequacy of the efforts of youth to adapt to their social environments has been identified in prior empirical work. For the most part, researchers have defined abilities in relatively narrow, task-specific terms (e.g., skills for conflict resolution with peers). Although this approach clearly is not without its merits, it does relatively little to point us toward a more generally applicable definition of the skills and competencies that are the core of social competence. Moving up several levels of analysis, Felner et al. (1990) sought to identify categories of superordinate or "bedrock" competencies that are essential elements of all human development. As shown in Figure 7.1, the four categories they identified include "(a) cognitive processing, decision-making, and/or judgment skills and abilities, including both the ability to learn and the acquisition of necessary information; (b) emotion-focused self-regulation and coping capacities; (c) behavioral skills; and (d) motivational sets and expectancies" (p. 251). Each of these component sets of skills and abilities is assumed to be a necessary, but not sufficient, domain of competence for attaining positive adaptive outcomes (Felner et al., 1990). A key implication of this viewpoint is that adequate levels of competence in any one of the domains will not be enough to ensure desired results when intervening with youth to enhance social competence. This suggests the need for a multidimensional or "profile-oriented" approach to the assessment of social competence and approaches to treatment that conjointly address any deficiencies found to exist in different focal domains.

By contrast to this multidimensional and comprehensive focus, one instead often finds that one or another of the four core elements of social competence referred to above is emphasized to the general exclusion of the others. Illustratively, the teaching of interpersonal problem-solving skills has been one of the most popular approaches to enhancing social competence among children and adolescents (e.g., Shure & Spivak, 1982). Here, the focus has been almost exclusively on enhancement of cognitive decision-making skills as a means of enhancing social competence and preventing or ameliorating disorder. By contrast, relatively little attention has been given to the motivational levels or "sets" of the target groups and how these may also influence program outcomes. It is not hard to imagine, for example, instances in which youth "know" what to do, but lack sufficient motivation or desire to implement the desired behaviors. Scenarios such as these may be especially likely to arise when target behaviors are not well matched to the characteristics and demand structure of the social environment in which they are to be employed. It also may be the case that the youngster in question both "knows" what to do and has sufficient motivation to engage in the desired behaviors. But, even when both knowledge and motivation are present, in order to predict the actual expression of the desired behavior, we also need information on whether the required behavioral skills are present in the youth's repertoire and on his or her emotional state at the time the behavior is required. Critically, with regard to the latter point, we must know his or her capacity to regulate any associated emotions in ways that will ensure they do not interfere with execution of the target behaviors. If the youngster is unable to modulate feelings of intense anger, for example, the accompanying affective arousal may effectively inhibit his or her ability to draw on previously acquired cognitive and behavioral skills, no matter how "overlearned" these skills are. We now turn to a more in-depth consideration of each of these four component sets of skills and abilities.

Cognitive Skills and Abilities

Cognitive skills and abilities, the first core domain of the quadripartite model, have received fairly extensive consideration in the social competence literature. Of central importance in this domain is the acquisition of cultural and social knowledge that youth must have in order to function effectively in society both as they develop and later as adults (Felner et al., 1990). Included here are academic skills and abilities required to succeed in school and, as development progresses, in a widening array of tasks, such as holding a job and the day-to-day transactions of adult life (e.g., buying goods, filling out forms, etc.). In addition, a great deal of information relating to other domains, such as health (e.g., behaviors that place one at risk for various diseases) and the rules of society, must be acquired. Although such information may be transmitted through a variety of channels, educational and familial contexts are arguably the most salient sources of socialization in this regard for youth (certainly, however, the media's input is also of ever increasing salience). To the extent that these socializing agents have been unavailable, or have otherwise failed to transmit the relevant information, youth may lack adequate grounding in this very basic and presumably necessary ingredient for social competence. Recent work concerned with the outcomes of youth from poor, urban environments, for example, has called attention to the ways in which both developmentally inappropriate, underresourced school settings (Carnegie Council on Adolescent Development, 1989) and an absence of adaptive role models in family and neighborhood contexts (Wilson, 1987) may prevent such youth from acquiring information and knowledge that is critical for their later success as adults. At the same time, to take advantage of the learning opportunities provided by family, educational, and other contexts, youth must have the ability to process and assimilate the relevant information in at least some "adequate" fashion. Moreover, youth must also recognize the need to become "culturally literate," a consideration that reminds us again of the importance of the motivational element of social competence.

A second major element in the domain of cognitive skills is decision-making ability. A distinction in this area can be made between interpersonal decision-making skills and impersonal ones (Felner et al., 1990). Interpersonal decision-making skills have received widespread attention in prior empirical work and intervention models for enhancing social competence (e.g., Elias et al., 1986; Kendall & Braswell, 1993; Shure & Spivak, 1982; Weissberg, Caplan, & Sivo, 1989). These skills, which have come to be called "interpersonal–cognitive problem solving" (ICPS), include the ability to (1) generate alternative problem solutions, (2) develop viable plans for attaining desired ends, (3) predict the consequences of behaviors selected for implementation, and (4) effectively evaluate potential outcomes.

Impersonal problem-solving skills have been conceptualized as including similar processes, but are not related as directly to interpersonal situations and concerns. The "generic" problem-solving frameworks outlined by D'Zurilla and Goldfried (1971) and others (e.g., Kanfer & Busemeyer, 1982) in the adult literature are examples of approaches that lend themselves to a focus on these latter types of decision-making skills. However, it is clear that even when problem-solving skills are applied to "impersonal" concerns, such as academic work, finances, and health decisions, they may have significant and far-reaching implications for social functioning and adaptation. In recognition of this type of interdependency, Felner et al. (1990) argued that it is essential for impersonal problem-solving skills to be included in any general model of social competence.

A third major area of cognitive skills relates to the processing of information and the accuracy and adaptiveness of resulting views and beliefs concerning the self, others, and the surrounding environment. Here, considerable attention has been given to the ways in which cognitive errors, distortions, and irrational beliefs held by individuals may give rise to negative emotional states and/or maladaptive behavioral responses when interpreting events (e.g., Beck, 1967, 1991; Ellis, 1962). The term "cognitive therapy" has been used to encompass clinical approaches to modifying maladaptive thinking patterns of this type. Numerous specific types of cognitive biases and irrational beliefs have been identified in this work. One recent volume on cognitive therapy (Freeman, Pretzer, Fleming, & Simon, 1990), for example, identified 12 different types of commonly observed cognitive distortions, including dichotomous thinking, overgeneralization, and catastrophizing. Investigators in this area (e.g., Beck, 1967; Young, 1990) have posited that the specific cognitive errors that individuals make cross-situationally may reflect more fundamental cognitive sets, or "schemas." Young (1990), for example, argued for 15 different schemas relating to three superordinate themes: autonomy, connectedness, and worthiness. It has generally been assumed that schemas have largely developmental and experiential origins. Hence, negative or maladaptive schemas may frequently be associated with noxious developmental contexts and experiences such as abuse and/or neglect by caretakers.

A related area of work concerned with the processing of information has focused on the role of attributions made for events. Here, attention has focused on the ways in which the attributions that individuals make for positive and/or negative events may affect mental health outcomes. Specifically, investigators have posited the existence of a "depression-prone" attributional style for both children (Seligman & Peterson, 1986) and adults (Abramson, Seligman, & Teasdale, 1978). According to this view, individuals who tend to attribute negative events to causes that are global, stable, and internal are at increased risk for depressive episodes. Given that many events will have a salient interpersonal component, attributional patterns may also exert considerable influence on the social behavior and adaptation of youth (Goetz & Dweck, 1980). Social adaptation may be seriously compromised, for example, when youth "externalize" and hence do not accept a realistic or adaptive degree of responsibility for their interpersonal difficulties; at the other extreme, overattributing interactional difficulties to internal deficits also may impair social adaptation, especially if youth view such deficits as "static" or unchangeable characteristics of their makeup (Goetz & Dweck, 1980). Attributional patterns also may influence social competence less directly through intermediary effects on mental health and disorder. Studies suggest, for example, that depressed individuals have an aversive interpersonal style that tends to elicit negative reactions from those with whom they interact (e.g., Coyne, 1976; Joiner, Alfano, & Metalsky, 1992).

More recently, attributional theorists have posited that expectancies about the likelihood of future positive and/or negative events are also critically important. Investigators pursuing this line of research have argued that individuals who have an expectation that positive events will not occur and/or that negative events will, are more susceptible to feelings of hopelessness and depression (Abramson, Metalsky, & Alloy, 1989). These types of "future-oriented" concerns are most closely relevant to the motivational/expectancy component of the proposed model, which will be considered later.

As with cognitive skills needed for the acquisition of relevant information, it is important when considering cognitive processing components (e.g., attributional style) to keep in mind that such elements may be shaped and potentially maintained by contextual circumstances and experiences that youth have in their day-to-day lives. We suggested above, for example, that significant acute events and/or prolonged exposure to various types of environmental experiences (e.g., dysfunctional family systems) can have important formative influences on the attributional and belief systems of developing youth. It is also the case, however, that the beliefs, expectations, or attributions that youth develop may, in a reciprocal manner, influence the events and interpersonal situations they encounter. For example, maladaptive beliefs may elicit predictable responses from others that, in turn, serve as evidence to further support the beliefs. Several investigators (e.g., Sameroff & Fiese, 1989; Wachtel, 1994) have emphasized the importance of attending to these types of transactional processes both in research on psychopathology and in the design of interventions. Although acknowledging that intrapsychic processes can be shaped by the events of daily life, Wachtel (1994) concluded that "it is equally the case that the events one encounters in daily living are a function of one's intrapsychic state" (p. 52). It should be kept in mind, however, when considering such viewpoints that youth typically enjoy significantly fewer degrees of freedom in choosing the primary contexts of their lives (e.g., school setting) than do adults. Hence, among younger populations, reciprocal effects of individual variables on contextual experiences may, in many instances, be notably less pronounced in comparison to the influences that developmental contexts and experiences have on emerging belief patterns and attributional styles. The issue of where to intervene in any cyclical person–environment patterns that are identified will, of course, often be dictated by the pragmatic limitations of the treatment framework. Still, attending to both directions of possible influence may remain important both for case conceptualization purposes and for forming an effective therapeutic alliance.

Behavioral Skills

Behavioral skills represent a second element of the quadripartite model. When a person selects a behavior to attempt to achieve a desired outcome, the behavior must be one that is available to the individual; that is, it must be one that the individual both knows of (as mentioned earlier) and also, critically, has acquired the requisite skills to emit. As we will discuss, a variety of situational and cultural conditions may limit the expression of a desired behavior once it is selected. Such considerations notwithstanding, the type and range of behaviors in which the individual is skilled still must be regarded as a critical cross-situational element that limits social competence (Felner et al., 1990). Consistent with the literature on problem- or action-focused coping (Lazarus & Folkman, 1984) and classic social learning formulations (Rotter, 1954), it is assumed that the greater the degrees of behavioral freedom (skills) an individual has in his or her repertoire, all other factors held constant, the more likely it is that he or she will cope effectively with situational demands.

The universe of specific behavioral skills that may be useful is, in principle, limitless. However, there are several overarching sets of behaviors that may subsume these larger numbers of specific skills and thus provide a helpful organizing framework. Overarching sets of skills that have been identified as important for the adaptive success of youth include negotiation, role or perspective taking, adaptive assertiveness, support and/or information acquisition, conversational skills for initiating and maintaining social interactions, knowledge acquisition/learning skills, and prosocial or "helping" behavior (cf. Durlak, 1983). The task of mapping specific relevant behaviors in these domains has also received attention. McGinnis and Goldstein (1984), for example, identified 60 specific behaviors that they regarded as important to teach in enhancing the prosocial skills of elementary school-age children. However, at this point a comprehensive taxonomy of behavioral skills relevant to social competence has not yet been offered and remains a future challenge for researchers.

Emotional Competencies

Affective regulation and coping capacities comprise a third core area of basic competencies (Felner et al., 1990). To function effectively in social contexts, youth must have the capacity to manage emotional arousal that may result from stress-, anxiety-, and anger-generating situations. Children and adolescents who find themselves unable to modulate their affective responses in such situations may be unable to implement previously acquired problem-solving strategies in an adaptive manner; that is, even though a youngster may be able to perform the necessary decision-making steps in emotionally "cold" situations, such as is typical in didactic situations, he or she may be unable to do so under conditions of heightened affective arousal in "real-world" contexts. In these circumstances, youth may behave impulsively and/or demonstrate other substantial impairment in accessing and processing of information, decision-making ability, or behavioral skills, even if all of the relevant competencies are available to them under conditions of lower threat/arousal.

A second set of emotional competencies impacting on the ability of youth to adapt socially involve affective capacities for forming positive relationships with others (Felner et al., 1990). Affect-based skills required for establishing fulfilling relationships include the capacity to bond positively with others (Bowlby, 1979; Sroufe, 1979), to develop trusting and mutually supportive relationships (Erikson, 1963), to identify and respond appropriately to emotional cues in social interactions (Gottman, 1994; Izard, 1977), and to affectively role take and be empathic (Eisenberg & Miller, 1987). Deficits in one or more of these domains may limit a youth's ability to adapt socially at any given point in his or her development. Furthermore, from a developmental perspective, it is also important to keep in mind that a failure to acquire affective relationship competencies appropriate for one's age level may have enduring negative consequences for social adaptation at subsequent stages of development. Longitudinal studies, for example, suggest that the quality of the infant's or young child's attachment to the primary caretaker is a powerful predictor of socioemotional functioning several years later. In this research, preschool-age youth for whom insecure attachment relationships had been evident prior to age 2 displayed lower levels of independence, effective problem solving, and positive sociability toward peers (Arend, Gove, & Sroufe, 1979; Pastor, 1981; Sroufe, Fox, & Pancake, 1983; Waters, Wippman, & Sroufe, 1979).

Motivational and Expectancy Sets

The fourth and final core domain of the quadripartite model relates to the "performance" aspect of social competence. Even when a youth is able to engage in cognitive problem solving to select certain behavior(s), has the capacity to exhibit the behavior(s) chosen, and is able to regulate emotional arousal in the situation at hand, he or she still may fail to execute if the actions involved are not seen as desirable, or as ones that will result in valued outcomes (Felner et al., 1990). This view has important implications for researchers or clinicians attempting to assess the relative contributions of the other three proposed core elements of social competence to problematic patterns of adaptation; that is, to accurately determine whether problems are the result of actual deficits in any of the other three focal areas, it is critical to ascertain whether any apparent deficits instead simply reflect a lack of motivation to perform (Felner et al., 1990).

Felner et al. (1990) identified three distinct domains of motivational and expectancy factors that may be important for socially competent behavior: the value structure of the individual, the individual's level of moral development, and the individual's sense of efficacy and control. The domain that has received the most attention is the value structure of the individual. Here, factors such as the motivation to achieve academically, to be successful in prosocial relationships, and to attain societally valued vocational goals all may be salient influences on behavior. Consider, for example, the ways in which motivational factors may help to account for the markedly increased levels of academic failure and school-related behavioral problems that are found among youth from economically disadvantaged family and community contexts. In many instances, such youth have not been exposed to adult "models" in their home and/or immediate neighborhood surroundings from whom they could learn the value of having achieved academically. Furthermore, those adults who are present may perceive conditions of prejudice and unfairness in the larger society that, when communicated to youth, reduce expectancies that hard work and persistence in school will pay off. For youths whose motivational sets for school are shaped in these types of environments, it is not surprising that they may expend little effort either on academic work or on conforming to the rules and requirements of the school setting.

The two additional sets of motivational/expectancy factors, moral development level and sense of efficacy and control, can be seen as special cases of the person's overall value structure (Felner et al., 1990). With regard to the former, the moral reasoning of the child or adolescent may lead him or her to engage in behaviors that are different from those defined as the appropriate or "correct" ones by researchers, clinicians, and/or society in general (Kennedy, Felner, Cauce, & Primavera, 1988). Although such occasions may reflect a lack of developmental progress toward various types and levels of reasoning (e.g., Kohlberg, 1976; Piaget, 1932/1965), it also must be kept in mind that apparent deficits or delays in moral reasoning may reflect variations associated with nondevelopmental factors such as gender, racial/ethnic, or other cultural differences in the predominant types and forms of thinking and analysis that are employed (see, e.g., Gilligan, 1982). This latter issue is especially important to attend to when working with persons from cultures that may have values that are not fully congruent with those of the context(s) to which they are presently trying to adapt.

The final motivational element to consider is whether the child or adolescent has a sufficient sense of self-efficacy or internal control to even attempt desired behaviors. An extensive body of literature addressing the role of self-efficacy, internal locus of control, and sense of mastery in shaping the behavior and adaptive efforts of both adults and youth (see Bandura, 1977; Dweck & Leggett, 1988; Harter & Connell, 1984) suggests that a deficiency in one's sense of one's ability to carry out acts that are important for behaving in a socially competent manner can thwart adaptive efforts, even when other focal elements (e.g., decision-making skills, motivational valuation) are present at necessary levels.

The four-part conceptual framework of core skills and abilities underlying social competence posited by Felner et al. (1990) has potentially important implications for clinical assessment and intervention. Specifically, it appears that an adequate understanding of social competence requires examination of the child or adolescent's profile of capacities across the entire set of core domains. Consider, for example, two children referred for treatment due to noncompliance with the directives of their parents and teachers. Such behavior might result in a similar diagnosis of oppositional-defiant or conduct disorder for each youth. But on assessing the overall profile of cognitive, behavioral, emotional, and motivational factors necessary for the execution of the desired behaviors, we may find that the youngsters' primary deficits lie in quite different areas. One child might, for example, lack key cognitive skills necessary for engaging in socially competent behavior, such as generating an adequate set of alternative behaviors, predicting the consequences of possible actions, and developing plans to effectively implement behaviors that are selected (i.e., in ICPS domains). In contrast, the other child might possess those skills. But, it may be the case that this youth lacks sufficient motivation to attempt to engage in the desired behaviors because he or she does not expect that they will result in positive outcomes. Clearly, the intervention strategies that would follow from these two assessments would be quite different, despite the "surface-level" similarity in presenting problems. The analyses also reveal that neither child is failing to comply simply due to an "oppositional set" or other pathology; rather, each youth's adaptive difficulties can be viewed as the result of the lack of a *positive* competence. For the first child, training in interpersonal cognitive problem-solving skills may be most effective. For the latter youth, it may be most helpful to identify factors that are shaping his or her motivational set and attempt to alter these in positive directions. For example, many youth with this type of profile may benefit from intervention strategies that increase positive recognition and praise from teachers and parents for prosocial behavior. Here, the primary instrument for change would be modifications in the social environment to better facilitate the normal developmental acquisition of necessary skills and competencies. Adopting a "competence-based" view in either case would also reduce the probability that the adults involved develop a negative "set" about the child. This may, in turn, reduce the likelihood that negative transactional patterns are generalized to other areas of the child's life. As we can see from this example, the type of profile analysis of competencies suggested by the quadripartite model may serve to highlight transactional and contextual issues involved in social competence. It is to these issues that we now turn.

Person–Environment Transactions and the Assessment of Social Competence

As noted previously, the quadripartite model emphasizes the importance of taking into account the contextual circumstances in which behaviors occur when attempting to define or assess social competence. Adaptation and socially competent functioning are viewed as dependent not only on the sets of skills and abilities acquired by the youth, but also on the degree to which these capacities are well suited or "matched" to the characteristics of the social environments in which they are employed. As such, it is not appropriate to attempt to define a youth as competent simply by assessing the absolute level of skills in each of the four core areas. Instead, such judgments require the evaluation of whether the youth is able to adapt appropriately to some task or set of tasks within a specific context. To illustrate, Felner et al. (1990) suggested that one might offer the following type of statement: "Youth X is highly competent in peer interaction with both same and opposite gender peers in both formal and informal settings when these peers are from the same socioeconomic class. However, when placed in a context with peers from [different] cultural or economic backgrounds, she has Y difficulties" (p. 257).

How can information about cross-situational differences be used when designing and implementing social competence enhancement strategies? Issues of "person–environment" fit are potentially relevant for understanding and assessing competencies in each of the four core skill areas. To illustrate, consider a youth who fails to demonstrate social behaviors that are adaptive in the school setting. In the cognitive domain, we would want to gain some understanding not only of absolute levels of relevant skills and abilities necessary for engaging in adaptive behavior (e.g., decision-making skills, study skills), but also situational and contextual factors that might impede adaptive efforts in this domain, regardless of absolute skill levels. For example, the youth may lack information about the norms and expectations of the setting in which the behaviors occur. The youngster also may hold and be generalizing assumptions about possible appropriate alternative actions, routes to action, or consequences for decisions that are viable for other settings in which he or she is concurrently involved (e.g., neighborhood), but not for the school context. Similar issues may arise when considering behavioral, emotional, and motivational elements. The youth might, for example, come from an ethnic or socioeconomic group in which displays of emotion are acceptable and valued, but now find him- or herself in an educational setting in which different norms and expectations exist with respect to the manner in which emotions are expressed. Furthermore, those behaviors that are called for in the new setting may be ones that the youth has had little prior exposure to or opportunity to practice, with the result that they are not yet a part of his or her repertoire of well-learned behaviors. From a motivational standpoint, the youngster may have such low expectations for success in school that he or she sees little to be gained by efforts to modify his or her behavior in ways that would address the difficulties encountered. It is important to note in this example that the same underlying processes of cognitive processing, behavioral learning, emotional regulation, and motivation would operate in both school and nonschool settings, but that adaptive outcomes may differ markedly because of contrasting norms and expectations in these settings.

To summarize our discussion to this point, we see that it is essential to assess levels of skills and abilities in each of the four core areas, as well as interdependencies and interrelationships among these skills that may shape their overall adaptive value. As a second step, it is also critically important to assess whether the behaviors that occur when skills are engaged are appropriate for the particular contexts to which the youth is attempting to adapt. Based on this information, it is possible to make a judgment concerning the relative degree to which adaptive problems stem from deficiencies in core skills or a lack of fit between the youth's behavior and contextual demands.

Social Competence and Positive Mental Health

The last major feature of the model is concerned with the relationship of social competence to adaptive outcomes and positive mental health. In prior work, investigators have often offered conceptualizations of social competence that include mental-health-related outcome criteria. Several investigators (e.g., Peterson & Leigh, 1990), for example, have argued for self-esteem as a component of social competence. Indeed, as noted by Luthar and Zigler (1991), for some researchers social competence has been viewed as the measure of choice for assessing levels of overall adjustment (e.g., Garmezy, Masten, & Tellegen, 1984; Masterpasqua, 1989). By contrast, Felner et al. (1990) argued that distinguishing between social competence and mental health is a more useful approach. They suggested that social competence is best viewed as "a necessary component of, but . . .

not equivalent to, positive mental health" (Felner et al., 1990, p. 260). This view suggests that some degree of social competence is expected to be necessary for positive mental health outcomes to be obtained. However, some individuals may possess social competence and still fail to achieve positive mental health for other reasons (Felner et al., 1990).

Empirical support for this position was obtained in a recent study (Luthar, 1991, cited in Luthar & Zigler, 1991) comparing levels of depression and anxiety among "resilient" adolescents (those who experienced high levels of environmental stress but demonstrated high levels of competence) and two other groups: high stress/low competence and low stress/ high competence. Results indicated that the "resilient" adolescents fared no better in terms of levels of emotional disturbance than those with lower levels of social competence, who also experienced high levels of stress (i.e., the high stress/low competence group). Furthermore, the "resilient" group was found to have significantly higher levels of depression and anxiety than those in the low stress/high competence group. Clearly, it would have been incorrect to view the high social competence of the so-called "resilient" group of adolescents as synonymous with positive mental health. These data also suggest the limitations of approaches that regard social or behavioral competence as the sine qua non of the definition of resiliency (cf. Felner, Silverman, & Felner, in press).

It is also important to note, as discussed earlier, that the linkage between social competence and positive mental health may be reciprocal in nature (Felner et al., 1990; Sameroff & Feise, 1989; Wachtel, 1994). As shown in Figure 7.1, social competence may influence mental health. However, the bidirectional arrow linking these constructs indicates that mental health also may have effects on social competence. Consider, for example, the nature of the relationship between self-esteem and social competence. Dealing effectively with the social world would be expected to foster a positive self-image. However, levels of self-esteem may also reciprocally affect various aspects of social competence, such as a youth's sense of efficacy for handling different types of social interactions, and hence the likelihood that he or she will attempt important adaptive strategies that, without such feelings of efficacy, might be inhibited (e.g., efforts to initiate and sustain positive interactions with peers). Empirical studies of the adaptive correlates of social competence among children and adolescents have generally indicated a significant positive association between indices of social competence and mental health (e.g., Compas, Malcarne, & Fondacaro, 1988; Higgins & Thies, 1981; Spivak, Platt, & Shure, 1976). With a few notable exceptions (e.g., Dubow, Tisak, Causey, Hryshki, & Reid, 1992; Glyshaw, Cohen, & Towbes, 1989), however, most of these studies have been cross-sectional in design. Consequently, there is a lack of longitudinal data needed to address possible bidirectional patterns of effects between mental health and social competence such as those reflected in the above example.

Having considered the major elements of the proposed model of social competence and relevant literatures bearing on them, we now apply the model to an illustrative case of a youth referred for mental health treatment.

CASE REPORT

Tommy G., a 14-year-old in the eighth grade, was referred for treatment by a child and family services caseworker due to his sadness and confusion regarding his status as a foster child, poor social skills, and what the caseworker referred to as "sexual identity issues." Tommy had been legally removed from his mother's care due to neglect 18 months prior to the referral and had been living with his current foster family for approximately 1 year. Sources of information for the initial assessment included interviews with Tommy, his foster parents and biological mother, classroom teacher, and caseworker. Psychological testing was also conducted.

Initial Assessment

Tommy's foster mother, Mrs. K., reported that he was severely lacking in age-appropriate academic and daily living skills when he first came to live with her and her husband. She noted, for example, that he wet his bed regularly, had to be taught to bathe himself, and did not know his alphabet or how to read beyond a rudimentary level. Consistent with these impressions, findings of a psychological evaluation conducted at that time indicated that although Tommy was in the eighth grade, he was reading at the first-grade level. Testing further revealed that Tommy was functioning intellectually in the borderline mentally retarded range (composite IQ of 71 on the Stanford–Binet). Mrs. K. also noted that following placement in her home, Tommy exhibited "inappropriate" social behavior with both same- and cross-gender peers, such as "hanging on" his teenage foster sisters and female baby-sitters and attempting to kiss other boys in bathrooms at school and at church. She further reported that she was concerned by what she perceived to be his display of numerous "effeminate" mannerisms and behaviors and by reports that because of these he had become a target of frequent teasing by peers at his new school. For example, she indicated that other students ridiculed him because he tended to sway his hips to an unusual degree when walking and because he laughed in a manner that they viewed as "girlish." In his interactions with Mrs.

K. and with adults in general, Tommy was described as "eager to please" and vigilant for indications of approval or disapproval.

Information obtained from Tommy's caseworker indicated that he had lived in conditions of severe poverty and neglect for most of his life. Case records detailed a long history of substandard and unsanitary living conditions in the home, inadequate care for the hygiene and basic material needs of Tommy and his three sisters, and a pattern of highly sporadic and inconsistent school attendance for all of the children. However, the caseworker also indicated that Tommy and his mother had a very close relationship and that she was highly committed to his well-being (this impression was subsequently supported by the therapist's interview with Tommy's mother and observations of her interactions with him). Rather, it appeared that due to her limited intellectual functioning (tested to be in the mild to moderate range of mental retardation), the compounding strains of poverty, and having been abandoned by the children's father, she had been unable to negotiate the demands of caring for Tommy or her other children. In initial interviews with Tommy, he reported that he had a strong sense of his mother's affection for him and that he was highly distressed by the "unfairness" of her not receiving the help that she needed to care adequately for him and his sisters.

Notable improvements occurred in Tommy's daily living skills and academic functioning during the year following his placement in Mr. and Mrs. K.'s home. His reading skills, for example, improved to approximately the third-grade level. However, information obtained at the time of the referral indicated that Tommy continued to experience significant problems in his interactions with peers, similar to those that had been evident when he first came to live with the K. family. His feelings of sadness relating to his separation from his mother had also persisted and were now punctuated by periods of marked depression and social withdrawal. Mrs. K. and Tommy's teacher reported that his sadness and withdrawal were most severe following his bimonthly supervised visits with his mother.

Also of concern were a number of externalizing behavior problems Tommy had begun to exhibit. He had, for example, run away from home on several occasions and returned only when found by the local police several hours later. In addition, Mrs. K. and her husband reported that Tommy was demonstrating increased oppositionality in his behavior toward them. Tommy's behavioral difficulties in these areas appeared to be closely tied to emotionally distressing events. On learning that he had received a detention at school, for example, he refused to go home and had to be placed in a youth shelter for several days before "calming down" enough to agree to return to his foster family. In view of these ongoing difficulties, Mrs. K. expressed doubts about her own and her husband's ability to care for Tommy and, on at least one occasion, had requested that the caseworker remove him from their home.

During his initial interview with the therapist, Tommy presented as a highly dysphoric and withdrawn youngster. He said little other than to repeat his desire to return to live with his mother. Tommy's three wishes were "to go home to my 'real' mother, to get a new car, and to get to know how to read better." Tommy's self-descriptive statements to the therapist suggested that he viewed himself negatively and as lacking competence and efficacy in the domains of behavioral control, schoolwork, and peer relations. A reassessment of Tommy's intellectual functioning at the time of the referral showed little change from the results obtained previously (full-scale IQ of 72 on the Wechsler Intelligence Scale for Children—Revised); thus, despite some progress in his academic skills during the year he had spent living with the K. family, testing continued to indicate significant limitations in his cognitive abilities.

Diagnosis and Conceptualization

Diagnostically, Tommy appeared to meet criteria in the fourth edition of the *Diagnostic and Statistical Manual of Mental Disorders* (DSM-IV; American Psychiatric Association, 1994) for a depressive disorder and borderline intellectual functioning. A psychologist who had assessed Tommy earlier suggested that he might also meet criteria for a gender identity disorder. However, the current assessment suggested that his somewhat effeminate behavior was likely due more to social factors (e.g., a lack of exposure to appropriate male role models) than a gender identity disturbance per se. For example, when asked about kissing other boys, Tommy insisted that he had done so only because he wanted to show them that he "liked them as friends." He denied experiencing any distress or confusion regarding his gender identity, and observations of his behavior by others (e.g., foster parents) did not suggest the presence of these types of feelings. Psychosocial stressors associated with the strain of separation from his mother and the demands of adapting to his new environment were significant and ongoing sources of distress for Tommy and, as noted, appeared to be directly linked to many of his externalizing behaviors. For example, Tommy indicated that his acting-out behavior was in part his way of attempting to let others know that he wanted to return to live with his mother. Furthermore, he believed that positive adjustment to his foster home might cast a negative light on his mother and jeopardize his chances of returning to her. From the standpoint of the quadripartite model of social competence, one might conceptualize Tommy's profile of deficits and areas of relative strength as follows:

Cognitive skills and abilities

- Borderline intellectual functioning for processing and acquiring information/knowledge
- Lack of age-appropriate fund of cultural knowledge
- Deficits in cognitive problem-solving/decision-making skills
- Dysfunctional schemas ("I am not as good as other kids," "I have to please and take care of adults to have their approval," "There is no hope for my future")

Behavioral skills

- Limited repertoire of age-appropriate behaviors for interacting with same-gender and cross-gender peers, especially for displaying affection and for gaining acceptance, inclusion, and support
- Environmental conditions that limit utility of more appropriate behaviors (e.g., little response to simply telling others he wants to go home)

Emotional competencies

- Difficulties with affect regulation
- Strong capacity for positive bonding with others

Motivational and expectancy sets

- Expectation that behaviors desired in his foster home and/or school may lead to negative or undesirable outcomes (i.e., continued separation from mother)
- Low sense of self-efficacy
- High level of motivation to conform to adult expectations and to achieve societally desired goals (e.g., wanted very much to graduate from eighth grade)

As is evident from this list, in many areas Tommy exhibited levels of skills and capacities that were "low" in absolute terms (i.e., in comparison with other children his age). From a transactional perspective, a lack of fit was also evident between the content and form of the behaviors generated by those skills Tommy did possess and the norms and demands of his new environment. Despite his separations, for example, Tommy was still highly affectionate toward others and thus could be regarded as having a strong capacity for positive bonding in relationships. The ways in which this emotional competency was expressed, however, were not appropriate for his new environment. High levels of physical contact and displays of affection had been a central feature of his relationship with his mother and apparently quite adaptive in the sense of allowing him to establish a strong bond with her. The generalization of similar behaviors to his new environment, however, was causing significant problems, especially at school and with his peers.

Course of Treatment

Given the foregoing conceptualization, a major component of treatment was to address deficits in Tommy's skills for interacting effectively with others. The initial focus was on enhancing Tommy's cognitive decision-making and problem-solving skills. We hoped that these skills would provide a useful framework for addressing other core areas of difficulty, such as behavioral deficits, problems with affective control, and limited feelings of self-efficacy. Despite Tommy's strong motivation to comply with this aspect of treatment, it quickly became apparent that it would not be feasible to use standard intervention protocols (e.g., Kendall & Braswell, 1993) without adapting them to take into account his level of intellectual functioning and social maturity. These modifications included efforts to provide for "overlearning" of skills through repetitive practice beyond suggested levels, concrete illustrations of abstract concepts using play therapy techniques (e.g., art, games, puppet shows, etc.), and daily tape-recorded messages from the therapist to facilitate maintenance and generalization of skill gains between sessions. Tommy's foster parents and teacher actively assisted with this aspect of treatment by helping him to implement decision-making skills at home and at school. Previous work (Shure & Spivak, 1988) has shown that in order to obtain generalization of acquired problem-solving skills and tactics to contexts beyond those in which they were initially learned, it is essential that the adults in generalization contexts elicit and model the targeted skills in their interactions with the child.

As Tommy developed a reasonably solid foundation of decision-making skills, he began to apply them with some success outside of sessions. Improvements were observed, for example, in his relations with peers at school and in other settings (e.g., church). Nevertheless, deficits in other "core" areas of his social competence limited the extent to which gains accrued in his overall adaptation to his new environment. For example, on several occasions it appeared that Tommy had been too affectively aroused (e.g., angry) to use the decision-making skills effectively; in other instances, he seemed to lack the behaviors in his repertoire (e.g., assertiveness skills) to select and implement effective solutions to his problems.

To address these concerns, additional intervention strategies were introduced. Affective regulation, for example, was addressed via training in labeling and differentiation of feeling states and by rehearsing coping strategies for modulating affective arousal (e.g., writing in a "feelings notebook"). Behavioral training focused on acquiring skills and behaviors that would be adaptive for interacting with same- and cross-gender peers in his new environment, including assertiveness and several other specific skills (e.g., expressing affection, responding to teasing, etc.). Rather than utilizing a potentially artificial social skills group, Mrs. K.'s other children were actively involved in attempting to facilitate Tommy's acquisition of the targeted skills and the generalization of these skills to natural settings. Here, Mrs. K.'s older teenage sons and daughters served as "expert consultants" on the norms and regularities of the local peer and school cultures and in this way helped Tommy to learn new, more adaptive ways of behaving in these settings. For example, Mrs. K.'s daughters helped Tommy to identify ways of expressing affection toward girls that would be viewed as acceptable. They also taught him how to alter some aspects of his behavior that were regarded by others as effeminate. This was done to reduce the likelihood of his being teased by classmates and other peers. Also important was a close relationship that Tommy formed with Mrs. K.'s college-age son. Within the context of this relationship, Tommy received modeling and reinforcement for age-appropriate expressions of assertiveness with others, guidance in the effective use of problem-solving and decision-making strategies, and opportunities to practice newly acquired skills in structured peer activities (e.g., Mrs. K.'s son arranged for Tommy to play on a youth basketball team that he coached).

To enhance feelings of self-efficacy and self-esteem, a structured reward program was instituted to help ensure tangible positive outcomes and recognition for Tommy's adaptive efforts (e.g., use of problem-solving skills). The reward program included both a home-based component delivered by Mrs. K. and a school-based component administered by Tommy's teacher. In addition to enhancing Tommy's sense of efficacy for exhibiting adaptive behaviors in both home and school settings, the program was aimed at increasing the frequency that persons in these settings would be involved in positive transactions with Tommy, so as to help protect against the formation of biased or negative "sets" about his behavior that might otherwise arise in the absence of interventions to increase the saliency of his positive adaptive efforts. As will be seen when considering transactional issues addressed in treatment, the success of the behavioral program was found to be largely dependent on the degree to which expectations held for Tommy were appropriately "matched" to the levels of performance that he could realistically be expected to exhibit.

As gains accrued across the four core competency areas, Tommy's adaptive functioning improved in several important areas. Particularly noteworthy was a reduction in externalizing behaviors (e.g., running away from home, sexualized behavior with peers) which, as noted previously, had reached the point of jeopardizing his foster placement. Altering these behavioral patterns seems to have required an integrated application of emerging competencies across all four core domains. Illustratively, during this phase of treatment, Tommy proudly related an incident in which he had used his "stop and think steps" to respond adaptively to a situation in which he had become highly emotionally distressed upon being informed by his caseworker that he would not be returning to live with his mother in the near future. Although his initial impulse had been to run away from his foster home, by employing his cognitive problem-solving "stop and think" strategy and other newly acquired behavioral skills, he was able to identify and implement several alternative coping strategies. These included modulating his affective arousal by writing an extensive entry in his feelings notebook, using assertiveness behaviors to raise the issue as a concern with his caseworker, seeking out adult support from his foster mother, and using positive self-statements to enhance his self-confidence and sense of efficacy for responding to the situation in an adaptive manner.

In addition to these individually focused interventions, other components of treatment sought to modify elements of Tommy's social environment that were impinging negatively on his ability to adapt successfully to his new surroundings. Here, as an adjunct to Tommy's individual therapy, parent training and guidance sessions were conducted on a regular basis with Mrs. K. Mrs. K.'s general style of parenting, which she had found to be effective in raising her own children, was characterized by an emphasis on discipline and firm expectations for appropriate behavior. This approach, however, was ineffective in dealing with Tommy because it did not pay sufficient attention to his emotional needs or the difficulties that were presented by his level of intellectual functioning and lack of prior socialization. For example, Mrs. K.'s stern and critical tone in many of her interactions with Tommy seemed to exacerbate his feelings of insecurity regarding his status in the foster home and thus precipitate further behavioral problems. Mrs. K. proved adept at modifying her parenting style with Tommy once these patterns were pointed out. It also proved useful to help Mrs. K. to recognize Tommy's cognitive limitations and to develop more reasonable standards and expectations for his behavior and schoolwork. Alternative interpretations for some of Tommy's problematic actions were also noted. For example, in exploring Mrs. K.'s impression that Tommy "lies all the time," it became apparent that at least some of these instances stemmed from his limited cognitive skills. He tended to become confused when attempting to recall facts and events and did not appear to be deliberately attempting to deceive her. After several sessions with Mrs. K. focusing on these issues, a noticeable change was evident in her overall tone and style of interacting with Tommy, such that she now "gave him a little more slack" because "he's had such a hard time of it" and "I understand him better." Moreover, whereas initial efforts to implement the behavior program referred to earlier had faltered due to Mrs. K.'s reluctance to adopt reward criteria that Tommy would likely be able to obtain, she now began to set goals that were more realistic and which Tommy was able to consistently achieve with some effort. Mrs. K. also began to provide Tommy with more support to develop skills and knowledge needed for adaptation at home and in school. She began, for example, to devote greater time to helping him complete homework assignments.

An additional component of treatment focused on providing services to Tommy's biological mother. These services were aimed at helping her to function more effectively as a parent. Through the state's department of rehabilitation services, arrangements were made for her to receive employment in a sheltered workshop environment, admission to a community-based residential program for developmentally disabled adults, and individual training in parenting skills. Tommy was quite pleased by these developments, which occurred several months into treatment, and appeared to be emotionally buoyed by the improved prospects for being reunited with his mother and his siblings. At the same time, however, he complained less about his status as a foster child and noted that he now felt very close to members of his foster family, "just like they are my real family." He seemed no longer to adhere strongly to the idea that adapting successfully to his foster home would jeopardize his chances for reunification with mother, a development that may in part be attributable to the increased efforts that were now being made on his mother's behalf. This motivational shift seems also to have been facilitated by Tommy's use of his new skills and competencies, which allowed him to adapt more successfully to his foster placement. In a reciprocal manner, Tommy's increased motivation to "bond" positively with his foster family, and the stronger ties with foster parents and siblings that were facilitated by this shift, were conducive to further learning of skills and competencies.

Therapy was terminated with Tommy after 33 sessions and approximately 1 year in treatment. During the final 2 months of treatment, sessions primarily took the form of a fading and follow-up process, becoming less frequent and devoted primarily to monitoring and consolidation of the gains that had been made during the active phase of treatment. At termination, Tommy no longer displayed notable symptoms of depression or social withdrawal, and the behavioral problems that remained were for the most part relatively minor and within normal developmental limits. Moreover, when such problems did arise, Tommy's foster parents tended now to respond more empathically, reducing the potential for escalation into serious incidents (e.g., running away). Although Tommy still expressed ambivalence regarding his status as a foster child, this concern was no longer the predominant influence on his mood and behavior that it had been at the outset of treatment.

DISCUSSION

Previous approaches for enhancing social competence among children and adolescents have lacked a primary focus on the integrated development of the core skills and capacities that constitute the quadripartite model presented here. Integration across various subsets of these domains, most notably cognitive and behavioral, has received consideration in prior work (e.g., Kendall & Braswell, 1993). In these efforts, however, discussion of the need to consider the potential influence of elements in domains viewed as nonprimary (e.g., motivational sets) typically has been limited to ancillary considerations of program design and implementation, such as "troubleshooting" reasons for a lack of desired results for skill enhancement efforts in areas viewed as primary. Even less attention has been paid to the ways in which a person–environment, transactional perspective may be key to assessment and the design of clinical interventions. As a result, relatively little consideration has been given to the differential requirements for intervention that are called for by adaptive difficulties that result from a poor fit between the youth's competencies and the requirements of the settings in which he or she lives versus dysfunction that results from more "absolute" deficits in competencies.

The case example illustrates the potential importance of attending to both of these sets of issues in clinical work with children and adolescents. With regard to the quadripartite set of skills, assessment data indicated significant deficits in all four domains. Furthermore, during the course of treatment, the most significant clinical gains were not achieved until intervention strategies aimed at enhancing all four domains had been put into place. It appeared that the most problematic aspects of Tommy's behavior were under the mutual influence of cognitive, behavioral, emotional, and motivational factors, such that positive changes in only one or a subset of these domains were not sufficient to allow new and more adaptive patterns of behavior to emerge fully. Attention to transactional issues played an equally critical role in the treatment program. Although Tommy's skill deficits were significant, it proved essential to additionally consider the ways in which his difficulties were exacerbated by differences between the norms and expectations of his new environment and those of the context in which he had spent the greater part of his development. It was also apparent that the absolute level of adaptive demands and expectations that Tommy faced in his new environment were unreasonably high in view of the significant limitations imposed by his level of intellectual functioning and lack of adequate socialization experiences. Consequently, rather than channeling all of the treatment resources toward the end of enhancing Tommy's social skills, our intervention strategy also entailed attempting to alter the adaptive demands he was experiencing at home and at school to make them more congruent with his capacities. Finally, because Tommy's mother continued to be a major figure in his life, it was essential to incorporate her into his treatment. To the extent that she became better able to provide for Tommy's needs and parent him in ways that would facilitate his development, he was well served by such interventions.

Additional empirical investigation of the quadripartite model would be helpful for clarifying its utility as a framework for understanding and enhancing social competence among children and adolescents. It would be interesting, for example, to investigate whether patterns of association observed among indices of social competence are consistent with the four-factor structure posited by the model. The transactional component of the model might be explored by examining context-specific measures of skills and abilities in the four core domains, such as competencies relating to adaptation in specific developmental settings (e.g., school) and varied types of community contexts. According to the model, these types of indices should be more sensitive and powerful predictors of adaptation and mental health than are generic indices that do not take into account cross-situational variability in skills and behaviors that are most critical for adaptive success. Also useful would be an examination of the model as it applies to clinical and other applied efforts to enhance social competence. Here, the model suggests relatively greater efficacy for intervention protocols that include components aimed at enhancements in all four domains. Systematic efforts to tailor intervention efforts to maximize fit between skills and abilities that are targeted for enhancement and the adaptive demands of the contexts in which children and adolescents will need to implement such skills would also be expected to increase positive effects on adaptation.

The last two decades have been characterized by significant progress in the development of models for understanding, treating, and preventing mental health problems. The arguments that have been made for a merging of cognitive and behavioral perspectives and, more recently, for even more broadly integrative approaches to psychotherapy are two salient markers of this trend. The quadripartite model of social competence presented here fits well with this renewed interest in forging integrative models and the view that such models have the potential to capture the complexity of human functioning more fully than the individual constituent models from which they are derived. Although the utility of the quadripartite model is not yet established, it offers a promising starting point on the journey to a more adequate and complete understanding of social competence and its adaptive correlates among children and adolescents.

REFERENCES

Abramson, L. Y., Metalsky, G. I., & Alloy, L. B. (1989). Hopelessness depression: A theory-based subtype of depression. *Psychological Review, 96,* 358–372.

Abramson, L. Y., Seligman, M. E. P., & Teasdale, J. D. (1978). Learned helplessness in humans: Critique and reformulation. *Journal of Abnormal Psychology, 87,* 49–74.

Achenbach, T. M. (1986). The developmental study of psychopathology: Implications for psychotherapy and behavior change. In S. L. Garfield & A. E. Bergin (Eds.), *Handbook of psychotherapy and behavior change* (pp. 117–154). New York: Wiley.

American Psychiatric Association. (1994). *Diagnostic and statistical manual of mental disorders* (4th ed.). Washington, DC: Author.

Arend, R., Gove, R., & Sroufe, A. (1979). Continuity of individual adaptation from infancy to kindergarten: A predictive study of ego resiliency and curiosity with preschoolers. *Child Development, 50,* 950–959.

Bandura, A. (1977). *Social learning theory.* Englewood Cliffs, NJ: Prentice-Hall.

Beck, A. T. (1967). *Depression: Clinical, experimental, and theoretical aspects.* New York: Harper & Row.

Beck, A. T. (1991). Cognitive therapy: A 30-year retrospective. *American Psychologist, 46,* 368–375.

Bowlby, J. (1979). *The making and breaking of affectional bonds.* London: Tavistock.

Carnegie Council on Adolescent Development. (1989). *Turning points: Preparing American youth for the 21st century.* New York: Author.

Cohen, R., & Schleser, R. (1984). Cognitive development and clinical interventions. In A. W. Meyers & W. E. Craighead (Eds.), *Cognitive behavior therapy with children* (pp. 45–68). New York: Plenum Press.

Compas, B. E., Malcarne, V. L., & Fondacaro, K. M. (1988). Coping with stressful events in older children and young adolescents. *Journal of Consulting and Clinical Psychology, 56,* 405–411.

Coyne, J. C. (1976). Depression and the response of others. *Journal of Abnormal Psychology, 85,* 186–193.

Dubow, E. F., & Tisak, J., Causey, D., Hryshko, A., & Reid, G. (1992). A two-year longitudinal study of stressful life events, social support, and social problem-solving skills: Contributions to children's behavioral and academic adjustment. *Child Development, 62,* 583–599.

Durlak, J. A. (1983). Social problem-solving as a primary prevention strategy. In R. D. Felner, L. A. Jason, J. N. Moritsugu, & S. S. Farber (Eds.), *Preventive psychology: Theory, research, and practice* (pp. 31–48). New York: Pergamon Press.

Dweck, C. S., & Leggett, E. L. (1988). A social–cognitive approach to motivation and personality. *Psychological Review, 95,* 256–273.

D'Zurilla, T., & Goldfried, M. (1971). Problem solving and behavior modification. *Journal of Abnormal Psychology, 78,* 107–126.

Eisenberg, N., & Miller, P. A. (1987). The relation of empathy to prosocial and related behavior. *Psychological Bulletin, 101,* 91–119.

Elias, M. J., Gara, M., Ubriaco, M., Rothbaum, P. A., Clabby, J. F., & Schuyler, T. (1986). Impact of a preventive social problem-solving intervention on children's coping with middle school stressors. *American Journal of Community Psychology, 14,* 259–275.

Ellis, A. (1962). *Reason and emotion in psychotherapy.* New York: Lyle Stuart.

Erikson, E. H. (1963). *Childhood and society* (2nd ed.). New York: Norton.

Felner, R. D., Lease, A. M., & Phillips, R. S. C. (1990). Social competence and the language of adequacy as a subject matter for psychology: A quadripartite trilevel framework. In T. P. Gullotta, G. R. Adams, & R. Montemayor (Eds.), *The development of social competence in adolescence* (pp. 245–264). Beverly Hills: Sage.

Felner, R. D., Silverman, M. M., & Felner, T. Y. (in press). Primary prevention: Conceptual and methodological issues in the development of a science in mental health and social intervention. In J. Rappaport & E. Seidman (Eds.), *Handbook of community psychology.* New York: Plenum Press.

Freeman, A., Pretzer, J., Fleming, B., & Simon, K. M. (1990). *Clinical applications of cognitive therapy.* New York: Plenum Press.

Garber, J. (1984). Classification of childhood psychopathology: A developmental perspective. *Child Development, 55,* 30–48.

Garmezy, N., Masten, A. S., & Tellegen, A. (1984). The study of stress and competence in children: A building block for developmental psychopathology. *Child Development, 55,* 97–111.

Gilligan, C. F. (1982). *In a different voice: Psychological theory and women's development.* Cambridge, MA: Harvard University Press.

Glyshaw, K., Cohen, L. H., & Towbes, L. C. (1989). Coping strategies and psychological distress: Prospective analyses of early and middle adolescents. *American Journal of Community Psychology, 17,* 607–623.

Goetz, T. E., & Dweck, C. S. (1980). Learned helplessness in social situations. *Journal of Personality and Social Psychology, 39,* 246–255.

Gottman, J. M. (1994). *What predicts divorce? The relationship between marital process and marital outcomes.* Hillsdale, NJ: Erlbaum.

Gullotta, T. P., Adams, G. R., & Montemayor, R. (Eds.). (1990). *The development of social competence in adolescence.* Beverly Hills: Sage.

Harter, S., & Connell, J. P. (1984). A model of children's achievement and related self-perceptions of competence, control, and motivational orientation. In J. Nicholls (Ed.), *Advances in motivation and achievement* (Vol. 3, pp. 219–250). Greenwich, CT: JAI Press.

Higgins, J., & Thies, A. (1981). Problem solving and social position among emotionally disturbed boys. *American Journal of Orthopsychiatry, 51,* 356–358.

Izard, C. E. (1977). *Human emotions.* New York: Plenum Press.

Joiner, T. E., Alfano, M. S., & Metalsky, G. I. (1992). When depression breeds contempt: Reassurance seeking, self-esteem, and rejection of depressed college students by their roommates. *Journal of Abnormal Psychology, 101,* 165–173.

Kanfer, F. H., & Busemeyer, J. R. (1982). The use of problem solving and decision making in behavior therapy. *Clinical Psychology Review, 2,* 239–266.

Kendall, P. C., & Braswell, L. (1993). *Cognitive-behavioral therapy for impulsive children* (2nd ed.). New York: Guilford Press.

Kendall, P. C., Lerner, R. M., & Craighead, W. E. (1984). Human development and intervention in child psychopathology. *Child Development, 55,* 71–82.

Kennedy, M. G., Felner, R. D., Cauce, A. M., & Primavera, J. (1988). Social problem-solving and adjustment in adolescence: The influence of moral-reasoning level, scoring alternatives, and family climate. *Journal of Clinical Child Psychology, 17,* 73–83.

Kohlberg, L. (1969). Stage and sequence: The cognitive-developmental approach to socialization. In D. A. Goslin (Ed.), *Handbook of socialization theory and research* (pp. 347–480). Chicago: Rand McNally.

Lazarus, R. S., & Folkman, S. (1984). *Stress, appraisal, and coping.* New York: Springer.

Luthar, S. S. (1991). Vulnerability and resilience: A study of high risk adolescents. *Child Development, 62,* 600–616.

Luthar, S. S., & Zigler, E. (1991). Vulnerability and competence: A review of research on resilience in childhood. *American Journal of Orthopsychiatry, 61,* 6–22.

McGinnis, E., & Goldstein, A. P. (1984). *Skill-streaming the elementary school child: A guide for teaching prosocial skills.* Champaign, IL: Research Press.

Pastor, D. (1981). The quality of mother–infant attachment and its relationship to toddlers' initial sociability with peers. *Developmental Psychology, 17,* 326–335.

Peterson, G. W., & Leigh, G. K. (1990). The family and social competence in adolescence. In T. P. Gullotta, G. R. Adams, & R. Montemayor (Eds.), *The development of social competence in adolescence* (pp. 97–139). Beverly Hills: Sage.

Piaget, J. (1965). *The moral judgement of the child.* New York: Free Press. (Original work published 1932)

Rotter, J. B. (1954). *Social learning and clinical psychology.* Englewood Cliffs, NJ: Prentice-Hall.

Sameroff, A. J., & Fiese, B. H. (1989). Conceptual issues in prevention. In D. Shaffer, I. Philips, & N. B. Enzer (Eds.), *Prevention of mental disorders, alcohol and other drug use in children and adolescents* (DHHS Publication No. ADM 89–1646, pp. 23–53). Rockville, MD: Office for Substance Abuse Prevention, Alcohol, Drug Abuse, and Mental Health Administration.

Seligman, M. E. P., & Peterson, C. (1986). A learned helplessness perspective on childhood depression: Theory and research. In M. Rutter, C. E. Izard, & P. B. Read (Eds.), *Depression in young people: Developmental and clinical considerations* (pp. 223–249). New York: Guilford Press.

Shure, M. B., & Spivak, G. (1982). Interpersonal problem-solving in young children: A cognitive approach to prevention. *American Journal of Community Psychology, 10,* 341–356.

Shure, M. B., & Spivak, G. (1988). Interpersonal cognitive problem-solving. In R. H. Price, E. L. Cowen, R. P. Lorion, & J. Ramos-McKay (Eds.), *Fourteen ounces of prevention: A casebook for practitioners* (pp. 68–82). Washington, DC: American Psychological Association.

Spivak, G., Platt, J. J., & Shure, M. B. (1976). *The problem-solving approach to adjustment.* San Francisco: Jossey-Bass.

Sroufe, L. A. (1979). The coherence of individual development: Early care, attachment and subsequent developmental issues. *American Psychologist, 34,* 834–841.

Sroufe, L. A., Fox, N. E., & Pancake, V. R. (1983). Attachment and dependency in developmental perspective. *Child Development, 54,* 1615–1627.

Sroufe, L. A., & Rutter, M. (1984). The domain of developmental psychopathology. *Child Development, 55,* 17–29.

Wachtel, P. L. (1994). Cyclical processes in personality and psychopathology. *Journal of Abnormal Psychology, 103,* 51–54.

Waters, E., Wippman, J., & Sroufe, L. A. (1979). Attachment, positive affect, and competence in peer group: Two studies in construct validation. *Child Development, 50,* 821–829.

Weissberg, R. P., Caplan, M. Z., & Sivo, P. J. (1989). A new conceptual framework for establishing school-based social competence promotion programs. In L. A. Bond & B. E. Compas (Eds.), *Primary prevention and promotion in schools* (pp. 255–298). Newbury Park, CA: Sage.

Wilson, W. J. (1987). *The truly disadvantaged: The inner city, the underclass, and public policy.* Chicago: University of Chicago Press.

Young, J. (1990). *Cognitive therapy for personality disorders: A schema-focused approach.* Sarasota, FL: Professional Resource Exchange.

Zigler, E., & Trickett, P. K. (1978). I.Q., social competence, and evaluation of early childhood intervention programs. *American Psychologist, 33,* 789–796.

SUGGESTED READINGS

Dodge, K. A. (1989). Problems in social relationships. In E. J. Mash & R. A. Barkley (Eds.), *Treatment of childhood disorders* (pp. 222–244). New York: Guilford Press.

Hops, H., & Greenwood, C. R. (1988). Social skill deficits. In E. J. Mash & L. G. Terdal (Eds.), *Behavioral assessment of childhood disorders* (2nd ed., pp. 263–314). New York: Guilford Press.

Kent, M. W., & Rolf, J. E. (Eds.). (1979). *Primary prevention of psychopathology: Vol. 3. Social competence in children.* Hanover, NH: University Press of New England.

Schneider, B. H., Attili, G., Nadel, J., & Weissberg, R. P. (Eds.). (1989). *Social competence in developmental perspective.* Boston: Kluwer Academic.

Weissberg, R. P., Caplan, M. Z., & Sivo, P. J. (1989). A new conceptual framework for establishing school-based social competence promotion programs. In L. A. Bond & B. E. Compas (Eds.), *Primary prevention and promotion in schools* (pp. 255–298). Newbury Park, CA: Sage.

8

Treatment of Separation Anxiety Disorder

Margot R. Levin
Serena Ashmore-Callahan
Philip C. Kendall
Masaya Ichii

S eparation anxiety disorder (SAD), one of the disorders of childhood identified in the fourth edition of the *Diagnostic and Statistical Manual of Mental Disorders* (DSM-IV; American Psychiatric Association, 1994) has been estimated to occur in approximately 4% of children in the general population (Costello et al., 1988; Anderson, Williams, Mcgee, & Silver, 1987). In an outpatient clinic for children with anxiety disorders, 27.1% of patients were diagnosed with SAD (Last, Hersen, Kazdin, Finkelstein, & Strauss, 1987). The central feature of SAD is a child's excessive anxiety concerning separation from an attachment figure, often the child's mother. The excessive anxiety must have a duration of at least 4 weeks and the child must exhibit at least three of the following eight possible symptoms:

1. Recurrent excessive distress when separation from home or major attachment figures is anticipated or involved.
2. Unrealistic and persistent worry about possible harm befalling major attachment figures or fear that they will leave and not return.
3. Unrealistic and persistent worry that an untoward calamitous event will separate the child from a major attachment figure (e.g., the child will be lost, kidnapped, killed, or be the victim of an accident).

4. Persistent reluctance or refusal to go to school or elsewhere in order to stay with major attachment figures or at home.
5. Persistent avoidance of being alone, including "clinging to" and "shadowing" major attachment figures.
6. Persistent reluctance or refusal to go to sleep without being near a major attachment figure or to go to sleep away from home.
7. Repeated nightmares involving the theme of separation.
8. Complaints of physical symptoms (e.g., headaches, stomachaches, nausea, or vomiting) on many school days or on other occasions when anticipating separation from major attachment figures.

In addition, the DSM-IV specifies that these symptoms must cause clinically significant distress or impairment in social, academic (occupational), or other important areas of functioning. Onset must occur before age 18 and more commonly occurs around preschool age. Approximately one-third of children with SAD also have a concurrent overanxious disorder (OAD), although SAD is usually the primary complaint (Last et al., 1987).

Developmental factors are important in understanding SAD, because behaviors that are considered normal at one age can be viewed as pathological at another. Separation distress first emerges between 9 and 12 months, peaks between 13 and 20 months, and then declines. Such distress is normal and may even serve an adaptive function. According to Kagan (1976), it emerges when a child is cognitively mature enough to notice the mother's departure but is not certain of her return. Other theorists have speculated that early separation distress helps the child to remain near the mother so that he or she is protected from external dangers (Bowlby, 1973). However, when such distress occurs beyond the expected developmental timetable, it is disruptive to the child's life and is cause for concern. For example, if the child refuses to engage in any activity that requires separation from the parent, many developmentally appropriate activities will be missed, leading to delayed development in some areas. The trigger for the onset of pathological separation anxiety is often a life stress, such as the loss of a relative or pet; an illness of the child or relative; or a change in the child's environment, such as a school change (American Psychiatric Association, 1994).

Developmental factors also influence how the SAD manifests itself. In a study of separation-anxious children ranging in age from 5 to 16, Francis, Last, and Strauss (1987) reported that the disorder manifests itself differently depending on the age of the child, but they did not find significant differences based on the sex of the child. Young children (ages 5 to 8) tended to worry about an attachment figure being harmed, or about themselves being harmed and thus separated from an attachment figure. They were also more likely to refuse to attend school and to become very distressed when separated from a parent. Youth in middle childhood (ages 9 to 12) tended to complain about physical symptoms on school days, to exhibit excessive distress when forced to separate, and to withdraw and appear sad when separated from an attachment figure. Adolescents (ages 13 to 16) were most likely to complain about physical symptoms on school days and to refuse to attend school. In addition, according to the DSM-IV, older children are likely to deny anxiety about separation, but will be reluctant to participate in independent activities outside of family life.

Family factors have also been implicated in the onset of SAD. Guidano (1987) identified parents' limitation of a child's exploratory behavior, either because of the parent's overprotectiveness or rejection of the child, as instrumental in the development of SAD. Several anecdotal studies described the mothers of school-phobic children (school phobia is sometimes viewed as a variant of SAD) as ambivalent about separation (e.g., Eisenberg, 1958; Levy, 1943). More recent empirical studies supported and amplified these findings, noting boundary problems among family members as well as difficulty adapting to new roles, such as increasing independence in the child (Bernstein & Garfinkel, 1988; Bernstein, Svingen, & Garfinkel, 1990).

A COGNITIVE-BEHAVIORAL MODEL OF ANXIETY

Certain core principles are common to the cognitive-behavioral approach to understanding and treating psychological disorders (Kendall, Chansky, et al., 1992). In a cognitive-behavioral model, it is assumed that the client responds primarily to cognitive representations of the environment rather than to the environment per se. Thoughts, feelings, and behaviors are causally interrelated, and none is considered to be primary. Client attitudes, expectancies, attributions, and other cognitive activities are central to producing, predicting, and understanding therapeutic interventions. With respect to treatment, it is both possible and desirable to combine cognitive treatment strategies with behavioral contingency management strategies. The role of the therapist is to assess the client's maladaptive cognitive processes and work with the client to design learning experiences that may alter the client's dysfunctional cognitions and the behavioral and affective patterns that accompany them.

In the cognitive model of adult anxiety, exaggerated perceptions of danger, threat, and fear, and an underestimation of one's ability to cope with these threats have been identified as central (Beck, 1976; Beck & Emery, 1985). Similarly, among children with anxiety disorders, the dominant schema or structure for anxious youth is threat—threat of loss, criticism, or harm. In addition, anxious youth hold expectations that are more critical, potentially harmful, and catastrophic than those of nonanxious children. Such dysfunctional cognitive activity usually takes the form of distortions or misconstruals and misperceptions of the social and interpersonal environment.

The results of efforts to assess cognitive processing in anxious children have been mixed. This may be due in part to the nature of the disorder. Thoughts produced by anxious children may be more difficult to access than those of other children because of their habitual use of avoidance and their tendency to want to "look good," both of which may make them less likely to report negative thoughts than other children (Kendall & Chansky, 1991). Kendall and Chansky found that anxious children do not differ significantly from nonanxious children in either their endorsement or report of negative thoughts. In addition, they rate themselves as better able to cope with difficulties than their parents rate them, suggesting that they may keep problems to themselves. In contrast, in a study that assessed cognitive activity in a nonclinical sample of children, researchers found that high-anxious children endorse or report more negative self-cognitions (e.g., "I'm going to mess up again") than low-anxious children (Ronan, Kendall, & Rowe, 1994). Finally, it has not been empirically demonstrated that the cognitions of children with different subtypes of childhood anxiety disorders differ from each other. For example, it is unclear whether children with OAD endorse different types of anxious cognitions than children with SAD. Although some support for the model has been found, a great deal more research is needed before an understanding of children's anxious cognitive processing is available.

OVERVIEW OF THE TREATMENT PROTOCOL

The cognitive-behavioral treatment program described here attempts to preserve the demonstrated positive effects of *in vivo* exposure and performance based approaches, while incorporating the cognitive activities of the client into the efforts to produce therapeutic change. The cognitive-behavioral analyses of child and adolescent disorders and adjustment problems, as well as related analyses of treatment-produced gains, include consideration of both the child's internal and external environment and represent an integrationist perspective (e.g., Meichenbaum, 1977). The model (1) places greatest emphasis on the learning process and the influence of the contingencies and models in the environment, while (2) underscoring the centrality of the individual's mediating and information-processing style in the development and remediation of psychological distress (Kendall, 1985).

The treatment consists of two segments, each requiring at least eight 1-hour sessions, resulting in a treatment duration of 16 to 20 sessions. The first half of treatment is primarily educational; therapists teach children to identify anxious feelings and somatic symptoms, to help themselves relax when anxious, to recognize and then to modify their self-talk in anxious situations, to make a coping plan and implement it, and to reward themselves when they cope with an anxious situation. These principles are condensed into the FEAR steps (explained in depth later), a coping mechanism taught via an acronym that facilitates children's recall of the various steps. Children use the *Coping Cat Workbook* (Kendall, 1990), and therapists follow the treatment manual (Kendall, Kane, Howard, & Siqueland, 1992).

The second half of treatment consists of sessions in which the child can practice the new skills using both imaginal and *in vivo* exposure to situations of increasing stress and anxiety. *In vivo* exposure exercises are anxiety-provoking experiences devised by therapists in which children practice using the FEAR steps to cope with their anxiety. They are tailored to the specific fears of the child. For example, a child who is fearful of elevators would gradually be exposed to the elevator for incrementally greater periods of time. Table 8.1 provides a sampling of *in vivo* exposure exercises that can be incorporated into the treatment program.

Rewards are an important component of this therapeutic program. As a part of their therapy, children receive notebooks in which to do homework assignments, called STIC ("Show That I Can") tasks. When children complete their assignments, they earn two stickers and after earning eight stickers, they receive a small reward they have previously chosen. During the *in vivo* segment of treatment, children are given behavioral homework assignments to practice during the week between sessions. An opportunity for children to be creative is also provided at the completion of treatment, when they videotape a "commercial" in which they describe using the FEAR steps. Children collaborate with their therapists, and their efforts have resulted in rap songs, talk shows, and puppet shows. In addition, an important component of both segments is the relationship that develops between the therapist and the child.

Cognitive therapists have begun to focus increasingly on the importance of the therapeutic relationship as a change agent in adult disorders (Safran & Segal, 1990). There has been less research on therapist variables within the child literature, although warmth, physical contact and verbal encouragement, ethnicity, and model similarity have all been discussed as possibly contributing to treatment effectiveness (Kendall & Morris, 1991). In our view, the cognitive-behavioral therapist serves the client as consultant, diagnostician, and educator.

TABLE 8.1. Examples of *In Vivo* Exposure Exercises Used with Anxious Children at the Child and Adolescent Anxiety Disorders Clinic (CAADC)

1. Having the child drop papers or trip in public in order to face evaluation fears. Initially, the therapist may participate as well.

2. Sending the child on errands to help get over fears of new situations.

3. Sending two or more children on a scavenger hunt together and asking them to find out information about each other in order to address social anxiety.

4. Speechmaking in front of progressively larger groups to help a child cope with performance anxiety. Perfectionistic children may be asked to intentionally make a mistake.

5. Trips alone to various parts of the campus to help children with separation fears.

6. Asking people directions or how to do something and then asking them to repeat their questions in order to address fears of looking foolish.

7. Taking the subway with the therapist. On the way to their destination, the therapist provides minimal prompts but does say when to get off of the subway. On the return trip, the child is responsible for getting them back to campus.

8. Having the child draw with his or her eyes closed. Anxiety can be heightened by having the child hang up the drawing in public or sign it.

9. Taking the child to a local mall to work with children who fear getting lost. This is also a place to address parents' fears of something happening to the child.

10. Riding the elevator and gradually increasing the level of exposure. Initially, the child may ride for one floor with the therapist present and work up to riding alone. Ultimately, the child may, with the therapist, push the elevator buttons to intentionally make the elevator stop between floors.

As in cognitive therapy with adults, the therapist-as-consultant approaches the client with an attitude of "collaborative empiricism" (Beck & Emery, 1985). The therapist guides the child toward independent problem solving, rather than providing specific solutions. The therapist may use personal experiences as either a mastery or a coping model for the child. For example, the therapist may use his or her own experience of successfully coping with a scary situation, or may enlist the child's help in coming up with strategies for coping. The therapist as diagnostician attempts to integrate the various sources of information about the problem—the parents, the child, the teacher—and judges these data against a background of his or her professional knowledge, and makes a determination as to the problem's nature and the optimal strategy for its treatment. The therapist-as-educator helps to communicate to the child the skills he or she is lacking and that may impede effective problem solving for the child. For example, the therapist might offer assertiveness training or social skills training when necessary.

CLIENT BACKGROUND AND PRESENTING PROBLEM

Allison, a 9-year-old Caucasian female, presented as slightly built and looked younger than her age. She had one older brother, age 13, lived in a lower-middle-class neighborhood with her brother and parents, and attended a private parochial school. Her father, age 45, was a high school graduate who completed some technical training and worked as an electrician. Her mother, age 44, completed training as a lab technician and worked at a local hospital. At the start of the child's treatment, the father reported agoraphobic concerns and past depressive episodes. The father was taking Zoloft and was in individual therapy. In addition to his work, the father's only contact outside the home was a bar at which he stopped one night each week. He never traveled or shopped with the family. The mother's social circle was more extensive, although her social life centered primarily around her children. The parents had long-standing marital difficulties and sexual problems that dated back to the birth of Allison, when her father was absent from her difficult birth because of his agoraphobia.

Allison's mother contacted our clinic because of Allison's difficulty separating from her parents. Information was obtained during diagnostic interviews (the Anxiety Disorders Interview Schedule—Revised [ADIS-R; Silverman, 1987]) with the parents and Allison. This structured interview, with forms for administration to both parents and child, focuses on anxiety disorders of childhood, while allowing the diagnostician to rule out other nonanxiety disorders. In addition, the parents, Allison, and Allison's teacher completed a variety of objective rating scales. For a complete list of paper-and-pencil measures, see Table 8.2. Based on both the parent and the child interviews, the diagnostician concluded that SAD was the primary diagnosis. Secondary diagnoses were OAD and simple phobias. It should be noted that Allison was present during the parent interview, so her responses may have been influenced by her parents' statements. However, Allison was interviewed alone, because when the interviewing clinician refused to conduct the child interview with the parents in the room, Allison agreed to have the parents wait outside the room. Following the intake interview, the interviewing clinician observed that Allison probably had more control over her fear of separation than she overtly revealed, since she was able to separate relatively smoothly once she realized that the interviewer would not conduct the interview with the parents in the

TABLE 8.2. Objective Rating Scales Administered at Pretreatment Diagnostic Intake

Child self-report measures

Revised Children's Manifest Anxiety Scale (RCMAS; Reynolds & Richmond, 1978). Designed as a measure of the child's chronic anxiety (trait), the scale reveals three anxiety factors: physiology, worry and oversensitivity, and concentration.

State–Trait Anxiety Inventory for Children (STAIC; Spielberger, 1973). These scales include two 20–item self-report scales that measure both enduring tendencies to experience anxiety (trait), and temporal and situational variations in levels of perceived anxiety (state).

Fear Survey Schedule for Children—Revised (FSSC-R; Ollendick, 1978). This measure assesses specific fears in children. Eight specific fear-content categories are measured by this scale: school, home, social, physical, animal, travel, classical phobia, and miscellaneous.

Children's Depression Inventory (CDI; Kovacs, 1981). This scale includes 27 items regarding the cognitive, affective, and behavioral signs of depression.

Coping Questionnaire—Child (CQ-C; Kendall, 1994). This measure was developed to assess change in children's perceived ability to manage specific anxiety-provoking situations. Three areas of difficulty for each child are chosen from the information in the diagnostic interview, and the child rates his or her ability to cope with the situation.

Children's Negative Affect Self-Statement Questionnaire (NASSQ; Ronan et al., 1994). This 55-item measure assesses the frequency of anxious self-talk over the past week.

Parent measures

Child Behavior Checklist (CBCL; Achenbach & Edelbrock, 1983) The CBCL is a 118-item scale that assesses an array of behavioral problems and social competencies.

Coping Questionnaire—Parent (CQ-P; Kendall, 1994). This measure parallels the child version described earlier.

State–Trait Anxiety Inventory for Children—Modification of Trait Version for Parents. This measure is a modification of the trait version of Spielberger's (1973) STAIC to be used as a parent report measure. It provides information specific to anxiety, in contrast to the global measures available from the CBCL.

Teacher measures

Child Behavior Checklist—Teacher's Form (TRF; Achenbach & Edelbrock, 1983). Similar to the parent CBCL, the teacher CBCL provides the therapist with a picture of the child's classroom functioning as viewed by a primary teacher.

room. The interviewing clinician also noted that the father tended to escalate the child's fears by his unmodulated expression of his own fears and anxiety.

According to her parents, although Allison was able to attend school, she phoned her mother frequently from school. In addition, she refused to go out to play unless she was sure that her mother was home and refused to join groups because her mother could not attend with her. At night, she would not sleep in her own bed and slept on the floor of her parents' room. When her parents refused to let her sleep in their room, Allison slept on the floor in the hallway and would come into her parents' room after they were asleep. In addition, they reported that Allison had a strong fear of being alone in the dark and a fear of elevators. Her parents reported concerns, such as Allison's worrying about her performance in sports, worrying about events before they happen, and needing frequent reassurance from her parents. Allison also experienced occasional somatic symptoms such as vomiting. On self-report measures, her scores appeared to be within normal ranges on most measures (see Table 8.3 for her scores at each assessment point). Children in this sample, particularly those as young as age 9, often score in nonclinical ranges on self-report measures and do not differ significantly from a normal group of children the same age (Ashmore-Callahan, 1993). This finding is consistent with research on other samples of anxious children. For example, Strauss, Lease, Last, and Francis (1988) found that children below age 12 endorse less severe symptoms on self-report measures. This may be due to the difficulty

TABLE 8.3. Scores from Child Self-Report Measures at Each Assessment Point

Self-report measure[a]	Assessment point		
	Pretreatment	Immediately posttreatment	1-year posttreatment
RCMAS	12	12	9
NASSQ	139	122	96
CDI	0	5	3
STAI—State version	33	29	29
STAI—Trait version	28	25	24
FSSC-R	92	88	88

[a]Revised Children's Manifest Anxiety Scale (RCMAS; Reynolds & Richmond, 1978); Negative Affectivity Self-Statement Questionnaire (NASSQ; Ronan et al., 1994); Children's Depression Inventory (CDI; Kovacs, 1981); State–Trait Anxiety Inventory for Children (STAIC; Spielberger, 1973); Fear Survey Schedule for Children—Revised (FSSC-R; Ollendick, 1978).

younger children experience in evaluating their own levels of anxiety. It is also possible that young children have difficulty understanding the subtle differences among choices such as *Often, Moderately Often,* and *Sometimes,* which are routinely found on children's self-report measures.

Similarly, Allison's teacher reported her to be within normal limits on the Child Behavior Checklist (Achenbach & Edelbrock, 1983). This finding, too, is consistent with the data from a larger sample of children (e.g., Kendall, 1994), for we have found that anxiety-disordered children do not always exhibit their anxiety in ways that are readily observed by teachers. Teachers may not be reliable reporters of anxiety symptoms because anxious children are usually not disruptive, and therefore do not call attention to their distress.

TREATMENT OVERVIEW

In many ways, Allison's case is typical of many separation anxiety cases. The child's sleeping in the parents' room is a common symptom of the separation-anxious children in our clinic, and it frequently suggests more entrenched family problems. For example, the child's sleeping in the parents' bed or room has implications for the marital relationship, and consequently cooperation with the parents is required for the symptom to be addressed.

Allison's case was atypical in her reported fears of sexual abuse. She made a number of sexual references (e.g., to naked bodies being disgusting), and during the fourth session, directly expressed a fear that the therapist would sexually abuse her. The therapist spoke to both the mother and Allison about these fears. Allison's mother expressed her confidence in the therapist and talked further with Allison, who denied ever being abused. The mother attributed Allison's fears to "hysteria" and to her reactivity to things that she saw on television. In addition to discussing the possibility of past abuse with both to Allison and her mother, the therapist administered the Thematic Apperception Test to Allison. The findings from the testing were inconclusive. After this incident, the issue of abuse never arose again, and Allison appeared to feel comfortable with the therapist.

Allison was initially resistant to therapy, and she also denied any anxiety problems. In our experience, children are sometimes uncomfortable during the early sessions discussing their own feelings and fears. The therapist proceeds slowly, emphasizing the feelings that other kids might have in difficult situations, as well as disclosing his or her own feelings of anxiety in certain situations. This normalizes the experience of anxiety and helps create an environment in which the child does not feel that he or she needs to be perfect. Another frequent manifestation of client resistance is a child's refusal or, more often, forgetting to complete behavioral homework assignments. When this happens, the therapist tries to understand the reasons behind the child's noncompliance. In addition, the therapist, together with the child, works to come up with assignments that are agreeable to them both. As in most cases, Allison eventually acknowledged some of her own fears. The therapist was then able to work more directly with those fears.

As noted previously, one reason that children do not disclose anxiety is a need to present themselves as "perfect" to the therapist. Such children frequently have great fears of making mistakes in other spheres of their lives. Therapists may address these perfectionistic beliefs through modeling how they cope when they make mistakes. Using examples that occur between the client and therapist can be especially meaningful for children. Therapists may also assign children homework assignments in which they must observe others' mistakes or intentionally make mistakes of their own. It is important to look for perfectionistic beliefs and fear of making mistakes in clients who are exceptionally compliant. A fear of displeasing the therapist and a need to be a "good client" may be behind a child's disclosure of "textbook" anxiety symptoms. When the therapist feels that a child is highly invested in pleasing, he or she may try to devise interventions in which the child must disobey or look foolish in front of him or her.

TEACHING THE FEAR STEPS

One of the cornerstones of our treatment is the FEAR steps, an acronym used to help children problem solve in new or anxiety-provoking situations. The steps, in order, are as follows:

Feeling Frightened?
Expecting Bad Things to Happen?
Attitudes and Actions That Can Help
Results and Rewards

In the following section, we elaborate on how the FEAR steps were used with Allison.

Feeling Frightened?

Frequently children do not recognize the relationship between the physical signs of anxiety in their bodies and their distress in a situation. We begin our treatment by teaching children to use their somatic feelings as cues: When they notice these cues, they know that they need to activate their problem-solving skills. For Allison, this was an important aspect of treatment. Prior to treatment, when faced with a frightening situation, Allison could not help herself—she would panic and be unable to think clearly. The therapist helped her connect her physical symptoms—nail-biting, swinging her feet, and chewing on her hair—with her anxiety. Later in treatment, she was able to use the deep breathing and relaxation exercises to calm herself down so that she was able to cope more successfully.

Expecting Bad Things to Happen?

Identifying the expectations behind the anxiety is the next step in developing a coping plan. For example, Allison was afraid of riding on elevators. Specifically, she was afraid that someone "bad" would get on the elevator while she was on it, and also that her parents might not be there when she returned. Self-identification of expectancies is a part of treatment with which many young children have difficulty. Because children's cognitive capacities may not be fully developed, the therapist assists in generating possible expectations. It is often easier for children to endorse a fear when the therapist says, "Some kids are afraid that the elevator might get stuck," than to come up with it themselves spontaneously. It is important that the therapist assess each child's cognitive abilities individually. For example, in younger children who may have difficulty understanding the idea of identifying expectations, it may be more useful for the child to acknowledge fear and then move on to the problem-solving step. Similarly, it may be best to concentrate on problem solving with ruminative children, who may become mired in all the negative possibilities. In Allison's case, she was able to identify her anxious thinking, but she had difficulty considering alternative thoughts. Instead, she would become involved in imagining potentially catastrophic consequences.

For example, early in treatment Allison asked her therapist about the program and whether she would have to "face her fears" later in the treatment. She became alarmed and said, "You're not going to make me get stuck on an elevator, are you?" The therapist tried to reassure her and said that she would not ask Allison to do anything before she was ready to do it. She also tried to help Allison to consider that she would be gradually facing fears, and by the time she was doing something that she now found terrifying, she would feel prepared.

Attitudes and Actions That Can Help

In this step, therapists teach children to question the validity and likelihood of the feared events occurring, as well as to generate more positive alternative outcomes that could also occur. For example, when working with an elevator phobia, the therapist might get the child to think about the odds of being locked in the elevator, and to investigate whether others have ridden in elevators without incident. When adults are told of the unlikely "probability" that an event will happen to them, they often respond, "Okay, but it could still happen this time to me." They tend to experience difficulty accepting this information uncritically. Children, however, are less likely to question this intervention, and they seem more able to use information about the probability of frightening events to feel more secure in these circumstances. Children are encouraged, for example, to consider the likelihood of the frightening event occurring as a coping method that they can use while they are in the scary situation.

Therapists help children to identify possible solutions to problems and then to choose the ones that best serve their needs. This was difficult for Allison, especially when she was emotionally stimulated. When the therapist role-played an anxious situation, for example, Allison became visibly upset and was unable to generate alternative solutions. This problem continued throughout treatment. Therefore, when the therapist was trying to get Allison to ride on the elevator, rather than focusing on cognitive techniques, she would encourage her by saying, "Let's just give it a try." Initially, they rode only one floor and would only get on if no one else was on the elevator. In a similar manner, the therapist helped Allison cope with her fears about "scary men" by talking with her about how she could distinguish between someone dangerous and someone unthreatening.

Another way that a therapist encourages a child to try out new behaviors is to frame the task as an "experiment," or a way of testing whether the child's hypothesis of a negative outcome or the therapist's hypothesis of a positive outcome is correct. Children generally respond quite positively to this because it provides a nonthreatening context in which to develop a new skill.

Results and Rewards

The final step in generating a coping plan is to determine what reward the child will receive after coping with the feared situation. Possible rewards include having a snack, watching a television program, telling parents about their accomplishment (and receiving praise), spending time with a parent, or simply congratulating oneself that he or she has done well. It is important to encourage children to think beyond rewards that are monetary. With children who are separation anxious, therapists emphasize rewards that involve positive interactions with parents, which may help children to give up some of their dependent, negative interactions with parents.

Upon completion of the task, the therapists help children to rate how well they coped with the situation, and children learn to rate themselves based on how hard they tried. For example, a good attempt that goes awry receives a high rating. This is an especially important concept to convey to perfectionistic children, who may have difficulty accepting the idea of an imperfect outcome constituting a success. Therapists coach children to understand what went well and what could be improved—information that is used to develop better coping plans for future situations.

USING THE FEAR STEPS

A condensed transcript reflecting the flavor of an exchange between Allison and her therapist about an anxious experience is provided here. They are discussing how Allison coped with an anxiety-provoking situation at school. The therapist is helping Allison to organize her experience so that she can see how her behavior reflected her knowledge of the FEAR steps. Allison had completed an assignment for school the day before, and then had taken it home with her that night. The next morning, she could not find the work, so she had to go to school without it. Initially, the therapist establishes that Allison felt nervous, or the first step in the FEAR steps: Feeling Frightened?

THERAPIST: So tell me, how did you know you were feeling frightened?

ALLISON: My heart started pounding.

THERAPIST: What else?

ALLISON: Umm . . . let's see. I started biting my nails.

THERAPIST: Uh huh. That's a sign isn't it?

ALLISON: Yeah.

Next, the therapist focuses on how Allison perceives the experience, and what her expectations are. This is the second step in the FEAR steps: Expecting Bad Things to Happen?

THERAPIST: So then what did you notice? What were you thinking about?

ALLISON: I could get in real big trouble here—get punished.

THERAPIST: That's what you're thinking about. Well, what bad things were going to happen to you? What were you worried about?

ALLISON: I was gonna get yelled at.

THERAPIST: You were gonna get yelled at, and if you got yelled at, what?

ALLISON: I would probably have to stay in for recess.

THERAPIST: Okay, what about your teacher? What would your teacher be thinking if you lost your health homework?

ALLISON: Boy, is she forgetful. He'd say, "Why did you take it home in the first place?"

THERAPIST: He would think you were forgetful?

ALLISON: Yeah, and he yells. You can hear him all the way down the hall.

THERAPIST: What does he say?

ALLISON: "You're so noisy; you always forget things." And when he yells, the kids down the hall can hear him.

THERAPIST: You might get yelled at, and other kids would know, and they might ask you about it.

ALLISON: Yeah.

THERAPIST: What would they think?

ALLISON: They'd just think I was weird.

THERAPIST: They'd think you were weird. Well, no wonder you were feeling a little scared!

At this point in the dialogue, the therapist moves to the third FEAR step: Attitudes and Actions That Can Help.

THERAPIST: Okay, so what did you do about that? How else could you have thought about that?

ALLISON: Maybe he won't want to go over them today, because he didn't. I asked him at lunch, and he said he didn't want to go over them until tomorrow.

THERAPIST: That was an action you took to help yourself out. Good for you, Allison; you went and asked the questions! How could you have changed your scary thoughts around a little bit?

ALLISON: I don't know. Maybe he'll just forget about going over them or something, and maybe if he doesn't, he won't yell at me.

Finally, the therapist reinforces the behavior that Allison has used to cope with her situation, and this is the final FEAR step: Results and Rewards.

THERAPIST: Well, I think that you should really be congratulated for that action that you took! That's like the best idea I could have thought of—go check it out, you found out what's going to happen.

ALLISON: Before you start worrying your head off.

THERAPIST: Before you start getting so upset and worried. Yeah, that was excellent!

"SHOW THAT I CAN" TASK

As part of her treatment, Allison was assigned "homework" to complete between sessions with her therapist. STIC tasks are assigned to increase the likelihood of generalization of the success experiences that occur in therapy to other aspects of life. During the first half of treatment, children usually write down their thoughts and feelings about an anxious experience that occurred during the week. Therapists are creative in tailoring STIC tasks to address each child's individual experience of anxiety. A therapist might ask a child who believes that no one else ever feels worried to observe one or two classmates and to report on their anxious behavior. A child whose identity appears to be solely based on his or her anxiety symptoms may be encouraged to write about the activities that he or she enjoys doing, rather than writing about fears. During the latter half of treatment, children are asked to record how they use the FEAR steps to cope with new situations. The STIC task can be especially useful for a subset of children who will not acknowledge anxiety during the session, but who will write about it in their notebooks. Allison's primary STIC task involved activities related to sleeping in her own room.

BEHAVIORAL COMPONENTS OF TREATMENT

The major goal of Allison's treatment was for her to sleep in her own room. This required substantial planning, as well as the cooperation of Allison and her parents. In this treatment program, after extensive discussions with both the parents and the child, the therapist chooses a date when the child will begin sleeping in her own room. This date is usually toward the middle or end of treatment, so that the child has had the opportunity to build coping skills and have some mastery experiences before tackling such a difficult task. As in Allison's case, this goal can be modified.

Allison's fears about sleeping in her own room centered around being harmed by others. She was terrified that someone would put a ladder to her window and break in and hurt her. To address these fears, the therapist attempted to help her see how unlikely it was that the harm she feared would actually occur. She encouraged Allison to find out if anyone else in the neighborhood had been robbed. Allison checked with her parents and in the newspaper and reported each week whether anyone had been robbed in the neighborhood. The therapist's use of this intervention is an example of the importance of the flexible application of a manualized treatment. Such a suggestion would have been countertherapeutic if Allison were a ruminative or obsessional child, because it would have encouraged her to focus too much on the negative possibilities.

The therapist also used humor to help Allison. She would ask Allison to imagine burglars walking through the neighborhood with a ladder. The child was able to visualize how conspicuous these people would be and how unlikely it was that they would get to her house unnoticed. The therapist also asked her to check outside of her window between sessions to see how many strange people with ladders walked by each week.

It is important to note that the therapist made these interventions only after establishing with the parents that the neighborhood was, in fact, safe and that Allison's fears were unreasonable. In situations in which the child's fears of harm are more realistic, therapists have worked with the parents to make the child's environment as safe as possible. In a case like Allison's, this might include putting bars on the windows or removing close branches from a nearby tree.

The therapist encouraged the family to make Allison's room comfortable, pleasant, and safe for her. Also, for her STIC task, she was asked to spend time alone in her room during the day, so that she would begin to feel more comfortable there. Next, a plan was developed that included rewards for time Allison spent in her room. For every hour that she spent in her room, she would get points, which she would accumulate toward earning a prize. For Allison, the prizes were time spent with her parents and buying things to fix up her room.

In this case, the behavioral plans were primarily positive reward systems. For Allison, the therapist did not set up any negative consequences of noncompliance, except that the parents would take her into her room, forcefully if necessary, if she came into her parents' bedroom at night. A date was set, after the 14th session, at which time the plan would be implemented. During the first week, Allison made good progress. She did not stay in her room all night, but she spent more hours in her own room than in that of her parents. An interim step was also included in the initial plan. Allison would spend a certain number of hours in her room and then sleep in the hallway, although she was not rewarded for this hallway time. At the next session, her parents reported that she had slept through the night in her own room one time during the week. At that point, the reward system shifted so that Allison would earn a prize only for staying in her room all night.

One month later, Allison had not made further progress in increasing the time spent in her own room during the night. A new goal was set: that she not awaken her mother for three nights during the week. In addition, the therapist arranged with Allison to call her during the week to update her on her progress. The reward was shifted again to rewarding her for awakening her mother no more than one time during the night and spending the rest of the night in her room.

A problem developed in this plan because, although her parents consistently took Allison back to her own room during the night, they only sporadically rewarded her for her successes. The therapist reiterated to them the importance of being consistent with rewards. When the rewards became more consistent, Allison began spending more and more nights in her own room. By the end of treatment, although she came into her parents' room at times, she was able to sleep primarily in her own room.

WORKING WITH THE PARENTS

Particularly when treating separation-anxious children, it is necessary to involve the parents in treatment. Parents often find it difficult to require their children to confront and overcome their fears, but by giving in to these fears, they undermine the child's sense of competence in difficult situations. In Allison's case, the therapist stressed to the parents that the central goal was furthering her independence. She emphasized that although, in the short run, it might seem harsh to prevent her from avoiding the fearful situation, ultimately Allison would feel resentment toward her parents if they did not equip her with the skills to cope with difficult situations in her life.

The therapist made other interventions with the parents as well. As noted earlier, the father was agoraphobic and had many fears and worries of his own. He would assess the safety of every situation and ruminate about negative events that could occur. He seemed unaware of how literally his daughter took his anxious ruminations. For example, Allison heard about an accident that occurred on a busy local interstate and then refused to ride in a car on this road. The therapist encouraged Allison's father to try to refrain from some of his anxious processing in his daughter's presence. When the effects of his behavior were made clear to him, he was able to modify his behavior somewhat.

When problems in the marriage seem to interfere with the child's potential to benefit from treatment, we often recommend marital therapy. In this case, it became apparent early in treatment that because of conflicts between Allison's parents, they were undermining each other's efforts to help their child. For example, when Allison's mother wanted to stand firm and prevent her from coming into her parents' room, Allison's father would disagree, saying that the child needed her sleep. Because of this problem between the parents, the therapist recommended couple therapy and provided them with referrals. In addition, when she became aware of their hesitation about marital therapy because of financial constraints, past negative experiences with such therapy, and a feeling that their daughter would just "grow out of" her fearfulness, the therapist met with them again to strongly reiterate the importance of treatment and to try addressing their concerns. The parents did go to a couple therapist, and appeared to find it helpful. They were able to be more consistent in their support of Allison's progress after beginning therapy for their own problems.

POSTTREATMENT AND FOLLOW-UP ASSESSMENT

When Allison's parents completed the diagnostic interview following the completion of treatment, they reported that Allison had improved dramatically and that she continued to sleep in her own room. Allison and her parents both reported that her coping problems in specific situations identified prior to treatment had significantly improved. One clear marker of improvement was that, in contrast to the pretreatment interview, Allison was easily able to separate from her parents during the posttreatment interview.

Based on the diagnostic interviews with both Allison and her parents, she no longer met criteria for OAD and SAD. Although she was still diagnosed with simple phobias, the severity of her fear of elevators and the dark had decreased (see Table 8.4 for diagnoses obtained at each assessment point). According to the Child Behavior Checklist (Achenbach & Edelbrock, 1983) completed by Allison's mother, Allison evidenced clinically significant change on the Depression scale and the Internalizing scale as she moved from the clinical range to within the normal range on these scales (Kendall & Grove, 1988). Little change was noted on Allison's self-report measures from before and after treatment. However, this is to be expected, because she did not disclose distress on these measures prior to treatment.

In a posttreatment meeting with the therapist, the parents reported being pleased with Allison's gains, although, like many parents, they ex-

TABLE 8.4. Allison's Diagnoses and Severity Ratings at Each Assessment Point, Based on ADIS-R

Assessment point	Reporter	Diagnoses	Severity	
Pretreatment	Parents	SAD	3	
			OAD	2.5
		Simple phobias	4	
	Child	SAD	4	
		OAD	3	
		Simple phobias	2	
Immediately posttreatment	Parents	Simple phobias	1	
	Child	Simple Phobia	1	
1 year posttreatment	Parents	Simple phobia	2	
	Child	No diagnosis		

pressed some concerns about her ability to maintain her gains or to handle stressful situations that would inevitably arise after treatment. Therapists prepare parents for the possibility of some relapse and alert them to the ways that relapse is most likely to occur. In Allison's case, the most likely problem was that she would begin having problems sleeping in her own room. Therapists attempt throughout treatment to keep parents actively involved in the treatment process so that they develop skills to assist their child and do not come to believe that someone else has "fixed" their child. Instead, therapists want to instill in parents the feeling that they have the skills to help their child cope with future challenges. Parents are viewed as "collaborators" in the treatment.

A final diagnostic interview was completed with Allison and her parents approximately 1 year after the completion of treatment. The parents' perception of the treatment 1 year later was that it had been very helpful. Interviews with the family indicated that Allison had maintained her gains and still did not meet criteria for SAD and OAD. Her parents did provide information leading to only one diagnosis of a simple phobia of the dark. During the ensuing year, Allison had continued to sleep in her own room.

CONCLUSION

In this chapter, we have selected one case from a randomized clinical trial evaluating a cognitive-behavioral treatment for anxiety-disordered children. Allison's treatment is representative of the techniques that we use in treating separation anxiety, as well as the level of success typically achieved with this treatment.

Allison's SAD and OAD symptoms were substantially reduced to the point that she no longer met criteria for either disorder. By the end of treatment, she was able to sleep in her own room. We consider this to be an important achievement, because sleeping in her parents' room would have increasingly interfered with her development. For example, we often find that children who sleep in their parents' room avoid sleeping at friends' houses or inviting friends to spend the night at their house. Such events become more important to children's social lives as they approach puberty, and avoiding them can affect their ability to make friends. In addition, Allison was able to apply her newfound coping skills in other situations, as evidenced by the way that she handled her anxiety over her homework assignment.

One potential limitation of our treatment program is the extent to which we are able to work with parents. As a child-focused program, with a research evaluation component, we cannot provide additional therapy to troubled parents or families. To the extent that parental issues interfere with the child's progress, we can and do intervene. As in this case, the parents received help for their marital concerns and they were then better able to support their daughter in her own treatment. Over the life of our clinic, we have become increasingly aware of the importance of parental involvement in treatment and of the problems that arise when there are serious family conflicts. As a result, our future plans include evaluating a family-focused cognitive-behavioral treatment for childhood anxiety disorders.

REFERENCES

Achenbach, T. M., & Edelbrock, C. S. (1983). *Manual for the Child Behavior Checklist and Profile*. Burlington, VT: University of Vermont.

American Psychiatric Association. (1994). *Diagnostic and statistical manual of mental disorders* (4th ed.). Washington, DC: Author.

Anderson, T. C., Williams, S., McGee, R., & Silver, P. A. (1987). DSM-III disorders in preadolescent children: Prevalence in a large sample from the general population. *Archives of General Psychiatry, 44,* 69–76.

Ashmore-Callahan, S. (1993). *Children's self-report measures of anxiety: Predictive accuracy for diagnosis of anxiety disorders*. Unpublished master's thesis, Temple University.

Beck, A. T. (1976). *Cognitive therapy and the emotional disorders*. New York: International Universities Press.

Beck, A. T., & Emery, G. (1985). *Anxiety disorders and phobias: A cognitive perspective*. New York: Basic Books.

Bernstein, G. A., & Garfinkel, B. D. (1988). Pedigrees, functioning, and psychopathology in families of school phobic children. *American Journal of Psychiatry, 145,* 70–74.

Bernstein, G. A., & Svingen, P. H., & Garfinkel, B. D. (1990). School phobia: patterns of family functioning. *Journal of the American Academy of Child and Adolescent Psychiatry, 29,* 24–30.

Bowlby, J. (1973). *Attachment and loss: Vol. 2. Separation, anxiety, and anger*. New York: Basic Books.

Costello, E. J., Costello, A. J., Edelbrock, C., Burns, B. J., Dulcan, M. K., Brent, D., & Janiszewski, S. (1988). Psychiatric disorders in pediatric primary care. *Archives of General Psychiatry, 45,* 1107–1116.

Eisenberg, L. (1958). School phobia: A study in the communication of anxiety. *American Journal of Psychiatry, 114,* 712–718.

Francis, G., Last, C. G., & Strauss, C. C. (1987). Expression of separation anxiety disorder: The roles of age and gender. *Child Psychiatry and Human Development, 18,* 82–89.

Guidano, V. (1987). *Complexity of the self*. New York: Guilford Press.

Kagan, J. (1976). Emergent themes in human development. *American Scientist, 64,* 186–196.

Kendall, P. C. (1985). Toward a cognitive behavioral model of child psychopathology and a critique of related interventions. *Journal of Abnormal Child Psychology, 13*, 357–372.

Kendall, P. C. (1990). *Coping cat workbook.* (Available from the author, Department of Psychology, Temple University, Philadelphia, PA 19122.)

Kendall, P. C. (1994). Treating anxiety disorders in youth: Results of a randomized clinical trial. *Journal of Consulting and Clinical Psychology, 62*, 100–110.

Kendall, P. C., & Chansky, T. E. (1991). Considering cognition in anxiety-disordered children. *Journal of Anxiety Disorders, 5*, 167–185.

Kendall, P. C., Chansky, T. E., Kane, M. T., Kim, R. S., Kortlander, E., Ronan, K. R., Sessa, F. M., & Siqueland, L. (1992). *Anxiety disorders in youth: Cognitive-behavioral interventions.* Boston: Allyn & Bacon.

Kendall, P. C., & Grove, W. M. (1988). Normative comparisons in therapy outcome. *Behavioral Assessment, 10*, 147–158.

Kendall, P. C., & Hollon, S. D. (1989). Development of the anxious self-statement questionnaire. *Cognitive Therapy and Research, 13*, 81–93.

Kendall, P. C., Kane, M., Howard, B., & Siqueland, L. (1992). *Cognitive-behavioral therapy for anxious children: Treatment manual.* (Available from the author, Department of Psychology, Temple University, Philadelphia, PA 19122.)

Kendall, P. C., & Morris, R. J. (1991). Child therapy: Issues and recommendations. *Journal of Consulting and Clinical Psychology, 59*, 777–784.

Kovacs, M. (1981). Rating scales to assess depression in school aged children. *Acta Paedopsychiatrica, 46*, 305–315.

Last, C. G., Hersen, M., Kazdin, A. E., Finkelstein, R., & Strauss, C. C. (1987). Comparison of DSM-III separation anxiety and overanxious disorders: Demographic characteristics and patterns of comorbidity. *Journal of the American Academy of Child Psychiatry, 26*, 527–531.

Levy, D. M. (1943). *Maternal overprotection.* New York: Norton.

Meichenbaum, D. (1977). *Cognitive-behavior modification: An integrative approach.* New York: Plenum Press.

Ollendick, T. (1978). *Fear Survey Schedule—Revised.* (Available from the author, Virginia Polytechnic Institute and State University, Blacksburg, VA 24061)

Reynolds, C. R., & Richmond, B. O. (1978). A revised measure of children's manifest anxiety scale. *Journal of Abnormal Child Psychology, 6*, 271–280.

Ronan, K., Kendall, P. C., & Rowe, M. (1994). Negative affectivity in children: Development and validation of a self-statement questionnaire. *Cognitive Therapy and Research, 18*, 509–528.

Safran, J. D., & Segal, Z. V. (1990). *Interpersonal process in cognitive therapy.* New York: Basic Books.

Silverman, W. K. (1987). *Anxiety Disorders Interview Schedule for Children (ADIS).* SUNY, Albany, NY: Graywind Publications.

Spielberger, C. D. (1973). *Manual for the State–Trait Anxiety Inventory for Children.* Palo Alto, CA: Consulting Psychologists Press.

Strauss, C. C., Lease, C. A., Last, C. G., & Francis, G. (1988). Overanxious disorder: An examination of developmental differences. *Journal of Abnormal Child Psychology, 16*, 433–443.

9

Treatment of Low Self-Esteem

Stephen Shirk
Susan Harter

Over the last decade, clinical and developmental investigators have uncovered associations between self-related cognitions and a variety of childhood emotional and behavioral disorders (Crick & Dodge, 1994; Hammen & Zupan, 1984; Kaslow, Rehm, & Siegel, 1984; Stark, Humphrey, Laurent, Livingston, & Christopher, 1993). This research has revealed distortions in self-attributions (Curry & Craighead, 1990), deficits in self-regulatory strategies (Garber, Braafledt, & Zeman, 1991), deviations in self-schematic beliefs (Hammen, 1988), and exaggerations in negative self-focus (Rabian, Petersen, Richters, & Jensen, 1993) among emotionally distressed children. One recurrent finding to emerge from this literature is that children with emotional or behavioral problems often evince low self-esteem (Battle, 1987; Harter, Marold, & Whitesell, 1991; Lochman & Lampron, 1986; Toth, Manly, & Cicchetti, 1992). In fact, a brief review of the current *Diagnostic and Statistical Manual of Mental Disorders* (DSM-IV; American Psychiatric Association, 1994) indicates that low self-esteem is an associated feature of a range of childhood disorders, including attention-deficit/hyperactive disorder, learning disorders, oppositional defiant disorder, dysthymic disorder, and bulimia nervosa. Yet despite its involvement in many childhood disorders, self-esteem has not been a prominent target for intervention among cognitive and cognitive-behavioral child therapists (cf. Kendall, 1991). Thus, it is of interest to ask why self-esteem has been neglected by cognitively oriented child clinicians.

One possibility is that the construct's inferential, and potentially global, nature makes it unacceptable for clinicians who have honed their clinical skills in a tradition in which the precise measurement of observable behavior is essential for effective intervention. In addition, self-report, the principal method for assessing self-esteem, may carry the mark of introspectionism, a taboo for behaviorists who have doubted the capacity of individuals to accurately report on their own behavior or internal states. Finally, the *functional* role of self-esteem was questioned by many behaviorists. The keystone of behavioral approaches, including cognitive-behavioral approaches, is the functional analysis of skills or behavior. In contrast, early models of self-esteem did little more than demonstrate correlations between low self-esteem and maladjustment. Consequently, self-esteem has often been viewed as a mere correlate of other critical pathogenic processes.

A review of recent developmental research invites a reconsideration of the foregoing assumptions. The field of self theory has become more sophisticated in that theorists have become more precise in their definitions of self-constructs (Harter, 1990). In turn, operationalizations of the self, including self-esteem, have reflected greater clarity. For example, early measures were based on the assumption that the self is unidimensional. Consequently, self-esteem measures were often a mélange of items from different domains and sources (cf. Coopersmith, 1967). Such an aggregate approach ignored the specific content of items under the assumption that a single score would adequately reflect one's sense of self across the variety of domains in one's life (cf. Harter, 1986). Of course, such a perspective flies in the face of the behaviorist's assumption of domain and situational specificity in skills and behavior. In recent years, developmentalists have emphasized both hierarchical and multidimensional models of the self that, in turn, have necessitated the construction of measures that are far more domain specific and precise (Harter, 1990; Marsh, 1986). In fact, these current models integrate domain-specific self-evaluations and more global impressions of one's value or overall worth as a person (Harter, 1986, 1990). Unlike earlier additive models of global self-worth, Harter and colleagues have shown that school-aged children and adolescents make judgments about their overall worth as a person in addition to more specific evaluations of their competencies and skills. Affectively toned judgments of self-worth or esteem, in turn, are highly related to emotional and motivational processes (Harter et al., 1991).

With regard to the use of self-report, research indicates that accuracy of self-evaluation is a function of both developmental and individual difference factors (Harter, 1988). In fact, the lack of convergence between self-evaluations and "objective" indices of performance may, itself, be clinically interesting. For example, Harter (1988) has identified three groups of students on the basis of a comparison of their perceived scholastic competence and more objective indices, such as teachers' ratings and grade point average. There are students who overestimate their competence, those who underestimate their competence, and those whose judgments appear to be relatively accurate. Interestingly, on behavioral measures of preference for challenge, both the underestimators and the overestimators selected significantly lower levels of challenge compared to the accurate students. It is understandable why underestimators who doubt their academic competence would select lower levels of challenge. Of particular interest are the overestimators who presumably must, at some level, be aware that their talents fall short of their self-reported competence and behave accordingly.

Perhaps of greater importance, self-reports of esteem have been shown to be predictive of variations on theoretically related constructs (e.g., both motivational and emotional). Noteworthy are the robust correlations between self-esteem and dimensions of depression, for example, depressed affect and energy level (cf., Harter, 1990; Renouf & Harter, 1990). Of course, cognitive-behaviorists have come to rely increasingly on self-report as a major assessment method as the "black box" of internal processes has been shown to be integral to effective clinical intervention.

Finally, there has been increasing emphasis on the *functional* role of self-representations, including self-esteem, in interpersonal behavior and emotion regulation with both children and adults (cf. Baldwin, 1992; Main, Kaplan, & Cassidy, 1985; Harter, 1986; Segal & Muran, 1993). Developmental research has indicated that self-esteem is not merely a predictor of future interpersonal functioning (Kahle, Kulka, & Klinger, 1980), but is also both a mediator and moderator of emotional and behavioral adaptation. For example, through path analytic methods, Harter (1986) has shown that self-worth mediates between children's experience of social support and competence and their motivational and affective orientation in a scholastic context. Research on risk and resilience has revealed that self-esteem is one of the most important moderators (buffers) of psychosocial stress (Garmezy, 1985). Thus, the status of self-esteem should not be limited to that of a mere correlate or consequence of pathogenic processes, although such status is by no means insignificant; rather, self-esteem is integrally involved in various forms of childhood psychopathology and merits new status as a target for clinical intervention.

This perspective, that self-esteem is an important target for intervention, has long been a basic tenet of the child play therapy tradition (Wright, Everett, & Roisman, 1986). It is possible that in an effort to distinguish themselves from traditional play therapists, cognitively oriented child clinicians have downplayed the role of self-esteem in maladjustment. We would suggest that such an inclination "throws the baby out with the bath water." This is not to say that cognitive behaviorists should adopt the model of self-esteem espoused by traditional play therapists. In fact, there is reason to believe that the model presented in the play therapy literature is in need of a substantial overhaul.

According to play therapists (Axline, 1947; Wright et al., 1986), emotional and behavioral problems are markers of underlying vulnerabilities in self-esteem that have resulted from inadequate acceptance, support, or love from caregivers. Deficits in self-esteem translate into observable problems with motivation, behavior, and emotion. The aim of treatment, then, is compensatory—to help the child establish positive feelings of self-regard through a warm, accepting relationship with the therapist. As such, the play therapist does not focus on attaining specific behavioral goals in treatment, but attempts to provide a *relationship* that will enhance self-esteem.

Although findings on the corrective role of the therapeutic relationship (Horvath & Luborsky, 1993), including the relationship in cognitive therapy (Burns & Nolen-Hoeksema, 1992) are consistent with the emphasis on interpersonal processes in play therapy, the traditional model of self-esteem development and remediation, although parsimonious, may be oversimplified. The most fundamental limitation involves the conceptualization of self-esteem as an outgrowth of a unitary process; in brief, the development and maintenance of positive self-worth is viewed exclusively in terms of children's experience of others' regard for them (Axline, 1947; Moustakas, 1959). In turn, this unitary etiological model results in a single treatment prescription, namely the provision of a warm, accepting relationship with a substitute caregiver, the therapist. Two major problems follow from this conceptualization.

First, a unitary treatment model for low self-esteem fails to account for important developmental parameters. Although parental care and responsiveness are essential ingredients of adaptive development (Bowlby, 1988), the provision of compensatory support or acceptance may be differentially useful for children at different developmental levels. As Pope, McHale, and Craighead (1988) have observed,

> The attention and responsiveness of adults may be more important to a three-year-old learning a new skill than the actual quality of her task performance. In contrast, a nine-year-old may be so concerned about getting the job done correctly that positive adult attention may be an ineffective substitute for task failure. (p. 15)

To propose that all children with low self-esteem will be equally responsive to a single form of intervention commits what has been called the "developmental uniformity myth" of psychotherapy (Kendall, Lerner, & Craighead, 1984). "Children" is far from homogenous category, and treatments that ignore important developmental differences in child competencies and focal concerns are likely to be too "generic" for optimal effectiveness (Kendall et al., 1984).

A related, and equally important, limitation is the assumption of a single developmental pathway to low self-esteem. Developmental research has revealed that self-esteem is affected by multiple factors. For example, Harter (1986) has shown that variations in children's self-esteem can be accounted for by two principal factors: the children's experience of others' support *and* their sense of competence in areas of importance. Moreover, there are important individual differences in the degree to which these factors contribute to positive self-esteem. Harter, Simon, and Johnson (1993) found four subgroups of children who differed in the degree to which they based their self-esteem on either support or competence exclusively, an additive combination of both factors, or neither factor. Thus, a child who experiences negative events or feedback in areas of competence that are important to the self is likely to show more deleterious effects in self-esteem than a child who experiences the same negative events but bases his or her self-worth on other sources, for example, the approval of significant others.

Moreover, multiple pathways to self-esteem can be observed with regard to the particular competence/adequacy domains judged important, as well as the particular sources of social support that are critical to the child. For some children, perceptions of academic competence may be the domain that is a vital determinant of their self-esteem, whereas for others, it may be perceptions of their physical appearance or their behavioral conduct. With regard to the sources of support, for some children, self-esteem is highly dependent on support from parents, whereas for others, peer support is the most critical antecedent. Thus, the potential combinations of domains and sources of support represent numerous pathways to self-esteem. As these examples suggest, the determinants of low self-esteem are not as simple as the traditional play therapists would have us believe. Instead, it is likely that there are multiple developmental pathways to low self-esteem.

For example, Dodge (1993) has proposed a complex developmental pathway that begins with biased social information processing and poor social skills, progresses on to disrupted peer relations (culminating in peer rejection), and terminates with negative affects and cognitions directed toward the self (low self-esteem). Alternatively, Lynch and Cicchetti (1991) have maintained that one of the consequences of child maltreatment is impaired self-esteem and deficits in the child's capacity to talk about internal states, including the self. Such a combination may make it difficult for maltreated children to engage in compensatory social relations, which in turn maintains or compounds their problems with self-regard.

When one gives up a unitary developmental model of self-esteem, the "diagnosis" of low self-esteem is no longer sufficient for the design and delivery of corrective interventions. The recognition of multiple developmental pathways creates problems for diagnostically driven models of intervention. Thus, a manualized treatment protocol, designed for the enhancement of low self-esteem, is not likely to be optimally effective because of significant variations in the factors that influence the development and maintenance of low self-worth.

How, then, is the cognitively oriented child therapist to approach the treatment of low self-esteem? Currently, there is a strong emphasis in the field on prescriptive or targeted therapies for specific disorders (Beutler & Clarkin, 1990). According to this approach, specific diagnostic entities (e.g., depression) should be matched with interventions that have demonstrated efficacy; thus, for each disorder there will be a prescriptive treatment. However, as Persons (1991) has observed, the prescriptive approach assumes that all individuals with a particular disorder have the disorder for the same reason. Increasing evidence of multiple pathways to similar outcomes (e.g., low self-esteem or depression) undermines the assumption of a one-to-one correspondence between disorder and pathogenic process. This has led some clinicians to embrace multicomponent treatment packages in an effort to address multiple pathogenic contributors to specific disorders. Although multicomponent treatments may encompass a broad range of pathogenic mechanisms, such packages are not without significant liabilities; that is, some components may be irrelevant or counterproductive, thereby undermining the treatment relationship (Persons, 1991).

As an alternative to standardized or multicomponent treatment approaches, Persons (1989, 1991) has recommended the "case-formulation" approach. Here the therapist develops a working hypothesis about the nature of the pathogenic processes underlying the patient's presenting problems (Persons, 1991). The working hypothesis is the case formulation, and interventions are planned on the basis of the formulation rather than the diagnosis. The major advantage of such an approach is that it is consistent with a multiple-pathway model of developmental psychopathology. For each patient, the clinician must move beyond *diagnostic* assessment to an evaluation of the factors that are contributing to the presenting problems. Thus, in the treatment of low self-esteem, the child therapist must develop a formulation concerning the underlying processes that produce or maintain the child's problems with self-worth. In turn, the treatment plan follows from the formulation of pathogenic processes.

For example, with a child whose low self-esteem appears to be a consequence of highly contingent parental support, the provision of an accepting relationship that is incongruent with the child's prior relationship experiences might compensate for deficits in parental care or could even alter the child's beliefs about the basis for his or her self-worth. In contrast, for the child who lacks specific interpersonal competencies for establishing and maintaining peer relationships, and who evinces low peer acceptance, a compensatory therapeutic relationship is not likely to be sufficient. Instead, the therapist will need to focus on the development of social competencies that could alter peer acceptance and translate into improved self-esteem. Thus, given the multiple determinants of low self-esteem, treatment must be based on a formulation of the processes that contribute to the child's problems with self-worth. A corollary of this perspective is that the therapist must distinguish between the *goal* of treatment, that is, enhanced self-worth, and the locus of treatment. Whereas our goal may be the enhancement of self-worth, the locus of our intervention will be those factors that represent the *determinants* of low self-esteem (Harter, 1988). For example, if the primary antecedents of low self-esteem were lack of approval or validation from significant others, then treatment should be directed toward those factors that might lead to improved social relations. Alternatively, if the primary determinant of low self-esteem was lack of competence in areas in which success was deemed highly important, treatment should focus on either enhancing the child's level of competence or lowering the level of importance attached to success.

In the following section, two cases will be presented in order to illustrate a cognitively oriented, case-formulation approach to the treatment of low self-esteem. Although both of these children presented with self-esteem problems, the developmental pathways that lead them to treatment varied substantially.

CASE STUDIES

David

David, a 10-year-old fifth grader, was referred to the first author (S.R.S.) for psychotherapy following a psychological assessment conducted at his school. Intellectual testing indicated that David was of high-average intelligence; nevertheless, he was underachieving in both math and science. Teacher reports stated that David was typically resistant in class, occasionally disruptive, and rarely completed homework assignments. The previous evaluator concluded that David's "self-image and self-esteem appear to be highly impaired." This conclusion was based on significant deviations on the "egocentricity index" of the Rorschach, and from narrative material elicited by the Thematic Apperception Test. In the latter, David revealed a preoccupation with themes of vulnerability while attempting to project a positive sense of self through fantasies of magical power and invincibility.

Initial Assessment

David's mother, who was raising her son alone, was interviewed about David's developmental, social, and medical history. Although concerned with school underachievement and problems with peer relations, David's mother was particularly distressed by episodic outbursts of anger directed toward the self. During the preceding 6 months, David had intentionally banged his head against a doorframe on several occasions. During one episode of self-directed anger, he broke a yardstick over his head. Administered the Diagnostic Interview for Children and Adolescents—Parent form (DICA-P), David surprisingly did not meet criteria for dysthymia or major depression, but instead showed many of the symptoms of oppositional defiant disorder. These results were consistent with findings from the Child Behavior Checklist (CBCL), which showed David to be clinically elevated on the aggressive and delinquent narrow bands. The narrow band for depression was in the borderline range. Inspection of specific items from the depression narrow band revealed a pattern of self-rejection; items endorsed included Self-Conscious or Easily Embarrassed, Feels Worthless or Inferior, Feels Too Guilty, and Talks about Killing Self. In addition, David showed deficits on the CBCL social competence scale. Here, there were signs of significant peer relationship problems.

The family history was noteworthy for its high level of marital instability. When David was 4, his mother and father divorced following several years of marital discord. David's relationship with his father was marked by significant inconsistency. Visitation was irregular and David frequently experienced disappointment when his father would not follow through on commitments to visit or attend special events (e.g., birthdays or David's baseball games). Similarly, his relationship with his mother was uneven, owing to her involvement with a series of romantic partners.

In his initial interview, David presented as a relatively small, but athletically built, boy who pulled his baseball cap over his eyes during the session. Although he eventually engaged in conversation about professional sports, David showed a strong disinclination to talk about himself. As we focused on his experiences, he was able to acknowledge that he had some trouble with his schoolwork, and that he frequently got into fights with peers. He could not identify a best friend. When asked about his feelings, David simply replied that he was fine. Reminded of the self-abusive episodes, he acknowledged that he got angry at himself, although he found it difficult to elaborate about the causes of his self-directed anger. He half-heartedly attempted to make a joke about the episode during which he broke the yardstick over his head, stating that he now referred to himself as "Ironhead" (a professional football player's nickname). He then talked of becoming a professional football player. When asked about his size, David assured me that he would achieve great stature during his teen years.

David was administered two self-report instruments, the Child Depression Inventory (Kovacs, 1980) and the Self-Perception Profile for Children and Adolescents (Harter, 1988). The latter instrument is a multidimensional self-concept scale that assesses children's self-evaluations across multiple domains of functioning (e.g., behavioral conduct, academic competence, as well as their global self-worth). David's responses to these measures were unremarkable. Although he acknowledged some problems with conduct on both scales, he did not *report* low self-esteem or dysphoric mood, despite the behavioral indicators. It was not until the middle phase of treatment that David actually reported feelings of low self-worth. Acknowledgment of these difficult thoughts and feelings was clearly contingent on the development of a positive therapeutic alliance, an issue to which we shall return.

Case Formulation

Diagnostically David met criteria for oppositional defiant disorder. Based on this diagnosis, the prescriptive treatment might include a contingency management program for noncompliance or social skills training to enhance peer relations. In fact, on the basis of the diagnosis and David's self-reports, one might be inclined to dismiss low self-esteem as a critical component of his clinical presentation. Nevertheless, the behavioral pattern of self-directed anger, his preoccupation with themes of vulnerability and magical powers in his narratives, and his mother's endorsement of items on the CBCL that are indicative of self-rejection point to problems with self-esteem.

One important clue to David's difficulties was the *precipitant* for the self-abusive episodes. Although the pattern was not evident until David became more disclosing as an alliance developed in therapy, the main precipitants for these episodes tended to center around perceived rejection or parental unavailability. Over the course of therapy, several themes emerged: "being left out" (by peers or his mother), "being teased" (by peers), or "being lonely." The lack of close peer relationships also suggested low levels of social acceptance, an important predictor of low self-esteem. In brief, David's difficulties appeared to be embedded in a network of problematic relationships. His low self-esteem was manifested in *behavioral self-rejection*, that is, in high levels of self-directed anger and self-abusive behaviors. In essence, David presented his self-esteem problems through punitive, self-directed behaviors. Thus, one formulation for the case was that David's low self-esteem followed from his perceptions of low peer acceptance and limited parental unavailability. It is likely that these perceptions were compounded, particularly given their duration, by a sense of hopelessness, perceptions of low self-efficacy, and expectations of rejection. In turn, his low self-regard was expressed in motivational deficits at school and in his irritability at home and with peers. Although one goal for treatment would be the enhancement of David's self-esteem, the locus of the intervention would center on deficits in social acceptance and support, consistent with a model in which one attends to the identified causes of low self-esteem.

Treatment Plan

Given the case formulation, the development of a treatment plan hinged on identifying the specific obstructions to adequate social support and acceptance. Cognitive approaches have tended to focus on internal, psychological processes that contribute to emotional dysfunction. However, as Coyne and Gotlib (1983) have warned, many individual's who are experiencing psychological distress are, in fact, caught in distressing environments. In the treatment of children, who are embedded in family contexts, this possibility must be taken seriously. Thus, the first task was to determine the relative contribution of David's perceptions and behaviors to his experience of low social support in relation to the role of actual environmental constraints.

As is often the case, both intraindividual and social–environmental factors appeared to be contributing to his difficulties. On the environmental side, David faced the reality of inconsistent parental care. David's relationship with his father appeared to be highly disrupted, and his mother was intermittently unavailable as she struggled to balance career demands and her own emotional needs. However, David also appeared to be contributing to his sense of isolation and rejection through a pattern of perceptions and behaviors that alienated potential, compensatory peer support. In brief, David's perceptions of peers were filtered through the lens of inferiority (low self-regard). As he was quick to note about classmates, "They all think they're better than me." Thus, David's emotions in peer interactions were often "primed" by the expectation of rejection ("They wouldn't give me the time of day"). Not surprisingly, he tended to respond to his classmates with "a chip on his shoulder." In turn, he was increasingly isolated by his peers. David was caught in what Safran (1990) has described as the "cognitive-interpersonal cycle" (p. 97): maladaptive expectations or assumptions ("I am inferior and will be rejected"), primed emotions, and behaviors that, in turn, produced confirming responses from others, thus perpetuating the cycle. One target for treatment, then, was alteration of the schema that fueled this interpersonal cycle. On the other hand, given the "reality" of parental inconsistency, intervention at the dyadic level also was indicated.

Therapy was conceptualized as involving three active ingredients: (1) a supportive, compensatory relationship with the therapist; (2) structural dyadic interventions aimed at changing the mother–son relationship (the father was unavailable for treatment because he lived out of town); and (3) cognitive interventions to alter David's maladaptive schema.

Course of Therapy

Although all three components of treatment seemed essential, the cognitive interventions will be emphasized. Therapy sessions were typically divided into two sections. During the first half, the therapist introduced treatment tasks, and during the second, David was given the option of selecting an activity (including continuation of the "work" initiated during the first half of the session). Joint sessions between David and his mother were conducted on a monthly basis. During these sessions, mother and son were assisted in negotiations around family conflicts. Contractual agreements were often the outcome of these meetings. In addition, David and his mother were given the following prescription: that they set aside 15 minutes prior to David's bedtime to review the important events of the day, and that once each week they plan a special activity (e.g., baking cookies together, taking the dog on a hike) in order to increase their interactional time. Finally, David's mother was given the task of charting David's "moods" (irritability/noncompliance), and David tracked his mother's availability during weekly therapy sessions. David opted to portray the ebb and flow of their relationship as an elaborate roller coaster. Each week he added an additional "stretch" to the ride. As alliances with David *and* his mother were consolidated, we juxtaposed their records in a joint session. The juxtaposition of David's behavior problems with his depiction of maternal availability clearly communicated the importance of this relationship to his mother. She clearly recognized the significance of the parallels and openly commented that they would need to work on their relationship.

On the individual front, the cognitive intervention involved several components—increasing David's self-monitoring of thoughts and affects (specifically in peer situations), improving his capacity for "testing" the reality of his cognitions, engaging him in a "developmental analysis" (Guidano & Liotti, 1983, p. 152) of the origins of his expectations, and teaching him anger control strategies. He was presented with the overall rationale that I suspected that at times his feelings took control of him, and that I wanted to help him "be in charge of his emotions." Initial sessions were directed toward improving David's capacity to monitor his own thoughts and feelings. He was introduced to the idea of becoming a "psychological detective," which involved moving through a series of mastery steps. Each step was given a corresponding name, for example, Feelings Expert, Master Thought Detective, and so on. Initially we focused on the feelings he was experiencing during sessions (e.g., during competitive play), and later he charted his feelings during lunch and immediately after school, when peer interaction was likely.

Anger was far and away the most common emotion to be recorded. Next, he was introduced to the idea that people often have thoughts that accompany such emotions, but that it would take outstanding detective work to identify these rapidly moving ideas. Initially, we used photos of individuals in different affectively charged situations, and David filled in "thought bubbles" with possible co-occurring cognitions. Not surprisingly, many of these ambiguous situations elicited schema-driven cognitions, for example, "They think they're so cool," "I'm sick of bein' dissed [being disrespected]," that appeared to reflect hostile biases. We then moved to charting the thoughts that co-occurred with his experience of anger during peer interactions. Surprisingly, despite David's oppositional tendencies, he cooperated with this task without extrinsic rewards. It was likely that his collaboration with these therapeutic tasks reflected the quality and strength of the therapeutic relationship that was developing between us.

As David accumulated a list of "automatic thoughts," I introduced the idea that a good detective always examines the "strength of his evidence." Initially, David was asked to rate his level of certainty about his automatic thoughts. Although he was generally confident in their veridicality, as might be expected at his developmental level, there was some variability in his ratings. I suggested that the variation was a signal that it was important for him to "stop and test" his thoughts before acting on them. The next sessions involved a series of role plays, during which I played various peer partners and David reacted and practiced the "stop-and-test" routine. After each role play, we "brainstormed" other appraisals of the situation that might be possible. Overall, as reflected in the role plays, it appeared that David was developing the compensatory skills of self-monitoring and reality testing that would be essential to interrupting the cognitive-interpersonal cycle.

With the list of "automatic thoughts" in hand, we were in position to consider the developmental origins of these ideas. The aim of such an analysis is to place the thoughts in a new cognitive context, the past, in order to modify their meaning. With David, I simply introduced this phase by pointing out the common themes to his thoughts (rejection, disrespect, inferiority), and then suggested that these ideas did not "come from the moon," but that, in fact, he must have learned to think this way for a good reason. Operating from the clinical hypothesis that David was primed to experience new interpersonal interactions as rejecting, based in part on his relationship history with his father, I attempted to draw parallels between these past experiences and his current expectations. However, David appeared "resistant" to this aspect of the cognitive treatment. His focus centered on current relationships and how the behavior of peers justified his expectations. It was likely that his disinclination to engage in this part of the intervention was a function of both developmental constraints and affective processes; that is, school-aged children tend to view their current behavior in terms of temporally proximal causes, rather than in relation to more distal influences (Harter, 1982; Shirk, 1988). David's strongly mixed feelings for his father made it very difficult for him to discuss this relationship in therapy. Consequently, the developmental analysis took a backseat to working on other compensatory skills, specifically, training in anger control.

Anger control skills appeared to be critical in this case insofar as David evinced periodic undercontrolled outbursts directed toward both self and others. As in most anger control programs (cf. Feindler, 1991; Novaco, 1975), we focused on (1) identifying both internal (physiological) and external (situational) cues to anger, (2) differentiating levels of anger (specifically, prompts for angry behavior), (3) utilizing verbal self-statements to prompt coping strategies, and (4) practicing both relaxation techniques (creating calming imagery) and problem-solving strategies. This skills were first role played in sessions, and later in joint sessions with David's mother. Although David reported periodic lapses in anger control, he also reported multiple situations at school in which he utilized his new strategies.

Treatment Outcome

David's treatment was carried out over an 8-month period. Maternal report indicated a significant decrease in conflicts at home and maintenance of more positive parent–child interaction. School reports also revealed an improvement in David's "attitude." As reported by David, he had found a small group of friends with whom he could "hang" on a regular basis. His mother observed that he was receiving more requests from peers to join in afterschool activities (e.g., going to the movies).

With regard to self-esteem, by both maternal and self-report at time of termination, David had not evinced a single episode of self-abusive behavior for over 2 months. This pattern remained stable at 3-month follow-up. A posttreatment CBCL revealed a sharp drop on items indicative of self-rejection. Finally, and perhaps most dramatically, David presented the therapist with a drawing during the final session. The picture was a before-and-after self-depiction. On one side was a muscular figure whose sharp teeth and clenched fists exuded anger. In the corresponding "thought bubble" was the phrase, "I hate myself." Next to this figure was a somewhat smaller—perhaps more realistic—depiction of a smiling boy in a baseball cap. His thoughts were strikingly different; they simply read, "I feel great, I'm doing great." The contrast left little doubt that David was feeling much better about himself.

Chris

Chris, a 16-year-old high school junior, was referred for psychotherapy by his mother following an emotional episode during which he expressed a wish to kill himself. Over the previous 2 years, Chris, who was an outstanding student/athlete, had shown signs of social withdrawal and self-deprecatory thinking. There had been no overt suicide attempts, but he had informed his mother that he had thought about ending his life on several occasions.

Initial Assessment

Chris was interviewed with his mother during the first session. It was evident that he was overwhelmed by strong feelings, and as his mother described her concerns, Chris began to cry. She reported that Chris was a "model son" who was near the top of his class academically, well-integrated socially, and a starter for the high school basketball team. She was both perplexed and concerned about "how hard Chris was on himself." During the last 2 years, she had observed that Chris seemed to think that he had to be "perfect." An A– on an exam would unleash harsh self-criticism and self-punishment. For example, when Chris failed to achieve the highest grade on a physics exam, he did not permit himself to see his close friends for over a week; instead, he spent the time sequestered in his room studying. Asked about the family's expectations for Chris, his mother noted that she and her husband would be happy with a solid B average. Chris acknowledged that the pressure he felt did not come from parental demands to excel; in fact, he felt that his parents, although proud of his performance, were worried about the amount of time that he spent studying.

On the Youth Self-Report (YSR), Chris showed clinically significant elevations on several of the internalizing narrow bands, including depression. The most prominent feature of his presentation was self-criticism. Diagnostically, Chris appeared to fit the parameters of what Blatt (1974) has called "introjective" or "self-critical depression." He set extremely high standards for himself and was sharply self-punitive when he failed to attain them. On several occasions he had actually slapped himself on the face following what he perceived to be academic "failure" (not getting an A). Not surprisingly, he reported low global self-worth on the Self-Perception

Profile. In brief, his self-esteem was extremely fragile. Acknowledged achievements brought limited feelings of satisfaction, whereas perceived failure resulted in sustained self-reproach.

The family history was noteworthy in that Chris had been adopted at 3 months of age. His biological mother, a teenager at the time, had initially attempted to raise him alone, but given her limited resources, including little family support, found the task to be overwhelming. For a brief period, Chris had been placed in foster care. According to his adoptive parents, social service reports did not indicate a history of abuse or neglect. In fact, when Chris was placed with the family, they were impressed with his physical size and robust demeanor. Chris had been informed of his adoption at an early age, but given the "closed" nature of the adoption, he had no contact with his biological mother. In interview, he reported no desire to locate her and expressed a strong sense of "belonging" in his adoptive family.

Case Formulation

The most prominent features of Chris's presentation were his high self-standards, strong self-critical tendencies, and depressed mood that appeared to follow from self-punitive thinking. Like David, Chris showed significant vulnerabilities in his sense of self; in fact, his problems with self-worth were more directly evident in his self-critical thinking and in his report of low self-esteem. Despite important differences in the two cases, both boys evinced self-rejecting tendencies: David on a behavioral level through his self-abusive episodes, and Chris on a cognitive level with his self-punitive thinking. It is possible that these differences in the manifestation of self-esteem problems—behavioral versus cognitive symptoms—reflect the impact of development level on symptom expression (Leahy, 1988), that is, developmentally one expects a "progression" from symptoms expressed directly into action to symptoms mediated by thought. Of equal importance, although David and Chris both presented with self-esteem problems, the pathogenic processes underlying their difficulties were quite different. For Chris, the central problem appeared to revolve around his unrealistic self-expectations and his tendency to utilize self-punishment as his primary method of self-regulation. For David, the source of his difficulties resided in ongoing problematic relationships, some of which followed from his maladaptive interpersonal expectations.

Treatment Plan

Chris seemed to be motivated to participate in therapy and expressed a strong desire to find relief from what he called "inside pressure." Our initial alliance was forged around a mutual attempt to find the "relief valve" for this internal pressure. Following the establishment of a contract around suicidal ideation, interventions were aimed at modifying his self-standards and self-critical thinking. As will be seen, the aims and methods of treatment evolved as therapy progressed, or more to the point, as the initial interventions failed to bring Chris sustainable relief.

Course of Treatment

During the first weeks of treatment, Chris and I (S.R.S.) explored his goals and expectations for himself. Consistent with the initial interview, his academic performance expectations were extraordinarily high and somewhat at odds with his long-term goals—to attend a state university and eventually become an architect. Neither goal required the level of performance Chris demanded from himself. In an effort to highlight the incongruity between his perfectionistic standards and his goals, I advised Chris to meet with his guidance counselor to review college requirements. In addition, his parents arranged for a visit to a local architectural firm. Despite feedback about what would be "realistically" required to attain his goals, little change in his self-expectations resulted from these "psychoeducational" interventions.

Chris was also asked to keep a log of his "inner pressure," noting any occasion when he acted punitively toward himself. He was an active recorder of his moods and thoughts, which typically included references to his "stupidity" and "worthlessness." At this point, I began to challenge the connection between his high expectations and his harsh self-criticism through role plays aimed at introducing a new perspective on his situation. After we clarified the connection between performance standards, self-reproach, and his inner pressure, I asked Chris if he held the same standards for his friends, and, of equal importance, if he treated them so harshly when they failed to perform perfectly. Not surprisingly, Chris was far more forgiving with his friends and certainly did not expect them to be perfect. We focused on this "double standard" for several sessions. During this time, I role played one of his friends. In a typical scenario, I would express disappointment in my performance. It was Chris's task to demonstrate how he would console or support a friend in distress. Again, Chris had little difficulty being highly supportive and had no trouble generating the type of calming statements he consistently failed to use with himself. It was easy to see why Chris had a network of friends. In relation to *others*, he demonstrated remarkable empathy and warmth, but in relation to himself, he was a harsh taskmaster. Thus, the aim of therapy came to be defined as "teaching Chris to be a friend to himself." In an effort to transfer the "skills" and attitudes Chris clearly demonstrated in relation to others, we recorded the calming statements he used with his friends (e.g.,

"Don't take it so hard; there'll be another test"; "So this one didn't go so well; think about everything else you have going for you"). In session, we continued the role plays, but this time Chris was asked to recall episodes of disappointment and to practice the self-calming statements. During the week, he was asked to practice "being a friend to himself." At one point, I prescribed "intentionally failing" an exam so that he could practice the self-calming strategies. With a wry smile, Chris acknowledged that he might be willing to study a little less.

Unfortunately, Chris continued to struggle with perfectionism and self-criticism. It was simply easier to be a good friend to others than to himself. Although it was clear that he had the "skills" needed to be less self-critical, the recalcitrant nature of this cognitive pattern appeared to be embedded in deeper assumptions about the self and others. A recurrent theme in Chris's thinking was a link between "failure" (lack of perfection) and interpersonal rejection. For example, Chris made numerous comments suggesting that his interpersonal security was tied to outstanding performances across multiple domains (e.g., "They'll laugh at me if I make a mistake"; "I don't measure up, so I have to show I'm better"; "No one wants to hang around with a loser." These expectations had all the hallmarks of cognitive distortions. First, they were overgeneralized and unqualified; second, they were incongruent with what I had learned about Chris's parents and friends. Unlike David, who faced an uncertain and inconsistent social environment, Chris was surrounded by supportive peers and family. It was my hypothesis that the schema linking perfection and rejection had its roots in Chris' developmental history. As Leahy (1988) has observed, from a cognitive perspective, the problem was not that something had happened in early childhood, but that Chris continued to believe the validity of the conclusions drawn from the early experience; thus, with this new formulation, the aim of treatment became schematic change.

Given the evidence that Chris's schematic expectation (imperfection = rejection) was not based on current interpersonal experiences, we began a "developmental analysis" of the origins of this belief. I assured Chris that he must have good grounds for holding such a belief, and that our new task was to discover how he came to believe in it. Unlike David, who lacked the cognitive capacities and inclination to explore links between past and present, Chris readily engaged in this process. He initially focused on the anxiety he experienced when he changed schools and peer groups at age 13. Not surprisingly, the theme of this memory revolved around anticipated rejection by new classmates and teachers. As we focused on possible bases for his expectation of rejection, our conversations quickly turned to Chris's adoption. Chris, and his parents, knew relatively little about the circumstances of his relinquishment; however, Chris was adamant that somehow he had played a role in the process. As we explored the possibilities, he alluded to being "too difficult," to "being a burden." Eventually, with a great outpouring of emotion he simply said, "Something must have been wrong with me." It appeared that beneath Chris's self-critical stance was the implicit belief, "If I had been flawless (perfect), she would have kept me." This core assumption, undoubtedly constructed during childhood to make sense of his early experience, found expression in his current schematic belief that "others will reject me (or I must reject myself), if I am not perfect."

The final phase of treatment involved gentle challenges to Chris's core assumption about his relinquishment. First, a series of joint sessions between Chris and his mother were held to review the known "facts" of his early placement. His adoptive mother emphasized the difficult situation of his biological parent, and underscored the fact that Chris was a "wonderful" baby when he joined his new family. In our individual sessions, we explored possible alternative accounts for his placement, noting that each was as plausible as the "theory" Chris had constructed. Interestingly, this approach resulted in a marked change in emotional expression. For the first time, Chris directed anger, not toward himself, but toward his birth mother, whom he now regarded as "weak." In later sessions, I noted that now he was turning his harshness in another direction, and although I was pleased to see him direct it away from himself, we needed to recall that his perception of his birth mother as "weak" was also only a theory. Although Chris initially reacted by directing some of his anger toward me, this intervention seemed to open the door to the process of grieving the early loss. The strength of the emotions expressed during the ensuing sessions provided strong testimony to the intrinsic link between core schemas and intense emotion. Although this portion of therapy had been guided by an analysis of cognitive assumptions, it was evident that schema transformation also involved the expression of associated emotion.

The final phase of treatment involved revisiting the parallels between his "theory" of his relinquishment, and his drive for perfection and self-punitive stance. During this period, I offered a cognitive reframe for this parallel by suggesting that it was "one way of remaining connected with his biological mother." This intervention led Chris to reconsider other ways of acknowledging his adoptive heritage, including further conversations with his adoptive mother about his arrival in the family. Near the end of treatment, Chris was beginning to show signs of schematic change, albeit indirectly. For example, he talked about the plight of teenage girls who got pregnant, and how difficult it might be for them to raise their children without family support. He wondered aloud whether that would be the best thing for the child. Simultaneously, his mood began to elevate and stabilize, and he increasingly directed his attention to non-achievement-related activities (e.g., serving as a peer counselor). In striking contrast to his initial presentation, he also began to show a sense of humor about his tendency to drive himself so hard.

Treatment Outcome

It was evident that Chris had attained significant distance from his maladaptive assumption linking perfection to interpersonal security or acceptance. Maternal report indicated increased involvement in social activities and an emerging interest in romantic relationships. In fact, for the first time, Chris began dating. The intensity of his achievement concerns and his drive for perfection were clearly in better balance with other age-appropriate interests and activities. More directly, Chris no longer showed the highly self-punitive cognitive pattern following "perceived failure" (not getting the top grade), although he remained highly motivated in the academic domain and his standards remained relatively, but not excessively, high. Perhaps of greatest relevance, at time of termination Chris reported feeling "more relaxed with himself," and not surprisingly, his self-report of global self-worth showed a noteworthy jump in a more positive direction.

CONCLUSIONS

At the heart of the cases of David and Chris were vulnerabilities in their senses of self. For each of them, low self-esteem was integrally involved in their respective emotional and behavioral problems. For David, social interactions were filtered through his thoughts of inferiority and worthlessness which, in turn, primed him for dysregulated interpersonal behavior. For Chris, the experience of self as "flawed" or "a burden" set the foundation for maladaptive assumptions linking perfection with security, and for self-criticism as a depressogenic cognitive process. Both of these youngsters showed strong self-rejecting tendencies, one through self-punitive actions, the other through self-punitive cognitions. Nevertheless, the developmental pathways that brought them to these similar outcomes were quite different.

Harter (1986) has demonstrated that the development and maintenance of children's self-esteem can be predicted from two major factors: (1) perceived competence in areas of importance and (2) the child's experience of social support. Moreover, children vary in the degree to which their self-esteem is linked to either or both of these factors. Thus, according to this model, threats to self-esteem and the obstacles that could lead a child off the path of normal self-development come in two broad forms: (1) perceived incompetence in domains of importance and/or (2) lack of support, validation, and acceptance from significant others. In the cases of David and Chris, we find clinical prototypes of these two pathogenic processes. For David, the experience of peer rejection and parental unavailability were critical determinants of his low self-regard; for Chris, self-criticism followed from the perception of incompetence in achievement areas that were highly valued. In essence, these cases represent the extension of normal developmental processes into the clinical domain.

Although both of these cases shared a common diagnostic feature—low self-esteem—given the important differences in the *determinants* of their respective difficulties, treatment methods were based on formulations of the pathogenic processes underlying their self-esteem problems. A basic tenet of the case-formulation approach is that treatment and assessment of underlying pathogenic processes—be they cognitive distortions, skills deficits, or the lack of social support—are intimately linked. As Persons (1991) has noted, diagnosis in medicine is not restricted to the observation of manifest symptoms, but includes an assessment of underlying pathogenic processes. In turn, treatment is based on the assessment and formulation of these processes. The same must hold true for psychosocial disorders; diagnosis of a disorder is a starting point for treatment planning, rather than the primary determinant of treatment prescriptions.

It is important to note that developmental differences between these youngsters played an important part in the design of the interventions. There is increasing recognition that developmental level may be an important moderator of clinical interventions with children, particularly with cognitive interventions (Shirk, 1990). In both of these cases, self-monitoring of thoughts and feelings played a pivotal role in treatment. Although both of these youngsters demonstrated the capacity to engage in this procedure—with different levels of scaffolding—younger children could find such a treatment task problematic. As Harter (1982) has observed, school-aged children often lack the capacity to distance themselves from their own thinking (engage in recursive thinking), and typically show little interest in focusing on internal events such as thoughts, feelings, or fantasies. One salient developmental contrast in these cases involved the differential utility of "developmental analysis." For David, the 10-year-old, there was little interest in revisiting earlier experiences in order to move forward. In contrast, Chris, who exhibited considerable abstract thinking abilities, was readily engaged in this task, and attained a new cognitive framework for and relief from his current problems by revisiting the past. It is likely that the usefulness of "developmental analysis" as a change process is constrained by the process of development itself.

These cases also highlight the role of the "real" social environment in case formulation and treatment planning. The degree to which each of these youngster's problems could be attributed primarily to internal, cognitive processes differed substantially. For example, Chris was surrounded by supportive peers and family members. His difficulties were rooted in the cognitive legacy of a past relationship. In David's case, however, though cognitive assumptions interfered with the development of compensatory peer relations, he was, in fact, faced with parental unavailability. Thus, as Braswell (1991) has noted, cognitively oriented therapists must not forget their behavioral heritage with its emphasis on the impact of the social environment on child psychopathology.

Finally, although both children manifested problems with self-esteem, they differed in their direct disclosure of these problems. Chris reported feelings of low self-worth at the start of treatment, whereas David inflated his self-report while exhibiting behavioral signs of self-rejection. Only after the formation of a positive alliance did David begin to reveal his "true" feelings of low self-regard. These cases underscore two important points. First, clinicians must be sensitive to both self-reported and behaviorally presented evidence of low self-esteem. Inconsistency between self-report and behavioral presentation is likely to be clinically significant and reflect the operation of defensive processes. It is also likely that difficulties with problem acknowledgment (self-report) in the face of manifest problems will constitute an obstacle to treatment collaboration (Shirk, Saiz, & Sarlin, 1993). Second, because self-report is the most direct method for assessing many internal psychological processes, including self-esteem, clinicians must establish an adequate level of rapport with their patients in order to ensure valid assessment. As David's case clearly demonstrates, his acknowledgment of self-esteem problems emerged with the development of a positive treatment alliance.

In conclusion, these cases demonstrate the potential efficacy of developmentally informed cognitive interventions for children with low self-esteem. Because there are multiple developmental pathways to low self-esteem, interventions must be based on an assessment and formulation of the pathogenic processes underlying the children's problems. Finally, these cases represent living examples of the recurrent finding that representations of self, specifically self-esteem, are intertwined with dysregulated emotional and behavioral processes. Thus, interventions for low self-esteem represent a promising new pathway to the treatment of child psychopathology.

REFERENCES

American Psychiatric Association. (1994). *Diagnostic and statistical manual of mental disorders* (4th ed.). Washington, DC: Author.

Axline, V. (1947). *Play therapy.* New York: Ballantine.

Baldwin, A. (1992). Relational schemas and the processing of social information. *Psychological Bulletin, 112,* 461–484.

Battle, J. (1987). Relationship between self-esteem and depression among children. *Psychological Reports, 60,* 1187–1190.

Beutler, L., & Clarkin, J. (1990). *Systematic treatment selection: Toward targeted therapeutic interventions.* New York: Brunner/Mazel.

Blatt, S. J. (1974). Levels of object representation in anaclitic and introjective depression. *Psychoanalytic Study of the Child, 29,* 107–157.

Bowlby, J. (1988). *A secure base.* New York: Basic Books.

Braswell, L. (1991). Involving parents in cognitive-behavioral therapy with children and adolescents. In P. Kendall (Ed.), *Child and adolescent therapy: Cognitive-behavioral procedures* (pp. 316–352). New York: Guilford Press.

Burns, D., & Nolen-Hoeksema, S. (1992). Therapeutic empathy and recovery from depression in cognitive-behavioral therapy: A structural equation model. *Journal of Consulting and Clinical Psychology, 60,* 441–449.

Coopersmith, S. (1967). *The antecedents of self-esteem.* San Francisco: Freeman.

Coyne, J., & Gotlib, I. (1983). The role of cognition in depression: A critical appraisal. *Psychological Bulletin, 94,* 472–505.

Crick, N., & Dodge, K. (1994). A review and reformulation of social information-processing mechanisms in children's social adjustment. *Psychological Bulletin, 115,* 74–101.

Curry, J., & Craighead, W. (1990). Attributional style and self-reported depression among adolescent inpatients. *Child and Family Behavior Therapy, 12,* 89–93.

Dodge, K. (1993, March). *Social information processing and peer rejection factors in the development of behavior problems in children.* Paper presented at meetings of Society for Research in Child Development, New Orleans, LA.

Feindler, E. (1991). Cognitive strategies in anger control interventions for children and adolescents. In P. Kendall (Ed.), *Child and adolescent therapy: Cognitive-behavioral procedures* (pp. 66–97). New York: Guilford Press.

Garber, J., Braafledt, N., & Zeman, J. (1991). The regulation of sad affect: An information processing perspective. In J. Garber & K. Dodge (Eds.), *The development of emotion regulation and dysregulation* (pp. 208–242). New York: Cambridge University Press.

Garmezy, N. (1985). Stress-resilient children: The search for protective factors. In J. E. Stevenson (Ed.), *Recent research in developmental psychopathology* (pp. 213–233). Oxford: Pergamon Press.

Guidano, V. F., & Liotti, G. (1983). *Cognitive processes and emotional disorders.* New York: Guilford Press.

Hammen, C. (1988). Self cognitions, stressful events, and the prediction of depression in children of depressed mothers. *Journal of Abnormal Child Psychology, 16,* 347–360.

Hammen, C., & Zupan, B. (1984). Self-schema, depression, and the processing of personal information in children. *Journal of Experimental Child Psychology, 37,* 598–608.

Harter, S. (1982). Cognitive-developmental considerations in the conduct of play therapy. In C. Schaefer & K. O'Connor (Eds.), *Handbook of play therapy* (pp. 95–127). New York: Wiley.

Harter, S. (1986). Processes underlying the construction, maintenance, and enhancement of the self-concept in children. In J. Suls & A. Greenwald (Eds.), *Psychological perspectives on the self* (Vol. 3, pp. 137–181). Hillsdale, NJ: Erlbaum.

Harter, S. (1988). Developmental and dynamic changes in the nature of the self-concept: Implications for child psychotherapy. In S. Shirk (Ed.), *Cognitive development and child psychotherapy* (pp. 119–160). New York: Plenum Press.

Harter, S. (1990). Causes, correlates and the functional role of global self-worth: A life-span perspective. In J. Kolligian & R. Sternberg (Eds.), *Perceptions of competence and incompetence across the life-span* (pp. 67–98). New Haven, CT: Yale University Press.

Harter, S., Marold, D. B., & Whitesell, N. R. (1991). A model of psychosocial risk factors leading to suicidal ideation in young adolescents. *Development and Psychopathology, 4,* 167–188.

Harter, S., Simon, V., & Johnson, E. (1993, March). *James vs. Cooley: Individual differences in the sources of young adolescents' self-esteem.* Poster presented at biennial meetings of the Society for Research in Child Development, New Orleans, LA.

Horvath, A., & Luborsky, L. (1993). The role of the therapeutic alliance in psychotherapy. *Journal of Consulting and Clinical Psychology, 61,* 561–573.

Kahle, L., Kulka, R., & Klingel, D. (1980). Low adolescent self-esteem leads to multiple interpersonal problems: A test of social-adaptation theory. *Journal of Personality and Social Psychology, 39,* 496–502.

Kaslow, N., Rehm, L., & Siegel, A. (1984). Social cognitive and cognitive correlates of depression in children. *Journal of Abnormal Child Psychology, 12,* 243–248.

Kendall, P. (Ed.). (1991). *Child and adolescent therapy: Cognitive-behavioral procedures.* New York: Guilford Press.

Kendall, P., Lerner, R., & Craighead, E. (1984). Human development and intervention in childhood psychopathology. *Child Development, 55,* 71–82.

Kovacs, M. (1980). Rating scales to assess depression in school-aged children. *Acta Paedopsychiatrica, 46,* 305–315.

Leahy, R. (1988). Cognitive therapy of childhood depression: Developmental considerations. In S. Shirk (Ed.), *Cognitive development and child psychotherapy* (pp. 187–206). New York: Plenum Press.

Lochman, J., & Lampron, L. (1986). Situational social problem-solving skills and self-esteem of aggressive and nonaggressive boys. *Journal of Abnormal Child Psychology, 14,* 605–617.

Lynch, M., & Cicchetti, D. (1991). Patterns of relatedness in maltreated and nonmaltreated children: Connections among multiple representational models. *Development and Psychopathology, 3,* 207–226.

Main, M., Kaplan, N., & Cassidy, J. (1985). Security in infancy, childhood, and adulthood: A move to the level of representation. In I. Bretherton & E. Waters (Eds.), *Growing points of attachment theory and research. Monographs of the Society for Research in Child Development, 50* (1–2, Serial No. 209), 66–104.

Marsh, H. W. (1986). Global self-esteem: Its relation to specific facets of self-concept and their importance. *Journal of Personality and Social Psychology, 51*, 1224–1236.

Moustakas, C. (1959). *Psychotherapy with children.* New York: Harper & Row.

Novaco, R. W. (1975). *Anger control: The development and evaluation of an experimental treatment.* Lexington, MA: D. C. Heath.

Persons, J. (1989). *Cognitive therapy in practice: A case formulation approach.* New York: Norton.

Persons, J. (1991). Psychotherapy outcome studies do not accurately represent current models of psychotherapy. *American Psychologist, 46*, 99–106.

Pope, A., McHale, S., & Craighead, W. E. (1988). *Self-esteem enhancement with children and adolescents.* Boston: Allyn & Bacon.

Rabian, B., Petersen, R., Richters, J., & Jensen, P. (1993). Anxiety sensitivity among anxious children. *Journal of Clinical Child Psychology, 22*, 441–446.

Renouf, A., & Harter, S. (1990). Low self-worth and anger as components of the depressive experience in young adolescents. *Development and Psychopathology, 2*, 293–310.

Safran, J. (1990). Towards a refinement of cognitive therapy in light of interpersonal theory. *Clinical Psychology Review, 10*, 87–105.

Segal, Z., & Muran, C. (1993). A cognitive perspective on self-representation in depression. In Z. Segal & S. Blatt (Eds.), *The self in emotional distress: Cognitive and psychodynamic perspectives* (pp. 131–170). New York: Guilford Press.

Shirk, S. R. (1988). Causal reasoning and children's comprehension of therapeutic interpretations. In S. Shirk (Ed.), *Cognitive development and child psychotherapy* (pp. 53–89). New York: Plenum Press.

Shirk, S. (1990). Cognitive processes in child psychotherapy: Where are the developmental limits? In J. deWit, W. Slot, & M. Terwogt (Eds.), *Developmental psychopathology and clinical practice* (pp. 19–31). Amsterdam: Acco.

Shirk, S., Saiz, C., & Sarlin, N. (1993, June). *The therapeutic alliance in child and adolescent treatment: Preliminary studies with inpatients.* Paper presented at meetings of the Society for Psychotherapy Research, Pittsburgh, PA.

Stark, K., Humphrey, L., Laurent, J., Livingston, R., & Christopher, J. (1993). Cognitive, behavioral, and family factors in the differentiation of depressive and anxiety disorders during childhood. *Journal of Consulting and Clinical Psychology, 61*, 878–886.

Toth, S., Manly, J., & Cicchetti, D. (1992). Child maltreatment and vulnerability to depression. *Development and Psychopathology, 4*, 97–112.

Wright, L., Everett, F., & Roisman, L. (1986). *Experiential psychotherapy with children.* Baltimore: Johns Hopkins University Press.

10

Treatment of an Adolescent Survivor of Child Sexual Abuse

Anne Hope Heflin
Esther Deblinger

C hild sexual abuse is a highly prevalent societal problem that cuts across all ethnic, racial, educational, and socioeconomic groups. Retrospective surveys of adults suggest that approximately 27% of adult females and 16% of adult males suffer sexual victimization by the age of 18 (Finkelhor, 1987; Finkelhor, Hotaling, Lewis, & Smith, 1990; Russell, 1986).

Research has demonstrated that sexual abuse survivors may be affected by their abusive experiences in a variety of ways, with some survivors exhibiting minimal, if any, apparent effects, whereas others develop severe social and/or psychiatric problems. Adolescents appear to be at risk for some of the most severe psychiatric and psychosocial difficulties. Some of the difficulties identified through prospective examinations of adolescents who have experienced sexual abuse include depression, suicide attempts, and self-injury; posttraumatic stress symptoms, psychotic symptoms, and acting-out behaviors such as running away, substance abuse, promiscuity, and delinquent behaviors (Anderson, 1981; Dembo et al., 1987; Sansonnet-Hayden, Haley, Marriage, & Fine, 1987).

A number of variables have been identified as mediating factors associated with the adjustment of children after a sexual abuse experience. For example, sexual abuse perpetrated by a father or stepfather has been associated with greater postabuse symptomatology (Briere & Runtz, 1988; McLeer, Deblinger, Atkins, Foa, & Ralphe, 1988). The nature of the abusive interaction has been found to be related to postabuse adjustment with more invasive or intimate sexual contact being linked with more negative outcomes (Peters, 1988; Tufts New England Medical Center, 1984). Similarly, the threat or use of force during the sexual abuse experience has been associated with more traumatic responses (Finkelhor, 1979; Russell, 1986).

The role of nonoffending parents also has been recognized as being important in mediating the effects of child sexual abuse. Children's post-abuse adjustment has been linked with the level of support they receive from nonoffending adults (Adams-Tucker, 1982; Conte & Schuerman, 1987; Everson, Hunter, Runyon, Edelson, & Coulter, 1989). Furthermore, children's postabuse outcomes have been associated with maternal levels of symptomatology (Deblinger, Taub, Schaal, Lippmann, & Stauffer, 1994; Runyon, Hunter, & Everson, 1992).

Until recently, little attention has been paid to cognitive variables that may serve as mediating factors in children's postabuse adjustment. However, a study by Mannarino and Cohen (1993) demonstrated the importance of examining the relationship between cognitive attributions and postabuse adjustment. These researchers found that negative, abuse-related cognitions such as feeling different from peers, self-blame, and low perceived credibility and interpersonal trust were associated with increased levels of postabuse symptomatology. Furthermore, locus of control predicted symptomatology, with a more external locus of control being associated with greater symptomatology.

The treatment of children and adolescents who have experienced sexual abuse is still in its developmental stages. The literature that exists regarding treatment generally lacks adequate empirical grounding as it consists primarily of case studies, anecdotes, and proposed treatment plans. Although several large treatment-outcome studies are currently underway (including one by E.D. focusing on treatment for latency aged children), the findings are not yet available. One preliminary study that included adolescents as well as younger victims of sexual abuse suggested that a short-term cognitive-behavioral treatment program may be quite effective in alleviating symptoms of posttraumatic stress disorder (PTSD; Deblinger, McLeer, & Henry, 1990).

Also relevant to the treatment of adolescent victims of sexual abuse are the treatment programs focused on providing care to adult rape victims (Foa, Rothbaum, & Ette, 1993; Foa, Rothbaum, Riggs, & Murdock, 1991). Cognitive-behavioral rape treatment programs have largely been based on the strategies of stress-inoculation training and exposure treatment. Stress-inoculation training focuses on the development of coping skills to manage anxiety and fear. Exposure treatment involves reliving the trauma and confronting memories and feelings associated with the traumatic experience.

ADOLESCENT TREATMENT ISSUES

Although the treatment plan outlined in the following case study of an adolescent victim of sexual abuse draws from both treatment programs for child victims of sexual abuse (Deblinger et al., 1990) and programs for adult rape victims (Foa et al., 1993), these treatment programs had to be adapted to be appropriate for adolescents. For example, many of the rape-treatment programs for adults include highly focused exposure work that requires great willingness and cooperation on the part of the patient. Although adult rape victims may be able to tolerate the immediate discomfort of that exposure while focusing on the long-term goal of symptom relief, children and adolescents are less able to commit to such arduous work. Thus, the exposure work we recommend for adolescents is more gradual and less anxiety provoking at each step. This adaptation is necessary to keep the adolescent involved and committed to therapy.

Cognitive-behavioral treatment programs developed for younger children also had to be adapted for use with adolescents. The greatest adaptation has to do with the inclusion of a large treatment component focused on sexuality and dating. Although younger children may be provided with basic sex education, that treatment component is expanded significantly for adolescent patients. This increased attention to the issue is felt to be important with adolescents, because issues of sexuality and dating are of such great concern for most adolescents. Furthermore, problems with sexual adjustment that have been identified as a potential consequence of child sexual abuse (James & Meyerding, 1977; Meiselman, 1978) may first become apparent during adolescence. During this developmental period, most youth are consolidating their attitudes and beliefs regarding sexuality; thus, this seems to be a pivotal time to address these potential problems. It is important that significant efforts be made to understand the adolescent's thoughts and attitudes toward sexuality, to identify how those cognitions influence behaviors, to dispute any dysfunctional thoughts, and to facilitate communication between the adolescent and a nonoffending parent about sexual issues.

THEORETICAL MODEL

The treatment approach utilized in this case study is based on a cognitive-behavioral theoretical model. This model offers a social learning conceptualization of the development, maintenance and treatment of abuse-related symptoms in sexually abused children and adolescents. The development of PTSD and related symptoms exhibited by sexually abused adolescents can be explained by two-factor learning theory, incorporating both classical and operant conditioning principles (Lyons, 1987). When an adolescent experiences sexual abuse (unconditioned stimulus), he or she often instinctively experiences negative emotions such as fear, shame, or anger (unconditioned response). Classical conditioning occurs when other neutral cues, such as certain clothes, a particular tone of voice, darkness, and so on (conditioned stimuli), present at the time of the sexual abuse become conditioned such that they too elicit negative emotions (conditioned responses), even though these cues are inherently innocuous. For example, an adolescent who was sexually abused in the darkness when she was wearing certain clothes may naturally experience fear at the time of the abuse. Unfortunately, she may continue to experience fear whenever she is in the dark or wears that particular outfit, due to the association of these neutral cues with the actual abuse. Operant conditioning comes into play when the sexually abused adolescent learns to avoid abuse-related cues in order to reduce the likelihood of experiencing conditioned fear. Each time she avoids the darkness and/or wearing the particular clothes, she experiences a reduction in fear, and thus her avoidance behaviors are strengthened through negative reinforcement. As avoidance behaviors are repeatedly reinforced, they may generalize, for example, from not wearing the short skirt worn at the time of the abuse to not wearing attractive clothes in general. Abuse-related memories and thoughts may also become conditioned stimuli that automatically elicit negative emotions as a result of the processes just described. Thus, it is not surprising that many child sexual abuse victims frequently work hard to avoid thoughts and memories of their own abusive experiences. However, even though adolescents as well as their nonoffending parents often feel that avoidance is an effective coping response because it leads to immediate reductions in anxiety, there is evidence that such behavior leads to increased long-term symptomatology (Leitenberg, Greenwald, & Cado, 1992). The cognitive-behavioral intervention referred to as "gradual exposure," therefore, is designed to assist sexually abused children and adolescents to gradually confront these anxiety-provoking, inherently innocuous, reminders of their abusive experiences. Through gradual but repeated attempts to confront abuse-related cues, children and adolescents learn that thoughts, memories, and reminders of the abuse are not harmful and need not be avoided.

Sexual abuse also may significantly influence a child's or adolescent's developing cognitive view of the world. Child sexual abuse victims may be prone to developing cognitive distortions, particularly with respect to relationships, sexuality, and personal safety. For example, a child sexual abuse victim may begin to think about sex in negative terms beginning at a very young age (e.g., "Sex is dirty"; "I'm never going to have sex"). Such dysfunctional thoughts about sex may impair their ability to enjoy healthy sexuality during adolescence and adulthood. In fact, there is considerable evidence that survivors of child sexual abuse suffer a significantly higher rate of sexual dysfunctions as compared to individuals without such a history (James & Meyerding, 1977; Meiselman, 1978). The treatment model described, therefore, incorporates a component on cognitive coping skills that aims to assist adolescents and their parents in effectively identifying and disputing dysfunctional, abuse-related thoughts. Because one's cognitive view of the world is in a constant state of development, it can be influenced by new information and experiences. Thus, this treatment model includes a large educational component designed to provide clients with accurate information regarding sexual abuse, healthy sexuality, and body safety skills.

Finally, the cognitive-behavioral model helps to explain the role of nonoffending parents in the maintenance and treatment of their children's abuse-related difficulties. There is considerable evidence that child/adolescent coping responses are significantly influenced by the models of coping presented by their parents (Seligman, 1991). In addition, the reactions of nonoffending parents to their children's abuse-related behavior problems may significantly influence the improvement or exacerbation of such difficulties. For example, nonoffending parents may inadvertently reinforce abuse-related difficulties by responding with increased or inappropriate attention to problem behaviors. Thus, the proposed treatment aims to (1) teach parents effective behavioral skills for responding to their children's abuse-related disclosures and difficulties and (2) help parents to learn more effective coping skills for managing their own distress, so they can model these skills for their children.

CASE REPORT

Presenting Problem

Michelle is a 14-year-old adolescent who was referred for an evaluation and treatment by child protective services (CPS). She is an only child who has been living with both biological parents in a middle-class suburb. The report from the CPS worker indicated that Michelle had been sexually abused for years by her biological father. Michelle eventually disclosed this abuse to a girlfriend who subsequently told her own mother. This mother called the school guidance counselor, who then made the required report to CPS.

A CPS worker and an investigator from the county prosecutor's office interviewed Michelle at school, where she tearfully and somewhat reluctantly disclosed that her father began fondling her at around age 5 or 6. Over time, the abuse escalated to oral sexual activities and vaginal–

penile intercourse, which had been occurring approximately weekly over the past several years. Michelle reported that she attempted to tell her mother, but that her mother did not seem to understand and therefore did little to prevent the ongoing abuse.

Following the interview with Michelle, the CPS worker and the investigator went to Michelle's home and interviewed her mother. Michelle's mother, Harriett, responded to the information about Michelle's disclosure with shock and disbelief. She denied that Michelle had ever told her of the abuse. However, she was clear about her willingness to do whatever was required to keep Michelle at home and to protect her appropriately. Based on Michelle's mother's response, the CPS worker decided to leave Michelle in the home with her mother, contingent on Michelle's father leaving the home and having no contact with Michelle. The county prosecutor's office continued to pursue its investigation of these allegations.

Initial Evaluation

In this case, the evaluation process focused on identifying how Michelle and her mother were responding to this situation in order to direct the course of therapy most effectively. Michelle's mother was included as an important component in the evaluation and treatment process because research studies have documented that support from nonoffending adults is a critical factor in children's adjustment following an experience of child sexual abuse (Adams-Tucker, 1982; Conte & Schuerman, 1987; Everson et al., 1989; Friedrich, Beilke, & Urquiza, 1987). The evaluation was completed over the course of three assessment sessions.

Evaluation Sessions with Michelle's Mother

Michelle's mother, Harriett, was interviewed to obtain background information regarding family history; Michelle's medical, developmental, and school history; as well as Harriett's thoughts and feelings regarding the allegations of child sexual abuse. Harriett reported that her husband was the primary wage earner for the family and had been employed for years with the same company in a corporate management position. Harriett had recently accepted a position as an elementary school teacher.

Harriett reported that the family had moved a number of times due to her husband's job transfers. They had lived in their current home for approximately 2 years. Harriett described Michelle as a generally compliant and cooperative child who was a good student at school; however, she did acknowledge that Michelle had been exhibiting more anger recently. When asked about her perceptions of the allegations of child sexual abuse, Harriett reported that she was shocked and confused about the entire situation. She said that Michelle did not lie, so she must believe her; however, she said it is hard to imagine her husband as a sexual offender. She became tearful during the interview and said that she did not know what was going to happen to her family. She went on to say that she did not know how she and her daughter would manage, either financially or emotionally, without her husband.

Harriett was asked to complete psychological measures assessing her level of depression, anxiety, and her symptoms of trauma related to the allegations of sexual abuse. These measures indicated that she was experiencing a moderate level of depression, as well as intrusive and distressing thoughts about the sexual abuse. Although she attempted to avoid thinking about the abuse, those efforts did not alleviate her distress.

Evaluation Sessions with Michelle

During her initial evaluation session, Michelle was interviewed regarding her school history, friends, and other interests. Subsequently, she was asked what she understood about why her mother brought her to the session. In response to that question, Michelle began to disclose the sexual abuse. That interview proceeded as follows:

THERAPIST: Why do you think your Mom brought you here today?

MICHELLE: Because of what happened with my Dad.

THERAPIST: What happened with your Dad?

MICHELLE: He used to touch me and do things.

THERAPIST: Where did he touch you?

MICHELLE: On my private parts.

THERAPIST: Did this happen one time or more than one time?

MICHELLE: Lots of times.

THERAPIST: How old were you when it first happened?

MICHELLE: I'm not sure. I guess I was around 5 or maybe 6. (*At this point, Michelle's eyes were downcast and her voice was low. Although she seemed uncomfortable discussing the abuse, she was able to respond thoughtfully and appropriate to the questions she was asked.*)

THERAPIST: How often would it happen?

MICHELLE: Well, usually it happened when my Mom had to go to a meeting at night, usually on Tuesdays. Sometimes on the weekends, too, if she went out shopping, but usually I tried to go with her.

THERAPIST: Where were you when it happened?

MICHELLE: Usually my Dad would call me into his room and tell me to lie down on his bed, and he'd do it there. But sometimes he'd do it out in the family room.

THERAPIST: You said he would touch your private parts. What did he touch them with?

MICHELLE: His hands, mostly.

THERAPIST: And how were your clothes arranged when he would touch you?

MICHELLE: Usually he pulled my pants down or told me to do it.

THERAPIST: How about his clothes? How were they arranged?

MICHELLE: Sometimes they were on and sometimes they were off.

THERAPIST: Did he ever touch your private parts with anything besides his hands?

MICHELLE: Yeah.

THERAPIST: What else did he use to touch you?

MICHELLE: Well, he would make me have sex with him. (*At this point in the interview, Michelle began crying.*)

THERAPIST: Is this hard to talk about?

MICHELLE: (*Nodded head to indicate "yes."*)

THERAPIST: I'm really glad that you were able to talk about what has happened because that's the only way we can help you feel better. I'm sorry that it's so hard to talk about now, but the more we talk about it the easier it will get. Let's talk a little more and then we can do some other things together.

The therapist did not end the discussion of the abuse while Michelle was in distress out of concern that she would be encouraged to stop discussing the issue whenever she was feeling upset. Thus, the therapist attempted to provide her with support so that she could continue the discussion briefly. Then, they would end the discussion when Michelle was less distressed. Through that experience, Michelle would learn that she could tolerate discussions of the abuse.

THERAPIST: You said that your father would make you have sex with him. Different people mean different things when they say they "have sex." What do you mean by that?

MICHELLE: Well, he would put his private into mine.

THERAPIST: Did that happen one time or more than one time?

MICHELLE: Lots of times. Almost every Tuesday.

THERAPIST: Did he touch you in any other way?

MICHELLE: Yeah, sometimes he . . . well, he licked my private parts.

THERAPIST: Did he ever have you touch him?

MICHELLE: Well, sometimes he would make me rub his private.

Although Michelle was able to discuss the abuse clearly, with significant detail, she was obviously anxious and uncomfortable during the discussion. She became tearful at times and seemed eager to end the discussion. The therapist praised her for her courage in disclosing the abuse and for her willingness to discuss it in spite of the discomfort it precipitated.

Michelle also was asked to complete psychological measures designed to assess her level of depression, anxiety, as well as specific symptoms related to her sexual abuse experience. Those measures revealed a mild level of depression and significant trauma symptoms related to the sexual abuse experience. She was bothered by intrusive memories of the abuse, nightmares related to the abuse, and symptoms of physiological arousal when confronted with reminders of the abuse. She acknowledged that she tried to avoid thinking of the abuse as much as possible. The assessment also revealed that Michelle's perceptions of sexuality in general were quite negative.

Finally, to complete the evaluation process, both Michelle and her mother were interviewed individually regarding any emotional or behavioral symptoms that Michelle might be exhibiting that would warrant a psychiatric diagnosis. Based on their mutual reports, Michelle met the criteria for the diagnosis of PTSD as well as the diagnosis of dysthymic disorder according to the fourth edition of the *Diagnostic and Statistical Manual of Mental Disorders* (DSM-IV; American Psychiatric Association, 1994). Her symptoms of PTSD included recurrent, distressing memories and dreams of the abuse; attempts to avoid thoughts and reminders of the abuse; feelings of increased distance from other people; problems sleeping and concentrating; and increased anger and irritability. These symptoms had been increasingly evident for the last year. Her symptoms of dysthymic disorder included depressed mood; disturbance of sleep, concentration, and appetite; and feelings of hopelessness. These symptoms had been evident for approximately 2 years.

Treatment

Michelle's Treatment

In Michelle's initial therapy session, the evaluation findings were reviewed. Subsequently, the treatment plan was presented to Michelle. The therapist explained that she would be teaching Michelle what is known about sexual abuse because it is generally easier to cope with an experience we know something about and understand. The therapist further stated that she would be teaching Michelle some skills for dealing with her own upsetting feelings about the abuse. Michelle was receptive to those recommendations for therapy. However, when the therapist next explained that they would be talking a lot about Michelle's sexual abuse experience in order to help her become more comfortable with her thoughts and memories of the abuse, Michelle expressed some reluctance. The therapist was sympathetic and stated that those discussions would occur gradually, without ever requiring more of Michelle than she could handle. Yet, the therapist was firm in stating that discussing the abuse would be a very important part of Michelle's therapy because such discussions were the most effective way to alleviate the distress Michelle currently felt when confronted with reminders of the abuse. Finally, the therapist explained that they would be discussing sexuality in general, dating relationships, and abuse-response skills. Initially, Michelle and her mother would be seen separately, but eventually they would be seen in joint sessions. The purpose of the joint sessions would be to facilitate communication between Michelle and her mother regarding the sexual abuse, as well as sexuality in general. The therapist stated that her intention was to encourage open communication so that Michelle and her mother eventually could continue the therapeutic process on their own.

Thus, Michelle's treatment plan consisted of a number of different components. These components generally were provided to Michelle in the order in which they are presented below. However, there is considerable overlap between the therapy components, and during therapy attention sometimes shifted back and forth between the components.

Education Regarding Child Sexual Abuse

The first component of Michelle's treatment was to provide her with education regarding sexual abuse. The purpose of providing this education was to dispel any distressing misconceptions Michelle might have regarding sexual abuse. Additionally, these educational discussions would allow Michelle to become comfortable discussing sexual abuse in a somewhat general way before focusing specifically on the details of her personal experience.

The sexual abuse education was provided with the use of an information sheet that has been developed specifically for this purpose. The information sheet is written in question-and-answer form. It addresses issues such as what sexual abuse is, who is responsible for the abuse, why sexual abuse occurs, how many and what types of children are abused, how children feel when they have been abused, and why children find it difficult to tell about abuse.

In use with Michelle, the questions initially were posed to Michelle in order to obtain her responses to them before providing the "correct" response. In that way, it was possible to elicit some of Michelle's inaccurate and distressing perceptions, so that they could be corrected. For example, when asked how many children she believed were sexually abused, Michelle reported that she thought there were probably one or two in each state per year. She was surprised and somewhat relieved to learn that, in fact, as many as one in three girls are sexually abused before they reach adulthood. That information seemed to reduce her sense of isolation and feeling that she was different from everyone else. After eliciting Michelle's own thoughts, the answers provided on the information sheet were discussed with her.

Coping Skills Training

The next component of Michelle's treatment was to provide her with some skills for coping with the emotional distress generated by her memories of the abuse. This training in coping skills was provided before engaging Michelle in focused gradual exposure exercises, which were anticipated to be the most emotionally taxing aspect of her treatment. Two full sessions were devoted to coping skills training early in Michelle's therapy. These skills subsequently were used again and again throughout therapy.

The first coping technique offered to Michelle was cognitive coping skills training. This training is based on the work of Beck (1976) and Seligman (1991). To initiate that training, a triangle illustrating the connections between thoughts, emotions, and behaviors was presented to Michelle. Examples were provided to demonstrate how thoughts may influence our emotions. Once Michelle understood the concept, her own emotions regarding her sexual abuse experience were elicited. Subsequently, she was encouraged to identify the thoughts underlying these emotions. We then analyzed her thoughts for accuracy and effectiveness. Michelle was able to identify several thoughts that were heightening her level of emotional distress. For example, one of the emotions she initially identified was a feeling of guilt. The following conversation took place as she and the therapist discussed her feeling of guilt, and Michelle learned to identify and dispute the inaccurate thought that was underlying her guilt.

THERAPIST: When something reminds you about the abuse now, what feelings do you have?

MICHELLE: I guess I mostly just feel bad.

THERAPIST: I'm not sure what you mean by "bad." Can you tell me a little more about which kind of bad feeling you have?

MICHELLE: Well, I just feel guilty about all of it.

THERAPIST: Okay, remember how we said that sometimes our thoughts influence how we are feeling? Can you tell me what you are thinking about when you feel guilty?

MICHELLE: I just feel like I must have done something to make my Dad decide to do it to me.

THERAPIST: What do you think you might have done?

MICHELLE: I don't know. He used to always yell at me for the clothes I wore, so I guess maybe I wore the wrong kind of stuff.

THERAPIST: What do you think was wrong with your clothes?

MICHELLE: I don't really know. I dress like all the other kids, but he said I was trying to look too grown up, too sexy. He even said sometimes that I made him do it to me because of the way I walked around in really short shorts and miniskirts.

THERAPIST: You know, Michelle, the clothes you wore had nothing to do with your father sexually abusing you. He sexually abused you because he has a problem with touching, not because of anything you did or anything you wore. I think he said that you made him do it to give himself an excuse and make himself feel better about doing something he knew was wrong.

MICHELLE: Well, I've heard people say that a girl was asking to be raped when she was wearing really tight or short clothes. I was thinking that I sort of did the same thing.

THERAPIST: Michelle, you don't control another person by the clothes you wear, you can't *make them* do anything. Think about it for a minute. Does anyone make you behave a certain way by the clothes they wear?

MICHELLE: No, I guess not.

THERAPIST: I think when you blame yourself for making your father sexually abuse you, you are making yourself feel much worse than you need to feel. Let's try to think of a more accurate thought you could use to replace the thought that you are to blame for the abuse because of the clothes you wore. Can you think of how you could replace that?

MICHELLE: Well, I could say what you did, that my clothes cannot make anyone behave in any particular way, so I could not have made my dad abuse me.

THERAPIST: Exactly! Now we need to practice using that replacement thought to get rid of the inaccurate thought that is making you feel badly.

Subsequently, the therapist used role plays to give Michelle opportunities to practice using these cognitive coping skills. The therapist pretended to be a friend of Michelle's who was sexually abused and struggling with the same guilt-producing thought. Michelle was asked to help the friend feel better by disputing her friend's dysfunctional thought. In a similar manner, the therapist worked with Michelle to identify other inaccurate and ineffective thoughts that were causing Michelle distress. The therapist also used cognitive coping homework sheets to structure Michelle's practice of these skills at home. The sheets provide columns for the identification of distressing emotions, the thoughts underlying those emotions, and the replacement thoughts that the patient generates. Michelle completed those sheets and returned them the following session for review. Michelle responded very well to this training.

The therapist also offered Michelle some training in the effective expression of emotions. Michelle acknowledged that she was feeling angry more frequently and with greater intensity than she had previously. Much of that anger was being expressed inappropriately, in outbursts toward her mother. With the therapist's help, she was able to generate some ideas about how she could more effectively express her anger. She began keeping a journal of her feelings and found that writing them down was helpful to her. Additionally, the therapist discussed with Michelle how she could present issues to her mother in a way that allowed Michelle to express her opinion, but did not anger or alienate her mother. The therapist and Michelle did role plays to practice those skills for the appropriate expression of anger.

Gradual Exposure

The gradual exposure process followed a rough hierarchy of increasingly anxiety-provoking stimuli associated with the sexual abuse experience. In work with children and adolescents, this hierarchy is a fluid model, developed as the therapist works with the child. Although adults may be able to identify their level of anxiety associated with various stimuli at the beginning of treatment, children and adolescents are much less able and willing to do that. Thus, the therapist must construct and revise the hierarchy incorporating his or her own observations of the client's anxiety level, as well as the client's own report of his or her level of distress. In work with Michelle, the therapist began work with the premise that general discussions of sexual abuse would be least anxiety provoking for

Michelle. The next step up the hierarchy would be to include more personalized discussions of Michelle's experience, but not yet focusing on the specific acts of sexual abuse. Subsequently, discussions would move to the specific episodes of abuse, but focused on those which were least distressing. At the top of the hierarchy would be detailed discussions of the most upsetting episodes of the abuse. The final step in the hierarchy would be to share information about the specific episodes of abuse with her mother.

The gradual exposure process with Michelle actually had been initiated during the sessions focused on education regarding sexual abuse and cognitive coping skills because those sessions allowed Michelle to discuss the general topic of sexual abuse, which was not particularly anxiety provoking. Having completed that work successfully, by the fifth session, it was time to move up the hierarchy of anxiety-provoking topics to begin discussing Michelle's own experiences.

As is true for most adolescents, Michelle seemed to dread the therapy sessions in which she would discuss the specifics of her experience of sexual abuse. She expressed her belief that she felt better when she just didn't think about the abuse. She said that she wanted to forget all about it. The therapist explained that although Michelle might temporarily distract herself from thinking about the abuse, it was unlikely that she would ever truly forget it. Furthermore, the therapist said that, given the fact that Michelle could not truly forget the abuse, the best thing to do would be to find a way to help Michelle be more comfortable with her memories.

The therapist began this work by asking for details of Michelle's disclosure of sexual abuse because that was not likely to be terribly anxiety provoking. Indeed, Michelle was able to discuss her disclosures to her friend and to investigating professionals without significant distress. However, when she began to discuss her disclosure to her mother, she became much more upset. Michelle was able to label her emotions as sadness as well as anger toward her mother. Through further discussion, it became clear that Michelle was angry with her mother for not being as supportive as Michelle would have liked. Furthermore, she was angry because she believed that she had previously told her mother about what was happening, and her mother had not acted to help her. As that earlier attempt at disclosure was discussed, Michelle realized that she actually had not clarified for her mother what was happening. Indeed, during the earlier disclosure, Michelle, who was angry about being punished by her father, had only told her mother that her father hurt her sometimes. In spite of the lack of information her mother had, Michelle expected that her mother would be able to help her, or "fix things," as Michelle said. Eventually, Michelle was able to understand that her expectations of her mother were unrealistic, although understandable, because many children expect parents to be able to accomplish anything. Michelle was able to recognize that her mother really had no way of knowing that Michelle was referring to sexual abuse. The therapist made mental notes that clearly this was an issue to discuss in the joint sessions.

In the sixth session, the therapist asked Michelle to recall the last episode of sexual abuse she experienced with her father. Michelle became anxious during that discussion and was tearful at times. However, with the support and encouragement of the therapist, Michelle was able to provide details about where, when, and how her father had touched her during the last episode. The therapist provided praise and congratulations to Michelle for having been able to discuss those details. Michelle left that session tired, but proud of her accomplishment.

Future sessions proceeded in a similar manner, with the therapist focusing the discussions on specific episodes of sexual abuse. Because Michelle had experienced so many episodes of abuse, she had a tendency to group episodes together, saying, "It always happened that way." As much as possible, the therapist tried to focus Michelle on specific episodes by linking the episodes with events or occasions such as holidays, birthdays, or the first time her father touched her in a different way. By focusing on specific episodes, the therapist was attempting to have Michelle reexperience the emotions and sensations of that experience. By confronting those often distressing memories, Michelle learned that the memories themselves were not harmful and need not be feared or avoided. During this work, the therapist refrained from asking questions requiring affective or cognitive processing that might distract Michelle from her memories of the episode. Although such questions were important to help Michelle make sense of her experience both emotionally and intellectually, they were saved for different times when they would not interrupt the actual gradual exposure work. During the processing exercises, the therapist encouraged Michelle to use her cognitive coping skills to cope with any distressing thoughts or feelings generated by the gradual exposure work. Additionally, the therapist pointed out to Michelle how much progress Michelle was making; the conversations seemed to become easier over the course of several sessions.

After four sessions focused on this type of gradual exposure work, the therapist discussed with Michelle the possibility of writing a book about her sexual abuse experience, with the possibility of using this book (with identifying information altered) to help younger children cope with a sexual abuse experience. Michelle responded positively to this suggestion and seemed to feel proud of her ability to help younger children. Thus, the next several sessions were devoted to writing a book outlining her experience of sexual abuse and how she had coped with this experience successfully. Completing this project gave Michelle a real sense of pride and accomplishment.

Education about Dating, Sexuality, and Body Safety Skills

Education regarding these topics was actually begun during the sessions focused on gradual exposure. In that way, it was possible to shift the discussions away from the anxiety-provoking gradual exposure work from time to time. The primary purposes of this education were to (1) make sure Michelle had appropriate factual information regarding sexuality and abuse response skills, (2) explore Michelle's beliefs and feelings regarding sexuality and prevent any confusion between the sexual abuse and healthy adult sexuality, and (3) facilitate communication between Michelle and her mother regarding these topics. Much of this work occurred during the joint sessions with Michelle and her mother.

Parent Treatment

During the initial treatment session with Michelle's mother, the evaluation findings and the proposed treatment plan were reviewed. Harriett's individual treatment sessions would essentially follow the same model as Michelle's sessions, with the addition of a module focusing on parenting skills specific to abuse-related behavior problems. Harriett also was informed that current research in the field suggests that the most important factor influencing the recovery of sexually abused children may be the level of support that they receive from a nonoffending parent (Adams-Tucker, 1982; Conte & Schuerman, 1987; Everson et al., 1989; Friedrich et al., 1987). Thus, her active participation in treatment would be strongly encouraged. At this point, Harriett tearfully broke down, questioning if she could be there for Michelle when she was barely managing to hang on herself.

Harriett was reminded that the initial treatment module would focus on helping her cope with her own emotional reactions. The therapist emphasized that discovering that your child has been sexually abused is highly traumatic for any parent. Moreover, she would not be asked to participate in sessions with her daughter for quite some time. In fact, joint sessions would not be initiated until she was feeling much less distressed and coping more effectively. However, the importance of her modeling effective coping strategies for Michelle was emphasized because there is evidence linking maternal and child cognitive coping styles (Seligman et al., 1984).

Education Regarding Child Sexual Abuse

Individual parent sessions began with the provision of some basic information. Michelle's mother had many specific questions about the criminal investigation, as well as general questions about child sexual abuse. Although some information about the standard investigatory procedures was provided, Harriett was directed to the county Victim Witness Coordinator for specific information concerning the current standing and the legal steps that could be expected in this case. Harriett also was provided with information about the prevalence, etiology, and impact of child sexual abuse. Much like her daughter, she seemed astounded to learn about the high prevalence rate associated with child sexual abuse. Additional information was provided via a Child Sexual Abuse Fact Sheet specifically designed for parents. The therapist encouraged Harriett to read the information sheet carefully and write down any additional questions she might have for the next session.

Coping Skills Training

Many of the early treatment sessions with Harriett focused on her emotional state and coping efforts. She was encouraged to verbalize her feelings and thoughts, particularly those she had been keeping to herself. Although she believed it was unlikely, she acknowledged occasionally thinking that she and her husband would get back together after he served his time. She reported that he had contacted her several times asking for her forgiveness and for her commitment to the marriage. At those times, she experienced all kinds of feelings toward him, including sympathy and love, as well as frustration and anger. Michelle's mother seemed relieved to focus on her own needs and seemed comforted by the knowledge that other mothers expressed similar feelings and concerns. However, she was encouraged to postpone making any decisions about reunification until she and her daughter had completed counseling. It was suggested that with time and counseling she would likely begin to feel stronger and more independent, and then she could make these important decisions from a position of strength rather than weakness.

The cognitive coping model (Seligman, 1991) was presented, utilizing the triangle diagram described earlier. Michelle's mother seemed to quickly grasp the interrelationships between thoughts, feelings, and behaviors. She acknowledged that her thoughts and feelings seemed to fluctuate dramatically, especially when she was at home with too much time to dwell on the situation. She reported that her behavior, particularly toward her daughter, seemed to reflect these erratic thoughts and feelings. She was not always as supportive toward her daughter as she would have liked to be.

As the therapist helped Harriett explore the thoughts that seemed to underlie her most depressed moods, it became clear that some of these moods were driven by dysfunctional thoughts and misconceptions.

Harriett, for example, was convinced that she was responsible for her daughter's abuse because of her occasional failure to respond positively to her husband's sexual advances. In addition, she feared that her daughter's inappropriate introduction to sexual activity would lead her to take sexual risks that would ultimately expose her to the AIDS virus.

The cognitive coping model was used as follows to help Harriett learn to dispute the thoughts she and the therapist identified as dysfunctional:

THERAPIST: I'd like to focus some time on those thoughts that seem to make you feel really guilty and responsible for your daughter's abuse. Tell me about the last time you were feeling that way.

HARRIETT: Well, I guess it was just yesterday. I was talking to my husband's sister on the phone. She tries to be supportive, but sometimes I think she blames me for this whole thing.

THERAPIST: How did you feel after that phone call?

HARRIETT: Guilty, responsible, absolutely awful.

THERAPIST: What do you recall saying to yourself when you are feeling that way?

HARRIETT: Well, I couldn't stop thinking that if I hadn't turned down my husband's sexual advances maybe he wouldn't have abused our daughter. I keep trying to remember the times when I did say no. It wasn't that often. My husband didn't seem interested in having sex frequently, and when he was interested I was usually delighted. Still, I wonder if he went to Michelle on the occasions that I did say no.

THERAPIST: What else were you thinking?

HARRIETT: I was thinking that maybe if I stayed trimmer he would have been more attracted to me. I just wasn't a good enough wife and I obviously completely failed as a mother. Why wasn't I there to protect my daughter?

THERAPIST: It's no wonder you are feeling awful, those are pretty harsh things to say to yourself. I bet you would not say those things to a good friend who was in your situation. I want you to try something with me now. I'm going to pretend I'm you and repeat some of the thoughts you just shared. I want you to be my best friend and convince me with the facts you know about child sexual abuse and the knowledge you have about effective cognitive coping that some of my thoughts are hurtful and just plain wrong. Do you think you can do that?

HARRIETT: I'll try.

Michelle's mother responded well to the "best friend" role play. She helped "her best friend" to recognize that her husband gave few, if any, direct indications that he was dissatisfied with their sexual relationship. Moreover, she argued that there were alternatives to sexually abusing a child if he was, in fact, dissatisfied. He could have talked to her about it, suggested counseling, or even had an affair with an adult woman rather than hurting his daughter. Harriett also was able to point out all the things that made her a good wife and a very caring and supportive mother. Harriett was able to use the positive replacement thoughts she came up with to dispute her repetitive thoughts of guilt and responsibility for her daughter's abuse.

Unfortunately, Michelle's mother had more difficulty disputing her thoughts concerning her daughter's potential exposure to AIDS and other sexually transmitted diseases. She was very concerned that her daughter would become promiscuous as a result of the abuse. When pushed, however, she was able to acknowledge that although her daughter was interested in boys, there was no evidence that she was sexually active. In addition, Harriett was informed that young adults who have more knowledge about sex are much less likely to experience sexually transmitted diseases and teenage pregnancy. Thus, she was encouraged to dispute her anxiety-provoking thoughts with those facts. Harriett also was comforted by the fact that she and the therapist would provide sex education and information about healthy sexuality to Michelle together during joint sessions. Michelle's mother was asked to monitor and record her thoughts when she felt particularly depressed between sessions. She then used the cognitive coping homework sheets described earlier to dispute the dysfunctional thoughts while replacing them with more accurate and positive thoughts.

Parenting Skills

During the evaluation, Michelle's mother reported that her husband was the disciplinarian in the family. She wondered whether she could effectively discipline Michelle on her own. Harriett expressed particular concern about some of the changes she observed in Michelle's behavior in recent months. She explained that Michelle increasingly exhibited angry outbursts directed toward Harriett. In addition, she expressed concern that Michelle was becoming "boy crazy" and that she dressed in a way that made her appear "loose." She felt that these might be precursors to sexual promiscuity.

Harriett's most pressing concerns seemed to be related to Michelle's sexual behaviors. She was, therefore, asked to provide a great deal of information about the quality and pattern of these behaviors. Harriett reported that she had responded to the seemingly sudden emergence of Michelle's sexuality with increasing restrictiveness. Not surprisingly, Michelle constantly complained about what she believed was an unreasonably early curfew, as well as her mother's reluctance to allow her to spend time with boys, even in the most closely supervised circumstances. Michelle, in fact, seemed to interpret the restrictions as punishment for her role in the sexual abuse. While ultimately this mother–daughter conflict would be discussed in joint sessions, Michelle's mother was encouraged to begin the process by exploring what the current adolescent norms seemed to be by consulting other mothers, teachers, and guidance counselors concerning their expectations for curfews and opposite sex interactions. Harriett, however, was given encouragement to continue to monitor Michelle's behaviors by requiring that she provide her with basic information concerning who she was with, where she was, what she was doing, and when she would be home. She was informed that parents who consistently maintain this type of simple information about their children's whereabouts tend to have children with fewer psychosocial problems.

In conjunction with the parenting sessions, Michelle's mother was encouraged to begin reading *Parents and Adolescents Living Together* by Gerald Patterson and Mary Forgatch (1987). While this book is not specific to the treatment of sexually abused adolescents, it offers a highly effective step-by-step approach for managing conflicts experienced between parents and teenagers. In fact, it is often helpful for parents to recognize that abuse-related behavior problems can be treated with the same proven methods that are effective in treating other typical problems of adolescence. Although Michelle's angry outbursts may have been a manifestation of the irritability and anger that is frequently a symptom of PTSD, her mood swings also may simply have reflected an exaggeration of the normal struggle that adolescents often experience between their dependency needs and their healthy striving toward autonomy. Regardless of whether Michelle's angry moods were a direct result of the abuse or a response to her mother's increased restrictiveness, it was agreed that her outbursts were inappropriate and dysfunctional. Thus, Harriett was encouraged to begin examining the pattern of angry disputes between herself and her daughter by recording the antecedents and consequences associated with these problematic episodes. The therapist then assisted Harriett in developing an effective plan for eliminating the angry outbursts, which included praising Michelle for appropriate expressions of anger while providing effective consequences for inappropriate angry outbursts. Simultaneously, the therapist taught Michelle more effective means of expressing her anger.

Gradual Exposure

For this mother, gradual exposure to specific information concerning her daughter's abuse was tackled during the final module prior to the initiation of the joint sessions. Michelle's mother needed considerable time to cope with her own feelings and to regain her confidence as a parent. Because she was reluctant to deal with the specifics of her daughter's abuse early on, the initial gradual exposure sessions focused on the general circumstances of the abuse, as well as her husband's emotional abusiveness toward herself and Michelle. Ultimately, however, with the client's permission, the book Michelle had written about her experiences was gradually shared with her mother. Although Harriett's reactions to these materials were highly emotional at first, by the time she began the joint sessions, she had read her daughter's book several times. Ultimately, she was able to read this calmly, with pride and respect for her daughter's courage in enduring and writing about the abusive experiences. Michelle's detailed descriptions of how her father used her feelings of love and fear to encourage her cooperation in the sexual abuse seemed to enhance Harriett's empathy for her daughter and clarified her understanding of the dynamics of sexual abuse. Harriett had never discussed the sexual abuse directly with her daughter and was very anxious about doing so in joint sessions. She was therefore encouraged to participate in role plays in which the therapist played Michelle. Although Harriett's natural instincts during the role plays seemed to be excellent, she was given some guidance to provide more direct support to her daughter in the form of clear and specific praise for her accomplishments in therapy.

Joint Sessions

The joint sessions were viewed as a critical component of Michelle's treatment for a number of reasons. The joint sessions provided an opportunity for Michelle and her mother to communicate openly about the abuse and their feelings regarding Michelle's father. Through that communication, Michelle and her mother were able to clarify any misunderstandings or confusion that existed between them and eliminate any secrets that were hindering their relationship. The sessions also allowed Michelle's mother to move more into the therapist's role so that the therapeutic process could continue after the formal therapy sessions were over. The focuses of the joint sessions were as follows: discussions regarding sexuality and dating, abuse response skills, and gradual exposure.

The joint sessions were initiated in the 12th therapy session. Following individual meetings with both Michelle and her mother, a 20-minute joint session was held. Both Michelle and her mother were quite anxious about meeting jointly. Therefore, it was decided that the initial discussions would be about sex education in general because that was not likely to heighten their anxiety too much. A book regarding sexuality and dating, *Asking about Sex and Growing Up* (Cole, 1988), was presented to them. It was explained that the therapist wanted to encourage them to discuss issues regarding sexuality openly, and that this book would help initially to structure those discussions. During that session, Michelle and her mother took turns reading aloud from that book. They were asked to continue that process for homework. Although some of the information presented regarding anatomy and sexual functioning was a review of information Michelle had received in school, these discussions gave her opportunities to ask questions, express concerns, and openly talk with her mother about these issues.

A similar format was followed for the next several sessions, with a brief joint meeting following Michelle and Harriett's individual meetings. During these sessions, an attempt was made to explore Michelle's attitudes toward sexuality in general. Research studies have provided evidence that child sexual abuse may be associated with avoidance of sexual activity, as well as with promiscuity (James & Meyerding, 1977; Meiselman, 1978). It seems likely that cognitive factors may mediate the effects of the abusive experience, thus, perhaps in part, determining whether and how the abuse influences later sexual adjustment. Indeed, one study demonstrated that college students who had been sexually abused as children had more negative perceptions of their own sexuality because they were more likely to view themselves as promiscuous than were nonabused women (Fromuth, 1986). Thus, it was thought to be important to explore Michelle's attitudes toward sexuality, with the aim of disputing any inaccurate or dysfunctional beliefs about sexuality.

Through these discussions, it became clear that Michelle was somewhat confused about healthy sexuality. Although she was interested in boys and had some curiosity about the experience of a sexual relationship with a peer, she also was very anxious about such a relationship. She expressed a desire to get married eventually and have children, yet she described sex as being dirty. In contrast to her mother's concerns, Michelle was not yet sexually active. However, her confusion about sexuality put her at some risk for making poor decisions regarding her own sexuality.

The therapist worked with Harriett to help Michelle make a clear distinction between her own experience of sexual abuse and healthy sexuality between two adults who love and are committed to each other. Although Michelle's mother initially was concerned about describing adult sexuality too positively, for fear of encouraging Michelle to become sexually active, the therapist pointed out during Harriett's individual sessions that Michelle had to overcome a preexisting negative orientation toward sexuality. Harriett felt strongly that she did not want to encourage any premarital sexual activity. The therapist stated that it was appropriate that Harriett communicate her values to Michelle, but that it was also important that Michelle understand that within the right relationship, adult sexuality is a very positive thing. Thus, after completing this individual work, Harriett was able to communicate to Michelle during joint sessions that sexuality within a marriage is healthy and positive, while emphasizing that the decision to enter into a sexual relationship is a serious decision that should be made with great thought and care.

The discussions during the joint sessions moved on to the topic of dating and what Michelle and her mother felt were appropriate levels of physical affection in dating relationships. As Michelle began to see that her mother could tolerate those discussions without becoming upset, she became increasingly open. Eventually the conversations turned to the issue of contraceptive methods. Harriett was able to provide Michelle with education regarding contraceptive methods. She acknowledged to Michelle that ultimately it was her decision as to when she became involved in a sexual relationship. Harriett indicated to Michelle that although it was her strong belief that Michelle should wait until marriage to be sexually active (and Harriett provided sound reasons for her belief), Harriett would prefer to know if Michelle did decide to enter a sexual relationship, so that Harriett could help her obtain appropriate contraceptives.

The conversations regarding dating naturally led to discussions of abuse response skills, focusing on aggressive sexual encounters in dating situations, as well as episodes of sexual abuse by adult perpetrators. Michelle was taught about body ownership, her absolute right to say "no" in any situation, the fact that she owed no one anything in terms of sexual touches, and the need to get away and tell someone about inappropriate sexual touches.

Because recent research suggests that modeling and role plays seem to be more effective than didactic instruction in encouraging the use of abuse response skills (Wurtle & Miller-Perrin, 1992), Michelle and her mother were asked to role play potentially abusive encounters. Like many adolescents in therapy, Michelle initially balked at the idea of participating in "silly" role plays of such unlikely encounters. The therapist responded with the staggering statistics on date rape and participated in a role play with Michelle's mother of a scenario that seemed relevant to Michelle. Ultimately, Michelle joined in on the role plays, first by critiquing her mother's performance and then by outperforming her. Following each role play, Michelle and Harriett were encouraged to share the feelings and thoughts they experienced during each simulated dating interaction. This gave the therapist an opportunity to help Michelle and her mother dispute any dysfunctional or inaccurate thoughts they may have experienced in reaction to the role play (e.g., "Maybe my date touched me like that because he could tell I had been touched before, when my Dad abused me").

After four joint sessions devoted to the topics just described, the therapist refocused Michelle and her mother on more formal gradual exposure work. This work began by having Michelle read her book regarding her experience to her mother during a joint session. Michelle's mother responded with praise and admiration for Michelle's courage and hard work. Then she began asking Michelle further questions about her experience. This was a pivotal session because it allowed Michelle to see that her mother could tolerate this discussion and, in fact, would be supportive of Michelle. Both Michelle and her mother seemed greatly relieved and proud of themselves at the end of this session.

As sessions progressed, the individual sessions were shortened, allowing more time in the joint sessions. Michelle and her mother continued to discuss specific episodes of the sexual abuse. Another important topic was Michelle's early attempt at disclosure to her mother and her feelings regarding her mother's lack of helpful response at that time. Michelle was able to express her anger toward her mother, and her mother explained her lack of understanding at the time and apologized for not being able to support Michelle then. The final critical issue for discussion concerned their feelings toward Michelle's father and their thoughts regarding future relationships with him. Michelle's mother was honest in expressing her conflicted feelings, but assured Michelle that she would never force Michelle to live with her father again. Michelle stated unequivocally that she did not want to see or talk to her father at that time and was uncertain whether she would ever want any contact with him.

By the 20th session, the therapist, Harriett, and Michelle were beginning to talk about the timing of termination. The therapist, therefore, asked Michelle and her mother to repeat some of the psychological measures they initially completed, so that their progress could be evaluated. For both Michelle and her mother, their PTSD symptoms were significantly reduced. Michelle's symptoms of depression also were significantly diminished. Her mother's level of depression was still above normal, but lower than it had been initially. The therapist encouraged Harriett to pursue individual counseling for herself if her depression became problematic; however, Harriett was not interested in that possibility at the time. Based upon the reevaluation, as well as the clients' sense of progress, it was decided to taper down the therapy process by spreading out the final sessions. The 21st session was scheduled for 2 weeks later, and the final session for 1 month after that.

Those last two sessions consisted largely of joint meetings with Harriett and Michelle in which their work in therapy was reviewed, their progress was emphasized, and suggestions were made for continuing the therapeutic work at home. For example, they were encouraged to continue discussing sexuality and dating issues, as well as the sexual abuse. Finally, they were encouraged to contact the therapist if at any point they felt it might be useful to come back for further sessions, for example, if they were experiencing stress regarding the legal proceedings.

SUMMARY

The treatment model presented in this chapter can be tailored to address the wide range of difficulties presented by adolescent survivors of sexual abuse. However, to effectively apply the intervention described, the clinician should be skilled in the application of cognitive-behavioral interventions and knowledgeable in the area of child sexual abuse. Cognitive-behavioral interventions are highly flexible and should be chosen and focused, based on the individual needs of the particular child and family. For example, in some cases, behavior-management training may not be necessary. However, in other cases, the parent may benefit a great deal from the parenting skills training. It should be noted, however, that we consider gradual exposure to be an essential therapy component in cases of child sexual abuse. Interestingly, however, this is the aspect of treatment that tends to be met with the greatest resistance. Most adolescents and parents enter therapy with the expectations that counseling will help them feel better. It is therefore quite disconcerting to some clients that the proposed gradual exposure exercises may cause some degree of discomfort. For some clients, this is simply unacceptable, and they may choose a less directive approach for treatment for themselves and their families. However, therapists can usually overcome such natural resistance by establishing a healthy and collaborative therapeutic relationship and explaining the treatment rationale in clear, sensitive, and developmentally appropriate terms to both parents and children.

An additional strength of this model is the heavy emphasis on involving the nonoffending parent as a therapeutic agent. However, it is important to consider referral to another individual therapist if the parent seems to be grappling with other personal and/or marital issues that require greater focus and attention. It is our contention that involving a nonoffending parent in the treatment of their child can extend the benefits of therapy beyond the therapy hour, as well as beyond the point of termination. In fact, there was no question in the case study described that Michelle's mother contributed dramatically to her daughter's recovery and positive adjustment.

Finally, it should be noted that although this case study describes a short-term treatment approach, child sexual abuse cases can be highly complex and may require follow-up counseling periodically. It is therefore important to offer parents and children anticipatory guidance to assist them in identifying when additional counseling might be needed.

Parents and children may need additional assistance in coping with their anxiety associated with the case going to court and/or when family reunification issues are being considered and/or discussed. Although the initial course of therapy is intended to provide clients with the necessary skills for coping with future stressors on their own, families are often comforted to know that therapeutic resources are available if needed.

REFERENCES

Adams-Tucker, C. (1982). Proximate effects of sexual abuse in childhood: A report on 28 children. *American Journal of Psychiatry, 139*, 1252–1256.

American Psychiatric Association. (1994). *Diagnostic and statistical manual of mental disorders* (4th ed.). Washington, DC: Author.

Anderson, L. S. (1981). Notes on the linkage between the sexually abused child and the suicidal adolescent. *Journal of Adolescence, 4*, 157–162.

Beck, A. (1976). *Cognitive therapy and the emotional disorders*. New York: International Universities Press.

Briere, J., & Runtz, N. (1988). Symptomatology associated with childhood sexual victimization in a nonclinical adult sample. *Child Abuse and Neglect, 12*, 51–59.

Cole, J. (1988). *Asking about sex and growing up*. New York: Beech Tree Books.

Conte, J. R., & Schuerman, J. (1987). Factors associated with an increased impact of child sexual abuse. *Child Abuse and Neglect, 11*, 201–211.

Deblinger, E., McLeer, S. V., & Henry, D. (1990). Cognitive behavioral treatment for sexually abused children suffering post traumatic stress: Preliminary findings. *Journal of the American Academy of Child and Adolescent Psychiatry, 29*, 747–752.

Deblinger, E., Taub, B., Schaal, A., Lippmann, J., & Stauffer, L. (1994). *Psychosocial correlates of symptomatology in sexually abused children*. Unpublished manuscript, University of Medicine and Dentistry of NJ School of Osteopathic Medicine.

Dembo, R., Dertke, M., LaVoie, L., Borders, S. Washburn, M., & Schmeidler, J. (1987). Physical abuse, sexual victimization and illicit drug use: A structural analysis among high risk adolescents. *Journal of Adolescence, 10*, 13–33.

Everson, M. D., Hunter, W. M., Runyon, D. K., Edelson, G. A., & Coulter, M. L. (1989). Maternal support following disclosure of incest. *American Journal of Orthopsychiatry, 59*(2), 197–207.

Finkelhor, D. (1987). The sexual abuse of children: Current research reviewed. *Psychiatric Annals: Journal of Continuing Psychiatric Education, 17*, 233–241.

Finkelhor, D. (1979). *Sexually victimized children.* New York: Free Press.

Finkelhor, D., Hotaling, G., Lewis, I., & Smith, C. (1990). Sexual abuse in a national survey of men and women: Prevalence, characteristics, and risk factors. *Child Abuse and Neglect, 14,* 19–28.

Foa, E., Rothbaum, B. O., & Ette, G. S. (1993). Treatment of rape victims. *Journal of Interpersonal Violence, 8,* 156–276.

Foa, E., Rothbaum, B. O., Riggs, D. S., & Murdock, T. B. (1991). Treatment of PTSD in rape victims: A comparison between cognitive-behavioral procedures and counseling. *Journal of Consulting and Clinical Psychology, 59,* 715–723.

Friedrich, W. N., Beilke, R. L., & Urquiza, A. J. (1987). Children from sexually abusive families: A behavioral comparison. *Journal of Interpersonal Violence, 2,* 391–402.

Fromuth, M. E. (1986). The relationship of childhood sexual abuse with later psychological and sexual adjustment in a sample of college women. *Child Abuse and Neglect, 10,* 5–15.

James, J., & Meyerding, J. (1977). Early sexual experience as a factor in prostitution. *Archives of Sexual Behavior 7,* 31–42.

Leitenberg, H., Greenwald, E., & Cado, S. (1992). A retrospective study of long-term methods of coping with having been sexually abused during childhood. *Child Abuse and Neglect, 16,* 399–407.

Lyons, J. A. (1987). Post-traumatic stress disorder in children and adolescents: A review of the literature. *Developmental and Behavioral Pediatrics, A*(6), 349–356.

Mannarino, A., & Cohen, J. A. (1993). *The psychological impact of child sexual abuse* (Final report for the National Center on Child Abuse and Neglect). Washington, DC: U.S. Department of Health and Human Services.

McLeer, S. V., Deblinger, E., Atkins, M. S., Foa, E. B., & Ralphe, D. L. (1988). Post-traumatic stress disorder in sexually abused children. *Journal of the American Academy of Child and Adolescent Psychiatry, 27,* 650–654.

Meiselman, K. C. (1978). *Incest: A psychological study of causes and effects with treatment recommendations.* San Francisco: Jossey-Bass.

Patterson, G., & Forgatch, M. (1987). *Parents and adolescents living together: Part 1. The basics.* Eugene, OR: Castalia.

Peters, S. D. (1988). Child sexual abuse and later psychological problems. In G. E. Wyatt & G. J. Powell (Eds.), *Lasting effects of child sexual abuse* (pp. 101–117). Newbury Park, CA: Sage.

Runyon, D. K., Hunter, W. M., & Everson, M. D. (1992). *Maternal support for child victims of sexual abuse: Determinants and implications* (Final report for the National Center for Child Abuse and Neglect). Washington, DC: U.S. Department of Health and Human Services.

Russell, D. (1986). *The secret trauma: Incest in the lives of girls and women.* New York: Basic Books.

Sansonnet-Hayden, H., Haley, G., Marriage, K., & Fine, S. (1987). Sexual abuse and psychopathology in hospitalized adolescents. *American Academy of Child and Adolescent Psychiatry, 26,* 753–757.

Seligman, M. (1991). *Learned optimism.* New York: Knopf.

Seligman, M., Peterson, C., Kaslow, N. J., Tanenbaum, R. L., Alloy, L. B., & Abramson, L. (1984). Attributional style and depressive symptoms among children. *Journal of Abnormal Psychology, 93,* 235–238.

Tufts New England Medical Center. (1984). *Sexually exploited children: Service and research project* (Final Report for the Office of Juvenile Justice and Delinquency Prevention). Washington, DC: U.S. Department of Justice.

Wurtle, S. K., & Miller-Perrin, C. L. (1992). *Preventing child sexual abuse: Sharing the responsibility.* Lincoln: University of Nebraska Press.

11

Treatment of Adolescent Eating Disorders

Wayne A. Bowers
Kay Evans
Laura Van Cleve

C ognitive therapy and cognitive-behavioral interventions for treating behavioral and emotional disorders among adult psychiatric and medical patients have attracted a great deal of interest during recent years. They have consistently been found effective in treating depression (Beck, Rush, Shaw, & Emery, 1979; Hollon, Shelton, & Davis, 1993), anxiety disorders (Chambless & Gillis, 1993), and eating disorders (Wilson & Fairburn, 1993). Cognitive models have been developed and therapeutic techniques have been derived from them to treat a wide variety of interpersonal problems (Freeman & Dattilio, 1992). Until recently, however, cognitive therapy with children and adolescents has received little attention (Kendall, 1985; Kendall & Braswell, 1985; Reinecke, 1992; Reynolds & Coates, 1986; Wilkes & Rush, 1988; Zarb, 1992).

The utility of cognitive therapy for treating eating disorders among adults, including bulimia nervosa and anorexia nervosa, has been widely studied (Wilson & Fairburn, 1993; Vitousek, 1991). Cognitive interventions, whether introduced in individual or group formats, have consistently yielded positive results for treating bulimia nervosa (Agras, Schneider, Arnow, Raeburn, & Telch 1989; Wilson & Fairburn, 1993; Wilson, Rossiter, Kleifield, & Lindholm, 1986). Focused, cognitive-behavioral treatment manuals have been developed that have standardized the treatment of this disorder (Agras et al., 1989; Fairburn & Cooper, 1989). Much less is known, however, about the effectiveness of cognitive therapy for treating anorexia nervosa (Bowers & Andersen, 1994; Vitousek, 1991). This disorder appears, in many ways, to be more complex and unyield-

227

ing. Adolescents with anorexia nervosa often do not believe that they have a problem, and frequently employ the food restriction as a means of controlling their environment or parents. The beliefs and attitudes about dieting and food held by teenagers with anorexia are typically ego-syntonic. They view attempts to change how they eat or what they weigh as reflecting others' jealousy or attempts to control them. Adding to the difficulty is the fact that treatment is often involuntary. Initial therapeutic interventions, as such, are typically met with little cooperation from the adolescent. As a consequence, treatment is usually longer in duration and may necessitate inpatient as well as outpatient management.

COGNITIVE THERAPY OF EATING DISORDERS

Bulimia Nervosa

Fairburn (1985) developed a cognitive model for conceptualizing and treating bulimia nervosa. He proposed that the extreme dieting, vomiting, and laxative abuse; preoccupation with food and eating; sensitivity to changes in shape and weight; as well as the frequent weighing, or avoidance of weighing that characterize this condition, stem from biased perceptions, cognitive distortions, and maladaptive beliefs or coping patterns that have been learned earlier in life. The cognitive model suggests that bulimic patients believe their shape and weight are of such fundamental importance that both must be kept under strict control. Binge eating can be understood as representing a secondary response to extreme dietary restraint. Rather than focusing solely on patients' desires to be thin, an emphasis is placed upon understanding the specific beliefs, expectations, and attitudes that maintain patients' attempts to control their weight and regulate their food intake. Beliefs and values, as such, are postulated to play a primary role in the maintenance of the condition. From this perspective, recovery from the disorder requires a change in the underlying beliefs and cognitive processes (Fairburn, 1983). Cognitive models of bulimia nervosa emphasize the importance of cognitive factors in the etiology and maintenance of the disorder, and treatment programs derived from these models are designed to produce such cognitive change. Cognitive therapy for bulimia nervosa is directed at changing underlying dysfunctional beliefs and values concerning food, body shape, and weight (Cooper & Fairburn, 1984).

Cognitive approaches for treating bulimia nervosa have been widely used in North America, Europe, and Australia (Agras et al., 1989; Fairburn & Cooper, 1989; Wilson & Fairburn, 1993; Wilson et al., 1986). Research suggests that these approaches can be effective in treating this disorder. As such, they have been recommended by some as the treatment of choice for bulimia nervosa (Wilson & Fairburn, 1993). Positive results have been obtained whether the therapy is delivered in small groups or through individual sessions. Therapy typically is brief—usually 20 sessions or less. Fairburn and Cooper (1989), for example, have developed a standardized cognitive-behavioral program for treating bulimia nervosa on an outpatient basis. Their program consists of 19 individual sessions over a 20-week period. As with cognitive therapy of other clinical disorders, their approach is problem oriented, focuses on the present and the future, and emphasizes the development of a strong, collaborative patient–therapist relationship. Treatment occurs in three phases, with the first phase focusing on educating patients about the disorder and socializing them to the cognitive model. During this "educational" portion of the treatment program, patients come to appreciate the role of beliefs and attitudes in the maintenance and modification of the disorder, as well as how the problem affects their current life. Information about food, nutrition, and weight regulation are provided. It is emphasized how these elements are crucial to the elimination of the disorder.

Behavioral interventions directed toward helping patients to monitor their eating habits also are introduced during the first phase of the treatment. These interventions are designed to identify "triggers" or cues for bingeing or purging, reduce the frequency of binge eating episodes, and normalize eating behaviors. A return to normal eating habits is a primary goal of this phase. As with the treatment of other disorders, cognitive therapies for bulimia place an emphasis on behavioral interventions at the outset of the treatment. Cognitive interventions come to play an increasingly important role as the therapy progresses.

The second phase of treatment is characterized by an increasing focus on the patients' beliefs, attitudes, and expectations. The primary goals are to reduce dietary restraint and to develop coping skills related to binge eating. These interventions are based on Beck's (1976; Beck et al., 1979) cognitive therapy of depression. Patients are taught to identify and examine negative automatic thoughts and distorted perceptions regarding weight, shape, and eating. Patients are encouraged to "collect evidence" for and against the validity of their specific beliefs, and to conduct behavioral experiments to evaluate the utility and validity of their dysfunctional thoughts and faulty assumptions.

The final stage of treatment focuses on relapse prevention. Explicit attempts are made to develop skills and strategies that will ensure the maintenance of therapeutic gains. This is accomplished by practicing the cognitive and behavioral coping skills that were developed earlier in treatment, and by anticipating situations or events that may place individuals at risk for relapse. It is postulated that recovery from bulimia nervosa is related to changes in attitudes, beliefs, and negative automatic thoughts that are associated with the disorder.

Anorexia Nervosa

The clinical features of anorexia nervosa commonly include excessive weight loss that results from restrictive eating, often accompanied by compulsive exercise. These difficulties are often complicated by binge eating, self-induced vomiting, or laxative abuse. Weight loss is driven by a profound fear of gaining weight or an overvalued desire to be thin. The weight loss may become life threatening. Distortion of body size and shape, cessation of menstrual cycle, and social withdrawal are common features of the disorder. The fourth edition of the *Diagnostic and Statistical Manual of Mental Disorders* (DSM-IV; American Psychiatric Association, 1994) criteria for this disorder are little changed from the revised third edition (DSM-III-R). Several subtypes have, however, been described. Specific criteria are presented in Table 11.1.

Other psychiatric and medical problems complicate the treatment of this disorder. Common comorbid disorders include major depression, obsessive–compulsive disorder, anxiety disorders, and personality difficulties. Suicidal ideations and severe binge- or purge-related symptoms also confound treatment. Moreover, significant medical complications often develop as a consequence of starvation and rapid weight loss.

TABLE 11.1. Diagnostic Criteria for Anorexia Nervosa

A. Refusal to maintain body weight at or above a minimally normal weight for age and height (e.g., weight loss leading to maintenance of body weight less then 85% of that expected; or failure to make expected weight gain during a period of growth leading to body weight less that 85% of that expected).

B. Intense fear of gaining weight or becoming fat, even though underweight.

C. Disturbance in the way one's body weight or shape is experienced, undue influence of body weight or shape on self-evaluation, or denial of the seriousness of the current low body weight.

D. In postmenarcheal females, amenorrhea, i.e., the absence of at least three consecutive menstrual cycles. (A woman is considered to have amenorrhea if her periods occur only following hormone, e.g., estrogen, administration.)

Specify type:

Restricting Type: during the current episode of Anorexia Nervosa, the person has not regularly engaged in binge-eating or purging behavior (i.e., self-induced vomiting or the misuse of laxatives, diuretics, or enemas).

Binge-Eating/Purging Type: during the current episode of Anorexia Nervosa, the person has regularly engaged in binge-eating or purging behavior (i.e., self-induced vomiting or the misuse of laxatives, diuretics, or enemas).

Note. From American Psychiatric Association (1994, pp. 544–545). Copyright 1994 by the American Psychiatric Association. Reprinted by permission.

The cognitive-behavioral model of anorexia nervosa is developmentally based and emphasizes the interaction of cognitive, affective, and behavioral variables in the etiology and maintenance of the disorder (Garfinkel & Garner, 1982; Garner, 1985; Garner & Bemis, 1982). The model incorporates both intrapsychic and social factors in conceptualizing the disorder, and acknowledges the importance of dynamic and biological factors in the etiology of the syndrome. The model postulates that specific tacit beliefs (known as "schemas") regarding the self, the world, and the future are consolidated over the course of development and create a vulnerability to anorexia nervosa. Investigators from a range of theoretical orientations concur that, at some point in the development of anorexia, causal factors converge in facilitating the emergence of the patient's belief that "It is absolutely essential that I be thin." This fixed idea typically is accompanied by a set of beliefs, attitudes, and assumptions about the meaning of body weight, shape, and personal competence or efficacy.

The cognitive model views anorexia nervosa as a final common pathway of a multiple series of events or experiences, beginning with a vulnerable adolescent arriving at the idea that weight loss will alleviate distress and dysphoria (Bowers & Andersen, 1994). Dieting and becoming thin come to serve as a means for individuals to exercise control over their environment. Additionally, thinness is often reinforced by the compliments of others and an enjoyable sense of success as individuals continue to lose weight. This weight loss ultimately results, however, in increased isolation from friends, family, and social interaction. This, in turn, can contribute to an increase in the distorted cognitions and maladaptive behaviors related to anorexia nervosa. Research supporting this model, although slow to develop, has been discussed by Garner and Bemis (1985) and Garner (1993).

Bruch (1962, 1985) noted that a range of cognitive factors may play a role in the development and maintenance of anorexia nervosa. She postulated that pathological cognitions centering on weight, shape, and a sense of autonomy may serve as contributing factors in the development of this disorder. Using principles of cognitive therapy originally developed by Beck (1976; Beck et al., 1979), Garner and Bemis (1982, 1985) extended Bruch's model by integrating cognitive strategies into a "multidimensional" treatment of anorexia nervosa. Following cognitive models originally developed for the treatment of depression, they proposed that cognitive interventions might be employed in addressing the specific thinking patterns found to characterize anorexia nervosa.

Central to cognitive models of emotional and behavioral disorders are "systematic errors in thinking" or faulty information processing (Beck, 1976). Garner and Bemis (1982) suggested that dysfunctional cognitive processes such as these may play an important role in the development and maintenance of anorexia nervosa. Cognitive errors associated with emotional disorders include arbitrary inference, selective abstraction, overgeneralization, magnification and minimization, personalization, and dichotomous thinking. They suggest that these disturbances in information processing provide ongoing support for relentless dieting, extreme ideas about food or body size, and overall negative self-perceptions. As in the treatment of depression, the therapist's ability to teach the patient to challenge and reframe these faulty assumptions becomes a focal point for cognitive therapy of eating disorders.

Although a great deal of work has been completed on the systematic use of cognitive therapy for treating bulimia nervosa, little research has been published on its use in treating anorexia (Bowers & Andersen, 1994; Wilson & Fairburn, 1993). This may be due to the more complex nature of the disorder and the emphasis placed by clinicians on the use of behavioral methods to assist in weight restoration. Complicating research in this area is the fact that the treatment of anorexia can be lengthy, and that patients with this disorder are often unmotivated to change their eating, weight, beliefs, and behaviors (Vitousek, 1991).

Nonetheless, the use of cognitive therapy fits well into an integrated treatment program (Bowers & Andersen, 1994; Wilson & Fairburn, 1993), especially while the patient with anorexia nervosa is hospitalized. Garner and Bemis (1985) have provided descriptions of how cognitive therapy can address the distorted cognitions and faulty assumptions that accompany anorexia nervosa, and Bowers (1993) has made suggestions on how these methods can be applied in inpatient settings.

When working with patients with anorexia nervosa, it is very important to assess the degree of cognitive impairment. With more severely impaired individuals, initial sessions may emphasize the use of behavioral interventions. Interventions such as activity scheduling, mastery and pleasure scheduling, and graded task assignments can increase patients' understanding of how their behavior contributes to and maintains their disorder. A reasonable early behavioral intervention, for example, might be a graded task assignment of eating a full meal. It is important to keep in mind that behavioral interventions set the stage for cognitive methods to address the thoughts and feelings surrounding food, weight, body image, and control over their environment.

Adaptations to Beck's cognitive model (Beck et al., 1979) are necessary when working with individuals with eating disorders. Garner and Bemis (1985) recommend that several specific features of eating disorders be addressed, including (1) the relative intractability of the disorder (including reluctance to enter into treatment), (2) interaction between physical and psychological elements, (3) prominence of deficits in self-concept related to the patient's lack of self-esteem and awareness of (and confidence in) internal states, (4) idiosyncratic beliefs related to food and weight, and (5) the patient's perception of the desirability of retaining certain focal symptoms (e.g., low body weight, control over others). Several of the interventions described by Beck (1976) can be utilized to address these features, including (1) monitoring thoughts and feelings and/or increasing the individual's awareness of thoughts; (2) becoming aware of and understanding the interaction among thoughts, feelings, and dysfunctional behaviors; (3) identifying negative automatic thoughts and challenging these cognitions; (4) increasing the patient's ability to accept more realistic and appropriate interpretations; and (5) identifying and modifying underlying schemas that maintain the disorder.

DEVELOPMENTAL CONSIDERATIONS

Evidence for the effectiveness of cognitive and behavioral interventions for treating anorexia and bulimia is derived almost exclusively from work with adult populations. Treatment of adolescents and children who have eating disorders has not been well researched. Studies suggest that family therapy can be useful in treating children and adolescents with eating disorders (Crisp et al., 1991; Dare, Eisler, Russell, & Szmukler, 1990; Hall, 1987). There is no reason to believe, however, that cognitive and behavioral interventions employed in treating adults might not also be useful in the treatment of adolescents and, possibly, children.

Cognitive therapy with adults emphasizes the importance of attending to an individual's cognitive contents—that is, their beliefs, attitudes, expectations, memories, goals, and attributions—and on assisting patients to change maladaptive or distorted perceptions and beliefs. The same is true for cognitive therapy with children and adolescents. Cognitive and behavioral techniques are employed to teach children to become more aware of their perceptions of specific events, and to aid them in monitoring and reevaluating recurrent maladaptive patterns of thinking. Cognitive problem-solving skills are taught, and behavioral coping strategies for approaching stressful or problematic situations are practiced. The ultimate goal is the development of alternative ways of looking at day-to-day events, as well as the consolidation of more effective ways of coping with potentially distressing problems that arise (Finch, Nelson, & Ott, 1993; Kendall, 1991; Reinecke, 1992).

In addition to developing alternative ways of interpreting events and coping with day-to-day problems, cognitive therapy attempts to change tacit beliefs or schemas (Freeman, 1993). Schemas are established during childhood and serve as templates for individuals' attributions and perceptions. They are believed, as such, to serve an organizing function for individuals' understanding of themselves and their world, and function to guide their behavior (Guidano, 1991; Safran, 1988). Schemas are strongly held and serve as a foundation for the ways individuals define themselves and their relationships with others. As in the treatment of depression and personality disorders, tacit beliefs are believed to play a central role in both the development and treatment of eating disorders. As Vitousek and Ewald (1993) stated, "Anorexia nervosa is fundamentally both a cognitive disorder and a disorder of the self. . . . The lives of anorexics are progressively dominated by a central, overdetermined idea about one aspect of the self: that one's self worth is represented in—or at least delimited by—the weight and shape of the body" (p. 224).

Tacit beliefs held by individuals with anorexia commonly include the perception that they are "flawed," "unworthy," and "ineffective." They typically manifest a poorly developed sense of personal identity and maintain rigid, perfectionistic standards. Weight loss, as a consequence, can serve as a source of pride and provides the individual with a sense of accomplishment, control, and uniqueness. It is postulated that the existence of tacit beliefs relating to self-concept, personal efficacy, weight, and physical appearance will lead individuals with anorexia to inaccurately process information about events in their lives. They come to view themselves and their world through the lens of meanings attached to weight. The existence of maladaptive schemas related to weight is associated with a range of distorted cognitive processes, including selective attention or perception, biased memory of events, overactivation of beliefs, and an attending to illusory correlations or confirmatory biases. Moreover, it is postulated that the maladaptive beliefs, attitudes, and expectations held by individuals with anorexia serve an adaptive function for them, providing them with a sense of identity, self-worth, and personal control. It is neccessary, as such, when treating individuals with eating disorders, to adopt a phenomenological stance; that is, it is important to make sense of the meanings they have attached to their behavior and the adaptive functions that weight loss serves for them. Change in dysfunctional schemas, as such, is believed to play a central role in the maintenance of therapeutic gains. Because these dysfunctional, tacit beliefs about the self are not believed to be fully consolidated during childhood, they may be somewhat more amenable to clinical interventions. As such, there may be more opportunity for success in working with children and younger adolescents in comparison to the treatment of older adolescents and adults.

As noted, there is an accumulating literature on the use of cognitive therapy with children and adolescents (Braswell & Kendall, 1988; Finch et al., 1993; Kendall & Braswell, 1985; Matson, 1989; Meyers & Craighead, 1984; Zarb, 1992). Few studies have focused, however, on its application to the treatment of eating disorders. It appears, nonetheless, that standard cognitive therapy techniques can be modified such that the model can be applied to adolescents. Several recent reports address the application of the cognitive model to young people (Reinecke, 1992; Schrodt, 1992; Wilkes & Rush, 1988). Each of these authors has emphasized the importance of tailoring techniques to the developmental level of the young person. It is often helpful, for example, to attempt to encourage children and adolescents to label their feelings and to monitor their ways of thinking, rather than to emphasize the identification and disputation of cognitive distortions. Because children and young adolescents have not typically developed skills in hypothetico-deductive reasoning, traditional approaches to "rational responding" are often difficult for them. Similarly, a developmentally informed cognitive model emphasizes developmental needs and tasks of children. There is a recognition of the role of the peer group as a support for a developing sense of autonomy from the family, the importance of attending to factors influencing the development of an adult identity, and the egocentric application of formal operational thought during later adolescence (Shirk, 1988).

ADAPTATIONS OF COGNITIVE THEORY AND TECHNIQUE

Adolescence is the time when abstract reasoning and an awareness of hypothetical alternatives begin to emerge. Cognitive interventions are able both to exploit and facilitate these developing skills. Although cognitive distortions and dysfunctional information processing are common among clinically referred children and adolescents, they are also often observed among normal or nonreferred children. It has been suggested by some that the development of more rational and flexible modes of thinking during later adolescence is associated with an improvement in self-concept and self-esteem. With this in mind, a goal of cognitive therapy with adolescents is to identify immature or flawed reasoning, and to support the development of more mature, flexible, cognitive problem-solving skills.

The active, goal-oriented, here-and-now focus of cognitive therapy is well suited for work with adolescents. The collaborative problem-solving approach of cognitive therapy helps to counter difficulties that adolescents with eating disorders often have in engaging in a working relationship with adult therapists. Moreover, the structured, supportive nature of cognitive therapy sessions can be reassuring to many teenagers. The clear expectations and consequences employed in cognitive-behavioral therapy serve to reduce oppositional behavior and destructive acting out. Finally, the egalitarian, empirical approach of cognitive-behavioral therapy encourages healthy skepticism. In some sense, the symptoms of anorexia nervosa not only represent how teenagers view themselves, but also are an attempt by adolescents to define a self. If the therapist can convey to the adolescent that his or her perceptions of a situation are but one possible alternative, and if the teenager can be encouraged to reciprocate by looking at his or her own thoughts with the same critical analysis, then collaborative empiricism can be attained and a more adaptive sense of self can emerge.

Cognitive-behavioral therapy stresses the need for specificity in identifying target symptoms and establishing therapeutic goals. Moreover, contemporary cognitive models of psychopathology recognize that dysfunctional attitudes and beliefs develop in a social context (Gotlib & Hammen, 1992). With this in mind, cognitive therapy with children and adolescents emphasizes the role of family instability in the etiology of behavioral disorders, as well as the importance of attending to the beliefs and attitudes of the children's parents during the treatment. Direct attempts are made to elicit and evaluate tacit beliefs, dysfunctional assumptions or appraisals, and maladaptive expectations held by family members. Our clinical experience suggests that treatment is most effective when the family, the adolescent, and the treatment team are able to understand each other's views and can collaborate in developing a treatment program. Dysfunctional attitudes, cognitive distortions, and maladaptive behavior patterns within the family system can be treated during family therapy sessions (see Chapter 14, this volume).

The process of cognitive therapy involves bringing automatic thoughts, schemas, and other cognitions into full awareness. Adolescents vary in their capacity for self-reflective thought, formal operational reasoning and, more specifically, in their capacity to reflect on their own thought processes. It is often helpful, as such, to encourage adolescents to articulate their thoughts by putting them into writing. This process assists teenagers to gain a more objective view of their beliefs and attitudes, as well as the situations in which they occur. This process of listing one's automatic thoughts, or of preparing a narrative of one's experiences, can provide insight into dysfunctional and distorted perceptions, and can lead to a sense of mastery over problematic situations.

Cognitive and behavioral approaches for treating adolescents with eating disorders are, in many ways, quite similar to those employed in working with adults. Interventions focus on identifying and changing specific beliefs, attributions, expectations, values, and cognitive distortions that contribute to the eating disorder. Cognitive and behavioral techniques are employed to teach adolescents to be more aware of their thoughts, feelings, and behaviors. As with adults, adolescents learn to identify and label their emotions, as well as recurrent patterns of thinking. Socratic questioning is used to assist adolescents in evaluating the validity of their automatic thoughts. For those adolescents who are not able to efficiently reflect on their specific automatic thoughts, an emphasis is placed on seeking logical alternatives for their thoughts about problematic situations (Reinecke, 1992).

As a rule of thumb, the degree of emphasis placed on the use of behavioral techniques is proportional to the severity of the disorder. For some patients with an eating disorder (especially anorexia nervosa), symptoms are so extreme that immediate behavioral change must be achieved. For these purposes, the initial interventions are primarily behavioral in nature. These early behavioral procedures set the stage for subsequent cognitive interventions by establishing situations that serve as cues for dysfunctional thoughts and feelings regarding food, weight, body size, and control over the environment.

Behavioral assignments typically can be graded to match the patient's level of understanding and motivation. It is important to remember that some teenagers experience difficulty understanding complex ideas or procedures. With this in mind, the behavioral tasks should be developed collaboratively and practiced with the therapist before they are attempted outside of the session. As in cognitive therapy with adults, it is important that the child or adolescent understand (at least in basic terms) the rationale and method for implementation of each assignment. Behavioral interventions, such as activity scheduling, mood monitoring (especially during food related activities), relaxation training, and exposure/desensitization can be quite useful early in therapy. The activity schedule is used to monitor teenagers' feelings of mastery or accomplishment and pleasure as they complete therapeutic tasks and encounter problematic situations. Mastery and pleasure ratings also may be used to generate homework assignments that challenge the patients' hypotheses of being fat or out of control. Graded task assignments can be used to complete difficult tasks. For example, an adolescent with anorexia nervosa might be encouraged to plan the steps necessary to finish a complete meal. He or she might begin by developing a script of the steps and *imagining* each successive step leading to the desired outcome. Similarly, a patient with bulimia might be encouraged to develop a list of situations in which he or she would be likely to binge and purge, then approach these situations *in vivo* with their therapist. They might, for example, purchase and eat a small amount of "junk food" in the presence of their therapist. The accompanying automatic thoughts, images, and emotions become the grist for the therapeutic mill.

The cognitive techniques used in treating adolescents with eating disorders are also similar to those employed in working with adults. The use of thought records, diaries, tape recorders, self-report questionnaires, and other techniques for identifying and challenging automatic thoughts and cognitive distortions is essentially similar with both groups. There are differences, however, with regard to the assessment and treatment of dysfunctional schemas. As noted, children and adolescents have not typically consolidated a coherent set of beliefs about themselves, their world, or their future. Moreover, their beliefs about themselves and their relationships with others tend to be strongly influenced by the social setting in which they are functioning and the psychosocial tasks they must address (Freeman, 1993).

Employing Erikson's (1950) psychosocial stage model, Freeman (1993) suggested that tacit beliefs surrounding specific developmental "crises" are consolidated at different ages. Like Gotlib and Hammen (1992), he suggests that beliefs and attitudes are acquired in a social context, and that these beliefs are activated and function in specific social settings. For the adolescent, these contexts are the home, school, church or community, and peer group. Freeman suggests that the development of dysfunctional schemas is influenced by the individual's ability to assimilate and integrate the socialization demands of each of these settings. As such, an assessment of schemas requires an understanding of the social stresses and developmental issues that the adolescent is confronting. In this way, the function of the specific belief for the teenager can be determined, and the social forces that are reinforcing or maintaining it can be identified.

Cognitive therapy for eating disorders with children places a greater emphasis on working with parents and other important persons in the child's life (Reinecke, 1992). It has been suggested, in fact, that the most appropriate intervention for children diagnosed with eating disorders is family therapy (Bowers & Andersen, 1994). Active attempts must be made to understand how parents may inadvertently contribute to the child's difficulties. Explicit attempts must be made to understand the parents' perceptions, beliefs, and expectations for their child, and whether they may be conveying maladaptive beliefs to their child.

CASE REPORT

Jane was a 14-year-old, eighth-grade student who was admitted to our psychiatric inpatient eating disorders unit. Jane's history is typical of many adolescent patients with anorexia nervosa. Her symptoms began in the sixth grade when she became focused on her appearance and began to believe that she was obese. As a result of these beliefs she started to restrict her calories, exercise heavily, purge, and abuse laxatives. These behaviors persisted through the seventh grade but were episodic in nature. In the eighth grade Jane experienced an increase in the intensity of her symptoms. During this time, she would go for several days without eating, then eat a bit of fruit for a few days, while refusing all other meals. For 1 week she would use 16–18 laxatives per day, stop for a week, and then repeat the cycle. The amount of exercise that Jane engaged in was dependent on her caloric intake. When she was not eating, her exercise program consisted of 20 minutes per day on her cross-country ski machine, in addition to her regular participation in basketball and softball. On days when she ate only fruit, she would increase her exercise on the cross-country ski machine to several times per day and add biking, running, and weight lifting.

Jane came to the attention of her local health care providers when she took 60 Correctol laxatives. The overdose was for weight loss rather than a suicide attempt. She was treated medically and admitted for 2 weeks to an adolescent psychiatry unit. Jane was discharged to outpatient follow-up care, but resumed engaging in her eating disordered behaviors. Within a short period of time, Jane was readmitted to the hospital due to her deteriorating health and dramatic mood swings. At this time, her physicians suggested an admission to a specialty unit for the treatment of eating disorders. Jane's physicians felt that her prognosis was quite poor. They emphatically described the intractibility of her symptoms and stated that they perceived Jane and her family as "totally unmotivated" for treatment.

When Jane entered the eating disorder unit she complained of poor concentration, was ruminating about food, and had a strong desire to be thin. She obsessed about what she was going to eat; what she had just eaten; and whether she was going to vomit, use laxatives, or exercise to get rid of the food. Jane also expressed difficulty accepting that her behaviors were disrupting her life.

Jane appeared physically older and presented as emotionally more mature than most 14-year-olds. Throughout her hospitalization, the treatment team had to remind themselves of her actual age in order to maintain reasonable goals and expectations for her. Her level of maturity became an ongoing theme during treatment. Although Jane was physically more mature than her peers and had prematurely developed something of an adult social identity, she was still struggling with issues surrounding the transition from adolescence to adulthood. Moreover, her level of cognitive maturity was similar to that of others her age.

Jane actually had good knowledge of the therapeutic skills required to work on changing her thoughts, feelings, and behaviors. However, she was not able to apply these concepts in her day-to-day life. Jane's inability to practice the skills she had learned appeared to stem from a reluctance to try anything new. This reluctance was fueled by her fear of being imperfect, which contributed to feelings of worthlessness. This reticence about using new skills appeared to be related as well to her automatic thoughts, basic assumptions, and schemas regarding herself and her role within her family. This is a common phenomenon for adolescent patients. One reason that cognitive-behavioral therapy may be effective in treating eating disorders is that it explicitly attempts to change specific beliefs, enhance understanding, and develop more effective coping skills. Moreover, it directly addresses the cognitive, social, and behavioral factors that may be hindering the use of these skills. In addition, cognitive-behavioral therapy provides a structure for change, both in the therapy hour and during the periods between sessions, that can be helpful for individuals who do not have the ability to effectively apply new coping skills in their lives.

Initial Assessment

Jane was evaluated by a multidisciplinary treatment team in our eating disorder unit. The team included psychiatrists, psychologists, psychiatric nurses, social workers, educators, and occupational and activities therapists. She was given a thorough physical and psychiatric examination and completed a battery of psychological tests to assess cognitive and motivational factors that might be contributing to her eating disorder, as well as level of intellectual functioning and personality characteristics. Nursing and social services assessed her family functioning and her ability to relate to others on the inpatient unit. Occupational and activities therapy assessed her understanding of exercise and leisure activities and knowledge of coping skills and food-related activities.

Upon admission Jane was 5'7" tall and weighed 107.6 pounds. She was started on a weight restoration program, with a target weight range of 127 to 131 pounds. Weight restoration was accomplished by starting Jane on a diet of 1,500 calories per day for 4 days and then increasing her diet by 500 calories every 4 days until 3,500 calories were ingested per day. When this target range was achieved, a maintenance level of calories was determined. Although Jane was medically stable upon admission, she appeared emaciated and was moderately dehydrated. Her electrolyte levels were checked and monitored to ensure there were no abnormalities.

Psychological testing revealed an adolescent who was in the superior range of intellectual functioning with no cognitive impairment. She was experiencing severe, self-reported symptoms of depression. As might be expected, Jane had a very high drive for thinness, displayed extreme body dissatisfaction, and set perfectionistic standards for herself. She had difficulty recognizing and responding appropriately to internal emotional states and forming close interpersonal relationships, and felt ineffective in coping with her problems. Jane presented as moralistic and sensitive to criticism. Moreover, she was highly resistant to alternative interpretations or perceptions of her predicament. She acknowledged experiencing subjectively severe levels of dysphoria and displayed little insight into her role regarding her current problems.

Jane described the symptoms of her eating disorder as coping mechanisms that allowed her to feel more in control of her life. She expressed a sense of isolation from her parents and stated, "The best we do is tolerate each other." She described her mother as being overinvolved physically, but not emotionally. By contrast, she felt that her father was underinvolved and very distant with the family. Our assessment of the family suggested that her parents were emotionally unresponsive and unexpressive, and that lines of communication between family members were almost nonexistent. Jane's family members appeared to share the belief that it is unacceptable to openly express strong emotions. Feelings were to be hidden not shared. Jane also stated that she did not have many friends her own age, for they were "too immature." She did, however, have several adult friends.

Diagnosis and Cognitive Conceptualization

Diagnostically, Jane met DSM-IV criteria for anorexia nervosa. These problems were superimposed upon family difficulties, extremely high personal expectations, a perfectionistic personality style, and a extreme fear of expressing her emotions. Jane's mood swings were related to difficulty in maintaining her expectations of herself and a fear that she had contributed to problems between her parents.

Raised in a family in which the expression of emotions was taboo, Jane began to hold negative emotions inside and did not express them. As this became more difficult, she turned to other behavioral strategies to subdue or regulate her feelings. She found that being thin, eating less, and purging were quick, easy ways to release tension, which made her feel better. She avoided peers because they were "immature" in their open expression of emotions. Because adults were somewhat less emotionally expressive than her peers, Jane came to feel safer and more comfortable in their company. As Jane's food restriction and purging behaviors became more established, her negative thoughts and feelings emerged. She began to feel bad, undeserving, and uncomfortable with her body image. As her eating disorder became more pronounced, she realized the anorexia nervosa seemed to pull her parents closer together. As a consequence, she came to believe that the eating disorder had taken on an importance "greater than anything else in her life." An excellent athlete, Jane was destined for a college athletic scholarship. Her eating disorder had physically weakened her, however, to the point she was no longer allowed to participate in sports.

Jane stated that she felt "like a terrible person" and that she fought frequently with her mother. The fights centered around issues of independence and autonomy. She began to believe that if she left home, her mother's life would be empty, and commented that her mother had been putting everything into their relationship and nothing into the relationship with her father. Jane acknowledged that she put tremendous pressure on herself to meet exceedingly high expectations. Although Jane excelled academically and athletically, she described herself as "never good enough." She consequently felt bad when she could not live up to her standards and expectations. This shift in mood and negative self-evaluation led to a greater desire to control her food intake. Jane also realized that she used sports to cope with stress. When she became too weak to participate in sports, she would focus on weight, shape, size, and food.

As Vitousek and Ewald (1993) observed, individuals with anorexia often feel that they are "perfectable," and that that they can derive a sense of uniqueness and superiority from their control over their weight. This was true of Jane. She pursued self-improvement activities and strove to be perceived as a "better person." Perfectionism was equated with confidence, and she would accept nothing less. Jane appeared to feel overwhelmed in complex social situations and was unsure of how she fit into her social and family roles. As a consequence, Jane was guarded with others and seemed to perceive emotional distance as necessary for her safety. As noted, Jane described her family members as detached and emotionally distant from one another. Jane did not, as a result, feel supported or understood.

Given this information about Jane, the treatment team began to conceptualize her problems as follows:

Behavioral coping strategies

Restriction of diet
Increased amounts of exercise
Attempting to spend much of her time with adults

Cognitive distortions

Dichotomous thinking
Catastrophizing
Mind reading

Automatic thoughts

"I'll never be good enough for my parents."
"I must be a better person."
"I'm obese."

Assumptions

"If I don't control my weight, then I'm a failure."
"If I express my emotions, then I'm a weak person."
"If I get close to people, then I will be hurt."
"If I put myself first, then I'm a selfish person."

Schemas

Relationships mean pain and being lost in the other person.
Showing emotions will mean negative outcomes.
I can show only positive emotions.

Jane's attempts to lose weight appeared to serve several functions for her. She viewed her diet and avoidance of expressing strong emotions as ways to control her future, her world, and herself. Jane's anorexia had become, in a real sense, central to her self-image and served as a "core" of her identity. When her weight was low, she felt in control and saw herself as meeting her expectations. She also saw the low weight as a way to keep her parents emotionally involved with each other. Our attempts to assist her in gaining and maintaining an adequate weight were interpreted, then, as threats to both her personal well-being and her family. She felt that others were attempting to remove the one thing that she felt confident about: being able to be thinner than others around her.

Course of Treatment

In addition to the weight restoration program, Jane participated in a number of therapeutic activities during her hospitalization. Cognitive therapy was employed as the primary psychotherapeutic approach (Wright, Thase, Beck, & Ludgate, 1993; Bowers, 1993). The unit's nursing staff was trained in both individual and group cognitive therapy, and other members of the treatment team (psychiatrists, family therapist, occupational therapist, recreational therapist) also used primarily a cognitive model when working with their patients.

The main psychotherapeutic interventions employed on the unit were a psychoeducation group, individual cognitive therapy, group cognitive therapy, and family therapy. Each was designed to complement the other interventions. The psychoeducational group explored various aspects of cognitive therapy (i.e., cognitive distortions, automatic thoughts) in a didactic fashion. The individual therapy was based upon Beck's model (Beck et al., 1979) with modifications specifically for an inpatient unit (Bowers, 1993). Group cognitive therapy combines Beck's theory and interventions in a process-oriented framework (Bowers & Andersen, 1994). The family therapy also employed a cognitive framework and was designed to facilitate communication among family members and address maladaptive beliefs, attributions, expectations, and schemas held by family members (Dattilio, 1994; Teichman, 1992). Each of the patients, including Jane, participated in some form of cognitive therapy for at least 3 hours per day.

As in therapy with adults, the first goal in cognitive therapy with adolescents is to develop a collaborative rapport. Jane initially expressed concern and fear over the amount of work she would need to do to recover from her eating disorder. As she stated, "I know *what* I need to do, I just don't know *how* to do it." She also identified family therapy as a needed intervention but did not want to pursue it, because it made her "uncomfortable." During group and individual therapy sessions, Jane developed trusting relationships and was able to address these beliefs. As these relationships developed, her dysfunctional cognitive and behavioral coping strategies became apparent. She came to recognize that her strict control over food and exercise, as well as the tight rein she held on the expression of emotions, were used to maintain her sense of self and affected her views of the world and her future.

As this data became available, it was necessary to present it to Jane in a way that she could utilize it. We needed to answer her basic question: "How can I do this?" We addressed this task by using interventions described by Beck et al. (1979) and Wright et al. (1993). Jane began most days by participating in a psychoeducational cognitive therapy group. It was here that many of the cognitive and behavior techniques that would be employed in individual and group therapy were introduced. This group focused on identification of automatic thoughts, cognitive distortions, basic assumptions, and schemas. Ways of monitoring these thoughts were reviewed and group members assisted each other, rationally evaluating and changing their thoughts, feelings, and behaviors.

Jane quickly became adept at using these cognitive techniques and often assisted others in the group with the interventions. The assistance that she offered others, however, served to keep her emotions from coming to the surface and allowed her to avoid discussing her feelings. It became apparent that Jane needed to discuss her thoughts and concerns first during group, rather than listening and helping others. Putting herself first created a great deal of discomfort for her, because it violated basic assumptions regarding the expression of emotions and "being selfish."

During her individual therapy sessions, Jane began to monitor her thoughts and behaviors in situations that were accompanied by shifts in her affect. This was particularly helpful, in that she came to understand the relationship between her feelings of dysphoria and her perfectionistic beliefs. She became more aware of these recurring thoughts, as well as the inordinately high standards on which they were based, as she completed a Daily Record of Dysfunctional Thoughts, a representative copy of which is presented in Table 11.2. As can be seen, Jane used this technique, as well as a daily journal, to track her basic assumptions for expressing emotions, forming close relationships, and what meaning a low body weight had for her. By rationally challenging these thoughts in therapy, Jane became better able to express her feelings openly and was able to develop close relationships with other patients on the unit. Both the individual and group therapy, then, focused on facilitating Jane's understanding of the relationships between thoughts, feelings, and her consequent behaviors. She became able to identify negative automatic thoughts and consistently challenged them before they provoked a shift in her mood or the desire to avoid eating. As a result of these interventions, Jane came to accept more realistic and appropriate interpretations of her life events.

Jane's cognitive therapy group served as her forum for using her new skills and exploring current developmental issues. Moreover, discussions of these issues with her peers allowed her to modify a number of the underlying schemas that maintained her disorder. By interacting with other group members, who encouraged her expression of feelings, Jane was able to challenge the idea that a close relationship meant giving up on her own person. She began to understand the origins of her fear of emotional intimacy and challenged her belief that intimate relationships were inevitably painful or risky. Jane was able to acknowledge that expressing her emotions did not always lead to negative outcomes. She found that it was, in fact, beneficial to express a full range of emotions to others. During

TABLE 11.2. Daily Record of Dysfunctional Thoughts

Situation	Emotions	Automatic thoughts	Rational response
Trying to talk to other patients	Sad	I'm a bad person if I don't do things perfect.	Having trouble with new things does not mean I'm bad.
Family therapy	Anxious, scared	My family won't be able to function without me.	My family has more strength than I really know. It takes all members of the family to really function well.
Eating a snack	Anxious	If I gain weight I'll be out of control.	My weight is not related to my ability to control my thoughts, behaviors. I'm okay regardless of what I eat or what I weigh.

group therapy sessions, Jane experienced how expressing anger, sadness, or fear served to strengthen her relationships with others. The group gave Jane a forum to be a young adolescent, without the responsibility of caring for others. She could be herself and display both strong and weak aspects of her character.

Family therapy sessions were initially very stressful for both Jane and her parents, because they were unfamiliar with the idea of expressing emotions openly and directly. They were eventually able, however, to begin the process of sharing their concerns and feelings with one another. This process was enlightening for Jane, because she had previously believed that her father "didn't have any emotions." She expressed shock when he began to express his feelings and share his inner thoughts.

As we have seen, Jane participated in several forms of cognitive therapy throughout her hospitalization that provided her with numerous opportunities for rehearsing cognitive-behavioral interventions, and offered many venues for identifying and changing her beliefs and attitudes. Cognitive principles guided her family, group, and individual therapy, and were utilized in occupational therapy, recreational therapy, and in her daily interactions with other patients and staff on the unit. The milieu strengthened and helped Jane generalize her learning and gave her a chance to work with her parents and friends outside of the hospital setting.

Jane's outcome was extremely positive. At discharge she felt that she had learned how to use the skills for change and, equally important, how to communicate them to others. She was able to identify how her own thoughts and perceptions contributed to her eating disorder and interfered in her life. She made significant changes in how she interacted with food and her world. To date, she has been able to maintain her restored weight and has maintained many cognitive-behavioral changes. She perceives and operates in her world differently and more positively than when she first entered treatment.

Aftercare is extremely important to the continued success of patients in their battle against anorexia nervosa. There is a need for support and structure within the therapeutic relationship to be able to maintain progress. Also, it is important that continued work be done to assist patients to recognize the cognitive distortions, basic assumptions, and schemas that have contributed to their eating disorders.

Jane continues treatment in outpatient individual therapy and in group psychotherapy that focuses on body perception. Her weight has been stable for several months—a feat that has not occurred outside of a hospital for many years. She continues to maintain her progress and appears to have made permanent changes in her perception of herself and her world.

CONCLUSION

This case example illustrates how cognitive, social and familial factors interact to influence the emotional problems experienced by adolescents with eating disorders. A hospital milieu based on cognitive therapy principles that focus on behavioral and cognitive interventions were highly effective in alleviating this young woman's emotional and behavioral problems. Our patient's beliefs, attitudes, and values regarding food, interpersonal relationships, and standards were similar to those experienced by adults with eating disorders. Jane's negative view of herself, her world, and her future, created a need in her to find a sense of control. This need was displayed in her strict eating patterns and fear of emotional involvement. These fears were partially lodged in her developmental view of how to be accepted in her family and in what she thought would create an image of being competent.

As the case example demonstrates, the principles and interventions of cognitive therapy can be applied effectively with adolescents. The structure of cognitive therapy allows for individualized care and developing strategies that fit the patient's needs. Even with this individualization of patient interventions, a cognitive model and theoretical framework was maintained, with a heavy emphasis on ideas developed by Beck et al. (1979) as guiding principles. Additionally, the cognitive milieu can potentially alter dysfunctional developmental patterns and encourage development of new and more functional schemas.

Treatment of adolescents with eating disorders generates some problems. Prominent among them are the level of understanding and maturity of the patient. Because the development of operational thought is uneven among adolescents, it is important to be cognizant of this when choosing what type of intervention, and in determining how soon to use any given intervention. Aftercare also creates difficulties. Without the cooperation of parents, gains made during a hospitalization may not persist. It is important to have the parents actively participate in their child's treatment, such that they can be enlisted to act as adjunct cognitive therapists at home. Future research must look at the role of cognitive processes in the etiology of eating disorders, as well as the process of change in therapy for these conditions. It is not known which combination of cognitive or behavioral interventions is associated with behavioral and emotional change over the course of treatment. Additionally, there needs to be a better conceptualization of adolescent eating disorders using cognitive and behavioral models.

Treatment of adolescents with eating disorders is a multifaceted endeavor. Many disciplines are involved in developing the treatment plan, and their efforts must be coordinated such that an effective, parsimonious program can be implemented. It is worth reiterating that during inpatient treatment the *entire* treatment team plays a role in patient change. Although an emphasis is placed on the utility of cognitive and behavioral techniques, other interventions and processes no doubt play an important role in the promoting therapeutic change. Treatment is most effective when the whole team operates from a cognitive therapy perspective. This means that all members of the team must have a basic knowledge of cognitive therapy, its theory, and interventions. We have found that adolescents have responded positively to cognitive-behavioral therapy concepts, and that these techniques are extremely effective in teaching and treating an adolescent eating disordered population.

REFERENCES

Agras, W. S., Schneider, J. A., Arnow, B., Raeburn, S. D., & Telch, C. F. (1989). Cognitive-behavioral treatment with and without exposure plus response prevention in the treatment of bulimia nervosa: A reply to Leitenberg and Rosen. *Journal of Consulting and Clinical Psychology, 57,* 778–779.

American Psychiatric Association. (1994). *Diagnostic and statistical manual of mental disorders* (4th ed.). Washington, DC: Author.

Beck, A. T. (1976). *Cognitive therapy and the emotional disorders.* New York: International Universities Press.

Beck, A. T., Rush, A. G., Shaw, B. F., & Emery, G. (1979). *Cognitive therapy of depression.* New York: Guilford Press.

Bowers, W. A. (1993). Cognitive therapy of eating disorders. In J. H. Wright, M. E. Thase, A. T. Beck, & J. W. Ludgate (Eds.), *Cognitive therapy with inpatients: Developing a cognitive milieu* (pp. 337–356). New York: Guilford Press.

Bowers, W. A., & Andersen, A. A. (1994). Inpatient treatment of anorexia nervosa: Review and recommendations. *Harvard Review of Psychiatry, 2,* 193–203.

Braswell, L., & Kendall, P. (1988). Cognitive-behavioral methods with children. In K. Dobson (Ed.), *Handbook of cognitive-behavioral therapies* (pp. 167–213). New York: Guilford Press.

Bruch, H. (1962). Perceptual and conceptual disturbances in anorexia nervosa. *Psychosomatic Medicine, 24,* 197–194.

Bruch, H. (1985). Four decades of eating disorders. In D. M. Garner & P. E. Garfinkel (Eds.), *Handbook of psychotherapy for anorexia nervosa and bulimia* (pp. 7–18). New York: Guilford Press.

Chambless, D. L., & Gillis, M. M. (1993). Cognitive therapy of anxiety disorders. *Journal of Consulting and Clinical Psychology, 61,* 248–260.

Cooper, P. J., & Fairburn, C. G. (1984). Cognitive behavior therapy for anorexia nervosa: Some preliminary findings. *Journal of Psychosomatic Research, 28,* 493–499.

Crisp, A. H., Norton, K., Gowers, S., Halek, C., Bowyer, C., Yeldhan, D., Levett, G., & Bhat, A. (1991). A controlled study of the effect therapies aimed at adolescents and family psychopathology in anorexia nervosa. *British Journal of Psychiatry, 159,* 325–333.

Dare, C., Eisler, I., Russell, M. R., & Szmukler, G. I. (1990). The clinical and theoretical impact of a controlled trial of family therapy in anorexia nervosa. *Journal of Marital and Family Therapy, 16,* 39–57.

Dattilio, F. M. (1994). Families in crises. In F. M. Dattilio & A. Freeman (Eds.), *Cognitive-behavioral strategies in crises intervention* (pp. 278–301). New York: Guilford Press.

Erikson, E. (1950). *Childhood and society.* New York: W. W. Norton.

Fairburn, C. G. (1983). Bulimia: Its epidemiology and management. In A. J. Stunkard & E. Stellar (Eds.), *Eating and its disorders* (pp. 235–258). New York: Raven Press.

Fairburn, C. G. (1985). A cognitive-behavioral approach to the treatment of bulimia. In D. M. Garner & P. E. Garfinkel (Eds.), *Handbook of psychotherapy for anorexia nervosa and bulimia* (pp. 160–191). New York: Guilford Press.

Fairburn, C. G., & Cooper, P. J. (1989). Eating disorders. In K. Hawton, P. M. Salkovskis, J. Kirk, & D. M. Clark (Eds.), *Cognitive behavioral therapy for psychiatric disorders* (pp. 160–192). New York: Oxford University Press.

Finch, A., Nelson, W., & Ott, E. (Eds.). (1993). *Cognitive-behavioral procedures with children and adolescents: A practical guide.* Boston: Allyn & Bacon.

Freeman, A. (1993) A psychosocial approach to conceptualizing schematic development for cognitive therapy. In K. T. Kuehlwein & H. Rosen (Eds.), *Cognitive therapies in action* (pp. 54–87). New York: Jossey-Bass.

Freeman A., & Dattilio, F. M. (1992). *Comprehensive casebook of cognitive therapy.* New York: Plenum Press.

Garfinkel, P. E., & Garner, D. M. (1982). *Anorexia nervosa: A multidimensional perspective.* New York: Brunner/Mazel.

Garner, D. M. (1985). Individual psychotherapy for anorexia nervosa. *Journal of Psychiatry Research, 19,* 423–433.

Garner, D. M. (1993). Pathogenesis of anorexia nervosa. *Lancet, 341,* 1631–1635.

Garner, D. M., & Bemis, K. M. (1982). A cognitive behavioral approach to anorexia nervosa. *Cognitive Therapy and Research, 6,* 1–27.

Garner, D. M., & Bemis, K. M. (1985). Cognitive therapy for anorexia nervosa. In D. M. Garner & P. E. Garfinkel (Eds.), *Handbook of psychotherapy for anorexia nervosa and bulimia* (pp. 107–146). New York: Guilford Press.

Gotlib, I., & Hammen, C. (1992). *Psychological aspects of depression: Toward a cognitive-interpersonal integration.* Chichester, UK: Wiley.

Guidano, V. F. (1991). *The self in process.* New York: Guilford Press.

Hall, A. (1987). The place of family therapy in the treatment of anorexia nervosa. *Australian and New Zealand Journal of Psychiatry, 21,* 568–574.

Hollon, S. D., Shelton, R. C., & Davis, D. D. (1993). Cognitive therapy for depression: Conceptual issues and clinical efficacy. *Journal of Consulting and Clinical Psychology, 61,* 270–275.

Kendall, P. (1985). Toward a cognitive-behavioral model of child psychopathology and a critique of related interventions. *Journal of Abnormal Child Psychology*, *13*, 357–372.

Kendall, P. C. (Ed.). (1991). *Child and adolescent therapy: Cognitive-behavioral procedures*. New York: Guilford Press.

Kendall, P., & Braswell, L. (1985). *Cognitive-behavioral therapy for impulsive children*. New York: Guilford Press.

Matson, J. (1989). *Treating depression in children and adolescents*. New York: Pergamon Press.

Meyers, A., & Craighead, W. (Eds.). (1984). *Cognitive-behavior therapy with children*. New York: Plenum Press.

Reinecke, M. A. (1992). Childhood depression. In A. Freeman & F. M. Dattilio (Eds.), *Comprehensive casebook of cognitive therapy* (pp. 147–158). New York: Plenum Press.

Reynolds, W. M., & Coates, K. I. (1986). A comparison of cognitive-behavioral therapy and relaxation training for the treatment of depression in adolescents. *Journal of Consulting and Clinical Psychology*, *54*, 653–660.

Safran, J. D. (1988). Feeling, thinking, and acting: A cognitive framework for psychotherapy integration. *Journal of Cognitive Psychotherapy*, *2*, 109–130.

Schrodt, R. G. (1992). Cognitive therapy of depression. In M. Shafi & S. L. Shafi (Eds.), *Clinical guide to depression in children and adolescents* (pp. 197–217). Washington, DC: American Psychiatric Press.

Segal, Z. (1988). Appraisal of the self-schema construct in cognitive models of depression. *Psychological Bulletin*, *103*, 147–162.

Shirk, S. (Ed.) (1988). *Cognitive development and child psychotherapy*. New York: Plenum Press.

Teichman, Y. (1992). Family therapy with an acting out adolescent. In A. Freeman & F. M. Dattilio (Eds.), *Comprehensive casebook of cognitive therapy* (pp. 147–158). New York: Plenum Press.

Vitousek, K. (1991, November). *Current status of cognitive-behavioral treatment of anorexia nervosa*. Paper presented at the 25th Annual Convention of the Association for Advancement of Behavior Therapy, New York.

Vitousek, K., & Ewald, L. (1993). Self-representation in eating disorders: A cognitive perspective. In Z. Segal & S. Blatt (Eds.), *The self in emotional distress: Cognitive and psychodynamic perspectives* (pp. 221–257). New York: Guilford Press.

Wilkes, T. C. R., & Rush, A. J. (1988). Adaptations of cognitive therapy for depressed adolescents. *Journal of American Academy of Child and Adolescents*, *27*, 381–386.

Wilson, G. T., & Fairburn, C. G. (1993). *Cognitive treatments for eating disorders*. *Journal of Consulting and Clinical Psychology*, *61*, 261–269.

Wilson, G. T., Rossiter, E. M., Kleifield, E. I., & Lindholm, L. (1986). Cognitive-behavioral treatment of bulimia nervosa: A controlled evaluation. *Behaviour Research and Therapy*, *24*, 277–288.

Wright, J. H., Thase, M. E., Beck, A. T., & Ludgate, J. W. (1993). *Cognitive therapy with inpatients: Developing a cognitive milieu*. New York: Guilford Press.

Zarb, J. (1992). *Cognitive-behavioral assessment and therapy with adolescents*. New York: Brunner/Mazel.

12

Treatment of Students with Learning Disabilities

Case Conceptualization and Program Design

Catherine Trapani
Maribeth Gettinger

COGNITIVE CHARACTERISTICS ASSOCIATED WITH LEARNING DISABILITY

"Learning disability" is probably the least-understood label used in educational and clinical practice today. Clinicians and educators agree that learning disabilities are manifested in significant academic and social difficulties among certain students. The field of learning disabilities is predicated on the assumption that students with disabilities learn differently than other students. This assumption has led to numerous investigations of the differences between students with and without disabilities, relative to a variety of behavioral, affective, and cognitive characteristics. Perhaps the most rapid growth in our knowledge in recent years concerns the cognitive characteristics of individuals with learning disabilities (Wong, 1991). Research describing cognitive characteristics associated with learning disabilities has provided a strong rationale for the use of cognitive therapies with this population of learners, and has also promoted a better understanding of how to devise cognitive approaches that are successful in enhancing the performance of individuals with learning disabilities. Studies of children with learning disabilities have identified a number of specific cognitive processes that differentiate them from their normally achieving classroom peers. Much of this work has focused on memory, attentional,

251

metacognitive, and attributional processes. The specific characteristics of students with learning disabilities have been labeled in many ways: passivity as learners, inadequacy of problem solving, learned helplessness, and inefficiency in the use of cognitive strategies. Broadly speaking, students with learning disabilities exhibit a variety of cognitive characteristics that may interfere with their acquisition and application of academic and social skills.

Memory

The importance of memory skills in academic and social learning cannot be underestimated. Research has linked memory deficits with reading and language problems, as well as difficulty in spelling and other content areas (Cohen, Netley, & Clarke, 1984). There is general consensus that memory constitutes a problematic area for most individuals with learning disabilities. Learning disability teachers often cite memory difficulties as the most frequent characteristic observed among their students (Torgesen, 1988a). Although there have been relatively few attempts to ascertain where in the memory process specific problems might occur, empirical research does lend support for classroom observations provided by teachers of students with learning disabilities. In fact, research is fairly consistent with regard to two major conclusions. First, children with learning disabilities exhibit difficulties on memory tasks in comparison to their non-learning disabled, same-age peers. Their performance on memory tasks often approximates that of younger, normally achieving children (Swanson & Trahan, 1990; Torgesen, 1988b). Second, memory problems among students with learning disabilities can be attributed, in part, to their failure to use strategies that facilitate memory. Torgesen (1988b) suggested that memory problems among children with learning disabilities derive primarily from their inefficient use of strategies, such as rehearsal and organization, as well as their limited motivation for engaging in intentional mental efforts.

Attentional Characteristics

Similar to memory difficulties, problems in attention have long been considered a critical characteristic of learning disability. Dykman and his colleagues (Dykman, Ackerman, Clements, & Peters, 1971; Dykman, Ackerman, Holcomb, & Bordreau, 1983) originally postulated that an attentional deficit underlies most learning disabilities. They employed a battery of experimental tests to assess various aspects of attention, including alertness, vigilance, and ability to focus. On all attentional measures, they found that children with learning disabilities performed less well than normally achieving students. Additional support for an attentional deficit has been offered over the years through observational studies of classroom behaviors of students with learning disabilities (Bender, 1987; McKinney & Feagans, 1983; Roberts, Pratt, & Leach, 1991). Children with learning disabilities spend significantly less time engaged in task-oriented behaviors and more time in non-task-oriented behaviors. Moreover, students with learning disabilities are rated by their teachers as being significantly less attentive than peers without disabilities (Fleisher, Soodak, & Jelin, 1984). Gerber (1988) has suggested that even when students with learning disabilities exhibit optimal attention or on-task behavior during learning situations, they may have difficulty allocating attention efficiently to information within tasks. This may account for a slower rate of learning among students with learning disabilities.

Of major significance in the study of attention among individuals with learning disabilities is the consistent finding that students tend to exhibit a lag in selective attention, or the ability to identify important stimuli and salient aspects of a stimulus (Brown & Wynne, 1984). Similar to findings from memory research, they found that children with learning disabilities do not spontaneously use strategies, such as verbal rehearsal and organization, that would enable them to perform more effectively on selective attention tasks. Furthermore, students with learning disabilities differ significantly from peers without learning disabilities in both the quantity and quality of their inner speech. Torgesen (1980) reviewed research to suggest that, compared to normally achieving students, children with learning disabilities do not give themselves self-instructions with the same frequency or degree of accuracy needed to focus on the most critical task parameters.

Metacognitive Abilities

The view that children with learning disabilities fail to use appropriate memory or attention strategies has received considerable empirical support over the last 15 years. We now understand that students with learning disabilities may possess the necessary strategies but do not recognize situations or tasks for appropriate strategy use. This type of difficulty falls within the domain of metacognitive processing. Metacognitive proficiency enables students to engage efficiently in academic tasks. Many researchers suggest that students with learning disabilities are lacking in an awareness of how their own cognitive processes can enhance their learning. Students with specific learning disabilities experience frustration and failure due to ineffective metacognitive skill development or application (Englert, Raphael, Anderson, Gregg, & Anthony, 1989; Short & Ryan, 1984; Wong, 1985, 1991; Wong, Wong, & Blenkinsop, 1989). Students with learning disabilities have been characterized as inefficient learners who are not aware of the processes associated with academic tasks, nor do they appear to have a repertoire of specific task strategies. In other words, the problems associated with learning disabilities may extend beyond a failure to use cognitive task strategies. What may be lacking is the ability to recognize that one task is like another, and that a strategy that was useful for one task may also be used or modified to solve another.

Differences in the metacognitive abilities between children with and without learning disabilities have been noted in several performance areas. For example, research suggests that students with learning disabilities are less competent in monitoring their own reading comprehension than children without learning disabilities (Baker & Anderson, 1982; Paris & Myers, 1981; Wong, 1982). Successful readers are aware of instances when they are not comprehending what they read. Comprehension monitoring, or knowing when comprehension is and is not occurring, is a critical metacomprehension skill that tends to differentiate between students with reading disabilities and students who are good comprehenders.

Self-Regulated Strategy Use

Although many memory, attention, and metacognitive characteristics of students with learning disabilities set them apart from their nondisabled peers, a critical difference lies in the extent to which students with learning disabilities engage in intentional, self-regulated learning that promotes success in academic and social situations (Paris & Oka, 1986). According to Palincsar and Brown (1989), self-regulated learners use their knowledge of strategies for accomplishing tasks efficiently. Self-regulated learners also use metacognitive awareness or knowledge of their own learner characteristics and task demands that enable them to select, employ, monitor, and evaluate strategy use. In addition, self-regulated learners demonstrate motivation to employ this knowledge effectively.

Successful learners, in summary, have acquired and demonstrated functional learning strategies. They have a repertoire of cognitive strategies that works for them (Ellis, Deshler, Lenz, Schumaker, & Clark, 1991; Wong, 1992). Students with learning problems, on the other hand, often lack the ability to regulate their own learning. They do not know how to control and direct their own thinking, how to gain new knowledge, or how to remember what they learn. Overall, research has documented that students with learning disabilities do not display the knowledge and behaviors that characterize self-regulated learners (Meltzer, Solomon, Fenton, & Levine, 1989). Students with learning disabilities fail to adopt a flexible, strategic approach to learning new material (Reid & Stone, 1991). In other words, it seems that children with learning disabilities are not strategy deficient per se, but rather are strategy inefficient or strategy inflexible.

Personal Control

Whereas metacognitive research focuses on an individual's awareness of particular cognitive strategies that are available for cognitive performance, the personal control literature focuses on a more global awareness of personal impact. In addition to research on memory, attention, and metacognition, there is evidence that many children with learning disabilities exhibit "learned helplessness," the belief that their efforts will not result in designated outcomes. For example, when they fail a task, children with learning disabilities are less likely to believe their failures are the result of a lack of effort (Licht & Kistner, 1986). Researchers have concluded that children with learning disabilities are generally pessimistic about their ability to influence academic and social outcomes, and may not derive feelings of self-efficacy from their accomplishments. They tend to minimize the value of effort. Additionally, children with learning disabilities are more likely to have a lower self-concept than other children, which, in turn, leads to fewer attempts to plan successful approaches to academic, social, or problem-solving situations (Schunk & Cox, 1986).

Another way to characterize this style of personal control is passivity in learning style. Not believing they can succeed, students with learning disabilities do not know how to go about the task of learning. As a consequence, they become passive and dependent learners, a style that is consistent with learned helplessness (Kavale & Forness, 1986; Torgesen & Licht, 1983).

Cognitive Strategies Deficiency Syndrome

Collectively, these descriptive studies have led researchers and clinicians away from searching for one underlying cognitive deficit as a contributor to inadequate performance among children with learning disabilities. Instead, research suggests that each deficiency, whether in attention, memory, metacognition, or attribution, should be viewed as a complex process. A deficiency in any one cognitive process can contribute to inadequate performance. Thus, each child's deficit must be analyzed individually when considering treatment options.

Despite this complexity, one commonality that emerges across all research is a clear deficit in the use of cognitive strategies among individuals with learning disabilities. Bender (1992) used the summary characterization of "cognitive strategies deficiency syndrome" to describe children with learning disabilities. This view places emphasis on cognitive strategies and underscores the well-documented failure of such children to produce and emit task-relevant cognitions to enhance their performance (Zimmerman, 1988). The perspective of a "syndrome" is offered to note the constellation of behavior symptoms and the interdependence of various processes involved in any given task.

In summary, children with learning disabilities differ significantly from children without learning disabilities in their cognitive or thinking processes, their cognitive strategies, and in the quantity and quality of their inner speech. The cognitive, metacognitive, and attributional problems associated with learning disabilities have led researchers to conclude that individuals with learning disabilities are passive or inactive learners who fail to involve themselves actively and efficiently in learning tasks.

DEVELOPMENT OF COGNITIVE THERAPIES
FOR LEARNING DISABILITY

Interest in the development and application of cognitive therapies for learning disabilities has increased in recent years. Although cognitive therapies have been used for many years with adults and children for a variety of clinical problems, it was not until evidence had accumulated characterizing the cognitive characteristics associated with learning disabilities that the field embraced a cognitive approach. Cognitive therapies are based on a belief in the interactive, reciprocal nature of cognitions, feelings, and behaviors. As such, cognitive approaches are highly compatible with the needs of students with learning disabilities, who exhibit characteristics such as learned helplessness, deficits in self-regulation, limited metacognitive awareness, and problems in attention and memory. Research identifying cognitive deficits among individuals with learning disabilities has provided a solid research base for the development of cognitive approaches (Harris, 1988).

Cognitive approaches are multifaceted and incorporate a wide array of strategies, programs, and techniques appropriate for students with learning disabilities. In general, cognitive approaches concentrate on activating students, and on giving them personal control or responsibility for planning solutions to problems. Clinicians and educators strive to activate individual cognitive processes to alter thinking as well as behavior. The focus of cognitive approaches is on covert, internal processes that are presumed to underlie overt behavior. The postulated relationship among private speech, thought, and behavior has been influential in the development of cognitive therapies and the application of these procedures with individuals who have learning disabilities. Although cognitive interventions consist of explicating a strategy or series of steps to use during problem-solving activities, the hope is that children will internalize strategies and use them in place of previously ineffective, disorganized, or inefficient thinking. Such a focus provides cognitive therapies with the potential for improved maintenance and generalization of change among students with disabilities (Finch, Nelson, & Ott, 1993).

Concomitant with a stronger research focus on cognitive characteristics of learning disabilities, there has been growing dissatisfaction with traditional behavioral interventions, which has also contributed to the current interest in cognitive approaches. Cognitive interventions are predicated on the view that behavior is influenced by unobservable and covert operations. Aimed at cognitions, rather than discrete skills or behaviors, cognitive approaches focus on systematically replacing inappropriate cognitions with effective, organized, and task-relevant thought (Rooney & Hallahan, 1991).

There are two major classes of cognitive therapies representative of current efforts to assist students with learning disabilities. The first major class of approach is broadly termed "cognitive-behavior modification," which involves detailed and explicit practice in a sequence of behaviors necessary to accomplish a task (Hallahan, Kneedler, & Lloyd, 1983). The basic premise underlying the application of cognitive-behavior modification for students with learning disabilities is that their thinking processes can be altered by connecting covert thoughts to overt behaviors through an individually tailored, tactical use of self-directed verbalizations or self-instruction.

The second broad class of cognitive approaches have been variously termed "cognitive training," "metacognitive training," or "strategy training" (Deshler, Schumaker, Lenz, & Ellis, 1984; Wong, 1985). This approach differs from cognitive behavior modification primarily in that it relies less on teaching and reinforcing covert thoughts and places more emphasis on the student as an active learner. Whereas cognitive behavior modification approaches provide students with strategies for learning, metacognitive approaches emphasize self-regulation or self-initiative. Instructional research has offered valuable contributions to the construction of metacognitive procedures for students with learning disabilities (Tobias, 1982). Specifically, research indicates that improving self-awareness and teaching students with learning disabilities *how* to think is at least as important as teaching them *what* to think (Rooney & Hallahan, 1991).

COMPONENTS OF COGNITIVE THERAPIES

Although many different types of therapeutic approaches fall under the label of "cognitive approaches," several treatment components are common among the majority of cognitive approaches used with learning disabilities. These include (1) self-instructional training, (2) self-monitoring, (3) problem-solving strategy training, and (4) metacognitive training.

Self-Instructional Training

One of the most widespread uses of cognitive approaches is based on the notion that children can be taught to verbalize their cognitive processes and use these verbalizations to guide their academic and social behavior. Self-instructional training was the first type of cognitive therapy to be used with learning-disabled students and remains a critical component of cognitive therapies. Self-instructional training is a procedure in which children learn to self-verbalize silently questions, directions, and judgments that affect their performance.

Meichenbaum and Butler (1980) pioneered the use of this approach for students with learning disabilities. Self-instructional training involves teaching children to (1) ask questions of themselves about the nature of a problem, the most effective approach to a task, the relevant stimuli or information, and the accuracy or quality of their performance; (2) give themselves self-instructions about performance; and (3) provide appropriate reinforcement and corrective feedback to themselves. The specific questions and statements vary depending on the nature of the task targeted for training and the characteristics of the individual students. Typically, training follows a sequence of activities beginning with the adult's demonstration of overt self-instruction and concluding with the child's covert self-instruction.

Self-Monitoring

Self-monitoring of behavior is a cognitive component that is directed at increasing appropriate behavior associated with academic and social success (Snider, 1987). Self-monitoring may be conceptualized as involving two stages: (1) self-assessment, and (2) self-recording. "Self-assessment" refers to the act of evaluating one's own behavior to determine whether a particular target behavior has occurred. Self-recording is the act of keeping tally of how many times the target behavior occurred. The bulk of the developmental and evaluative research on self-monitoring of students with learning disabilities has been conducted by Hallahan and associates (e.g., Hallahan & Sapona, 1983), using a system that teaches children with learning disabilities. They have studied the effects of self-monitoring on children's attentional behavior and academic productivity. Children with learning disabilities are instructed to monitor their attentional behavior by repeatedly asking themselves whether they are paying attention and by recording their behavior.

Several major findings have emerged from this work. First, self-monitoring during academic tasks does lead to increases in attentional behavior and, to a lesser extent, academic productivity. These benefits can be maintained without reliance on external reinforcement. Furthermore, training in self-monitoring appears to be most effective when children are engaged in tasks for which they have the necessary skills and when they are engaged in activities at their seats.

Teaching Problem-Solving Strategies

Successful problem solving is an important factor in social adjustment and academic performance. Problem-solving ability is related to coping skills, independence, self-regulation, and task success, and can prevent future social and learning problems. According to Deshler and Schumaker (1986), "problem-solving strategies" are techniques, principles, or rules that enable students to learn, solve problems, and complete tasks. For a variety of reasons, many students with learning disabilities do not spontaneously employ or generate task-specific strategies when they are needed. For this reason, the use of cognitive approaches with students who have learning disabilities has now expanded beyond an inner-language component to include self-planning of learning tasks. The most comprehensive efforts to develop programs involving learning or problem-solving strategies have been those of Deshler, Schumaker, and their colleagues. These researchers have been particularly interested in developing learning strategies appropriate for adolescents with learning disabilities, which can be applied across a wide variety of school content and learning situations.

Metacognitive Training

In recent years, there has been a burgeoning interest in metacognition and metacognitive problems among students with learning disabilities. The fact that many children with learning disabilities need to be explicitly told to use particular strategies suggests that at least part of their difficulty lies in their lack of awareness of when and how to use strategies. This conclusion has led to an increase in research to evaluate the effectiveness of interventions designed to incorporate a metacognitive training component. For example, there have been significant efforts in applying metacognitive principles to children's reading disabilities. The goal of these procedures is to have children with learning disabilities think about the content of what they are reading. For example, training children to generate and direct questions to themselves about why they are reading the material and what they are understanding has been shown to have positive effects on comprehension (Wong, 1985). As with most cognitive therapies, a metacognitive component has been applied to social skills as well as academics. Smith, Finn, and Dowdy (1993), for example, described programs for students with social difficulties that focus on training students to think about their own behavior and develop alternatives.

Conclusion

Overall, students with learning disabilities are not agile in organizing and prioritizing the academic and social information to which they are exposed. Their academic performance and social behavior are limited by an informational base that is not easily accessed and is further constrained by dependence on poorly defined, inflexible strategies (Meltzer, 1993). Additionally, they often experience difficulty identifying and describing the processes they actually use to learn and to interact with others (Campione, Brown, Ferrara, Jones, & Steinberg, 1985; Ferrara, Brown, & Campione, 1986; Swanson, 1990). Because of important research describing the cognitive characteristics of students with learning disabilities, there have been extensive efforts to develop cognitive approaches for this population (Bos & Anders, 1990; Deshler & Schumaker, 1986; Ellis & Lenz, 1987; Rooney & Hallahan, 1991; Swanson, 1989).

Inasmuch as it has been widely documented that the performance of many students with learning disabilities improves on some tasks when they are directly instructed to use strategies (Torgesen, Murphey, & Ivey, 1979), there is no universal approach to successful strategy instruction (Wong & Jones, 1982). It is important for educators and clinicians to consider what the use of cognitive strategies may or may not accomplish for individuals with learning differences. Paris, Wasik, and Turner (1991) differentiate between strategies that are purposefully devised and utilized to achieve a particular goal, and skills that are unconscious and automatic. This is an important distinction. Even with the use of cognitive strategies, idiosyncratic learning styles and performance differences may still exist between students with learning disabilities and their counterparts without learning problems (Gelzheiser, Cort, & Sheperd, 1987). In other words, the use of learning strategies may not transform the student with learning disabilities into an expert, or advance the student from being strategy-dependent to possessing automaticity in skill (for a review of this topic, refer to the August/September 1993 issue of the *Journal of Learning Disabilities*). Therefore, it may be that cognitive interventions for youths with learning disabilities are best designed and implemented after comprehensive assessment of individual needs. The purpose of such an assessment is to gather information to identify the level of basic skills individuals have achieved and the ways in which individuals solve problems.

ISSUES IN ASSESSMENT AND DESIGN
OF COGNITIVE STRATEGIES

The assessment of students with learning disabilities is as highly debated as the label itself, with discussions deeply rooted in the controversies over definition and diagnosis. Because the emphasis of current practice in education remains on classification and labeling, assessments are not often used to explore the learning styles of individual students. Similarly, the literature on cognitive interventions is replete with discussions of its application in treatment settings. Nonetheless, increasingly more demands are made of educators and clinicians who address the problems of students with skill deficiencies. The comorbidity of learning disabilities with other disorders of childhood and adolescence, such as depression, attention-deficit/hyperactivity disorder, and conduct and behavioral disorders suggests the need to document not only the cognitive abilities, but also the cognitive strategies utilized by these youth and the interactive effect on academic and social learning.

Identifying the "best" assessment practices for designing cognitive interventions for this population, however, is extremely complex. Salient questions emerge: How is capacity for learning versus what has been learned best identified? How is the learning process orchestrated by the individual, and when can manipulations of the environment maximize the benefits of instruction? How are strategies designed and taught? How can the efficacy of strategy training be evaluated? Despite the presence of varied approaches to these questions, most proponents of the use of cognitive learning strategies agree that the assessment of preexisting skills is essential before the use of a cognitive strategy is considered (Ellis, Lenz, & Sabornie, 1987; Meltzer, 1993; Swanson, 1990).

Assessment Methods

Over the course of 25 years, two fundamental perspectives in approaching the assessment of students with special needs have emerged. One major perspective is broadly termed the "medical model," which assumes that learning disabilities are attributed to the individual, are biologically based, and are genetically determined. In this model, "product"-oriented measures are used to assess the attributes of the individual (Sattler, 1988). The other major perspective is broadly termed the "behavioral–ecological model," which assumes a relationship among the environment, affect, behavior, and cognitive function (Vygotsky, 1978). In this model, "process"-oriented measures assess the adaptation and interaction of the individual to learning and to the social demands of the environment. Represented in both models are four basic approaches to assessment: (1) norm-referenced measures, (2) criterion-referenced measures, (3) observations, and (4) interviews.

1. *Norm-referenced measures.* Norm-referenced measures are standardized and are assumed to be reliable and valid to the extent that they can determine individual differences between students. Additionally, it is assumed that results can be plotted on a continuum within a standard error of measure (Sattler, 1988). Unfortunately, intervening variables that influence the results on standardized tests are often not considered in scoring and interpretation procedures. Such variables include the influence of the testing setting on the results obtained, the interference of deficits in attention and executive function on test taking, and the effects of limited task demands that are the hallmark of most standardized measures (Telzrow, 1990). These limitations make the exclusive use of norm-referenced measures less than optimal in providing information about the learning styles, behaviors, and needs of students with learning differences.

Recently, more global views of intelligence have supported a shift in the conventional assessment paradigm (Gardner, 1983). Because assessment has not been used either to define the underlying strategies that students employ or to determine appropriate interventions, it has been difficult to shift assessment practices (Campione, 1989; Meltzer, 1993). It is suggested that these measures be used differently and include the use of cues, probes, and "testing the limits" techniques (Graham & Harris, 1989).

2. *Criterion-referenced assessment.* This approach considers the attributes of the learner, but accounts for the expectations or demands of the curriculum and the quality of the instructional methods that are utilized. Criterion-referenced measures are not used to compare the progress of a student with that of others, but to determine if a student possesses requisite skills to succeed in the curriculum and to define levels of instruction (Shinn, 1989). Assessments analyze the curriculum and instruction as much as they do the characteristics of the individual.

3. *Observations.* Direct observation of learning and social interactions can be implemented when target behaviors are defined operationally and measured according to frequency and duration. Setting events and consequences of behaviors are assessed to determine the function that a behavior serves in the individual's repertoire. Preferred reinforcers are also determined to facilitate substituting an unwanted behavior with a desired one. The generalization of learning from one setting to the next is also considered (Gardner, 1977; Ollendick & Hersen, 1984).

4. *Interviews.* Structured and unstructured interviews provide information that is not typically provided by norm- and criterion-referenced

measures, or by direct observations. An interview enables students, teachers, families, and other caregivers to present their views on the nature and development of the presenting problems. Additionally, an interview can provide insight into prioritizing education and treatment goals and identifying an appropriate course of intervention (Welsh, 1987).

Regardless of the approach, assessment is limited to the samples of information collected at a fixed point in time. In some respects, the ramifications of learning disabilities become more subtle and complex as a person matures. It is conceivable that an array of traditional and nontraditional approaches may be incorporated in assessing learning differences and learning strategies. In keeping with Bender's (1992) concept of "cognitive strategies deficiency syndrome," and the existence of a constellation of intervening learning differences, it is critical that the design and use of cognitive interventions be guided by information derived from a comprehensive assessment using multiple methods of evaluating cognitive abilities, academic achievement, and social and behavioral attributes. Additionally, the interaction of learning tasks and learning environments can be ascertained through direct observations of academic and social behavior, as well as from consultation with students, teachers, and families.

To acknowledge the complexity of learning disabilities, assessment must be viewed as a research process. Measures should be used to test hypotheses about what individuals have learned and how they acquire and retain new information. Quantitative and qualitative data derived from this process should drive the design and evaluation of cognitive interventions. Thus, the purpose of assessment shifts from labeling students to identifying instructional goals, methods of intervention, and the efficacy of intervention techniques (Trapani, 1990).

DESIGN AND INSTRUCTION
OF LEARNING STRATEGIES

Cognitive abilities, academic achievement, and behavior are not fixed entities. Information obtained from individual assessments can be applied to modify performance through manipulating the content and presentation of tasks (Lidz, 1987). There are several approaches currently utilized in the instruction of cognitive learning strategies; no single approach serves all needs. Inasmuch as the use of cognitive strategies with students with learning disabilities is relatively new, no data are available to support the longitudinal success of any one model.

Instructional Elements

It has been well documented that teaching cognitive learning strategies can be useful when strategies are developmentally appropriate (Weinstein & Mayer, 1986). Students are effective in using strategies when they have been taught a few strategies well. Academic instruction and therapy that incorporates learning strategies focus on helping students to actively form rules and use procedures for following rules (Swanson, 1989). Teaching students to use metacognitive or self-regulation techniques assists them in monitoring their use of learning strategies (Meltzer, 1987). Additionally, positive belief systems are needed regarding the efficacy of learning strategies (Licht, Kistner, Ozkaragoz, Shapiro, & Clausen, 1985) as is the motivation to use them. Proponents of the use of cognitive approaches seek to effect changes in responses that are self-generated and highly generalizable. It is hoped that students will not limit their use of the strategy to the training task or to the training setting, but will apply what is learned to similar tasks in a variety of settings. Learning to formulate and follow rules and procedures, to be flexible in the application of these techniques, and to self-monitor learning and behavior are critical toward empowering students to be efficient, active, responsible, and independent (see Borkowski, Estrada, Milstead, & Hale, 1989; McLoone, Scruggs, Mastroperi, & Zucker, 1986; Palinscar & Brown, 1987, for further discussion).

Design Elements

Regardless of the purpose of the strategy, it is widely agreed that a few critical elements are essential to strategy design if the goals of cognitive strategy training are to be realized. Once the skills needed to use a specific strategy are identified, a set of steps can be organized hierarchically to culminate in a specific outcome. Task-specific strategies should not utilize more than seven components. First, each step should be short and easy, beginning with a verb relating directly to the task. The strategy should be presented in a developmentally relevant mnemonic to facilitate easy recall of the individual steps and to motivate students to use the strategy. Additionally, a metacognitive device should be designed to provide the opportunity for self-instruction, self-regulation, and self-evaluation. Instruction of learning strategies should consider baseline performance in the targeted academic or social domain to properly evaluate the efficacy of strategy instruction on later performance. A description of the strategy and its importance should also be discussed (Bursuck, 1994; Ellis et al., 1987; Swanson, 1993). Finally, the strategy should be reviewed and practiced before the student uses the strategy independently.

CASE STUDY

The following case study was selected as an illustration of the cognitive characteristics of a student with learning disabilities and related disorders, and the multimethod approach to assessment. This case presents a child with difficulties in memory, attention, and metacognition. The child is not aware of the strategies she possesses and does not purposefully employ them in learning and social situations. A comprehensive assessment of cognitive ability, academic achievement, and behavior is presented using standardized and criterion-referenced measures. Interviews and self-reports were also incorporated in the evaluation. The multirater, multisetting approach to assessment was employed in order to identify the specific areas contributing to her difficulties at school and at home. Incorporating the information obtained from the assessment, a simple learning strategy was designed to assist in the organization of homework and studying. A self-monitoring checklist related to the strategy was incorporated as a measure to introduce "self talk" and the self-regulation that is lacking. It is hoped that the assessment and the design of this simple cognitive strategy will introduce the patient to a method of recognizing and creating other strategies both independently and with others.

History of Presenting Problems

Abby is an attractive, dynamic, and strong-willed 13-year-old girl who was diagnosed in 1990 with Tourette's syndrome. There is a positive family history for Tourette's syndrome, depression, and obsessive–compulsive disorder (OCD). Over the past 4 years, Abby has also been identified as having OCD, attention-deficit/hyperactivity disorder (ADHD), and learning disability.

Her tics are characterized by frequent involuntary vocalizations, as well as the presentation of subtle motor movements. Consistent with the syndrome, the tics constantly change and their frequency and intensity wax and wane. Inasmuch as the daily administration of 2 mg of haloperidol (Haldol) has been successful in suppressing the majority of Abby's tics, she experiences side effects, including fatigue, short-term memory problems, and slowed motor responses. Occasionally, these side effects interfere with her cognitive and academic performance.

Psychopharmacological intervention is provided by a child psychiatrist who assists Abby in developing self-monitoring skills, so that she may observe her tics and actively participate in managing her medication. Current areas of concern include academic progress, lack of independence in organizing schoolwork, behavioral lability, and parenting problems.

School Placement

Abby attends eighth grade at a prestigious private school in a large city. The curriculum is accelerated and demanding, and provides no formal special education resource services. Like the majority of the normally achieving and gifted students who attend the school, Abby receives three 1-hour private tutoring sessions weekly to prepare and complete homework assignments, papers, and projects.

Assessment Findings

Interviews and Self-Reports

Unstructured interviews with Abby reflect the concerns of a middle child between two gifted sisters. She likes school and wants to succeed academically, but at times, she is frustrated by her effort to do so. Many of the side effects of the medication aggravate her. For example, she reports that she is often tired and that it is hard to recall math facts and spelling rules. Similarly, directions must be repeated numerous times before she completes a task. Typically, she forgets to bring finished assignments to school or to bring home materials needed for studying. Although she has difficulty with planning and organization, she rejects systems that have been designed to assist her stating, "I don't want somebody else's way to do things. I want to find my own way!" Despite such proclamations, she is very dependent on the support she receives from adults. In fact, Abby's academic success is often influenced by the relationships that she has formed with teachers.

She is close to her parents, especially her mother, but they have a volatile relationship. Abby complains that her mother is too involved in her life, particularly in regard to monitoring school activities. At times, Abby becomes verbally and physically aggressive at home, especially when her mother is attempting to monitor her studies or her behavior. Abby would like to address these concerns, but does not believe that anything will help.

In addition to the interviews, Abby completed questionnaires addressing her behavior (Youth Self-Report [YSR]; Achenbach, 1991b), social skills (Social Skills Rating System [SSRS]; Gresham & Elliot, 1991), and self-esteem (Self-Esteem Inventories [SEI]; Coopersmith, 1981). No significant concerns regarding her behavior were noted from the results of the YSR (T score = 47). On the SSRS, she reported that her social skills were high (standard score = 128) compared to her same-age peers. The lie scale embedded in the SEI indicated that Abby was a reliable historian on this measure and placed her in the 90th percentile for self-esteem.

Family Background

Both parents are accomplished professionals and set high standards for school achievement. Her mother assumes primary responsibility for managing Abby's needs. She worries about Abby's maintaining academic progress, transitioning to high school, and receiving support from teachers and classmates. On the one hand, Abby's mother perceives her to be highly intelligent, sensitive, and accomplished. On the other, she reports that Abby has cognitive difficulties, is irresponsible, unorganized, and lacking in social skills (SSRS standard scores = 72 in social skills and 113 in problem behaviors). However, scale scores on the (Child Behavior Checklist—Teacher Form [CBCL]; Achenbach, 1991a) were not elevated. At times, her mother is overprotective; at other times, she is highly critical. No behavioral protocols, rewards, or consequences have been implemented, and, as a result, her mother is embroiled in the difficulties that Abby experiences. When Abby demonstrates frustration, hurt, or anger, her mother does not distance herself from Abby's affect, but reacts to it. Together, their emotions spiral, often culminating in Abby's physical or verbal aggression toward her mother.

School Information

Interviews, behavior checklists, and social skills questionnaires were completed by counselors and teachers. The results indicated that Abby is well liked and is perceived by school personnel as a bright, hardworking, average-achieving student who tries hard to please. Some concerns included dependence on adults, poor peer interactions, and low self-esteem (SSRS standard scores social skills ranged from 94–104, and from < 85–114 on problem behaviors.)

Direct Classroom Observation

A 45-minute observation was made during a mathematics class, and a 15-minute observation during a small, social, lunchtime gathering. A time-sampling procedure was utilized to observe following instructions, class participation, and social interactions. Abby followed all instructions, actively participated in class, and completed all seat work independently. Her social interactions were appropriate. It was noted, however, that when transitioning from the structure of the mathematics class to the informal lunchtime gathering, Abby demanded far more teacher attention than did her peers.

Test Results

Cognitive abilities as measured by the Weschler Intelligence Scale for Children—III (WISC-III; Wechsler, 1991) fell within the average range of intelligence (Full Scale IQ = 90–101). In part, slowed motor speed compromised scores on the Performance Scale, resulting in a significant discrepancy (17 points) between the Verbal and Performance IQ. Scores within the Verbal subtests were consistent, but, among Performance subtests, a relative weakness was disclosed in Picture Arrangement. It appears that Abby has some difficulties with nonverbal reasoning, visual organization (without motor activity), and planning ability. Short- and long-term memory scores were in the low-average to average range, as indicated by the Cognitive Abilities portion of the Woodcock–Johnson—Revised (Woodcock & Johnson, 1989). A language screen (Clinical Evaluation of Language Fundamentals—Revised [CELF-R]; Semel, Wigg, & Secord, 1987) revealed average to above-average language skills overall, with a significant discrepancy (16 points) noted between the receptive and expressive language scores. This difference is explained by relative weaknesses in recalling lengthy sentences containing clauses, and in formulating sentences. Inasmuch as reading vocabulary scores were good, Abby had difficulty comprehending items on a listening vocabulary task (Test of Adolescent Language—2 [TOAL-2]; Hamill & Larsen, 1988).

Both norm- and criterion-referenced measures of academic achievement disclosed subtle learning differences. Overall, Abby's reading scores obtained from the Stanford Diagnostic Reading Test (Karlsen & Gardner, 1984) and Survey of Problem-Solving and Educational Skills (SPES; Meltzer, 1987) were within the average range for her grade, but were below the 50th percentile. Her reading rate was markedly slow. Decoding of isolated words was grade appropriate. After reading a passage silently, she recalled only one third of the key points, but answered structured comprehension questions at grade level.

Written language was average, with relative weaknesses noted in spelling and in the thematic maturity of the spontaneous paragraphs Abby composed (TOWL-2, SPES). An error analysis of spelling items indicated that she made numerous phonetic substitutions. In constructing paragraphs, Abby limited her writing to the construction of short, simple sentences. The conditions under which a task is presented are important to Abby. For example, she wrote all of the elements of a sentence she heard, but transposed their order. In recalling and writing a sentence that she had read silently, words were substituted or omitted. Inasmuch as teacher reports and direct observations indicated excellent skills in mathematics, results on the SPES revealed relatively poor automaticity in accessing mathematics facts and in computing problems correctly (grade equivalent

= 4.0–5.0). She did not attend to details when solving problems or self-monitor her errors.

Administration of the SPES disclosed a strong pattern of problem-solving strategies on nonacademic tasks. Abby understood the concepts and formulated strategies slowly, but accurately. On a task of conceptual/thematic flexibility, she demonstrated relative difficulties selectively attending to details and explaining the shift from one organizing theme to its alternative (category shifts).

Summary and Recommendation for Strategy Training

Test results on a variety of measures obtained from multiple sources in several settings indicated that Abby possesses average intelligence, with discrepancies noted between verbal and nonverbal skills. Relative difficulties in selective attention, motor speed, and automaticity in recalling rule-governed information were evidenced throughout the assessment. Consistent with the literature regarding students with learning disabilities (Denkla & Rudel, 1976), Abby demonstrated weaknesses in automatic processing and spent extensive time identifying letters and numbers during reading and math tasks. Consequently, some difficulties were noted on complex cognitive components, such as literal and inferential reading comprehension (LaBerge & Samuels, 1974). Difficulties in silent reading, retrieving main ideas, and summarizing concepts were also noted. Written language measures revealed difficulties in visual retention of correct spelling and using spelling rules (not emphasized in school curriculum). Spontaneous writing samples revealed better spelling skills, but sentence and theme construction and vocabulary usage were simplistic. In addition to poor automatic retrieval of math facts, Abby did not correctly solve or self-monitor completion of mathematical operations.

Inasmuch as Abby demonstrated relative weaknesses in at least one area within each of the basic skills domains, the most pervasive problem was in Abby's lack of efficiency in organizing and executing independent learning tasks (i.e., homework and studying). These difficulties were magnified by the accelerated pace and emphasis of the curriculum on independent learning. School-related pressures necessitated her mother's monitoring of task completion, but her mother's involvement was an antecedent for Abby's verbal and physical aggression. Therefore, the acquisition of independent skills and managing assignments emerged as the primary target of intervention.

A strategy to guide independent organization and completion of assignments was designed (see Table 12.1). Additionally, a self-monitoring checklist was incorporated into the overall strategy (see Figure 12.1). Couched in a personally relevant mnemonic, the BACK OFF strategy pro-

TABLE 12.1. Cognitive Strategy for Independent Management of Assignments: "BACK OFF"

B	*Bring* completed assignments in the assignment folder.
A	*Ask* questions about assignments that were difficult.
C	*Copy* down new assignments in the assignment book.
K	*Keep* the assignment book, assignment folder, texts, and important papers in a backpack so assignments can be completed at home.
O	*Organize* and prioritize assignments at home.
F	*Finish* all of the work as copied in the assignment book.
F	*File* the completed assignment in the assignment folder and bring it with you the next day.

vided Abby with a framework to assume responsibility for assignments, while affording her the prompt to self-monitor her use of the strategy. We hoped Abby would identify the structure of the assignment strategy, recognize the utility of using other strategies, and begin to formulate her own strategies. Once she demonstrated mastery and independence in the use of this simple strategy, other issues in strengthening basic skills could be addressed. When Abby recognized the problem-solving strategies that she already possessed, scaffolding techniques could also be introduced (Palinscar, 1986).

SUMMARY

Students with learning disabilities display cognitive characteristics that may hinder their acquisition of academic and social skills. Learned helplessness, deficits in self-regulation, limited metacognitive awareness, and problems in attention and memory form a constellation of learning and social behaviors that hinder independent and efficient learning. Proponents of cognitive strategy interventions believe that strategies can be designed and incorporated in a variety of learning and social situations to engage such students in the learning process and to modify learning and behavioral outcomes. To accomplish this, it is essential that the design and implementation of such procedures be guided by the results of comprehensive assessments that sample cognitive abilities, academic achievement, and behavioral attributes. These data should be collected using multiple methods and multiple observers from multiple environments. The intention for cognitive strategy intervention is to replace inefficient, nondirected learning, with a rule-governed, self-regulated approach to knowledge acquisition and problem solving.

Dates of week: _____	Monday	Tuesday	Wednesday	Thursday	Friday
B Did I *bring* all of my finished assignments with me today?	Y N F	Y N F	Y N F	Y N F	Y N F
A Did I remember to *ask* questions about assignments that were difficult?	Y N F	Y N F	Y N F	Y N F	Y N F
C Did I *copy* all of my assignments accurately in the assignment book?	Y N F	Y N F	Y N F	Y N F	Y N F
K Did I *keep* the assignment book, assignment folder, and texts needed to complete assignments in my backpack so that I was prepared to complete my assignments independently?	Y N F	Y N F	Y N F	Y N F	Y N F
O Did I *organize* and prioritize my work so that I had time to complete my work?	Y N F	Y N F	Y N F	Y N F	Y N F
F Did I *finish* my work?	Y N F	Y N F	Y N F	Y N F	Y N F
F Did I *file* all of the completed assignments in the assignment folder so that I was prepared for the next day?	Y N F	Y N F	Y N F	Y N F	Y N F

Key: Y = Yes, N = No, F = Forgot. Time when completed:

FIGURE 12.1. Self-monitoring checklist for independent management of assignments.

There are many issues related to the use of cognitive strategies that extended beyond the limits of this chapter, but are important to the use of cognitive approaches with this student population. The current emphasis on including students with learning disabilities in regular education programs underscores the immediate need to better understand the assessment and teaching technology in order to assist these students in becoming effective, independent, and well-adjusted individuals. Despite the emphasis of the chapter on the problems associated with the learning styles of students with learning disabilities, it must be noted that strategy instruction may neither be needed by, nor be an effective solution for all students with learning disabilities. Thus, the individual nature of the difficulties of such students suggests that the use of a "canned-strategy curriculum" may not be the best approach to cognitive strategy intervention. Rather, it is essential that the design of individualized strategy interventions consider the unique and creative approaches to learning that many students with learning disabilities utilize. It is also critical that cognitive strategy interventions also consider the culture, ethnicity, and the goals of such individuals and their families in the design and delivery of instruction.

REFERENCES

Achenbach, T. M. (1991a). *The Child Behavior Checklist*. Burlington: University of Vermont.

Achenbach, T. M. (1991b). *Youth Self-Report*. Burlington: University of Vermont.

Baker, L., & Anderson, R. I. (1982). Effects of inconsistent information on text processing: Evidence for comprehension monitoring. *Reading Research Quarterly, 17*, 281–294.

Bender, W. N. (1987). Behavioral indicators of temperament and personality in the inactive learner. *Journal of Learning Disabilities, 20*, 280–286.

Bender, W. N. (1992). *Learning disabilities: Characteristics, identification, and teaching strategies*. Boston: Allyn & Bacon.

Borkowski, J. G., Estrada, M. T., Milstead, M., & Hale, C. (1989). General problem-solving skills: Relations between metacognition and strategic processing. *Learning Disability Quarterly, 12*, 57–70.

Bos, C., & Anders, P. L. (1990). Interactive teaching and learning: Instructional practices for teaching content and strategic knowledge. In T. E. Scruggs & B. Y. L. Wong (Eds.), *Intervention research in learning disabilities* (pp. 116–185). New York: Springer-Verlag.

Brown, R. T., & Wynne, M. E. (1984). An analysis of attentional components in hyperactive and normal boys. *Journal of Learning Disabilities, 17*, 162–167.

Bursuck, W. D. (1994, October). *Designing and teaching your own learning strategies*. Presentation to the Orton Dyslexia Society, Oakbrook, IL.

Campione, J. C. (1989). Assisted assessment: A taxonomy of approaches and an outline of strengths and weaknesses. *Journal of Learning Disabilities, 22,* 151–165.

Campione, J. C., Brown, A. L., Ferrara, R. A., Jones, R. S., & Steinberg, E. (1985). Breakdown in flexible use of information: Intelligence-related differences in transfer following equivalent learning performance. *Intelligence, 9,* 297–315.

Cohen, R. L., Netley, C., & Clarke, M. A. (1984). On the generality of the short-term memory/reading ability relationship. *Journal of Learning Disabilities, 17,* 218–221.

Coopersmith, S. (1981). *The Self-Esteem Inventories.* Palo Alto, CA: Consulting Psychologist Press.

Denkla, M., & Rudel, R. (1976). Rapid automatized naming: Dyslexia differentiated from other learning disabilities. *Neuropsychologia, 14,* 471–479.

Deshler, D. D., & Schumaker, J. B. (1986). Learning strategies: An instructional alternative for low-achieving adolescents. *Exceptional Children, 52,* 583–590.

Deshler, D. D., Schumaker, J. B., Lenz, B. K., & Ellis, E. (1984). Academic and cognitive interventions for learning disabilities adolescents: Part II. *Journal of Learning Disabilities, 17,* 170–179.

Dykman, R. A., Ackerman, P. T., Clements, S. D., & Peters, J. E. (1971). Specific learning disabilities: An attentional deficit syndrome. In H. R. Myklebust (Ed.), *Progress in learning disabilities* (Vol. 2, pp. 145–189). Orlando, FL: Grune & Stratton.

Dykman, R. A., Ackerman, P. T., Holcomb, M. A., & Bordreau, B. A. (1983). Physiological manifestations of learning disability. *Journal of Learning Disabilities, 16,* 46–53.

Ellis, E., Deshler, D., Lenz, K., Schumaker, J., & Clark, F. (1991). An instructional model for teaching learning strategies. *Focus on Exceptional Children, 23*(6), 1–23.

Ellis, E. S., & Lenz, B. K. (1987). A component analysis of effective learning strategies for learning disabilities students. *Learning Disability Focus, 2*(2), 94–107.

Ellis, E. S., Lenz, B. K., & Sabornie, E. S. (1987). Generalization and adaptation of learning strategies to natural environments: Part 2. Research into practice. *Remedial and Special Education, 8*(2), 6–23.

Englert, C. S., Raphael, T. E., Anderson, L. M., Gregg, S. L., & Anthony, H. M. (1989). Exposition: Reading, writing, and the metacognitive knowledge of learning disabled students. *Learning Disabilities Research, 5*(1), 5–24.

Ferrara, R. A., Brown, A. L., & Campione, J. C. (1986). Children's learning and transfer of inductive reasoning rules: Studies of proximal development. *Child Development, 57,* 1087–1089.

Finch, A. J., Nelson, W. M., & Ott, E. S. (1993). *Cognitive-behavioral procedures* with *children and adolescents.* Boston: Allyn & Bacon.

Fleisher, L. S., Soodak, L. C., & Jelin, M. A. (1984). Selective attention deficits in learning disabled children: Analysis of a data base. *Exceptional Children, 51,* 136–141.

Gardner, H. (1983). *Frames of mind: The theory of multiple intelligences.* New York: Basic Books.

Gardner, W. I. (1977). *Learning and behavior characteristics of exceptional children and youth.* Boston: Allyn & Bacon.

Gelzheiser, L. M., Cort, R., & Sheperd, M. J. (1987). Is minimal strategy instruction sufficient for learning disabilities children? Testing the production defending hypothesis. *Learning Disability Quarterly, 10,* 267–276.

Gerber, M. M. (1988). Cognitive-behavioral training in the curriculum: Time, slow learners, and basic skills. In E. L. Meyen, G. A. Vergason, & R. J. Whelan (Eds.), *Effective instructional strategies for exceptional children* (pp. 45–64). Denver, CO: Love.

Graham, S., & Harris, K. R. (1989). The relevance of IQ in the determination of learning disabilities: Abandoning scores as decision makers. *Journal of Learning Disabilities, 22,* 500–503.

Gresham, F. W., & Elliott, S. N. (1991). *Social Skills Rating System.* Circle Pines, MN: American Guidance Service.

Hallahan, D. P., Kneedler, R. D., & Lloyd, J. W. (1983). Cognitive behavior modification techniques for learning disabled children: Self-instruction and self-monitoring. In J. D. McKinney & L. Feagans (Eds.), *Current topics in learning disabilities* (Vol. 1, pp. 78–95). Norwood, NJ: Ablex.

Hallahan, D. P., & Sapona, R. (1983). Self-monitoring of attention with learning disabled children: Past research and current issues. *Journal of Learning Disabilities, 16,* 616–620.

Hammill, D. D., Brown, V. L., Larsen, S. C., & Wiederholt, J. L. (1987). *Test of Adolescent Language.* Austin, TX: Pro-Ed.

Hammill, D. D., & Larsen, S.C. (1988). *Test of Written Language—2.* Austin, TX: Pro-Ed.

Harris, K. R. (1988). Cognitive-behavior modification: Application with exceptional students. In E. L. Meyen, G. A. Vergason, & R. J. Whelan (Eds.), *Effective instructional strategies for exceptional children* (pp. 216–242). Denver, CO: Love.

Karlsen, B., & Gardner, E. F. (1984). *Stanford Diagnostic Reading Test* (3rd ed.). San Antonio, TX: Psychological Corporation.

Kavale, K. A., & Forness, S. R. (1986). School learning, time, and learning disabilities: The disassociated learner. *Journal of Learning Disabilities, 19,* 130–138.

LaBerge, D., & Samuels, S. J. (1974). Toward a theory of automatic information processing on reading. *Cognitive Psychology, 6,* 293–323.

Licht, B., & Kistner, J. (1986). Motivational problems of learning disabled children: Individual differences and their implications for treatment. In J. Torgesen & B. Wong (Eds.), *Psychological and educational perspectives on learning disabilities* (pp. 225–255). New York: Academic Press.

Licht, B. G., Kistner, J. A., Ozkaragoz, T., Shapiro, S., & Clausen, L. (1985). Causal attributions of learning disabled children: Individual differences that their implications for persistence. *Journal of Educational Psychology, 77,* 208–216.

Lidz, C. S. (Ed.). (1987). *Dynamic assessment.* New York: Guilford Press.

McLoone, B. B., Scruggs, T. E., Mastropieri, M. A., & Zucker, S. F. (1986).

Memory strategy instruction and training with learning-disabled adolescents. *Learning Disability Research, 2,* 45–53.

McKinney, J. D., & Feagans, L. (1983). Adaptive classroom behavior of learning disabled students. *Journal of Learning Disabilities, 16,* 360–367.

Meichenbaum, D. H., & Butler, L. (1980). Toward a conceptual model for the treatment of test anxiety: Implications for research and treatment. In I. G. Sarason (Ed.), *Test anxiety, theory, research and applications* (pp. 187–208). Hillsdale, NJ: Erlbaum.

Meltzer, L. J. (1987). *Surveys of problem-solving and educational skills.* Cambridge, MA: Educators Publishing Service.

Meltzer, L. J. (1993) Problem-solving strategies and academic performance in learning disabled students: Do subtypes exist? In L. Feagans, E. J. Short, & L. J. Meltzer (Eds.), *Subtypes of learning disabilities* (pp. 163–188). Hillsdale, NJ: Erlbaum.

Meltzer, L. J., Solomon, B., Fenton, R., & Levine, M. D. (1989). A developmental study of problem-solving strategies in children with and without learning difficulties. *Journal of Applied Developmental Psychology, 10,* 171–193.

Ollendick, T., & Hersen, M. (Eds.). (1984). *Child behavioral assessment.* New York: Pergamon Press.

Palinscar, A. (1986). The role of dialogue in providing scaffolded instruction. *Educational Psychologist, 21,* 73–98.

Palincsar, A. M., & Brown, A. (1987). Enhancing instructional time through attention to metacognition. *Journal of Learning Disabilities, 20,* 66–76.

Palincsar, A. M., & Brown, A. L. (1989). Instruction for self-regulated reading. In L. B. Resnick & L. E. Klopfer (Eds.), *Toward the thinking curriculum: Current cognitive research* (pp. 19–39). Alexandria, VA: Association for Supervision and Curriculum Development.

Paris, S. G., & Myers, M. (1981). Comprehension monitoring, memory, and study strategies of good and poor readers. *Journal of Reading Behavior, 13,* 5–22.

Paris, S. G., & Oka, E. R. (1986). Self-regulated learning among exceptional children. *Exceptional Children, 53,* 103–108.

Paris, S. G., Wasik, B. A., & Turner, J. C. (1991). The development of strategic readers. In P. D. Pearson (Ed.), *Handbook of reading research* (2nd ed., pp. 609–640). White Plains, NY: Longman.

Roberts, C., Pratt, C., & Leach, D. (1991). Classroom and playground interaction of students with and without disabilities. *Exceptional Children, 57,* 212–224.

Rooney, K. J., & Hallahan, D. P. (1991). Future directions for cognitive behavior modification research: The quest for cognitive change. *Remedial and Special Education, 6,* 46–51.

Sattler, J. (1988). Assessment of learning disabilities, attention-deficit hyperactivity disorders, conduct disorder, pervasive developmental disorders, and sensory impairments. In J. Sattler (Ed.), *The measurement of children* (pp. 597–645). San Diego: Sattler.

Schunk, D. H., & Cox, P. D. (1986). Strategy training and attributional feedback with learning disabled students. *Journal of Educational Psychology, 78,* 201–209.

Semel, E., Wiig, E. H., & Secord, W. (1987). *Clinical evaluation of language fundamentals—Revised.* San Diego: Harcourt Brace Jovanovich.

Shinn, M. R. (1989). Identifying and defining academic problems: Cognitive behavior modification screening and eligibility procedures. In M. R. Shinn (Ed.), *Curriculum-based measurement: Assessing special children* (pp. 90–129). New York: Guilford Press.

Short, E. J., & Ryan, E. G. (1984). Metacognitive differences between skilled and less skilled readers: Remediating deficits through story grammar and attribution retraining. *Journal of Educational Psychology, 76,* 225–235.

Smith, T. E. C., Finn, D. M., & Dowdy, C. A. (1993). *Teaching students with mild disabilities.* Philadelphia: Harcourt Brace Jovanovich.

Snider, V. (1987). Use of self-monitoring of attention with learning disabilities students: Research and application. *Learning Disability Quarterly, 10,* 139–151.

Swanson, H. L. (1989). Strategy instruction: Overview of principles and procedures for effective use. *Learning Disability Quarterly, 12,* 3–14.

Swanson, H. L. (1990). Instruction derived from the strategy deficit model: Overview of principles and procedures. In T. Scruggs & B. Y. L. Wong (Eds.), *Intervention research in learning disabilities* (pp. 34–65). New York: Springer-Verlag.

Swanson, H. L. (1993). A cognitive assessment approach 11. In D. K. Reid, W. P. Hresko, & H. L. Swanson (Eds.), *A cognitive approach to learning disabilities* (pp. 275–294). Austin, TX: Pro-Ed.

Swanson, H. L., & Trahan, M. (1990). Naturalistic memory in learning disabled children. *Learning Disability Quarterly, 13,* 82–89.

Telzrow, C. F. (1990). Best practices in reducing error in identifying specific learning disabilities. In Thomas, E. & Grimes, J. (Eds.), *Best practices in school psychology—II* (pp. 607–620). Washington, DC: NASP.

Tobias, S. (1982). When do instructional methods make a difference? *Educational Researcher, 11,* 4–9.

Torgesen, J. K. (1980). The use of efficient task strategies by learning disabled children: Conceptual and educational implications. *Journal of Learning Disabilities, 13,* 364–371.

Torgesen, J. K. (1988a). The cognitive and behavioral characteristics of children with learning disabilities: An overview. *Journal of Learning Disabilities, 21,* 587–589.

Torgesen, J. K. (1988b). Studies of children with learning disabilities who perform poorly on memory span tasks. *Journal of Learning Disabilities, 21,* 605–612.

Torgesen, J. K., & Licht, B. G. (1983). The learning disabled child as an inactive learner: Retrospect and prospects. In J. D. McKinney & L. Feagans (Eds.), *Current topics in learning disabilities* (Vol. 1, pp. 3–31). Norwood, NJ: Ablex.

Torgesen, J. K., Murphy, H., & Ivey, G. (1979). The effects of an orienting task on the memory performance of reading disabled children. *Journal of Learning Disabilities, 12,* 396–401.

Trapani, C. (1990). *Transition goals for adolescents with learning disabilities.* Austin, TX: Pro-Ed.

Vygostky, L. S. (1978). *Mind in society.* Cambridge, MA: Harvard University Press.

Wechsler, D. (1991). *Wechsler Intelligence Scale for Children* (3rd ed.). San Antonio, TX: Psychological Corporation.

Weinstein, C. F., & Mayer, R. F. (1986). The teaching of learning strategies. In M. C. Wittrock (Ed.), *Handbook of research on teaching* (pp. 315–327). (American Educational Research Association). New York: Macmillan.

Welsh. B. L. (1987). The individualized Family Plan: Bridge between the school and the family. *Social Work in Education, 9*(4), 230–239.

Wong, B. Y. L. (1982) Understanding the learning disabled student's reading problems: Contributions from cognitive psychology. *Topics in Learning and Learning Disabilities, 1*(4), 43–50.

Wong, B. Y. L. (1985). Metacognition and learning disabilities: A review of a view. *Journal of Special Education, 20,* 9–29.

Wong, B. Y. L. (1991). *Learning about learning disabilities.* San Diego: Academic Press.

Wong, B. Y. L. (1992). On cognitive process-based instruction. An introduction. *Journal of Learning Disabilities, 25,* 105–115.

Wong, B. Y. L., & Jones, W. (1982). Increasing metacomprehension in learning disabled and normally-achieving students through self-questioning training. *Learning Disability Quarterly, 5,* 228–240.

Wong, B. Y. L., Wong, R., & Blenkinsop, J. (1989). Cognitive and metacognitive aspects of learning disabled adolescents' composing problems. *Learning Disability Quarterly, 12,* 300–322.

Woodcock, R. W., & Johnson, M. B. (1989). *The Woodcock–Johnson Psychoeducational Assessment Battery: Part 1. Tests of cognitive ability.* Allen, TX: Developmental Learning Materials.

Zimmerman, S. O. (1988). Problem-solving tasks on the microcomputer: A look at the performance of students with learning disabilities. *Journal of Learning Disabilities, 21,* 637–641.

13

Adolescent Inpatient Treatment

G. Randolph Schrodt
Barbara A. Fitzgerald
Alan J. Ravitz
Mark A. Reinecke

The practice of inpatient adolescent psychiatry has undergone a radical transformation in recent years. In the 1960s and 1970s the average length of stay for adolescents in psychiatric hospitals was usually measured in months. Today, under pressure from managed care companies and other economic and social forces, the typical hospitalization of an adolescent is less than 2 weeks, and often just a few days' duration. This change has necessitated a reconsideration of the goals of inpatient treatment and the development of new treatment philosophies and methods.

In the majority of cases the primary objectives of hospitalization are as follows:

1. Stabilization of the crisis situation that prompted hospitalization
2. Rapid biopsychosocial diagnostic evaluation
3. Initiation of treatment
4. Development of an aftercare plan that can be implemented in a less restrictive environment

The attainment of these goals requires the coordination of effort of a multidisciplinary team with a clear conceptualization of the treatment plan and a shared treatment philosophy. Over the past 12 years at the Norton Psychiatric Clinic, we have found that cognitive-behavioral therapy has provided an effective, pragmatic organizational model for the adolescent inpatient program. We have previously described this approach in detail (Schrodt & Wright, 1987; Schrodt, 1993). In this chapter we illustrate the inpatient treatment, using a cognitive-behavioral approach, of a severely depressed young woman. Regardless of one's theoretical orientation or technical approach, it is vital that all members of the treatment team share a common, integrated treatment philosophy. Without a shared conceptual framework, it is difficult, if not impossible, for a team to work in concert to provide efficient, short-term interventions.

Over the last several years, clinicians have developed a number of intensive outpatient interventions that have decreased the likelihood of adolescents being admitted to the hospital unless they present with extremely severe symptomatology. Nevertheless, criteria for hospitalization are essentially the same today as they were 10 to 20 years ago. Most often, adolescents are admitted for inpatient treatment because they present an imminent risk of harming themselves or others. Patients who meet these criteria frequently are psychotic, suicidal, violent, or behaviorally out of control. Adolescents are also often admitted due to the presence of an inadequate, neglectful, or abusive support system. The family environments in which these patients find themselves are unable to protect them or are ineffective in controlling their behavior. An inability to benefit from less intensive, outpatient treatment may also prompt a referral for admission. Finally, patients may require psychiatric hospitalization due to the presence of a co-occurring medical illness that requires 24-hour monitoring by medical staff. In many cases, patients who present for hospitalization meet several of these criteria for inpatient care. In the great majority of cases, the clinician is confronted with a patient who has a complex set of difficulties, and who manifests long-standing problems that have proven refractory to several prior treatment attempts.

Usually, the behavior patterns with which these patients present represent an adaptive response to other, even longer standing intrapsychic, interpersonal, or environmental problems. As a consequence, these patients have developed adaptive rationalizations that allow them to maintain their maladaptive adjustment. They view their behavior as a reasonable response to events in their lives. Although the problems that bring the adolescent to the hospital are almost always ego-syntonic, rather than ego-dystonic, they invariably are seen as maladaptive by outside observers. It is important to remember that although the symptomatic behavior manifested by the patient may be maladaptive, it is purposeful and is guided by a specific set of beliefs, attitudes, expectations, attributions, and goals. In almost every case, problematic behaviors are reinforced because they serve the function of avoiding or ameliorating emotional pain. As clinicians, we need to understand the sources of our patients' pain and the adaptive function of their beliefs and actions. We must also, however, endeavor to assist patients to participate in an analysis of their beliefs and actions that will ultimately lead to the development of more effective adaptive strategies.

The fact that these behaviors are ego-syntonic often leads the patient to be resistant to therapeutic interventions. These patients often do not believe that change is either necessary or possible. Whereas they may recognize that there are difficulties in their lives, they tend to place the responsibility for these problems on others and tend not to believe that they have the capacity to influence others or bring about meaningful change. Although they often have little faith in their future and demonstrate limited perceptions of self-efficacy, they may attempt to camouflage these beliefs with grandiose posturing. These patients are, in short, relatively hopeless, pessimistic, and helpless. In point of fact, many adolescents referred for inpatient treatment have experienced failure at home, in school, and with their peer group. They often have little confidence in the sensitivity, reliability, or nurturance of their caretakers. They may, as such, perceive others as unsupportive and believe that their parents or peers do not fully understand or appreciate their predicament. Up to this point in their lives, their caretakers have been unable to protect them from experiencing the failures noted. They may, as a consequence, become pessimistic regarding the effectiveness of treatment, and not believe that they or their families can truly change. As a group, these children have been traumatized by their life experience. They have adapted by assuming a stance of denial of a need for help. Their maladaptive defenses or coping strategies are ego-syntonic, and as much as they may want to change, they cannot admit to this desire because they anticipate further failure and disappointment.

The typical hospitalized adolescent may present with any one of several Axis I, Axis II, or even Axis III diagnoses. As noted by several authors (Angold & Costello, 1992; Caron & Rutter, 1991; Kendall & Clarkin, 1992), comorbidity of diagnoses appears to be the rule, rather than the exception, for psychiatrically referred children and adolescents. Adolescents referred for hospitalization typically present with a number of readily identifiable personality traits. Most of these children are highly oppositional, sullen, and defiant. As much as they want help, they are mistrustful of adults. These children often, as a consequence, respond to interventions made by adults in a negative manner. As a corollary to their oppositional tendencies, many of these patients suffer from dysphoria, irritability, and a tendency to become hopeless in the face of obstacles. Moreover, they often manifest a range of social skills deficits, which can take the form of social withdrawal or antisocial tendencies. Their network of social supports, as such, is often limited. Most adolescent inpatients have experienced a range of stressful life events, including acute or chronic school failure. Most have experimented with drugs or alcohol, and a significant proportion have become dependent on these substances to help them modulate their moods. The assessment and treatment of alcohol and substance abuse, as such, plays a important role in the inpatient program (see O'Connell & Patterson, Chapter 5, this volume). Finally, the majority of adolescent inpatients experience difficulty identifying and labeling their emotional states, and thus are unable to express their feelings and needs directly to others. This presents us with a therapeutic challenge in that, unlike many adult patients, it is often difficult for adolescents to identify the relationships between their thoughts or beliefs and their consequent emotional reactions and behaviors. This often leads them to appear to be "manipulative," in that they experience difficulty expressing their desires in a forthright manner. The ability to identify emotions and to recognize their relationship to thoughts and attitudes is a skill that must be developed over the course of their inpatient stay.

How does the hospital function to assist adolescents with these difficulties? First, the treatment milieu provides a protected, structured environment, so that these very disturbed and anxious patients can feel emotionally and physically secure. Many of these patients experience difficulty regulating the expression of affect. The therapeutic milieu serves to support the development of this skill. The rules, regulations, and rituals of the program (including regularly scheduled community meetings, group psychotherapy, activity therapy, and school) all serve to provide the patient with a sense of stability, predictability, and security. Second, the structure of the treatment milieu provides emotional support for the patients and their families. Quite often, children and parents feel overwhelmed, confused, and frightened by the severity of the behavioral and emotional problems. The provision of a secure, supportive milieu and the development of a coherent treatment plan can be quite reassuring in this regard. It is all but impossible to form collaborative treatment alliances if the participants in the treatment process do not feel respected and understood. Clinically, we have found it useful to directly ask patients and their parents whether they feel that their feelings, concerns, and goals are fully understood by the treatment team. Third, the treatment milieu must be highly structured and predictable. Rules and regulations should be clearly described and administered in a consistent manner by all staff members. While patients should have input into the ways the milieu is managed, exceptions to rules should be rare and should only be made under exceptional circumstances. Although the provision of structure is valuable, it is even more important that the patients experience the structure as responsive to their needs and relevant to their problems. Consistent with the cognitive model, patients should be aware of the rationale for the interventions that are being made. Operant contingency paradigms should be established that reward genuine therapeutic work and punish avoidance or resistance. It must be kept in mind that the underlying rationale for each of our interventions should be to engineer an environment in which the maladaptive, albeit ego-syntonic, beliefs, attitudes, and behaviors become sufficiently painful that they become ego-dystonic. The therapeutic milieu initially challenges patients by placing them in an environment in which their customary, maladaptive coping strategies are no longer effective. It is only at this point that patients will be able to see the inadequacy of their defensive maneuvering.

Cognitive models of psychopathology recognize that maladaptive beliefs, attitudes, and behaviors develop in an interpersonal context (Gotlib & Hammen, 1992; Safran & Segal, 1990). This is nowhere more important than in clinical work with seriously disturbed children and adolescents. The maladaptive beliefs and behaviors displayed by these children are often modeled and reinforced by family members or peers. The developmental experiences of emotionally or behaviorally disturbed adolescents are often less than optimal, in the sense that they do not adequately support the consolidation of skills for forming trusting relationships, regulation of affect; maintaining a sense of personal security, self-control, or frustration tolerance; and the development of an adult-vocational or interpersonal identity. As a consequence, adolescents referred for inpatient treatment frequently display deficits in one or more of these domains. With this in mind, cognitively based family therapy (see Epstein & Schlesinger, Chapter 14, this volume) often plays an important role in the inpatient treatment program.

Because maladaptive schemas or tacit belief systems typically underlie maladaptive behavior, cognitive interventions play a central role in the treatment program. Due to the brevity of inpatient stays, however, there typically is not enough time to gently move a patient away from these dysfunctional beliefs. Therefore, the contemporary therapeutic milieu must be structured in such a way that maladaptive beliefs and attitudes can be identified and confronted directly. This is readily accomplished by preventing the patient from utilizing maladaptive coping strategies and by highlighting cognitive distortions and irrational or maladaptive beliefs as they become apparent. Patients are actively encouraged, both through writing assignments and therapeutic discussions, to address their underlying concerns by thinking and talking about them. They are actively discouraged from acting upon them in maladaptive ways. Behavioral, psychodynamic, and gestalt interventions may be incorporated into a cognitively based treatment program as a means of eliciting affect and encouraging reflection. The goal is to help adolescents acknowledge that they are, in fact, in a great deal of pain and that their customary coping strategies have been ineffective. A goal, as such, is to engender an optimum amount of anxiety so that patients are uncomfortable enough that they will want to change. They are not, however, confronted or pressed to the point that they become hopeless or resistant, because this would ultimately jeopardize the development of collaborative therapeutic relationships. The treatment team endeavors, through the use of supportive, expressive, and rationally based interventions, to destabilize the patients' maladaptive belief and coping systems. As they relinquish these maladaptive beliefs and behaviors, new cognitive and behavioral coping skills are acquired. This process of destabilization and reorganization can be initiated in a highly structured, cognitively oriented adolescent inpatient milieu. Once this process is initiated in the hospital, patients and their families can continue on an outpatient basis.

CASE PRESENTATION

Julie is a 17-year-old, white female who had been seen by a licensed clinical social worker in individual outpatient psychotherapy for 3 months prior to her admission for depression and an atypical eating disorder. She had become increasingly depressed over the Christmas holidays, and approximately 8 weeks prior to admission had been started on Prozac (20 mg per day) with some initial improvement in her mood. However, over the 2 weeks prior to her admission, she had become quite regressed. She had been unable to attend school, would rarely leave her bed, had deteriorating personal hygiene, and failed to care for herself in other ways. Due to her inability to function and the emergence of suicidal ideation, she was referred for admission. In the initial interview in the hospital, she related a sense of almost total hopelessness and helplessness. Her initial Child Depression Inventory (CDI) score was 31 and her Hopelessness Scale (HS) score was 16, both indicative of a severe depression and profound sense of pessimism about the future.

Julie's parents had been divorced for several years, and she lived with her father and younger sister. Her mother resided out of the country and had been diagnosed with schizophrenia, although her history was suggestive of a bipolar affective disorder. Julie reported that she had been "torn" for many years about which parent to live with. Although she had chosen to stay with her father, she reported extreme guilt "because my mother needs me." Over the past several years, Julie had danced with a regional ballet company and had a promising career. However, her recent depression and binge eating had interfered with her ability to participate actively, and she had not been going to ballet for some weeks. She was a high school senior and had previously been doing well in honors courses but was failing two of the subjects required for graduation. She had the prospect of getting a dancing scholarship to college, but would need to "get back in shape," return to active performance, and compete in tryouts.

Psychological testing supported the diagnosis of major depressive disorder with a secondary eating disorder, characterized by binge episodes and distorted body image. She was high-average in intelligence, although was experiencing cognitive impairment due to her depression and psychomotor retardation. In her on-admission physical examination, a cardiac murmur was detected. Chest X ray indicated possible cardiac enlargement. A cardiology consultation was requested, and further diagnostic tests failed to reveal cardiomegaly or an atrial septal defect, and she was diagnosed with a benign cardiac murmur.

Initial Individual Session

The initial therapy session with a hospitalized adolescent often deals with an agenda focused on issues related to hospitalization, separation from family and friends, rules, ward routine, the restriction of freedom, and the most frequently asked question, "When can I go home?" Issues of therapeutic alliance are difficult, particularly with adolescents who are admitted involuntarily. However, cognitive-behavioral therapy appears to provide a framework for establishing a collaborative working relationship (Schrodt & Fitzgerald, 1986; Schrodt & Wright, 1987; Schrodt, 1993). In this case, Julie was highly distressed by her depressive symptoms and had voluntarily sought treatment. Although understandably anxious about the disruptive impact of hospitalization, she was ready to launch into therapeutic issues in the first session.

DR. F.: What would you say is the major problem that led you to seek treatment?

JULIE: I'm fat and weigh too much and can't dance well.

DR. F.: Can you be a little bit more specific about that?

JULIE: Well, how else can I be more specific but to say that I weigh more than I have ever and that this makes it impossible for me to dance?

DR. F.: First, can we take a look at how you gained the weight? And second, what leads you to that it's "impossible" to dance?

JULIE: Well, I feel so bad I don't want to get up in the morning. I don't eat breakfast, and I don't eat lunch. When I come home, I pig out because I'm so upset. I feel like if I've had such a bad day I deserve to have whatever I want to eat, and what we generally have in the house is junk food. So, I pig out on that and then I feel bad, which then leads me, you know, almost to be even tireder, so I go to bed, cover up my head, don't want to think about any of this, go to sleep. The

next thing I know my dad's coming in the door calling me lazy, asking me if I've done my homework, and of course I haven't, so I feel
even worse. I fight with him, then just go to bed and don't do my
homework. I get up the next day and the whole thing starts over again.
My ballet teacher called me the other day and asked if I was ever
coming back to practice, and that made me even feel worse. I knew
he thought I was just a dumb kid who never was gonna amount to
anything or else I'd be there at practice.

DR. F.: Is there any other reason why he might have called?

JULIE: Well, he's always been somewhat nice. He told me that I have a
good future and maybe he just is concerned. Maybe he has a role for
me in the Christmas production and wants me to get back there so
he can decide whether to give it to me or somebody else.

DR. F.: From what you've described it sounds like there's a cycle that goes
on. Can you describe that cycle?

JULIE: I have a problem. When I feel bad I eat too much, then I am dis-
gusted with myself and end up eating more. I get real depressed and
lose my motivation to dance, so I skip practice. I'm such a failure.
Then I ignore my schoolwork and go out with friends to distract
myself, but just end up picking fights with them.

DR. F.: Let's try to diagram this cycle of events, thoughts, feelings, and
behaviors and see if we can make some sense out of it and maybe
come up with some ideas of how to change it. (Dr. F. takes a piece of
paper and diagrams Figure 13.1.) When a person is depressed we
typically see a vicious cycle develop where events trigger a negative
set of thoughts. Now it seems like you have several cycles going on
at different times of the day, but let's just take a look at one event,
"getting home from school." Now you've told me that you feel weak
and tired and start to eat. What thoughts go through your mind at
this point?

JULIE: I am such a slug. I'm so fat I can't do anything. I may as well eat
some more. I deserve to do something I like. I can't do anything right.
I'm worthless.

DR. F.: Okay. I've been jotting some of these thoughts down as you were
talking. Let's take a look at them. How do you feel when you think
this?

JULIE: I feel depressed and angry at myself. I want to climb in bed.

DR. F.: And what do you do then?

JULIE: I skip rehearsal and go to bed.

DR. F.: Alright, now let's review for minute. What do you see happening?

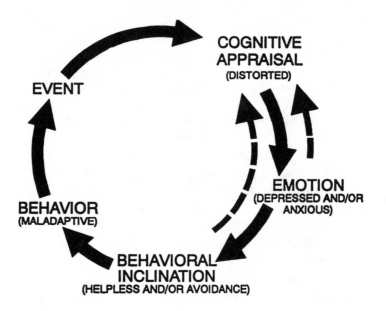

FIGURE 13.1. A cognitive model of depression. From Wright (1988). Copyright 1988 by Jesse H. Wright. Reprinted by permission.

JULIE: Well, it seems like I get a lot of negative thoughts and feelings when I get home. I start to eat to get more energy, but when I binge it just ends up sapping my energy and I don't get anything accomplished.

DR. F.: Can we look at some possible ways to restructure this? Do you have any ideas about what would give you some more energy through the day?

JULIE: I guess if I had a little bit more time in the morning, and maybe put some fuel in my body like we talked about earlier, I might feel like doing something. Then maybe I'd be less likely to eat all that junk food when I got home from school.

DR. F.: That sounds like a very reasonable idea. How would you start off?

JULIE: I guess I would need to plan some meals, go to the grocery store, talk to my dad about how we might do that, and organize my time better at night so I can make my lunch. But I really am not exactly sure what to eat.

DR. F.: I wonder if talking with the nutritionist might help you get some menu plans done?

JULIE: Sure. That sounds like a good idea.

DR. F.: It also sounds like it would help to start getting up a little earlier in the morning. Now this might be hard at first, but the staff can help. There is a physical part of depression as well. I think a change in your antidepressant will help you sleep better at night and play a part in getting your biological clock reset. Let's talk about what I have in mind.

In this first session the therapist's actions were guided both by the material presented and certain "generic" objectives (Schrodt, 1992):

1. Establish a collaborative therapeutic alliance.
2. Maintain a problem-oriented approach.
3. Identify negative automatic thoughts and their relationship to dysphoric mood and maladaptive behavior.
4. Pinpoint cognitive errors.
5. Test distorted automatic thoughts and underlying assumptions.
6. Replace, modify self-defeating cognitive style with a more realistic and adaptive perspective.
7. Improve sense of self-efficacy by development of a problem-solving strategy.
8. Design self-help assignment to be completed between therapy sessions.

Although Julie was severely depressed, she was able to participate in cognitive therapy quite well in this first session. With other hospitalized adolescents, therapy will progress more slowly at first, and the therapist might focus on behavioral techniques or less detailed cognitive exercises, such as making a problem list. The skilled cognitive therapist will modify the therapy to the level of ability and willingness of the adolescent.

Pharmacotherapy is commonly combined with cognitive-behavioral therapies in the treatment of hospitalized patients. Julie did not have any negative reactions to combined treatments, and relatively little time was needed on this topic in therapy sessions beyond presenting basic educational material and monitoring for side effects and therapeutic response. With other adolescents and their families, pharmacotherapy triggers many unrealistic negative (or positive) automatic thoughts. Cognitive-behavioral therapy provides an excellent format to test and modify dysfunctional attitudes and beliefs about medication that may affect compliance with prescribed medication (Wright & Schrodt, 1989; Schrodt, Adams, & Siegel, 1993; Schrodt, 1993).

Group Therapy

Group therapy is a major component of most adolescent inpatient programs. Hospitalization often intensifies the natural tendency of teenagers to bond with their peers, and group therapy may provide a sense of security and familiarity in an otherwise alien environment. Adolescents will often accept support and feedback from peers that they are unwilling to accept from adults. In group therapy, the hospitalized teen may obtain support, validation, and feedback. Perhaps more important, the group may stimulate new perspectives on problem situations and ways of dealing with them.

At first, Julie was reluctant to participate in group. She believed that "No one else has my kind of problem" and was embarrassed with self-disclosure. She later admitted that she was slightly intimidated by her first group session and reluctant to be assertive and bring up her own issues (a schema that later emerged in outpatient group). Nevertheless, with nursing staff encouragement she agreed to attend "and just listen."

Inpatient cognitive-behavioral therapy (CBT) groups follow different formats (Freeman, Schrodt, Gilson, & Ludgate, 1993). Julie attended an "open-ended cognitive-behavioral therapy group" that began with setting an agenda. After introductions, each member was asked if there were any issues he or she wanted to focus on in the group. In the beginning of this group session, the therapist distilled the general agenda issue of "self-concept," with particular reference to another young woman (Gail), who was hospitalized with anorexia nervosa.

THERAPIST: You've had a lot of complaints about your treatment program, the monitored meals, the staff watching you, the locked bathroom door, and the like. What kind of thoughts are you having in these situations?

GAIL: I am scared of gaining weight and getting fat. I won't look good.

THERAPIST: Yesterday you told us that there were a lot of medical problems that prompted your hospitalization, like passing out in school and feeling sick all the time. The doctors tell you it's because you're underweight. Would you rather feel good or "look good"?

GAIL: I'd rather look good.

KATE: You look good now, and you'd look better if you weren't so skinny.

LISA: I know what you mean. I'd rather look good than feel good.

GAIL: It's really important in my school. Everybody tries to look good. You have to look good to be popular, and in our family my mom and sisters were in pageants and people are always telling her, "Your daughters are so beautiful."

THERAPIST: I don't think that anyone is saying that attractiveness is a negative characteristic, but is it the main way that you'd like to be known?

GAIL: It's the most important thing.

SCOTT: You mean you'd rather be known as "pretty" than as "smart" or "nice"?

GAIL: Yes.

THERAPIST: (*to the group*) What are the adjectives that you'd like others to use to describe you? What do you think are the most valued traits? (*At this point the therapist goes around the group to elicit each member's list of valued personal attributes.*)

JULIE: I'd like people to think of me as a good dancer, smart, caring, a good friend. I guess I want people to think of me as pretty, too (*turning to Gail*). It's weird. I've had the same thoughts about my weight that you have. That my weight was why I was unhappy and that it was the most important thing. It's just strange to hear you say it. I think that my appearance is so important, but it's not the thing I care most about in my friends and other people.

The group session progressed with a discussion of the consequences of elevating a single attribute (e.g., appearance) to all-or-nothing significance. The idea of "programming" (schema) was introduced, and group members shared how they came to value certain characteristics such as "intelligent," "nice," or "athletic." Many referred to cultural or family attitudes and beliefs. The therapist encouraged the adolescents to question and evaluate their own attitudes and "decide for themselves." The therapist also discussed how behavioral habits reinforce these beliefs. For example, Gail revealed how she got up at 5 A.M. each morning to exercise and change her clothes "four or five times" so that she'd "look good" for school.

Julie continued to be active in further inpatient group sessions and often brought issues back to her individual sessions with her doctor. The group process greatly diminished her sense of isolation in the hospital. To her surprise, she discovered that others were not as "together" or critical as she had imagined. The opportunity to objectively evaluate others' thoughts and attitudes prompted a reevaluation of her own characteristic cognitive style. She was able to identify her tendency to think in "black and white," and began to modify her own perfectionistic standards by "thinking in shades of gray." Her therapist suggested that she consider attending an outpatient group after discharge. She quickly agreed and actually attended an outpatient group prior to discharge from the inpatient unit. This proved to be of considerable benefit, because she was able to discuss "reentry stress" and return to home, school, and friends with the outpatients, many of whom had previously "survived" hospitalization.

Nursing Interventions

The nursing staff has a major role in the treatment of hospitalized adolescents. Nurses and psychiatric aides have multiple daily interactions with teenagers and perform a variety of critical tasks on the inpatient unit (Schrodt, 1993):

1. Assessment
2. Orientation to the treatment program
3. Management of the therapeutic activity schedule and level system for privileges
4. Implementation of specific behavioral procedures (e.g., eating disorders protocol)
6. Enforcement of ward rules, including assignment of room restriction for inappropriate behavior
6. Patient and family education
7. Assistance in completion of therapy homework
8. Modeling of adaptive social skills, including communication, assertiveness, problem solving, negotiation, and conflict resolution

Julie developed a very positive relationship with several staff members during the first week of her hospitalization. The written treatment plan was reviewed and updated with Julie on a regular basis, and the staff played a significant role in helping her get up on time in the morning. Julie was placed on a modified eating disorder protocol that involved meals monitored by a staff member. During meals, Julie was encouraged not to discuss food or "getting fat." Additionally, the staff monitored and limited her snacking at other times.

The nursing staff also helped Julie complete Daily Records of Dysfunctional Thoughts and other therapy homework assignments. A regularly scheduled "room reflect" time is part of the adolescent inpatient routine. This time, spent alone in the teenager's room, provides an opportunity for therapy homework, writing, or reading of material assigned in individual therapy sessions.

Ward Meeting

The ward meeting is the largest formal group meeting on the adolescent inpatient unit and is presided over by Dr. F., the medical director of the unit. All patients attend this weekly meeting (unless they are severely psychotic or extremely agitated), as well as most of the psychiatry residents, medical students, nursing staff, recreational therapists, and social workers. The ward meeting is structured, task oriented, and focuses on unit community issues rather than individual problems. A broader agenda of the ward meeting is the integration and orientation of new patients into the unit routine. It provides a forum for the discussion of ward policies and rules, and clarification of the purpose of these procedures. After all members introduce themselves, the ward chief asks if there are any issues that need to be discussed.

TOM: The staff never listens.

DR. F.: Tom, could you be a little more specific?

TOM: I was trying to make an important phone call and I was cut off and sent to my room. Then, when I came out of my room to try again, I got restricted.

DEREK: They just don't understand how important these phone calls are to us.

DR. F.: It sounds like this is a very important issue, but I wonder if we could get a few more details. Can you be a little more specific, Tom?

TOM: I was talking to my parents about our last family conference and whether I was going to go home, and one of the staff pointed to the 10-minute time limit posted by the phone. I know that we're only supposed to be on the phone 10 minutes, but this was really important, and there wasn't really anybody waiting to talk on the phone.

DR. F.: Maybe we could check out with the rest of group how important that 10-minute phone limit is.

GAIL: It's really hard sometimes to make phone calls, but if somebody really has an important phone call, like Tom, I guess most of us would understand and not be so anxious to get him off.

DR. F.: That's really very supportive of you, Gail. If you did have an important phone call of your own, how would you get Tom's attention to let him know that you needed to make that call?

GAIL: Well, it's pretty hard for me to let people know that I need something important when their issues are probably more important than mine, but I guess I could either give him a note or tap him on the shoulder.

DR. F.: How easy would that be for you to do?

GAIL: Not very easy.

JULIE: Remember when we talked about assertiveness in our other group?

TOM: I'd sure want you to let me know if you had an important call. Though I guess I have gotten mad at times in the past and blown up at you.

DR. F.: So, it sounds like what we have here is the staff enforcing a rule that is there for a good reason. When people first come into the hospital and they are getting to know each other, it may be harder for them to be more assertive and let you know that they need to make a phone call. On the other hand, it sounds like we might need a way to take a look at phone calls that may need to be longer than 10 minutes in duration, particularly when it deals with important therapeutic issues, so that you don't feel that you have to be cut off when there is something important to talk about. I wonder, Tom, Julie, Gail, if you could get a group together and come back to us with some suggestions about what we might want to do about this?

TOM: Sure.

JULIE: Sure.

GAIL: Sure.

This ward meeting vignette illustrates several important components of a cognitively oriented inpatient unit. Group leaders attempt to maintain a collaborative, flexible, problem-solving approach in therapeutic interactions. Adolescents are particularly prone to feel helpless and to behave in a disruptive or oppositional fashion if staff are perceived as controlling or dictatorial. Dr. F. guided the group toward clarification of a problem, challenged cognitive distortions (e.g., "The staff never listens"), identified options, and took action to share responsibility and power with the teenagers.

Family Conference

Given the short length of stay in the hospital, the family therapist may only have two or three conferences with an adolescent and his or her family. The major objectives (Schrodt, 1993) of inpatient family therapy are as follows:

1. Establish a therapeutic alliance with the family.
2. Identify the reciprocal interaction of distorted perceptions and dysfunctional behavioral patterns within the family system.
3. Modify the beliefs, attitudes, and expectations that interfere with effective parenting.
4. Develop parenting skills, including communication, negotiation, conflict resolution, and ability to establish age-appropriate supervision and limits.

DAD: I'm really frustrated and I don't know what to do. I feel like I've tried everything. Julie's biggest problem is she is so disorganized. I've tried to get her to set up study times and have made her stay home rather than go out with her friends, but instead of studying she lays in bed and listens to her stereo or eats. I just know if she got on a schedule . . .

JULIE: There you go again, always criticizing me and putting me down. I was feeling better until you came here.

DAD: (*to the therapist*) See what I mean? I don't know why she has that attitude.

THERAPIST: Julie, in the hospital you've spent a lot of time with your doctor, the staff, and in group trying to sort out your problems and to make some changes. It might help if you caught your dad up on your progress and he'd have an idea of what your goals are and how he can help after you get home.

JULIE: I've learned that I have to make some changes, like getting up earlier in the morning so I have time to eat breakfast. I've decided I need to be careful about negative thinking and being such a perfectionist, but it doesn't help if you're on my case all the time.

DAD: I just can't stand to see you screw up school right before graduation and blow your chances for a scholarship and dance career. I thought that was what you wanted, too.

JULIE: It is.

THERAPIST: It really doesn't seem like there are disagreements over the long-term goals. You both want to get along better, for Julie to be less depressed and happier with herself, to finish school and to go to college. Am I right?

DAD: Absolutely.

JULIE: Yeah.

THERAPIST: The problems seem to come up with the kind of help your dad tries to offer.

JULIE: He's always so critical. He acts like I'm such a loser. You can tell by the look on his face. He doesn't like my friends, so he won't let me go out, and he doesn't understand that's the only time I'm happy.

DAD: Wait a minute. I've never thought you were "a loser" or ever said anything like that.

JULIE: You're always asking, "Why didn't you go to dance class?" "Why haven't you done your homework?" "Are you just going to sit around and eat all night?" I can't do anything to please him.

DAD: I come home and see you looking and feeling so miserable, and I'm just trying to help. It seems like anything I say or do is rejected. You get mad and just shut me out.

THERAPIST: Julie, how do you think your dad can help?

JULIE: Not be so negative all the time.

THERAPIST: So what kind of positive things can he do to help you continue the progress you've started in the hospital?

JULIE: Well, there's different things that have helped here. I've gotten on a good schedule and I'm getting things done.

DAD: But I've talked about a schedule before.

JULIE: I know . . . but it's different. I know when it's time to study or go to practice. I'm not stupid. I guess I just want some kind of encouragement or something.

DAD: I know it's been real hard and you've been having a real hard time. You are a great person and have so much going for you. I just want you to know I'm totally behind you and will do anything I can to help.

The therapist worked with Julie and her father to identify their misperceptions of each other's statements and intentions. In an earlier history-gathering session with Julie's father, the therapist had introduced basic cognitive therapy concepts and had given him a copy of *Coping with Depression* (Beck & Greenberg, 1974). In this session, the interplay of automatic thoughts and cognitive distortions became apparent. When Julie's father attempted to "help," she perceived him as critical and controlling. In turn, her father thought Julie had "a bad attitude," leading him to feel helpless and frustrated.

The family therapist helped Julie and her father make a list of changes in the home routine. They agreed that he would help her get up on time on the morning, because she had a tendency to sleep through her alarm clock. They also talked about buying healthier food at the grocery store. Plans for a therapeutic out-of-unit pass were developed, and for the first time in months, Julie and her father planned to spend some time together.

Individual Therapy Session (10 Days Later)

DR. F.: A lot has been going on here in the hospital, and you seem to be a little bit more energetic these days. As we try and sort through what you'd like to put on our agenda today, what would be on that list?

JULIE: Well, you're right, I am feeling better. I've been eating three meals a day and getting up at regular times. Having a structured time for homework certainly has given me some hope that I can get some things done. However, my concentration is still bad and I'm really worried about going back to school and getting everything done that I need to get done.

DR. F.: So it sounds like "how to organize school time and evaluate what I can and can't do" would be a good use of our time today. Is that right?

JULIE: Yes. I just feel so overwhelmed every time I think about it that I want to get back in bed. I've learned that getting back in bed really doesn't help anything, but it still is a pretty attractive alternative when I think of all these things I have to get done.

DR. F.: Let's make a list of exactly what it is you have to get done.

JULIE: Well, I have six honors classes and have a term paper in English and a research paper in American History. I have two tests to make up in Advanced Algebra. Choir—really no problem; I just have to go to the Christmas performance on the two times that it is planned, and this will give me enough extra credit. In Psychology I have two tests to make up and a paper to do, and in Keyboarding I have millions of assignments to do.

DR. F.: That certainly does sound like a number of assignments to do. Can you prioritize any of these?

JULIE: Well, I only need two credits for graduation and one of those that I have to pass is English. My school counselor and my dad have talked to me about dropping two courses since I don't really need them. I've already been accepted to a couple of schools, but I've always wanted to get that Commonwealth Diploma, and unless I finish those courses I won't get that.

DR. F.: Certainly that is an important decision. Could we take a look at the advantages and disadvantages of doing all those courses and getting the Commonwealth Diploma?

JULIE: The advantages of getting the Commonwealth Diploma are that it's something that I've always wanted to do. I guess among my friends there is a certain amount of prestige. I always thought colleges looked at it in some way special, but I guess since I've already been accepted to these colleges it might not make as much difference as I thought.

DR. F.: And what are the possible disadvantages?

JULIE: The disadvantages are . . . I guess, just what I'm feeling. I'm very overwhelmed. Even though I'm feeling a lot better, there is really no way that I can see me getting all those papers done by the deadline. Since I've already been accepted to the colleges where I could go, it might be more important to see if I can spend my time dancing. I'm more likely to get a scholarship for that than I am academically.

DR. F.: It sounds like you need to sit down with your counselor and take a look at a realistic plan of action, including maybe dropping a couple of courses or auditing. At least you can see what your choices are.

JULIE: You know, that really sounds like a good idea. But I'm having a hard time giving up that I can't do everything I want. I guess that's one of the lessons that I've learned. I can try and do everything and get nothing done or I can have a more realistic attitude and get done what needs to be done.

DR. F.: That certainly is one of those lessons or rules that we've talked about that needed to be challenged and replaced with a more realistic one. It sounds like getting in touch with your counselors and setting up a time to meet with them would be a good homework assignment for you between now and our next session.

JULIE: Sounds good to me.

Aftercare

Julie was discharged from the inpatient unit after 18 days. Her Children's Depression Inventory score at discharge was 16, a significant improvement over her admission score but still indicative of prominent depressive symptomatology. However, her hopelessness score was 4, reflective of a much more optimistic outlook toward the future.

Julie continued in weekly outpatient adolescent group for 6 months. She was an active participant and frequently discussed important issues such as school related stress, her return to dancing, and decisions about college. Her mother returned for her graduation ceremony, which activated considerable anxiety. She also seriously considered moving out of the country with her mother. On another occasion, she shared a letter with the group that she had written to her boyfriend, who had distanced himself after she was hospitalized. In each instance, she employed the cognitive-behavioral technique she had first learned during hospitalization. Self-monitoring, activity scheduling, weighing pros and cons, and graded task assignments became an integral part of her problem-solving repertoire.

Julie and her father had several more outpatient family sessions in the weeks following hospitalization and their relationship and communication improved. She also continued on antidepressants and decided to remain on prophylactic pharmacotherapy at least for her first semester away from home. Arrangements were made for her to contact the student health services at her college, and follow-up was arranged with Dr. F. for Christmas break.

SUMMARY

Cognitive therapy can be utilized on an adolescent inpatient unit as a specific format for individual, group, and family therapies. Moreover, with intensive staff training, supervision, and experience, inpatient units may adopt cognitive-behavioral theory as an organizing treatment philosophy. Julie was treated in such a "cognitive milieu" (Wright, Thase, Beck, & Ludgate, 1993).

This case illustrates the advantages of a single, cohesive treatment approach. When all therapists share the same "language," conflicts between therapies and disciplines are minimized. Patients and their families are less likely to be confused in interactions with various staff members. The collaborative and goal-oriented nature of cognitive therapy minimizes struggles over power and control that can undermine the progress of therapy on an adolescent inpatient unit. The cognitive approach also supports the development of adaptive coping strategies.

No controlled-outcome research has been completed with adolescents treated in a cognitively oriented inpatient program. Nevertheless, these programs can provide a short-term, cost-effective treatment for seriously disturbed adolescents, particularly if they are closely integrated with intensive outpatient services.

REFERENCES

Angold, A., & Costello, E. (1992). Comorbidity in children and adolescents with depression. *Child and Adolescent Psychiatric Clinics of North America*, 1(1), 31–51.

Beck, A. T., & Greenberg, R. L. (1974). *Coping with depression*. New York: Institute for Rational Living.

Caron, C., & Rutter, M. (1991). Comorbidity in child psychopathology: Concepts, issues and research strategies. *Journal of Child Psychology and Psychiatry*, 32(7), 1063–1080.

Freeman, A., Schrodt, G. R. Jr., Gilson, M., & Ludgate, J. W. (1993). Group cognitive therapy with inpatients. In J. H. Wright, M. E. Thase, A. T. Beck, & J. W. Ludgate (Eds.), *Cognitive therapy with inpatients: Developing a cognitive milieu* (pp. 121–153). New York: Guilford Press.

Gotlib, I., & Hammen, C. (1992). *Psychological aspects of depression: Toward a cognitive-interpersonal integration*. Chichester, UK: Wiley.

Kendall, P., & Clarkin, P. (1992). Introduction to special section: Comorbidity and treatment implication. *Journal of Consulting and Clinical Psychology*, 60, 833–835.

Safran, J., & Segal, Z. (1990). *Interpersonal process in cognitive therapy*. New York: Basic Books.

Schrodt, G. R. Jr. (1992). Cognitive therapy of depression. In M. Shafii & S. L. Shafii (Eds.), *Clinical guide to depression in children and adolescents* (pp. 197–217). Washington, DC: American Psychiatric Press.

Schrodt, G. R. Jr. (1993). Adolescent inpatient treatment. In J. H. Wright, M. E. Thase, A. T. Beck, & J. W. Ludgate (Eds.), *Cognitive therapy with inpatients: Developing a cognitive milieu* (pp. 273–294). New York: Guilford Press.

Schrodt, G. R. Jr., Adams, C. E., & Siegel, A. J. (1993). Pragmatic approaches to the treatment of depressed adolescents. In H. S. Kopelwicz & E. Klass (Eds.), *Depression in children and adolescents* (pp. 219–234). New York: Harwood Academic Publishers.

Schrodt, G. R. Jr., & Fitzgerald, B. A. (1987). Cognitive therapy with adolescents. *American Journal of Psychotherapy, 41,* 402–408.

Schrodt, G. R. Jr., & Wright, J. H. (1987). Inpatient treatment of adolescents. In A. Freeman & V. Greenwood (Eds.), *Cognitive therapy: Applications in psychiatric and medical settings* (pp. 69–82). New York: Human Sciences Press.

Wright, J. H. (1988). Cognitive therapy of depression. In A. J. Frances & R. E. Hales (Eds.), *American Psychiatric Press review of psychiatry* (Vol. 7, pp. 554–570). Washington, DC: American Psychiatric Press.

Wright, J. H., & Schrodt, G. R. Jr. (1989). Combined cognitive therapy and pharmacotherapy. In A. Freeman, K. M. Simon, H. Arkowitz, & L. Beutler (Eds.), *Handbook of cognitive therapy* (pp. 267–282). New York: Plenum Press.

Wright, J. H., Thase, M. E., Beck, A. T., & Ludgate, J. W. (Eds.). (1993). *Cognitive therapy with inpatients: Developing a cognitive milieu.* New York: Guilford Press.

14

Treatment of Family Problems

Norman Epstein
Stephen E. Schlesinger

T he hallmark of family therapy is its attention to *interpersonal* factors that make it difficult or impossible to resolve people's difficulties by treating the people involved solely on an individual basis. Very commonly, families identify problems by describing undesirable behavior of one member rather than viewing their difficulties as the result of problems in interactions among members. However, the initial explanation that they may offer for consulting a therapist does not necessarily turn out to be, on closer examination, the actual basis of their distress. This chapter describes a variety of intra- and interpersonal factors that are important in a cognitive-behavioral approach to the assessment and treatment of family problems. Although it can be tempting to focus on cognitions and behaviors of one family member that appear to contribute to a family problem, the chapter emphasizes that it often is the combination of cognitions and behaviors of two or more members that results in relationship problems.

Cognitive-behavioral approaches to family therapy are derived from cognitive mediation models of individual functioning (e.g., Beck, 1976; Ellis, 1962), which stress that an individual's emotional and behavioral reactions to life events are shaped by the particular interpretations that the person makes of the events, rather than solely by objective characteristics of the events themselves. Therapists who have applied cognitive mediation principles to couples (e.g., Baucom & Epstein, 1990; Beck, 1988; Dattilio & Padesky, 1990; Ellis, Sichel, Yeager, DiMattia, & DiGiuseppe, 1989; Epstein, 1982; Jacobson, 1984; Schlesinger & Epstein, 1986) and to families (e.g., Dattilio, 1993, 1994, 1995; Epstein & Schlesinger, 1991;

Epstein, Schlesinger, & Dryden, 1988; Huber & Baruth, 1989; Schwebel & Fine, 1994) have focused on how the behaviors of family members constantly serve as "life events" that are interpreted and evaluated by other family members.

In a cognitive-behavioral view of family relationships, cognitions, behaviors, and emotions are seen as exerting *mutual* influences upon one another. For example, a cognition (e.g., inferring that one's child is *willfully* disobeying one's orders) can produce emotions (e.g., anger) and behaviors (e.g., spanking). In contrast, an emotion (e.g., anger) can influence cognitions (e.g., selectively noticing or recalling unpleasant actions by one's child and overlooking positive ones) and behaviors (e.g., yelling, rather than speaking in a firm but calm manner). Finally, a behavior (e.g., withdrawing from one's family members) can affect one's emotions (e.g., decreased feelings of intimacy due to few shared pleasant activities with the other family members) or cognitions (e.g., drawing the conclusion, "I must not care about them any longer, or else I wouldn't be acting this way").

Consistent with a systems approach to family therapy (e.g., Watzlawick, Beavin, & Jackson, 1967), cognitive-behavioral approaches postulate that members of a family simultaneously influence and are influenced by each other. Consequently, a behavior on the part of one member leads to behaviors, cognitions and emotions in other members. In return, the other members' responses elicit cognitions, behaviors, and emotions in the former individual. Once such a cycle among family members is in motion, a dysfunctional cognition, behavior, or emotion at any point can lead to a negative spiral. For example, if one member misinterprets another's behavior as due to malicious intentions and therefore responds by disparaging the other, the other member may in turn think, "I try my best, and all I get in return is criticism," and may therefore leave the house in anger. Then, the former individual might interpret the other's withdrawal in a negative manner, such as, "Well, he or she obviously can't stand being caught trying to take advantage of me." Each member experiences and reacts to his or her cognitions about the other person as if they represent the absolute truth, and conflict can escalate quickly, as in this example.

When more than two individuals are involved in an interaction, the events that members observe, as well as the resulting cognitions about those events, become more complex than is the case with dyadic interactions (Epstein & Schlesinger, 1991). Each family member may observe at least four kinds of events:

1. The individual's own cognitions, behaviors, and emotions regarding family interaction (e.g., the person who notices him- or herself withdrawing from the rest of the family).

2. The actions of individual family members toward him or her.
3. The combined (and not always consistent) reactions that several members have toward him or her.
4. The characteristics of the relationships among other family members (e.g., noticing that two other family members usually are supportive of each other's opinions).

Thus, there is a vast array of events occurring during family interactions that serve as stimuli for the family members' cognitive appraisals, emotional reactions, and behavioral responses. The next section describes several types of cognitions that family members may experience concerning each of the four types of events listed previously.

TYPES OF COGNITIONS INVOLVED IN FAMILY DYSFUNCTION

As noted, the forms of cognition that have become foci of cognitive-behavioral approaches to marital and family problems are derived, in part, from cognitive models of individual psychopathology (e.g., Beck, 1976; Ellis, 1962) and from social psychological models of social cognition (cf. Arias & Beach, 1987). Five major types of cognition have been implicated in marital and family dysfunction: (1) *selective perceptions* about what events have occurred during family interactions, (2) *attributions* about why particular events occur, (3) *expectancies* (predictions) about the probabilities that certain events will occur in the future, (4) *assumptions* about the characteristics of family members and their relationships, and (5) *standards* about the characteristics that family members and their relationships "should" have (Baucom & Epstein, 1990; Baucom, Epstein, Sayers, & Sher, 1989; Epstein & Baucom, 1989, 1993). The following is a summary of research bearing on the roles that these types of cognitions can play in creating and maintaining conflict in family relationships. It is beyond the scope of this chapter to comprehensively review how these cognitive variables contribute to specific family problems (e.g., communication problems, role conflicts, difficulties with extended family). Table 14.1 presents a matrix with examples of the five types of cognitions associated with each of the four previously described types of family *events* that the individual may observe (own responses, actions of individual members, combined actions of two or more other members, and relationships among other members). The table refers to members of the family in the case example presented later in the chapter.

TABLE 14.1. Types of Cognitions

Kinds of events	Attributions	Expectancies	Assumptions	Standards	Perceptions
Own thoughts, emotions, and behaviors	Jane: "I'm not as good as Robert."	Frank: "If I don't scream, I'll get an ulcer."	Frank: "My concern about my teenage daughter is no different from any other father's."	Robert: "A good child obeys his parents."	Jane: "I never get to have any fun."
Actions of individual relatives toward him or her	Alice: "Frank doesn't listen to me because he doesn't respect me."	Robert: "If I do what Dad says, he'll give me more privileges."	Alice: "Teenagers can learn to control themselves without their parents' help."	Jane: "Parents have no right to give their children orders."	Frank: "Jane never is nice to me."
Combined reactions of several members toward him or her	Jane: "Dad and Robert treat me like this because they don't understand teenage girls."	Robert: "If I comply, Mom and Dad won't bother me."	Jane: "Parents can't understand kids because of the generation gap."	Alice: "Mothers should be treated as experts in child rearing."	Frank: "The women in the family always gang up on me."
Observations of relationships among other members	Jane: "Robert can do anything he wants because Mom and Dad think he's perfect."	Robert: "If Jane keeps this up, she'll break up our parents' marriage."	Alice: "Fathers don't know how to raise girls."	Frank: "Everybody in a family ought to get along."	Robert: "Jane never has a kind word to say."

Note. Frank, father; Alice, mother; Jane, daughter; Robert, son.

Selective Perceptions

Theorists such as Kelly (1955) and Heider (1958) stressed that perception is an active rather than a passive process. When in the role of observer, an individual cannot possibly notice all of the information available in a situation. There is a considerable body of research evidence that people engage in selective attention, noticing some of the available stimuli and overlooking others (cf. Nisbett & Ross, 1980). *Selective perceptions* are those aspects of the available information that an individual notices. For example, Patterson and Reid (1984) found that parents who tend to use coercive parenting strategies also tend to attend selectively to their children's negative behaviors.

Both clinical observation and empirical research (e.g., Beck, Rush, Shaw, & Emery, 1979; Fiske & Taylor, 1991; Turk & Speers, 1983; R. A. Wessler & R. L. Wessler, 1980) suggest that perceptions or interpretations of events can be influenced by a variety of factors, including the perceiver's current emotional state, fatigue, and tacit cognitive structures (schemas) that the individual has available for classifying and understanding experiences. Concerning cognitive structures (which will be described more fully in our discussions of assumptions and standards), Kelly's (1955) seminal writings on "personal constructs" emphasized how the concepts that one has developed through past experience for categorizing people and events determine what one notices in daily life situations. For example, an individual whose life experiences have left him or her sensitive to differences in individuals' levels of power in close relationships may be likely to notice behaviors of family members that might reflect their potential or actual attempts to exert control in family interactions. With this in mind, cognitive-behavioral approaches to family problems commonly include therapeutic interventions designed to improve family members' perceptual accuracy.

Attributions

A large body of empirical work has accumulated focusing on attributions that family members make about the causes of the events in their interactions (Baucom, 1987; Baucom et al., 1989; Bradbury & Fincham, 1990, 1992; Thompson & Snyder, 1986). Clinical and empirical evidence supports the theoretical notion (e.g., Heider, 1958; Kelley, 1967) that people spontaneously draw conclusions about possible causes of events in their lives (Baucom, 1987; Holtzworth-Munroe & Jacobson, 1985). Baucom (1987) described the functions that these attributions serve in a close relationship, such as giving one a sense (accurate or not) of understanding another person and his or her actions, a sense of control over the relationship due to that understanding, and a means for minimizing future disappointments in a dissatisfying relationship by attributing stable negative traits to one's partner (e.g., "I don't expect [my relative] to act in a caring manner, because he or she is a selfish person").

Numerous studies have examined the attributions that distressed and nondistressed spouses make about the determinants of positive and negative events in their relationships (see reviews by Baucom & Epstein, 1990, and by Bradbury & Fincham, 1990). The most consistent findings from these studies are that distressed spouses are more likely than nondistressed spouses to attribute negative partner behavior to trait-like (global, stable) characteristics of the partner, including malicious intent, selfish motivation, and lack of love. Concerning positive partner behaviors, nondistressed spouses are more likely to attribute them to global, stable causes. Furthermore, evidence that physically abusive husbands are more likely than both distressed and nondistressed husbands to attribute their wives' negative behaviors to negative intentions (e.g., trying to hurt the husband's feelings or put him down) suggest that particular types of attributions may be especially common in abusive relationships (Holtzworth-Munroe & Hutchinson, 1993).

Research also has been conducted concerning attributions that family members other than the marital partners make about other members' behaviors, and the results tend to be consistent with the findings from marital studies. For example, Morton, Twentyman, and Azar (1988) report that in their clinical work with child abusing parents, it is common for the abusers to believe that their children misbehave intentionally in order to annoy and spite them. Herzberger (1983) has argued that parents who interpret their children's negative behavior as willful and spiteful are likely to retaliate toward the children in an aggressive manner. In a study by Larrance and Twentyman (1983), a group of physically abusive mothers, a group of neglectful mothers, and a comparison group of mothers with no known history of abuse or neglect each rated the causes of their own children's positive and negative behaviors. The abusive mothers rated the causes of their children's negative behaviors as more internal and stable (i.e., due to traits) than did the comparison group, and they rated the causes of their children's positive behaviors as more external and unstable than did comparison mothers. The neglectful mothers' ratings had a more complex pattern but tended to fall between those of the abusive and comparison groups. Larrance and Twentyman note that abusive mothers' views emphasize their children's responsibility (and minimize the possible role of environmental factors) for problematic behavior. However, they also stress that the results of their study do not answer the question of whether the negative attributions of the abusive mothers represent cognitive distortions or are accurate descriptions of their children (given that there is evidence that abused children exhibit more temperament and behavior problems from a very young age than do comparison children). Nevertheless, it seems likely that once a parent develops such a negative cognitive set about his or her child, the parent's view of the child may lead him or her to discount positive behavior changes that the child may make, even when these changes occur due to family therapy. Azar (1986) found that within samples of abusive parents the tendency to make negative trait attributions about children was associated with more negative and less positive parental behavior toward the children. Thus, family therapists need to assess whether or not parents' attributions about their children's behavior are accurate, but in either case they also need to help the parents be aware of (and reward) positive behaviors and changes in negative behaviors.

Expectancies

Based on past experiences, people develop expectancies or predictions about the probabilities that certain events will occur in the future under particular circumstances (Bandura, 1977; Rotter, 1954). An individual continuously makes decisions to act or not act in certain ways, due to the outcomes that he or she anticipates from each action. Rotter (1954) made a distinction between *specific expectancies*, which are situation-specific (e.g., "If I ask Mom to help me with my homework right after she gets home from work, she will get angry and refuse"), and *generalized expectancies*, which are more global and stable (e.g., "My children won't cooperate with anything that I might ask of them"). The individual's choices of behavior toward other family members depend on the predictions that he or she makes about the outcomes *and* the degree to which he or she finds each outcome pleasant or unpleasant.

Bandura (1977) notes that expectancies are a normal and efficient aspect of learning from one's experiences. The crucial issue concerning family problems is that family members' expectancies are often accurate, but they can become distorted in important ways. An inaccurate expectancy may lead an individual to behave in a dysfunctional manner toward other family members, initiating negative behavioral spirals and blocking conflict resolution (Doherty, 1981). An inaccurate expectancy also can elicit inappropriate emotional responses within the individual who holds it, as when a person predicts an aversive response from another family member and feels anxiety about the anticipated trouble.

Two major types of expectancies described by Bandura (1977) are "outcome expectancies" and "efficacy expectancies." Outcome expectancies are predictions about the probability that a particular action will lead to a particular outcome. In contrast, efficacy expectancies involve estimates about the likelihood that one will be able to perform those actions successfully, which would lead to a particular outcome. Thus, a father may have an optimistic outcome expectancy, "If we all take turns expressing our opinions about an issue, we are likely to find some common ground for making a decision acceptable to everyone in the family," but may also have a pessimistic efficacy expectancy such as, "It is unlikely that members in this family will stop talking about their own ideas long enough to listen to others' opinions."

Results of preliminary studies (e.g., Kurdek & Berg, 1987; Pretzer, Epstein, & Fleming, 1991; Vanzetti, Notarius, & NeeSmith, 1992) indicate that family members' negative expectancies are associated with greater relationship distress. However, there is a need for much more research, particularly investigating the degree to which individuals' expectancies influence their actual behaviors toward other family members.

Assumptions and Standards

Both assumptions and standards are forms of "cognitive structures," "tacit beliefs," "knowledge structures," or "schemas" (Fiske & Taylor, 1991; Nisbett & Ross, 1980; Seiler, 1984; Turk & Speers, 1983). Assumptions are those cognitive structures concerning characteristics of objects and events that an individual believes *do* exist, whereas standards are the person's conceptions of how objects and events *should* be (Baucom & Epstein, 1990).

Assumptions

An assumption about a person or relationship typically includes a set of "descriptors," or characteristics that are interrelated, and beliefs about the degree to which those characteristics are correlated. Consequently, once an individual assigns a person or object to a category based on an observed characteristic, the individual tends to make inferences about unseen characteristics. For example, a person may assume that a "father" is someone who is kind, works hard to provide for his family, is strict, and is protective. The person also may assume that all of these characteristics are highly correlated with each other. Therefore, when this person meets a man who is identified as a father and is strict with his children, the observer is likely to conclude that this father is also very protective. The inference may or may not be accurate. It is possible, for example, that this particular father's strict behavior reflects his irritation about having children and his attempt to stop his children from bothering him. Correlational findings indicate associations between family members' assumptions and both their attributions and expectancies about family interactions (cf. Baucom & Epstein,

1990; Epstein & Baucom, 1993). Further research is needed to determine whether cognitive structures that exist before an individual enters a relationship shape the attributions and expectancies that he or she subsequently makes about events in the relationship.

Standards

Unrealistic or extreme standards have been implicated in a wide variety of family problems, such as child abuse, adjustment difficulties in stepfamilies, poor coping with an addicted family member, and ineffective control of children with conduct disorders. Rational–emotive therapy focuses on the distress that family members experience when (1) events in their relationships do not meet their unrealistic, extreme standards and (2) they evaluate the failure to meet those standards very negatively (e.g., as "awful" or "intolerable") (Dryden, 1985; Ellis et al., 1989). Beck's cognitive model (Beck, 1976; Beck et al., 1979) also emphasizes the role of extreme standards in producing distress in individuals' lives, viewing these relatively stable schemas as the bases of distortions in inferential processes such as attributions.

Standards can be based on experiences that people had in their own families as they grew up, as they observed other families, or in past family relationships that they had as adults. For example, a person whose family of origin was characterized by frequent aversive, hostile arguments may have developed a standard that members of a family should avoid expressing conflict.

There appear to be a variety of ways in which family members' assumptions and standards can influence the quality of family relationships. Robin and Foster (1989), for example, describe a variety of "absolute assumptions" (some of which appear to be standards and some to be assumptions in the taxonomy we are using) commonly held by parents and adolescents that contribute to parent–child conflict. Recurrent themes involve perfectionism (e.g., "Teenagers should always behave responsibly"), ruination (e.g., "If we permit him to stay out late, he will become an irresponsible adult"), fairness (e.g., "My parents should be at least as lenient as my friends' parents"), love/approval (e.g., "If my mother really loved me, she wouldn't question what I do"), obedience (e.g., "Young people have no right to challenge their parents' decisions"), self-blame (e.g., "If he fails at school, I'm a bad mother"), malicious intent (which appears to involve attributions; e.g., "My daughter is trying to drive me crazy"), and autonomy (e.g., "I'm all grown up at 16 and should be able to go out with anyone I like"). Robin and Foster note that such extreme views polarize family members into inflexible positions that impede problem solving and increase anger, which itself interferes with the use of constructive communication skills and increases reciprocal negative exchanges.

BEHAVIORAL FACTORS IN FAMILY DYSFUNCTION

Therapists who adopt a cognitive-behavioral approach to understanding and treating family dysfunction generally focus on behavioral aspects of family interactions as major targets of therapy (cf. Falloon, 1991; Jacobson & Margolin, 1979; Robin & Foster, 1989). These include (1) excesses of negative behaviors and deficits in pleasing behaviors exchanged by family members, (2) expressive and listening skills used in communication, (3) problem-solving skills, and (4) negotiation and behavior change skills. The theoretical models underlying behavioral approaches to family therapy are social learning theory (e.g., Bandura, 1977) and social exchange theory (e.g., Thibaut & Kelley, 1959). Both models assume that family members exert mutual influences over each other's behavior. Social learning theory emphasizes that interpersonal behavior is learned, both through operant conditioning and vicarious observation or other people's actions, and that current behavior is controlled by its actual or expected consequences. Social exchange theory describes an interpersonal relationship as an economic exchange in which each person's satisfaction is a function of the ratio of the benefits received to the costs incurred. It is assumed that in a satisfying relationship, the parties exchange rewards in a reciprocal manner and restrain the escalation of negative exchanges. In contrast, relationship distress is associated with relatively uncontrolled reciprocity in exchanges of aversive, coercive behavior (Falloon, 1991).

Social learning theory and social exchange theory have strongly influenced behaviorally oriented research and clinical practice with families. The following are representative findings concerning the four types of behaviors that are foci of cognitive-behavioral assessment and treatment with families.

Pleasing and Displeasing Behavior Exchanges

As noted, social exchange theory postulates that exchanges in a relationship tend to be reciprocal; that is, each party tends to give what he or she receives from the other person. For example, parents may reinforce their children's negative behavior by selectively paying attention to it and by failing to notice and encourage positive behavior. Furthermore, many parents attempt to reduce their children's negative behavior by means of aversive behavior, such as insults, threats, and physical punishment. Patterson (1982) notes that, at best, such parental strategies typically suppress unwanted child behavior only temporarily (while the punisher is present), and that they teach the children that aggression is an acceptable means of expressing anger and dissatisfaction with other people. The behavioral interventions that Patterson and his colleagues have developed (e.g., Patterson, 1975; Patterson & Forgatch, 1987) focus on changing in both children and parents the behaviors that contribute to coercive cycles.

Communication Skills Deficits

Some problems in communication among family members involve misinterpretations, wherein messages that one person intends to send are received inaccurately. These discrepancies can result from faulty (e.g., vague) expression by the person sending the message, or from ineffective listening on the recipient's part (e.g., formulating responses to the other person rather than attending carefully to what he or she is saying). At other times, family members complain that they cannot communicate when, in fact, they receive messages from each other clearly but find them unacceptable, either because the messages are sent in an aversive manner (e.g., a sarcastic tone, threatening words) or because the recipient does not agree with the ideas expressed. When assessing family communication, it is crucial to distinguish among these different kinds of communication problems. When there are real deficits in expressive and listening skills, communication skills training can be used. In contrast, when family members send aversive verbal and nonverbal messages, skills training may also be appropriate, but it also may be important to identify and modify emotions (e.g., strong anger) and cognitions (e.g., attribution that a child's misbehavior is caused by malicious intent) that can influence an individual's tendency to send aversive messages. Furthermore, when a complaint of poor communication stems from conflict among family members' preferences or values, intervention would focus much more on conflict resolution.

Constructive and Destructive Communication

Research on family communication behavior typically has involved coding family interactions according to a standard system (see Grotevant & Carlson, 1989, and Markman & Notarius, 1987, for reviews). Studies using these behavioral coding systems suggest that distressed families exhibit higher rates of negative communication behaviors and lower rates of positive communication behaviors than those who are nondistressed (Baucom & Adams, 1987; Markman & Notarius, 1987; Patterson, 1982). Furthermore, investigations of behavioral *sequences* between spouses and between parents and children (Gottman, 1979; Margolin & Wampold, 1981; Patterson, 1982; Revenstorf, Hahlweg, Schindler, & Vogel, 1984) have identified interaction patterns common in distressed relationships, particularly *mutual* escalating aversive exchanges. Given the consistent theoretical and empirical support for the importance of clear and constructive communication in family relationships, the assessment and modification of communication problems is an important component of cognitive-behavioral therapy for family problems.

Problem-Solving Skills Deficits

Families inevitably are faced with a variety of problems that require them to work as a unit to devise and implement solutions. These problems range from the relatively trivial (e.g., how to coordinate transportation when one of the family cars is inoperable) to major issues affecting family life (e.g., how the family should cope with a parent's unemployment and the associated financial problems). Problem solving is a cognitive-behavioral process that involves the abilities to (1) clearly define the nature of a problem in behavioral terms, (2) identify alternative solutions, (3) evaluate the relative costs and benefits of the alternative solutions, (4) reach family consensus on a solution, (5) implement the solution (with each family member fulfilling his or her specific role), and (6) evaluate the effectiveness of the solution and modify it as needed (Baucom & Epstein, 1990; Bornstein & Bornstein, 1986; Jacobson & Margolin, 1979; Robin & Foster, 1989; Stuart, 1980). Consequently, training in problem-solving skills is an important focus of behavioral interventions for family conflict (Epstein et al., 1988; Falloon, 1991; Robin & Foster, 1989).

COGNITIVE INTERVENTIONS

Cognitive restructuring procedures are intended to help family members test whether their cognitions about aspects of family interaction are adaptive or valid. Because people generally do not question the validity of their thoughts, one of the therapist's major goals is to increase each family member's sensitivity as an *observer* of his or her own cognitions. A second goal is to help each family member become a systematic and relatively objective *evaluator* of those cognitions, developing skills for collecting data concerning their appropriateness and validity. The following are common strategies used in cognitive restructuring work with distressed families.

Building Cognitive Self-Monitoring Skills

Family members can be assisted in increasing their attention to their own cognitions by teaching them about the ways in which cognitions can influence one's emotions and behaviors. The therapist can begin by presenting a brief, didactic "minilecture" describing a cognitive mediation model and concrete examples of how individuals' responses to life events can be influenced by their interpretations of those events. It is important to introduce the concept of "cognitive distortion" gradually and tactfully, in order to minimize defensiveness on the part of family members. Members of distressed relationships tend to blame their partners for relationship problems and can become defensive if a therapist suggests that part of the problem lies in their own thought processes. Perhaps the best way to demonstrate the subjectivity of cognitions is to elicit a cognition from a family member and then elicit information from that person, supplemented by data from other family members, that disconfirms that cognition. In other words, family members are more likely to accept the validity of the cognitive mediation model if the therapist can demonstrate its operation with concrete examples from the clients' daily experiences. This socialization process is also employed in cognitive therapy with individual patients (cf. Beck et al., 1979). The presence of other family members in conjoint sessions provides both the advantage of external sources of data concerning an individual's cognitions, and the risk that the other members' responses may elicit defensiveness on the part of the individual whose cognitions are being evaluated.

Family members commonly are assigned the "homework" of recording their automatic thoughts (word for word), associated emotions, and behaviors in written logs such as Beck et al.'s (1979) Daily Record of Dysfunctional Thoughts (DRDT). As in individual cognitive therapy, the therapist reviews these records with each family member during sessions, identifying the specific content of automatic thoughts that is associated with particular emotions. Having family members observe this analysis of each other's situation–cognition–emotion links can increase empathy, and members can give each other feedback that can alter interpretations of each other's behavior.

Another important aspect of improving monitoring skills involves logging *sequences* of interactions between the self and other family members. Cognitive-behavioral family therapists coach family members in avoiding unidirectional causal observations (seeing one's own behavior as caused by behaviors of other family members). Instead, family members are aided in observing how their own behaviors elicit responses from other members as well, such that causes of negative family interactions tend to be circular. As noted earlier, members of distressed families are likely to blame each other for problems, so the therapist must exercise care in focusing on circular causality in order to minimize defensiveness.

Altering Selective Perceptions

During therapy sessions it often becomes evident that two or more family members have different perceptions either of a past event or even of an event that has recently occurred. The therapist can draw this perceptual discrepancy to their attention, emphasizing that it is natural for people to notice different aspects of a complex interaction, but noting that it is important for each family member to avoid assuming that he or she has noticed everything. When a therapist is able to videotape a therapy session, it is possible to first ask each family member for his or her recollections of an interaction that just took place and then to replay the tape in order to examine the accuracy and comprehensiveness of the perceptions.

Family members also can be coached in monitoring and recording their cognitions concerning interactions with other family members in daily life. They can be sensitized to selective perception through comparisons of the perceptions that family members recorded concerning the same events. For example, it is common for family members to record different perceptions of who started an argument, with each person commonly perceiving a linear, causal process in which his or her negative behaviors were elicited by another person's negative behavior. As is the case when the therapist points out instances of reciprocal causality in family interactions that occur during therapy sessions, the therapist can note possible mutual influences in family members' reports of negative exchanges at home. Also, when an individual's written logs include all-or-nothing perceptions of another family member's behavior, such as "He or she *always* . . ." or "He or she *never* . . . ," the person can be coached in considering evidence concerning exceptions to such an absolute view.

Modifying Inaccurate Attributions

There are several skills that family members can be taught for testing the accuracy of the causal inferences that they make about family events. These approaches are similar to those used in individual cognitive therapy (e.g., Beck et al., 1979; Beck & Emery, 1985), although the presence of other family members provides additional sources of data that may be lacking in individual treatment.

Using Socratic questioning, a therapist can guide family members in a "logical analysis" of attributions, essentially answering the question, "Does it make logical sense that this event was due to the particular cause that you have inferred?" A second form of logical analysis is coaching family members in thinking of "alternative explanations" (attributions) for an event. Consistent with the collaborative empirical approach of cognitive therapy, the therapist notes that an individual's attribution may be accurate, but that it is important to consider other possibilities in order to avoid making a faulty inference that leads to emotional upset and negative behavioral interactions. One of the most powerful ways of demonstrating the negative effects of inaccurate attributions is to "catch" these when they occur during family therapy sessions. When one family member attributes another's negative behavior to negative causes (e.g., unpleasant personality traits, malicious intent), the latter individual can provide feedback about what he or she sees as the actual cause of the behavior. Although such an explanation may be viewed with skepticism by the family member who made the original negative attribution, especially when it appears to be self-enhancing or a "rationalization," the therapist can stress the importance of considering all possible attributions seriously. At times, family members' feedback concerning alternative explanations for their own behavior can broaden each other's perspective and result in more benign attributions.

Modifying Inaccurate Expectancies

Cognitive restructuring of problematic expectancies is similar in form to the interventions used to modify negativistic attributions. Logical analysis of an expectancy involves examining whether it makes sense that other family members will react as anticipated if the individual behaves in a particular manner, as well as identifying other possible outcomes. Other data concerning the validity of an expectancy can be derived from family members' memories of past outcomes and logs of current outcomes in similar situations. *In vivo* behavioral experiments are the most powerful tool for addressing maladaptive expectancies. Although the experiments can be quite anxiety provoking for the person who expects negative consequences for his or her behavior, these experiments (enacted during therapy sessions and at home) provide vivid, incontrovertible evidence that the outcome is not as predicted.

Modifying Unrealistic or Inappropriate Assumptions and Standards

Several cognitive restructuring methods used to test and alter perceptions, attributions, and expectancies can be applied with assumptions and standards as well. These include logical analysis, examination of alternative assumptions and standards that may be more adaptive given the family's current circumstances, and identification of experiences (including behavioral experiments devised during therapy sessions) that are or are not consistent with the assumptions and standards. In addition, family members can be coached in examining the *utility* of living according to a particular standard (e.g., "Children should never question their parents' rules regarding the children's responsibilities"). This involves generating lists of the advantages and disadvantages of adhering to the standard, deciding whether the balance of disadvantages versus advantages suggests that a revised standard may be appropriate, substituting a more realistic or appropriate standard when that seems prudent, and experimenting with living according to the new standard (Epstein et al., 1988). Therapists should be sensitive to the discomfort that commonly arises when individuals' longstanding assumptions and standards about family relationships are challenged, understanding the need for a supportive environment in which family members can explore alternative beliefs that are palatable to them.

BEHAVIORAL INTERVENTIONS

As noted, dysfunctional behavioral patterns commonly are associated with family problems, regardless of the specific nature of the problem (e.g., child abuse, stepfamily conflicts), and they typically involve excessive exchanges of negative behaviors, deficits in exchanges of positive behaviors, communication skills deficits, and problem-solving skills deficits. The following are descriptions of interventions that cognitive-behavioral family therapists use to address each type of behavioral problem.

Altering Behavioral Exchanges

Members of some families are able to increase their exchanges of positive affectional and instrumental behaviors with no guidance other than a therapist stressing to them how much daily exchanges affect the subjective quality of close relationships. Other families, however, have low rates of positive exchanges, because they spend little time together. Not only can a lack of shared activities detract from long-standing relationships, but it also can interfere with the establishment of cohesion in newly formed relationships, such as those of stepfamilies (Leslie & Epstein, 1988). Consequently, therapists can help family members to identify activities that they could share, and to agree to engage in certain activities from the list between therapy sessions. For clients who have difficulty generating lists of potentially pleasurable activities, therapists can provide written lists of activities that other couples and families have tended to enjoy (Baucom & Epstein, 1990).

Similarly, therapists can coach family members in generating lists of aversive behaviors that they exchange. They can then reach agreements that all family members will attempt to decrease particular negative behaviors, in conjunction with their efforts to increase positive exchanges.

Contingency contracting can be used when families have difficulty adhering to informal agreements to change their behaviors. When used with families, contracting sometimes is presented as if the parents were trained as therapists who reinforce positive changes in their children's behavior. However, Goldenberg and Goldenberg (1991) note that these procedures also change the parents' behavior toward their children (e.g., reducing parents' inconsistency and use of aversive behavior to control their children). There are excellent texts (e.g., Patterson & Forgatch, 1987) that can be used as instructional aids in teaching clients parenting skills, including the monitoring of children's behaviors and the implementation of reward systems.

Contracts can vary, as such, in their degree of structure, and the extent to which one person's behavior changes are contingent on another person also making desired changes. However, what contracts have in common is that they direct family members to identify specific pleasing and displeasing behaviors that they would like each other to increase or decrease. Furthermore, contracts emphasize collaborative efforts toward making desired behavior changes.

Communication Skills Training

Most commonly, family therapists focus on behavioral skills involved in (1) expressing thoughts and feelings accurately to other family members and (2) listening effectively to messages sent by others. Skills training typically involves giving family members specific instructions about problematic and constructive forms of communication. This may include handouts and other reading material, and is accompanied by specific feedback about the family's own communication behaviors. Specific, constructive communication behaviors are then modeled, and the family is coached in communication skills during therapy sessions (Baucom & Epstein, 1990; Epstein et al., 1988; Robin & Foster, 1989). Guerney's (1977) relationship enhancement program provides specific guidelines for expressive and empathic listening skills. For example, a person expressing his or her thoughts and emotions is to be brief and specific, acknowledge the subjectivity of the feelings, note positive as well as negative aspects of situations being described, and convey empathy for the listener's position. The listener's goal is to understand the expresser's subjective experience and convey that understanding to him or her by paraphrasing the message back to the expresser. The listener is to avoid introducing his or her own thoughts and emotions about the topic discussed by the expresser.

In addition to focusing on expressive and listening skills, therapists commonly conduct individualized assessments of excesses and deficits in a particular family's communication behaviors. For example, in their work with families that include a schizophrenic member, Falloon, Boyd, and McGill (1984) look for problems such as deficits in eye contact, confusing body posture and gestures, lack of variation in facial expressions and vocal tone, poverty of content in verbal messages, vagueness, mixed messages, overgeneralized statements, interruptions, and hostile threats. Robin and Foster's (1989) communication training with adolescents and their parents also focuses on teaching constructive alternatives to a variety of negative behaviors (e.g., making "I" statements rather than accusing or blaming, suggesting alternative solutions rather than threatening the other person).

Problem-Solving Skills Training

Training families in problem solving skills incorporates the same components of instruction, feedback, modeling, and coaching in behavioral rehearsal used in the training of expressive and listening skills. The emphasis is on collaborative efforts to define a problem in terms of observable behaviors, "brainstorm" possible solutions, evaluate the costs and benefits of solutions, select a solution that will be implemented, specify who in the family is responsible for enacting each component of the solution, attempt to implement the solution, and evaluate its effectiveness in resolving the problem. Problem-solving skills training is widely used in the treatment of marital and family problems (e.g., Baucom & Epstein, 1990; P. H. Bornstein & M. T. Bornstein, 1986; Epstein et al., 1988; Falloon et al., 1984; Jacobson & Margolin, 1979; Robin & Foster, 1989).

CASE EXAMPLE

Frank and Alice (ages 40 and 38, respectively) sought assistance at an agency providing child and family mental health services because of their 13-year-old daughter Jane's behavior problems. Jane had been getting into trouble at school for smoking and truancy, and at home she was uncooperative with parental requests, stayed out beyond her curfew, and used disrespectful language with both parents. Diagnostically, Jane appeared to meet criteria of the fourth edition of the *Diagnostic and Statistical Manual of Mental Disorders* (DSM-IV; American Psychiatric Association, 1994) for oppositional defiant disorder. Frank and Alice's 15-year-old son Robert also accompanied them to the first session, and both parents noted that he had no history of behavior problems at home or at school. During the therapist's initial interview with the family, Jane alternated between arguing with her parents and withdrawing from them. Robert was fairly quiet and responded to questions by his parents and the therapist in a polite manner.

The therapist conducted a systematic inquiry about (1) the family members' definitions of the problem for which they had sought help; (2) the history of the problem, including its development over time and the ways in which the family had attempted to solve it up to this point, and (3) the family's overall developmental history, including any significant positive and negative life events that had occurred since the time when the parents first met and established their relationship. This information was collected in order to help the therapist understand the nature of the presenting problem within its family context. In other words, the therapist took it at face value that Jane's behavior was problematic for her parents (and for school officials) but also began to look for characteristics of family interactions that might have contributed to the development and/or maintenance of the aversive behavior. Thus, the therapist's evaluation of the family during the initial interview and subsequent sessions was based not only on what they described during the interview, but also on how they interacted with each other in the therapist's office.

Although Frank and Alice had presented their problem as "Jane's nasty, defiant behavior, caused by her poor attitude about taking on responsibilities in life," the therapist's systematic assessment revealed that the family's problems were more complex than that. The following were some of the salient patterns observed by the therapist:

1. The father–daughter relationship had been close until Jane reached adolescence and sought greater independence from the family. As Jane spent less time talking with her father or accompanying her parents on family outings, and more time visiting her friends, Frank increasingly attempted to restrict her independence. Jane responded to her father's restrictiveness by arguing with him and disobeying him.

2. The mother–daughter relationship was strained, but not to the same extent as the father–daughter relationship. In fact, Alice was more accepting of Jane's becoming independent than was Frank. Alice related to the therapist that she remembered her own need to be independent during adolescence, and her own struggles with her parents. At times, she sided with Frank concerning Jane's negative behavior, but on other occasions, she expressed disagreement with him in front of Jane. During one heated exchange between Frank and Jane in the therapist's office, Alice interrupted Frank, telling him that he was too strict and that Jane needed to develop friendships apart from the family.

3. Jane complained that her parents, particularly her father, applied a double standard for her behavior versus her brother Robert's behavior, and this appeared to the therapist to be true. Neither parent questioned Robert about his activities outside the home to the extent that they inquired about Jane's plans and activities. Alice told the therapist that her

husband seemed especially protective of Jane, and Frank agreed that this was so, because he did not think that a young girl could handle "difficult situations" that might come up in dealing with other people.

4. The parents appeared to have had some chronic conflict in their marital relationship, particularly concerning their roles as parents and their philosophies about childrearing. Alice tended to base her childrearing practices on her belief that children need to have opportunities to learn from their own mistakes, whereas Frank acted on his belief that it is the parents' responsibility to protect their children from misfortune, even if that means restricting the children's freedom. The couple often had loud verbal fights about these issues. Jane described their fights to the therapist and said that she found them very upsetting, especially when her parents made comparisons between herself and Robert. Robert said that he did not like to hear his parents fighting, but that it really was not any of his business.

5. One area in which the parents were united in their concern about Jane involved her academic problems. They both restricted her social activities when they received negative reports from school officials, which Jane felt was "unfair."

The initial assessment revealed that although Jane's negativistic behavior was problematic in itself, the interactions among the members of her family exacerbated her "acting out." Further assessment was focused on identifying cognitive and behavioral factors that contributed to the escalation of conflict in the family.

One of Jane's *perceptions* about her family was revealed in her statement, "I *never* get to have any fun." Although she truly believed this to be an accurate perception, when she was asked to describe her activities over the course of a week she was able to identify a number of experiences (particularly time spent with friends) that had been pleasurable. Similarly, Alice's statement about her husband's relationship with their children, "He's so rigid with the rules and doesn't give of himself to the children," failed to take into account instances of flexible and nurturant behavior that he exhibited.

Interviews revealed a variety of *attributions* that family members were making related to Jane's behavior. Alice, for example, stated that Frank was especially restrictive with Jane "because he has old-fashioned values, a double standard for boys and girls." When the therapist asked Jane for her thoughts about her parents' reasons for allowing Robert more independence, she said, "They love him more than me; they trust him more than me." It was important for the therapist to help the family examine the validity of each of these distressing attributions.

Concerning *expectancies* that were associated with problematic family interaction, Frank expressed the idea, "If I don't scream at Jane to let out my frustration, I'll develop an ulcer. I know it's unhealthy to keep your feelings bottled up." Unfortunately, the actual outcome of his screaming was to elicit anger, screaming, and withdrawal from Jane (which frustrated Frank further). When discussing parental disagreements about childrearing practices, Alice expressed the expectancy, "If I try to negotiate with Frank about childrearing, it will be futile." Not only did this turn out to be an inaccurate overgeneralization, but it was a thought that made Alice angry on many occasions.

Jane expressed an *assumption* she held that parents cannot understand their children due to the age difference between them. This assumption clearly reduced her willingness to listen to her own parents' views about her behavior. Frank revealed that although he readily argued with Jane, he avoided open conflict with his wife, because he believed that disagreements are a sign of marital problems. He also held an assumption that his concerns about his daughter were "no different from any father's concerns." Frank was not aware that his restrictiveness had reached an unreasonably high level. As is generally the case with basic cognitive structures, the members of the family did not consider questioning their long-standing assumptions about family relationships; they took the validity of their cognitions for granted.

The therapist uncovered a variety of *standards* held by the family members that appeared to influence their interactions. For example, Robert expressed the belief that "A good child always obeys his or her parents." As a consequence, he was excessively conforming to his parents' requests and became very angry at his sister whenever she questioned their parents' authority. Frank, in turn, believed that "Mothers should *always* support fathers when the fathers are attempting to discipline their children." As a consequence, Frank became angry at Alice whenever she disagreed with his strict discipline of Jane. Frank also believed that children should adopt the values, beliefs, and preferences of their parents. Whenever there was evidence that the family did not share a common worldview, Frank became quite upset.

There was clear evidence of a marked drop in *positive affectional and instrumental behaviors* exchanged by the family members, particularly between father and daughter, but also between the spouses. The family members spent little time together, and when they were together, their interactions focused on problems concerning Jane. It was not surprising that none of the family members felt much satisfaction about their relationships.

Frank and Jane perceived each other as inflexible, so neither listened carefully to the other's opinions, and both began any discussion with defensive and attacking messages. In contrast, each of them expressed feelings and listened well when talking individually with the therapist.

Another communication problem identified was a high rate of coercive messages (threats, criticism, insults) between father and daughter, and between the spouses. Furthermore, samples of the family's conversations indicated that they used vague terms when attempting to express their concerns and requests to each other. Finally, they typically became caught in escalating cycles of negative exchange that they were only able to interrupt when one of the involved family members escaped the interaction (e.g., Jane running out of the house).

The therapist learned that both parents used effective problem-solving skills in their jobs, but not at home. As a group, the family tended to criticize each other's suggested solutions to problems, and when the parents felt pressured, they tended to try to implement the first solution that came to mind.

Frank and Alice had tried to institute their own version of a quid pro quo behavioral contract, specifying positive actions that they would take if Jane exhibited particular positive behaviors. Unfortunately, as soon as Jane failed to comply with any aspect of the contract, her father withdrew all of his positive behavior toward her. She responded to his punitiveness with oppositional behavior (creating a new negative escalation).

As noted, Jane attributed her father's restrictive behavior to a lack of love for her. The therapist helped her to modify this inaccurate and maladaptive attribution by generating alternative explanations, such as "He is very worried about some harm possibly coming to me" and "He is very attached to me and finds it hard to have me leave home." When she described past occasions when she shared leisure activities with her father and kept a log of similar events for 2 weeks, there were several instances in which Frank had expressed his caring for Jane. Furthermore, during a family therapy session, the therapist was able to elicit Frank's fears that his daughter could be harmed in what he saw as an increasingly dangerous world. The therapist also helped the family to plan and conduct a behavioral experiment in which Jane calmly proposed an outing for herself with her friends, describing to her father the precautions she would take to protect her well-being. She listened calmly while her father expressed his concerns to her, and then made sure that she was home on time. After the family had conducted the experiment, all expressed satisfaction with the outcome. Jane remarked that she could see that her father's restrictiveness was more likely due to worry than to a lack of caring.

The therapist helped Alice modify her expectancy that any attempts to negotiate with Frank would be futile. Her expectancy shifted when the therapist coached the couple in problem solving about ways of dealing with Jane's oppositional behavior, and Frank agreed to a compromise that was acceptable to Alice. Although it was clear to the therapist that Frank and Alice did not want to focus on their marital relationship, these interventions that improved their functioning as a "parental team" appeared to improve their overall relationship as well.

Frank held the standard that children should adopt the values and preferences of their parents. Consistent with the rational–emotive therapy concept of an "irrational belief," Frank concluded that it would be "awful" if his children did not conform to his values and standards. The therapist attempted, as a consequence, to help Frank modify his standards. When the therapist explored the logic of the standard with Frank, he readily saw that it was unrealistic to expect children to become replicas of their parents. Frank acknowledged that no two people are exactly alike, due to a complex interaction of innate temperament and unique life experiences. Furthermore, when asked to review what he had observed about other families whom he knew, he described some families in which the children clearly had developed some values and preferences that were different from those of their parents, with no apparent ill effects on the children or the parent–child relationships.

In spite of these interventions, Frank continued to cling to his belief that his children should share his values and preferences. When the therapist coached him in listing advantages and disadvantages of the standard, it became clear that, from Frank's perspective, there were some compelling advantages to maintain it. Frank noted, for example, that it was advantageous to have everyone agree about standards, because this would alleviate conflict (which was important to him, because he was very uncomfortable with overt conflict). He also noted that having his children mirror his views was comforting and bolstered his self-esteem. Finally, having such predictable children minimized a parent's need to worry about the children's welfare, another issue quite salient to Frank.

On the other hand, Frank was able to see that pressuring children to conform could impair their personal development, leaving them with lower self confidence and little ability to think for themselves. He saw this as a serious deficit, because he viewed the world as a difficult place in which to live that demanded self confidence and an ability to make decisions in the face of potentially harmful outside pressures. Another disadvantage that Frank saw in his standard was that a household in which everyone agreed actually could become boring.

Frank concluded that although there were advantages to his standard, the disadvantages pointed to a need to soften his views. With the help of the therapist and his family, he devised a more tolerant revised standard— "Parents should share with their children the knowledge that they have gained through their experiences of living in the world, including information about opportunities and dangers; however, they also should encourage each child to develop a healthy identity and self-esteem, which at times is likely to involve the child's testing him- or herself against the world, including the parents." Frank found the revised standard acceptable and agreed to devise behavioral experiments consistent with the alternative philosophy that he, Jane, and Robert could enact. After repeated successful experiments, Frank began to *believe* the alternative philosophy.

The therapist helped this family plan some shared leisure time during which there would be no discussion of problems. Given Jane's emerging need for independence, the therapist attempted to structure just enough joint activity to increase cohesion but not so much as to threaten Jane's developing sense of autonomy. Furthermore, communication training was used to decrease the aversive messages, interruptions, and other dysfunctional behaviors common in this family. All of the family members felt more respect from each other when they were able to use expressive and listening skills effectively. The therapist also taught the family problem-solving skills, which they applied to responsibilities for household chores, independent activities by the children, and decision making about family leisure activities. Finally, the therapist helped the parents enact a contract with Jane, in which she received specific rewards that she desired in return for completing her chores and being home on time.

REFERENCES

American Psychiatric Association. (1994). *Diagnostic and statistical manual of mental disorders* (4th ed.). Washington, DC: Author.

Arias, I., & Beach, S. R. H. (1987). Assessment of social cognition in the context of marriage. In K. D. O'Leary, (Ed.), *Assessment of marital discord: An integration for research and clinical practice* (pp. 109–137). Hillsdale, NJ: Erlbaum.

Azar, S. T. (1986, November). *Identifying at-risk populations: A research strategy for developing more specific risk indicators and screening devices.* Paper presented at the annual meeting of the Association for Advancement of Behavior Therapy, Chicago.

Bandura, A. (1977). *Social learning theory.* Englewood Cliffs, NJ: Prentice-Hall.

Baucom, D. H. (1987). Attributions in distressed relations: How can we explain them? In S. Duck & D. Perlman (Eds.), *Heterosexual relations, marriage and divorce* (pp. 177–206). London: Sage.

Baucom, D. H., & Adams, A. (1987). Assessing communication in marital interaction. In K. D. O'Leary (Ed.), *Assessment of marital discord* (pp. 139–182). Hillsdale, NJ: Erlbaum.

Baucom, D. H., & Epstein, N. (1990). *Cognitive-behavioral marital therapy.* New York: Brunner/Mazel.

Baucom, D. H., Epstein, N., Sayers, S., & Sher, T. G. (1989). The role of cognitions in marital relationships: Definitional, methodological, and conceptual issues. *Journal of Consulting and Clinical Psychology, 57,* 31–38.

Beck, A. T. (1976). *Cognitive therapy and the emotional disorders*. New York: International Universities Press.

Beck, A. T. (1988). *Love is never enough*. New York: Harper & Row.

Beck, A. T., & Emery, G. (1985). *Anxiety disorders and phobias: A cognitive perspective*. New York: Basic Books.

Beck, A. T., Rush, A. J., Shaw, B. F., & Emery, G. (1979). *Cognitive therapy of depression*. New York: Guilford Press.

Bornstein, P. H., & Bornstein, M. T. (1986). *Marital therapy: A behavioral-communications approach*. New York: Pergamon Press.

Bradbury, T. N., & Fincham, F. D. (1990). Attributions in marriage: Review and critique. *Psychological Bulletin, 107*, 3–33.

Bradbury, T. N., & Fincham, F. D. (1992). Attributions and behavior in marital interaction. *Journal of Personality and Social Psychology, 63*, 613–628.

Dattilio, F. M. (1993). Cognitive techniques with couples and families. *Family Journal, 1*(1), 51–65.

Dattilio, F. M. (1994). Families in crisis. In F. M. Dattilio & A. Freeman (Eds.), *Cognitive-behavioral strategies in crisis intervention* (pp. 278–301). New York: Guilford Press.

Dattilio, F. M. (1995). A cognitive-behavioral approach to family therapy with Ruth. In G. Corey (Ed.), *Case approach to counseling and psychotherapy* (4th ed., pp. 282–298). Pacific Grove, CA: Brooks/Cole.

Dattilio, F. M., & Padesky, C. A. (1990). *Cognitive therapy with couples*. Sarasota, FL: Professional Resource Exchange.

Doherty, W. J. (1981). Cognitive processes in intimate conflict: II. Efficacy and learned helplessness. *American Journal of Family Therapy, 9*(2), 35–44.

Ellis, A. (1962). *Reason and emotion in psychotherapy*. New York: Lyle Stuart.

Ellis, A., & Grieger, R. (Eds.) (1977). *Handbook of rational–emotive therapy*. New York: Springer.

Ellis, A., Sichel, J. L., Yeager, R. J., DiMattia, D. J., & DiGiuseppe, R. (1989). *Rational–emotive couples therapy*. New York: Pergamon Press.

Epstein, N. (1982). Cognitive therapy with couples. *American Journal of Family Therapy, 10*(1), 5–16.

Epstein, N., & Baucom, D. H. (1989). Cognitive-behavioral marital therapy. In A. Freeman, K. M. Simon, L. E. Beutler, & H. Arkowitz (Eds.), *Comprehensive handbook of cognitive therapy* (pp. 491–513). New York: Plenum Press.

Epstein, N., & Baucom, D. H. (1993). Cognitive factors in marital disturbance. In K. S. Dobson & P. C. Kendall (Eds.), *Psychopathology and cognition* (pp. 351–385). San Diego, CA: Academic Press.

Epstein, N., & Schlesinger, S. E. (1991). Marital and family problems. In W. Dryden & R. Rentoul (Eds.), *Adult clinical problems: A cognitive-behavioural approach* (pp. 288–317). London: Routledge & Kegan Paul.

Epstein, N., Schlesinger, S. E., & Dryden, W. (Eds.) (1988). *Cognitive-behavioral therapy with families*. New York: Brunner/Mazel.

Falloon, I. R. H. (1991). Behavioral family therapy. In A. S. Gurman & D. P. Kniskern (Eds.), *Handbook of family therapy* (Vol. 2, pp. 65–95). New York: Brunner/Mazel.

Falloon, I. R. H., Boyd, J. L., & McGill, C. W. (1984). *Family care of schizophrenia.* New York: Guilford Press.

Fiske, S. T., & Taylor, S. E. (1991). *Social cognition* (2nd ed.). New York: McGraw-Hill.

Goldenberg, I., & Goldenberg, H. (1991). *Family therapy: An overview* (3rd ed.). Pacific Grove, CA: Brooks/Cole.

Gottman, J. M. (1979). *Marital interaction: Empirical investigations.* New York: Academic Press.

Grotevant, H. D., & Carlson, C. I. (1989). *Family assessment: A guide to methods and measures.* New York: Guilford Press.

Guerney, B. G. Jr. (1977). *Relationship enhancement.* San Francisco: Jossey-Bass.

Heider, F. (1958). *The psychology of interpersonal relations.* New York: Wiley.

Herzberger, S. D. (1983). Social cognition and the transmission of abuse. In D. Finkelhor, R. J. Gelles, G. T. Hotaling, & M. A. Straus (Eds.), *The dark side of families: Current family violence research* (pp. 317–329). Beverly Hills, CA: Sage.

Holtzworth-Munroe, A., & Hutchinson, G. (1993). Attributing negative intent to wife behavior: The attributions of maritally violent versus nonviolent men. *Journal of Abnormal Psychology, 102,* 206–211.

Holtzworth-Munroe, A., & Jacobson, N. S. (1985). Causal attributions of married couples: When do they search for causes? What do they conclude when they do? *Journal of Personality and Social Psychology, 48,* 1398–1412.

Huber, C. H., & Baruth, L. G. (1989). *Rational–emotive family therapy: A systems perspective.* New York: Springer.

Jacobson, N. S. (1984). The modification of cognitive processes in behavioral marital therapy: Integrating cognitive and behavioral intervention strategies. In K. Hahlweg & N. S. Jacobson (Eds.), *Marital interaction: Analysis and modification* (pp. 285–308). New York: Guilford Press.

Jacobson, N. S., & Margolin, G. (1979). *Marital therapy: Strategies based on social learning and behavior exchange principles.* New York: Brunner/Mazel.

Kelley, H. H. (1967). Attribution theory in social psychology. In D. Levine (Ed.), *Nebraska Symposium on Motivation* (Vol. 15, pp. 192–238). Lincoln: University of Nebraska Press.

Kelly, G. A. (1955). *The psychology of personal constructs.* New York: Norton.

Kurdek, L. A., & Berg, B. (1987). Children's beliefs about parental divorce scale: Psychometric characteristics and concurrent validity. *Journal of Consulting and Clinical Psychology, 55,* 712–718.

Larrance, D. T., & Twentyman, C. T. (1983). Maternal attributions and child abuse. *Journal of Abnormal Psychology, 92,* 449–457.

Leslie, L. A., & Epstein, N. (1988). Cognitive-behavioral treatment of remarried families. In N. Epstein, S. E. Schlesinger, & W. Dryden (Eds.), *Cognitive-behavioral therapy with families* (pp. 151–182). New York: Brunner/Mazel.

Margolin, G., & Wampold, B. E. (1981). Sequential analysis of conflict and accord in distressed and nondistressed marital partners. *Journal of Consulting and Clinical Psychology, 49,* 554–567.

Markman, H. J., & Notarius, C. I. (1987). Coding marital and family interaction: Current status. In T. Jacob (Ed.), *Family interaction and psychopathology: Theories, methods, and findings* (pp. 329–390). New York: Plenum Press.

Morton, T. L., Twentyman, C. T., & Azar, S. T. (1988). Cognitive-behavioral assessment and treatment of child abuse. In N. Epstein, S. E. Schlesinger, & W. Dryden (Eds.), *Cognitive-behavioral therapy with families* (pp. 87–117). New York: Brunner/Mazel.

Nisbett, R., & Ross, L. (1980). *Human inference: Strategies and shortcomings of social judgment.* Englewood Cliffs, NJ: Prentice-Hall.

Patterson, G. R. (1975). *Families.* Champaign, IL: Research Press.

Patterson, G. R. (1982). *Coercive family process.* Eugene, OR: Castalia.

Patterson, G. R., & Forgatch, M. S. (1987). *Parents and adolescents living together: Part 1. The basics.* Eugene, OR: Castalia.

Patterson, G. R., & Reid, J. B. (1984). Social interaction processes within the family: The study of moment-by-moment family transaction in which human social development is embedded. *Journal of Applied Developmental Psychology, 5,* 237–262.

Pretzer, J., Epstein, N., & Fleming, B. (1991). The Marital Attitude Survey: A measure of dysfunctional attributions and expectancies. *The Journal of Cognitive Psychotherapy: An International Quarterly, 5,* 131–148.

Revenstorf, D., Hahlweg, K., Schindler, L., & Vogel, B. (1984). Interaction analysis of marital conflict. In K. Hahlweg & N. S. Jacobson (Eds.), *Marital interaction: Analysis and modification* (pp. 159–181). New York: Guilford Press.

Robin, A. L., & Foster, S. L. (1989). *Negotiating parent–adolescent conflict: A behavioral–family systems approach.* New York: Guilford Press.

Rotter, J. B. (1954). *Social learning and clinical psychology.* Englewood Cliffs, NJ: Prentice-Hall.

Schlesinger, S. E., & Epstein, N. (1986). Cognitive-behavioral techniques in marital therapy. In P. A. Keller & L. G. Ritt (Eds.), *Innovations in clinical practice: A source book* (Vol. 5, pp. 137–156). Sarasota, FL: Professional Resource Exchange.

Schwebel, A. I., & Fine, M. A. (1994). *Understanding and helping families: A cognitive-behavioral approach.* Hillsdale, NJ: Erlbaum.

Seiler, T. B. (1984). Development of cognitive theory, personality, and therapy. In N. Hoffman (Ed.), *Foundations of cognitive therapy: Theoretical methods and practical applications* (pp. 11–49). New York: Plenum Press.

Stuart, R. B. (1980). *Helping couples change: A social learning approach to marital therapy.* New York: Guilford Press.

Thibaut, J. W., & Kelley, H. H. (1959). *The social psychology of groups.* New York: Wiley.

Thompson, J. S., & Snyder, D. K. (1986). Attribution theory in intimate relationships: A methodological review. *American Journal of Family Therapy, 14,* 123–138.

Turk, D. C., & Speers, M. A. (1983). Cognitive schemata and cognitive processes in cognitive-behavioral interventions: Going beyond the information given. In P. C. Kendall (Ed.), *Advances in cognitive-behavioral research and therapy* (Vol. 2, pp. 1–31). New York: Academic Press.

Vanzetti, N. A., Notarius, C. I., & NeeSmith, D. (1992). Specific and generalized expectancies in marital interaction. *Journal of Family Psychology, 6,* 171–183.

Watzlawick, P., Beavin, J. H., & Jackson, D. D. (1967). *Pragmatics of human communication.* New York: Norton.

Wessler, R. A., & Wessler, R. L. (1980). *The principles and practice of rational–emotive therapy.* San Francisco: Jossey-Bass.

15

Facilitating Parental Understanding and Management of Attention-Deficit/ Hyperactivity Disorder

Arthur D. Anastopoulos

Attention-deficit/hyperactivity disorder (ADHD) is a chronic and pervasive condition characterized by developmental deficiencies in sustained attention, impulse control, and the regulation of motor activity in response to situational demands (American Psychiatric Association, 1994). When present in childhood, ADHD very often can be extremely disruptive, adversely affecting family relations, school performance, peer relations, and many other areas of psychosocial functioning (Barkley, 1990).

Although cognitive restructuring and other cognitive therapy techniques have not routinely been utilized as a treatment for ADHD, clinical experience would seem to suggest that such intervention strategies do have a place in the overall clinical management of children with this disorder. The purpose of this chapter is to illustrate how cognitive therapy procedures can be used to alter faulty assumptions and beliefs that impede parental acceptance of the diagnosis, as well as parental motivation to implement recommended pharmacological and/or cognitive-behavioral interventions on behalf of the child. To provide a foundation for understanding the therapeutic role that these procedures might play, this chapter begins with a brief overview of ADHD. Against this background, it then presents a case discussion, highlighting the manner in which cognitive restructuring techniques were used in the ongoing clinical care of a young child with ADHD.

OVERVIEW OF ADHD

Primary Symptoms

In clinical practice, it is not uncommon for parents or teachers to be unclear about what constitutes an ADHD diagnosis. For example, when asked to identify those behaviors that led them to believe that their child may have ADHD, many parents cite noncompliance, emotional immaturity, or unsatisfactory academic progress. Although such characteristics certainly can be associated with an ADHD diagnosis, they are not the core features of this disorder. For this reason, clinicians must often clarify what is and what is not an ADHD problem.

Most child health-care professionals agree that inattention, impulsivity, and hyperactivity are the primary features of ADHD. Clinical descriptions of children with ADHD frequently include complaints of "not listening to instructions," "not finishing assigned work," "daydreaming," "becoming bored easily," and so forth. Common to all of these referral concerns is a diminished capacity for vigilance, that is, difficulties sustaining attention to task (Douglas, 1983). Such problems can occur in free-play settings (Routh & Schroeder, 1976), but most often surface in situations demanding sustained attention to dull, boring, repetitive tasks (Milich, Loney, & Landau, 1982).

Clinic-referred children with ADHD may exhibit impulsivity as well. For example, they may interrupt others who might be busy, or display tremendous difficulty waiting for their turn in game situations. They may also begin tasks before directions are completed, take unnecessary risks, talk out of turn, or make indiscreet remarks without regard for social consequences.

When hyperactivity is present, this may be displayed not only motorically but verbally as well. Descriptions of physical restlessness might include statements such as "always on the go," "unable to sit still," and so forth. As for the verbal component, more often than not these complaints center around the child's "talking excessively" or being a "chatterbox or motormouth." Whether mild or severe, what makes all of these behaviors manifestations of hyperactivity is their excessive, task-irrelevant, and developmentally inappropriate nature.

Although not yet widely accepted, difficulties with rule-governed behavior and excessive performance variability may also represent primary deficits (Barkley, 1990; Kendall & Braswell, 1985). Several studies have demonstrated that children with ADHD display significant problems adhering to rules or complying with requests (Rapport, Tucker, DuPaul, Merlo, & Stoner, 1986). In line with these findings are the clinical reports of parents and teachers, who commonly voice concerns about the inability of children with ADHD to "follow through on instructions." Such difficulties may arise in a variety of contexts, but most often occur in situations when adults are not present, that is, when there are increased demands for behavioral self-regulation.

Children with ADHD may also display tremendous inconsistency in their task performance, both in terms of their productivity and accuracy (Douglas, 1972). Such variability may be evident with respect to their in-class performance or test scores, or it may involve fluctuations in their completion of homework or routine home chores. Although it can be argued that all children display a certain amount of variability in these areas, it is clear from clinical experience and research findings that children with ADHD exhibit this to a much greater degree. Thus, instead of reflecting "laziness," as some might contend, the inconsistent performance of children with ADHD may represent yet another manifestation of this disorder.

Diagnostic Criteria

Just as its diagnostic terminology has changed over time, so too have the criteria for diagnosing what we now label ADHD (American Psychiatric Association, 1980, 1987). The currently accepted criteria for making this diagnosis appear in the fourth edition of the *Diagnostic and Statistical Manual of Mental Disorders* (DSM-IV; American Psychiatric Association, 1994). At the heart of this decision-making process are two nine-item symptom listings: one pertaining to inattention symptoms, the other to hyperactivity–impulsivity concerns. Parents and/or teachers must report the presence of at least six of nine problem behaviors from each list to warrant consideration of a full ADHD diagnosis. Furthermore, such behaviors must have an onset prior to 7 years of age, a duration of at least 6 months, and a frequency above and beyond that expected of children of the same mental age.

As is evident from these criteria, the manner in which ADHD presents itself clinically can vary from child to child. For some children with ADHD, symptoms of inattention and impulsivity may be of relatively greater concern than hyperactivity problems; for others, impulsivity and hyperactivity difficulties may be more prominent. Most child health-care professionals do not find this variability in clinical presentation confusing, yet many parents and teachers do. For this reason, clinicians very often must provide such individuals with a general description of how the diagnostic criteria are employed, so as to increase their understanding and acceptance of this disorder.

Of the three primary symptoms, the hyperactivity component is by far the one most often misunderstood. For example, at the beginning of an evaluation, a clinician might ask, "What does your child do that makes you think he or she might have attention-deficit/hyperactivity disorder?" Not uncommonly, parents might answer, "Well, he or she definitely has problems paying attention, but he or she is not hyperactive." More often than not, implicit in this response is the faulty belief that motor restlessness has to be in its extreme form before it can be labeled hyperactivity. Moreover, there is an underlying assumption that hyperactivity can only be expressed through physical actions. Due to such misconceptions, parents might later have difficulty accepting diagnostic feedback, if indeed the clinician concludes that ADHD is present.

To help correct such thinking and thereby facilitate parental acceptance of the diagnosis, clinicians must clarify why they believe a hyperactivity component is present. For example, they might need to call attention to the fact that hyperactivity can be displayed motorically or vocally. They should also acknowledge that in extreme cases, children who are hyperactive can indeed be "in constant motion," "bouncing off the walls," and so forth. At the same time, however, they must point out that although most people think of hyperactivity in this way, it can also present itself in less severe forms, such as "fidgeting when seated," or "talking excessively."

Associated Features

In addition to their primary symptoms, children with ADHD frequently display secondary or comorbid difficulties. For example, noncompliance, argumentativeness, temper outbursts, lying, stealing, and other manifestations of oppositional defiant disorder and conduct disorder may occur in up to 65% of the clinic-referred ADHD population (Loney & Milich, 1982). Virtually all children with ADHD experience some type of school difficulty. An especially common problem is that their levels of academic productivity and achievement are significantly lower than their estimated potential (Barkley, 1990). As many as 20% to 30% of children may also exhibit dyslexia or other types of specific learning disabilities (Barkley, DuPaul, & McMurray, 1990). As a result of such complications, a relatively high percentage typically receive some form of special education assistance (Barkley, 1990). Significant peer socialization problems may occur as well (Pelham & Bender, 1982). At times, such difficulties involve deficiencies in establishing friendships (Grenell, Glass, & Katz, 1987). More often than not, however, maintaining satisfactory peer relations is of even greater clinical concern. Due to their inability to control their behavior in social situations, children with ADHD frequently alienate their peers, who in turn respond with social rejection or avoidance (Cunningham & Siegel, 1987). Possibly as a result of such behavioral, academic, and/or social problems, children with ADHD very often exhibit low self-esteem, low frustration tolerance, symptoms of depression and anxiety, and other emotional complications (Margalit & Arieli, 1984).

Impact on Family Functioning

As noted, ADHD is frequently accompanied by various behavioral, academic, social, and emotional complications. Together, such difficulties can have a significant impact on the psychosocial functioning of parents and siblings. Research has shown, for example, that parents of children with ADHD very often become overly directive and negative in their parenting style (Cunningham & Barkley, 1979). In addition to viewing themselves as less skilled and less knowledgeable in their parenting roles (Mash & Johnston, 1990), they may also experience considerable stress in their parenting roles, especially when comorbid oppositional–defiant features are present (Anastopoulos, Guevremont, Shelton, & DuPaul, 1992). Depression and marital discord may arise as well (Lahey et al., 1988). Whether these parental and family complications result directly from the child's ADHD is not entirely clear at present. Clinical experience would suggest that they probably do, at least in part, given the increased caretaking demands that children with ADHD impose on their parents. These include more frequent displays of noncompliance, related to the child's difficulties in following through on parental instructions (Cunningham & Barkley, 1979). In addition, parents of these children often find themselves involved in resolving various school, peer, and sibling difficulties that occur throughout childhood (Barkley, 1990) and into adolescence as well (Barkley, Anastopoulos, Guevremont, & Fletcher, 1991).

Etiology

Within the field today, there is a consensus that neurochemical imbalances play a central role in the etiology of ADHD. More specifically, there may be abnormalities in one or more of the monoaminergic systems involving either dopamine or norepinephrine mechanisms (Zametkin & Rapoport, 1986). The locus of this dysfunction purportedly lies within the prefrontal–limbic areas of the brain (Lou, Henriksen, Bruhn, Borner, & Nielsen, 1989). For a majority of children with ADHD, such neurological circumstances presumably arise from inborn biological factors, including genetic transmission, pregnancy, and birth complications (Biederman et al., 1987; Deutsch, 1987; Streissguth et al., 1984). For relatively smaller numbers of children carrying this diagnosis, it can be acquired after birth via head injury, neurological illness, elevated lead levels, and other biological complications (Ross & Ross, 1982).

Despite their widespread public appeal, there is relatively little support for the assertions of Feingold (1975) and others that the ingestion of sugar or various other food substances directly causes ADHD (Wolraich et al., 1994). Likewise, although a few environmental theories have been proposed to explain ADHD (Block, 1977; Willis & Lovaas, 1977), these have not received much support in the research literature. Thus, there would seem to be little justification for claiming that poor parenting, chaotic home environments, or fast-paced lifestyles are in any way causally related to ADHD. Such circumstances, however, certainly can serve to exacerbate a preexisting ADHD condition.

One of the first questions that many parents ask after learning of their child's ADHD diagnosis is "What caused this?" Although clinicians generally cannot supply a definitive answer to this question, they can at least speculate about possible causes based on their knowledge of whether the child has any of the etiological risk factors noted earlier. Emphasizing the biological nature of this disorder very often serves to help parents see their child's problems in a different light. This, in turn, sets the stage for them to let go of any faulty beliefs that they may have had (e.g., "I must be a bad parent"), thereby reducing any associated guilt feelings or other types of personal distress.

Onset and Developmental Course

In line with the previous etiological discussion, some children begin to show evidence of ADHD in early infancy (Hartsough & Lambert, 1985). Most, however, first display clear signs of developmentally deviant behavior between 3 and 4 years of age (Ross & Ross, 1982). For a smaller number of children, ADHD symptoms may not surface until 5 or 6 years of age, coinciding with school entrance.

During middle childhood, ADHD symptoms often become more chronic and pervasive, even though they may appear somewhat improved at times. It is during this same period that secondary complications, such as academic underachievement or oppositional defiant behavior, frequently arise.

Contrary to popular opinion, most children do not outgrow their ADHD problems upon reaching adolescence. As many as 70% will continue to exhibit inattention, impulsivity, and/or restlessness during their teen years to a degree much greater than that observed in peers (Weiss & Hechtman, 1986). Of additional clinical significance is that the pattern of secondary complications accompanying ADHD in adolescence is highly similar to that found in younger ADHD populations (Barkley et al., 1990).

Although many children with ADHD continue to display these symptoms well into adolescence and adulthood, the vast majority will learn to compensate for these problems and therefore make a satisfactory adult adjustment (Weiss & Hechtman, 1986). For those who do not, it is often the case that their comorbid problems, such as depression or alcoholism (Farrington, Loeber, & van Kammen, 1987), are of relatively greater clinical concern than their ADHD symptoms.

Situational Variability of Symptoms

Contrary to the belief of many individuals, ADHD is not an all-or-none phenomenon, either present all the time or not at all. Instead, it is a condition whose primary symptoms show significant fluctuations in response to different situational demands (Zentall, 1985). One of the most important factors determining this variation is the degree to which children with ADHD are interested in what they are doing. ADHD symptoms are much more likely to occur in situations that are highly repetitive, boring, or familiar, versus those that are novel or stimulating (Barkley, 1977). Another determinant of situational variation is the amount of imposed structure. In free-play or low-demand settings, in which children with ADHD have the freedom to do as they please, their behavior is relatively indistinguishable from that of normal children (Luk, 1985). Significant ADHD problems may arise, however, when others place demands on them or set rules for their behavior. Presumably due to increased demands for behavioral self-regulation, group settings are far more problematic for children with ADHD than would be the case in one-to-one situations. There is also an increased likelihood for ADHD symptoms to arise in situations in which feedback is dispensed infrequently and/or on a delayed basis (Douglas, 1983).

Being aware of the situational variability of ADHD symptoms is central to understanding the frequently irregular clinical presentation of this disorder. There are, of course, numerous examples of how ADHD symptoms might occur in one setting but not another. One of the more common discrepancies that might arise is when teachers observe the symptoms in school but parents report no such problems at home. At face value, this might cause parents a tremendous amount of difficulty in accepting their child's ADHD diagnosis, not to mention anger and mistrust toward the teacher. By pointing out that ADHD is not an all-or-none clinical phenomenon and that the conditions at school (e.g., less interesting activities, large groups) are more conducive to eliciting the symptoms, clinicians very often can replace faulty assumptions with more accurate beliefs, thereby facilitating not only parental understanding and acceptance of the disorder, but also their willingness to work cooperatively with their child's teacher.

Assessment

Clinical evaluations of children with ADHD must be comprehensive and multimodal in nature, so as to capture ADHD's situational variability, comorbid features, and impact on home, school, and social functioning (Barkley, 1990). This may include, for example, not only the traditional methods of parent-and-child interviews, but also standardized, child-behavior rating scales, parent self-report measures, direct behavioral observations of ADHD symptoms in natural or analogue settings, and clinic-based psychological tests. All sources of information about the child are of clinical value, but input obtained from parents and teachers is generally more reliable and valid than that obtained from the child via interview or psychological testing. For this reason, parents and teachers' input typically carries greater weight in the overall interpretation of obtained results.

Many parents find the aforementioned approach to assessment incompatible with what they thought might be done to determine the presence or absence of ADHD. "After all," they might reason, "if you're trying to find out whether my child has ADHD, why are you spending so much time interviewing me and having me fill out questionnaires? . . . Why aren't you spending more time testing my child?" Left unanswered, such matters can cause a parent to feel threatened or to question the competence of the evaluating clinician. This, in turn, can interfere with their acceptance of any diagnostic feedback, as well as their willingness to implement treatment recommendations.

In anticipation of such problems, clinicians must explain the rationale for their assessment approach. In particular, they need to mention that directly testing their child involves relatively novel and interesting psychological test materials that are administered under closely supervised, high-feedback, one-to-one conditions. Such circumstances decrease the likelihood that ADHD symptoms will surface. For this reason, therefore, the most accurate sampling of a child's behavior stems from parents' and teachers' input, based on observations of the child in situational contexts (e.g., large group settings) that are more likely to elicit ADHD symptomatology. This type of explanation very often serves to alleviate any parental concerns or doubts that might interfere with their receptivity to diagnostic and treatment feedback.

Treatment

The clinical management of ADHD often demands many different therapeutic modalities in combination, no single one of which can address all of the difficulties likely to be experienced by such children. Among the many available treatments, stimulant medication, parent training in contingency management, classroom behavior modification methods, and, in some cases, child cognitive-behavioral interventions appear to have the greatest efficacy or promise of such (Barkley, 1990). Nevertheless, to be effective in altering prognosis, such interventions must be highly individualized and maintained over extended periods of time.

CASE EXAMPLE

The following case was referred to the ADHD Clinic, a subspecialty child unit in the Department of Psychiatry at the University of Massachusetts Medical Center. It was selected for presentation because it so nicely illustrates many of the ways in which cognitive therapy techniques can be used as an adjunctive procedure in the diagnostic assessment and ongoing clinical management of a child with ADHD.

Reason for Referral

Nathan is an 8-year-old boy who was initially referred to the ADHD Clinic for an evaluation of long-standing home and school difficulties. Of particular concern to his parents and third-grade teacher at the time of his referral were his problems finishing assigned tasks, his frequent interruptions of others, and his constant fidgeting.

Background Information

Nathan's prenatal history, delivery, and neonatal course were unremarkable. His infant health and temperament were well within normal limits. According to his parents, he reached all of his major developmental milestones at age-appropriate times.

Throughout his lifetime, Nathan had maintained excellent physical health. He had no allergies or chronic illnesses, nor had he sustained any serious physical injury. His speech, hearing, vision, and motor coordination were age appropriate. His eating, sleeping, and elimination patterns were within normal limits as well. He was not taking any prescription medication regularly at the time of his evaluation.

The middle child of three children, Nathan and his siblings lived with their biological parents in a middle-class suburban home. Nathan maintained fairly typical relations with his siblings, neither of whom posed any major medical, learning, behavioral, or emotional problems. Both of Nathan's parents were in good health. Neither had a history of significant childhood or adult problems. Nathan's father was college educated and working full time as an engineer. His mother had 2 years of college training but had not worked outside of the home for several years. Nathan's parents had been married for 15 years, during which time there had been some strains in their relationship, but not to the point of separations or marital counseling. No major lifestyle changes or psychosocial stressors had occurred within 12 months of Nathan's diagnostic evaluation.

Nathan attended nursery school for 2 years prior to entering kindergarten. From kindergarten to his current enrollment in third grade, he had been enrolled in the same public school setting. Throughout his schooling, Nathan's teachers had described him as "bright but lazy, more interested in playing, and not working up to his ability." Of particular concern was that his academic productivity and achievement in almost all subject areas were well below grade level in quality. Moreover, Nathan's classmates were beginning to shy away from him because they did not appreciate his intrusiveness or his tendency to get into trouble with the teacher. Due to such concerns about his academic performance and classroom behavior, Nathan's third-grade teacher requested school-based testing. Because this revealed him to be functioning within the average range of intelligence in the absence of specific learning disabilities, no special education services were deemed necessary. Instead, the school assessment team recommended that he begin receiving individual counseling outside of the school setting, based on the assumption that his school problems stemmed from underlying emotional disturbance and/or family relationship problems.

Diagnostic Formulation and Treatment Recommendations

Input about Nathan and his family was obtained from multiple sources: his parents' responses to interview questioning, child behavior rating scales, and self-report rating scales; his third-grade teacher's responses to various child-behavior rating scales; Nathan's interview responses and performance on clinic-based psychological tests; and a review of prior school and medical records. The results of this multimethod assessment confirmed that he did indeed meet DSM-IV criteria for a diagnosis of ADHD, which was moderate in overall severity and manifested across both home and school settings. No other DSM-IV diagnostic concerns emerged with respect to other areas of Nathan's learning, behavioral, emotional, or psychiatric functioning. In the absence of such findings, Nathan's ADHD was viewed to be a major factor contributing to his diminished academic productivity and achievement, his emerging peer-relationship problems in school, and his parents' extremely high levels of parenting stress.

To address Nathan's ADHD both at home and at school, several intervention strategies were recommended for incorporation into his overall treatment plan, including parent and teacher education about ADHD as a disorder; numerous curriculum, teaching-style, and classroom-environment modifications; school-based social skills training; behavioral parent training; and pharmacotherapy, using Ritalin or some other form of stimulant-medication therapy.

Feedback Session

Feedback about Nathan's diagnostic status and treatment plan was shared with his parents on the same day as his intake evaluation. In anticipation of possible parental resistance to accepting their son's diagnosis, the criteria for making an ADHD diagnosis were first clarified. This was followed by a detailed review of all of the raw data that had been collected as part of the multimethod assessment. Despite the fact that all of the DSM-IV criteria had been met and that he himself had rated his son's ADHD symptomatology as developmentally deviant—above the 95th percentile relative to same-aged boys—Nathan's father still had a great deal of difficulty in accepting this diagnosis. After all, as he stated, "How can he have ADHD when he can sit and play computer games for hours on end?" Readily apparent in such a statement was the dichotomous nature of Nathan's father's thinking. Such faulty thinking was easily corrected by informing him of the situational variability of ADHD symptomatology.

Another clinical concern that arose during the feedback session was Nathan's mother's guilt about his diagnosis. She herself had often wondered whether she was doing something wrong in her parenting of Nathan. Some of her friends and relatives had even gone so far as to tell her that she was indeed doing something wrong. Hearing the diagnosis, therefore, served to confirm her worst fears: She had done something wrong; she was a bad parent and her son's future was bleak, all of which served to increase her sense of guilt, frustration, and despair. To help diffuse this situation, it was quickly pointed out that research had shown that faulty parenting was not a cause of ADHD. On the contrary, most of the current research pointed in the direction of biological causes, including genetic transmission, prenatal complications, and so forth. Although this information did not fully eliminate her negative self-perception and feelings that day, it definitely began the process of reframing her view of her contribution to her son's problems.

Similar restructuring was employed to address both parents' fears and worries about Nathan's future, and with respect to their reluctance to incorporate the recommended treatment plan. Given that they had "tried everything and nothing works" and that Nathan seemed "destined" to a life a failure and frustration, they were not especially eager to begin the behavioral parent-training program. Likewise, they expressed a great deal of frustration and pessimism about the prospects of enlisting the support and cooperation of Nathan's third-grade teacher, given that all other teachers up to that point had not been very responsive to meeting his individual classroom needs. Based on stories that they had read in their local newspaper, they were not at all interested in considering stimulant-medication therapy as a treatment option for Nathan.

As for their assessment of the efficacy of the parent-training program, it was first necessary to point out that what they had tried previously were traditional parenting techniques, which work well for normal children but not so well for children with ADHD. What they needed to be using were specialized parenting techniques to meet Nathan's special behavioral needs. Several examples of how the recommended parent-training strategies were very different from what they had tried before were presented, as were research findings pertinent to the efficacy of this form of treatment. Such information served to increase their willingness to participate in this program. Similar cognitive-restructuring strategies were employed to address the fortune-telling nature of their negative expectation that they would not be able to enlist the cooperation of Nathan's teacher. As for their concerns about medication, it was agreed that their preference not to medicate would be honored. At the same time, however, they were encouraged to take on an empirical approach to this matter. More specifically, they were advised to implement the recommended home- and school-based psychosocial treatments. After a period of 4 to 6 months, they and Nathan's teacher would need to evaluate his response to these treatments. If his level of improvement was less than satisfactory at that time, they would need to reconsider the merits of a stimulant medication trial. In the meantime, they agreed to begin receiving counseling about the advantages and disadvantages of using stimulant-medication, so as to acquire an understanding of this form of treatment that was more accurate and comprehensive than that available from the popular media.

Course of Treatment

The aforementioned treatment plan was implemented over a period of several months. At various points during their participation in the behavioral parent-training program (Anastopoulos & Barkley, 1990; Barkley, 1987), Nathan's parents occasionally slipped into unrealistic, negative thinking patterns that interfered with their willingness to try out new parenting strategies. For example, the recommended home poker chip system initially reminded them of something that they had previously tried unsuccessfully, and therefore they were disinclined to consider its use. Once again, it was necessary to point out how what was being recommended was different from what they had done before. With the clinician's encouragement, this information made it easier for them to put to test the hypothesis that these new parenting strategies might indeed work better.

Although the poker-chip system worked well for several weeks, Nathan began to display some resistance and deterioration in his behavior. This led both parents to the faulty conclusion that they were indeed right: The program did not work. It was pointed out that this was not an unusual occurrence for children with ADHD, given that they are prone to become bored easily. Nathan's parents were encouraged to make minor modifications in his poker-chip system, so as to increase its novelty, salience, and meaningfulness to Nathan. It was hypothesized that if they did, he very likely would regain interest in the program. When put to the test, this prediction indeed was supported.

In the midst of this parent-training program, a school meeting was conducted involving Nathan's teacher, principal, and parents. The purpose of this meeting was to educate school personnel about ADHD in general, to alert them as to how it affected Nathan, and to emphasize the need for collaborative teamwork between school personnel and his parents. Contrary to their earlier expectations, Nathan's parents were pleasantly surprised to discover that his teacher and principal were highly receptive to this suggestion, and that they would begin immediately incorporating modifications to meet his ADHD needs in the classroom and in other areas of the school in which behavior problems might arise (e.g., recess).

After several months, it was clear that these home- and school-based interventions had brought about many improvements in Nathan's psychosocial functioning. There was still ample room for improvement, however. This, coupled with the fact that they had acquired a better understanding of the potential benefits and side effects of stimulant-medication therapy, set the stage for Nathan's parents to request that he undergo a double-blind, placebo-controlled stimulant trial to determine if this form of treatment might bring about further normalization of his behavior.

CONCLUSION

What should be readily apparent from the preceding discussion is that there are indeed many ways in which cognitive therapy techniques can be used as adjunctive procedures in the overall clinical management of a child with ADHD. Although this particular case presentation illustrated how a large number and variety of such cognitive therapy techniques might be applied with parents, many other possible applications exist as well.

For example, clinicians working with ADHD populations might also find it useful to incorporate cognitive restructuring techniques in their dealings with teachers and other school personnel. Some teachers, for example, are highly resistant to recommendations that special modifications be made in the classroom. After all, the reasoning goes, "If I change things for one child, then I'll have to change things for everyone." Pointing out the overgeneralization in this statement and reminding them that the other students in the classroom do not have ADHD often serves to alter teachers' perceptions of this situation, thereby increasing their willingness to implement modifications that will facilitate the overall classroom behavior and performance of a child with ADHD. As was the case with Nathan's parents, cognitive restructuring may also play an important role in reducing a teacher's resistance to incorporating classroom modifications, based on the assumption, "I've tried that before and it doesn't work."

Children with ADHD themselves may also benefit a great deal from cognitive therapy interventions. Many, for example, may experience a great deal of failure or chronic feelings of underachievement, leading to diminished self-esteem and other symptoms of depression. Although there certainly can be a reality base for such feelings, at least in part, many children with ADHD begin to view themselves in ways that go beyond what is a realistic appraisal, and therefore engage in distorted thinking patterns that exacerbate their emotional distress. For example, they may conclude, "I can't do anything right" or "Nobody likes me." Here again, cognitive restructuring techniques can be immensely helpful in altering such distorted thinking, thereby reducing such mild depressive symptomatology. As was the case in the previous example, cognitive therapy procedures can also be used quite successfully in alleviating the anxiety that a child with ADHD might feel in anticipation of an upcoming stimulant-medication trial.

There are, of course, no bounds on the ways in which clinicians might employ cognitive therapy in their ongoing assessment and treatment of children with ADHD and their families. At present, however, very little information of this sort is available. Clearly, there is a need for ADHD experts and cognitive therapy experts to join forces for the purpose of developing assessment procedures that tap into parental assumptions about ADHD as a disorder, including parental attributions about its causes, and parental beliefs about the efficacy of various treatments. Similar assessment devices might also be developed for use with affected children and their teachers. Once developed, such measures could then be used to examine what role cognitive therapy variables might play in predicting treatment outcome or in mediating previously reported treatment-induced changes in parental functioning, such as decreased parenting stress following participation in cognitive-behavioral parent-training programs (Anastopoulos, Shelton, DuPaul, & Guevremont, 1993).

These are but a few of the many possible directions that future research might take. In addition to these suggestions, it is hoped that clinicians and researchers who read this chapter will begin thinking of other avenues for using a cognitive therapy approach in their clinical management of children and adolescents with ADHD.

REFERENCES

American Psychiatric Association. (1980). *Diagnostic and statistical manual of mental disorders* (3rd ed.). Washington, DC: Author.

American Psychiatric Association. (1987). *Diagnostic and statistical manual of mental disorders* (3rd ed., rev.). Washington, DC: Author.

American Psychiatric Association. (1994). *Diagnostic and statistical manual of mental disorders* (4th ed.). Washington, DC: Author.

Anastopoulos, A. D., & Barkley, R. A. (1990). Counseling and training parents. In R. A. Barkley, *Attention-deficit hyperactivity disorder: A handbook for diagnosis and treatment*. New York: Guilford Press.

Anastopoulos, A. D., Guevremont, D. C., Shelton, T. L., & DuPaul, G. J. (1992). Parenting stress among families of children with Attention Deficit Hyperactivity Disorder. *Journal of Abnormal Child Psychology, 20*, 503–520.

Anastopoulos, A. D., Shelton, T., DuPaul, G. J., & Guevremont, D. C. (1993). Parent training for Attention Deficit Hyperactivity Disorder: Its impact on parent functioning. *Journal of Abnormal Child Psychology, 21*, 581–596.

Barkley, R. A. (1977). A review of stimulant drug research with hyperactive children. *Journal of Child Psychology and Psychiatry, 18*, 137–165.

Barkley, R. A. (1987). *Defiant children: A clinician's manual for parent training*. New York: Guilford Press.

Barkley, R. A. (1990). *Attention-deficit hyperactivity disorder: A handbook for diagnosis and treatment*. New York: Guilford Press.

Barkley, R. A., Anastopoulos, A. D., Guevremont, D. C., & Fletcher, K. E. (1991). Adolescents with ADHD: Patterns of behavioral adjustment, academic functioning, and treatment utilization. *Journal of the American Academy of Child and Adolescent Psychiatry, 30*, 752–761.

Barkley, R. A., DuPaul, G. J., & McMurray, M. (1990). A comprehensive evaluation of Attention Deficit Disorder with and without Hyperactivity defined by research criteria. *Journal of Consulting and Clinical Psychology, 58*, 775–789.

Biederman, J., Munir, K., Knee, D., Armentano, M., Autor, S., Waternaux, C., & Tsuang, M. (1987). High rate of affective disorders in probands with attention deficit disorders and in their relatives: A controlled family study. *American Journal of Psychiatry, 144*, 330–333.

Block, G. H. (1977). Hyperactivity: A cultural perspective. *Journal of Learning Disabilities, 110*, 236–240.

Cunningham, C. E., & Barkley, R. A. (1979). The interactions of hyperactive and normal children with their mothers during free play and structured task. *Child Development, 50*, 217–224.

Cunningham, C. E., & Siegel, L. S. (1987). Peer interactions of normal and attention-deficit disordered boys during free-play, cooperative task, and simulated classroom situations. *Journal of Abnormal Child Psychology*, *15*, 247–268.

Deutsch, K. (1987). *Genetic factors in attention deficit disorders*. Paper presented at the symposium on Disorders of Brain, Development, and Cognition, Boston, MA.

Douglas, V. I. (1972). Stop, look, and listen: The problem of sustained attention and impulse control in hyperactive and normal children. *Canadian Journal of Behavioural Science*, *4*, 259–282.

Douglas, V. I. (1983). Attention and cognitive problems. In M. Rutter (Ed.), *Developmental neuropsychiatry* (pp. 280–329). New York: Guilford Press.

Farrington, D. P., Loeber, R., & van Kammen, W. B. (1987, October). *Long-term criminal outcomes of hyperactivity–impulsivity, attention deficit and conduct problems in childhood*. Paper presented at the Society for Life History Research meeting, St. Louis, MO.

Feingold, B. (1975). *Why your child is hyperactive*. New York: Random House.

Grenell, M. M., Glass, C. R., & Katz, K. S. (1987). Hyperactive children and peer interaction: Knowledge and performance of social skills. *Journal of Abnormal Child Psychology*, 1–13.

Hartsough, C. S., & Lambert, N. M. (1985). Medical factors in hyperactive and normal children: Prenatal, developmental, and health history findings. *American Journal of Orthopsychiatry*, *55*, 190–201.

Kendall, P. C., & Braswell, L. (1985). *Cognitive-behavioral therapy for impulsive children*. New York: Guilford Press.

Lahey, B. B., Piacentini, J., McBurnett, K., Stone, P., Hatdagen, S., & Hynd, G. (1988). Psychopathology in the parents of children with conduct disorder and hyperactivity. *Journal of the American Academy of Child Psychiatry*, *27*, 163–170.

Loney, J., & Milich, R. (1982). Hyperactivity, inattention, and aggression in clinical practice. In D. Routh & M. Wolraich (Eds.), *Advances in developmental and behavioral pediatrics* (Vol. 3, pp. 113–147). Greenwich, CT: JAI Press.

Lou, H. C., Henriksen, L., Bruhn, P., Borner, H., & Nielsen, J. B. (1989). Striatal dysfunction in attention deficit and hyperkinetic disorder. *Archives of Neurology*, *46*, 48–52.

Luk, S. (1985). Direct observations studies of hyperactive behaviors. *Journal of the American Academy of Child Psychiatry*, *24*, 338–344.

Margalit, M., & Arieli, N. (1984). Emotional and behavioral aspects of hyperactivity. *Journal of Learning Disabilities*, *17*, 374–376.

Mash, E. J., & Johnston, C. (1990). Determinants of parenting stress: Illustrations from families of hyperactive children and families of physically abused children. *Journal of Clinical Child Psychology*, *19*, 313–328.

Milich, R., Loney, J., & Landau, S. (1982). The independent dimensions of hyperactivity and aggression: A validation with playroom observation data. *Journal of Abnormal Psychology*, *91*, 183–198.

Pelham, W. E., & Bender, M. E. (1982). Peer relationships in hyperactive children: Description and treatment. In K. D. Gadow & I. Bialer (Eds.), *Advances in learning and behavioral disabilities* (Vol. 1, pp. 365–436). Greenwich, CT: JAI.

Rapport, M. D., Tucker, S. B., DuPaul, G. J., Merlo, M., & Stoner, G. (1986). Hyperactivity and frustration: The influence of control over and size of rewards in delaying gratification. *Journal of Abnormal Child Psychology, 14,* 191–204.

Ross, D. M., & Ross, S. A. (1982). *Hyperactivity: Current issues, research, and theory* (2nd ed.). New York: Wiley.

Routh, D. K., & Schroeder, C. S. (1976). Standardized playroom measures as indices of hyperactivity. *Journal of Abnormal Child Psychology, 4,* 199–207.

Streissguth, A. P., Martin, D. C., Barr, H. M., Sandman, B. M., Kirchner, G. L., & Darby, B. L. (1984). Intrauterine alcohol and nicotine exposure: Attention and reaction time in 4-year-old children. *Developmental Psychology, 20,* 533–541.

Taylor, E. A. (1986). Childhood hyperactivity. *British Journal of Psychiatry, 149,* 562–573.

Weiss, G., & Hechtman, L. (1986). *Hyperactive children grown up.* New York: Guilford Press.

Willis, T. J., & Lovaas, I. (1977). A behavioral approach to treating hyperactive children: The parent's role. In J. B. Millichap (Ed.), *Learning disabilities and related disorders* (pp. 119–140). Chicago: Yearbook Medical Publications.

Wolraich, M. L., Lindgren, S. D., Stumbo, P. J., Stegink, L. D., Appelbaum, M. I., & Kiritsy, M. C. (1994). Effects of diets high in sucrose or aspartame on the behavior and cognitive Cognitive Therapy and ADHD 31 performance of children. *New England Journal of Medicine, 330,* 301–307.

Zametkin, A. J., & Rapoport, J. L. (1986). The pathophysiology of attention deficit disorder with hyperactivity: A review. In B. Lahey & A. Kazdin (Eds.), *Advances in clinical child psychology* (Vol. 9, pp. 177–216). New York: Plenum Press.

Zentall, S. S. (1985). A context for hyperactivity. In K. D. Gadow & I. Bialer (Eds.), *Advances in learning and behavioral disabilities* (Vol. 4, pp. 273–343). Greenwich, CT: JAI Press.

16

Treatment of Academic Problems

Edward S. Shapiro
Kathy L. Bradley

Many students within the educational system do not meet the expected academic gains in the regular instructional setting. Examination of the differences between those individuals who are successful in their ability to learn compared with those who have difficulties often shows that the way in which these individuals approach tasks differs. Successful learners, when faced with challenging problems, tend to systematically gather information, planfully evaluate the data they obtain, select the best response, and carefully respond to the challenge. In contrast, unsuccessful learners may respond impulsively and in a disorganized manner. Others may exert a great amount of effort in responding, but because their response lacks a systematic plan to examine possible alternatives, they often fail. Essentially, many low-achieving students, as well as those with mild learning disabilities, often perform poorly in the educational settings due to their purported deficiency in using strategies needed to enable successful learning and performance (Ellis & Lenz, 1990).

Numerous approaches have been devised for the remediation of academic skills problems. Many are targeted specifically at teaching a new skill in order to remediate a deficiency. For example, if a student lacks phonemic awareness, then one may devise a strategy to teach that student the relationships between letters and their respective sounds. If a student lacks the skills in understanding the rules of capitalization, then one may devise a remediation program that specifically targets this skill. A large number of students with learning problems, however, continue to have difficulties despite remediation of specific skills. In particular, many have problems with organizational skills and performance of skills already in their repertoire (Fox & Kendall, 1983). Whereas approaches to remediation that target specific skills can certainly be successful, another approach to remediating academic skills problems is to teach students general strategies and methods to approach the problems. These strategies are based on a proactive perspective, trying to reduce the number of students who may potentially fail. In other words, the focus is on teaching students *how* to learn rather than *what* to learn. By doing this, students may be successful across a wide variety of academic domains simply by learning to apply these techniques to novel situations. Such a preventative approach to remediation is clearly appealing (Shapiro, 1988).

Cognitive-behavioral therapy represents one type of preventative remediation for academic skills. Through these interventions, students are taught various methods to aid them as they encounter new curriculum and learning environments. There are two types of cognitive-behavioral therapy as applied to academic skills problems: one that emphasizes antecedent control, and one that emphasizes control of consequences.

In antecedent control, the point of the intervention occurs prior to the occurrence of the academic behavior. Here, emphasis is placed on the cognitive events that precede the behavioral difficulty. Self-instructional training (Meichenbaum & Goodman, 1971; Miller & Brewster, 1992) and strategy training (Deshler, Alley, & Carlson, 1980) are examples of cognitive-behavioral therapy techniques for academic skills problems that focus on antecedent control.

In control of consequences, the point of the intervention occurs after the behavior has occurred. Emphasis is on the analysis and response to the academic skills problem. Use of self-monitoring and or self-evaluation (Shapiro & Cole, 1994) represents examples of cognitive-behavioral therapy procedures that are based on control of consequences.

One additional advantage of cognitive-behavioral therapy in the remediation of academic skills problems is the potential efficiency of these procedures. As more students enter the general education system with special learning needs, methods are needed that will allow teachers to manage their instructional time and encourage the cognitive proficiency of the learners within the classroom setting (Gerber, 1986). Because cognitive-behavioral therapy is designed to teach students how to approach new and challenging tasks themselves, once these techniques are mastered by those students considered to be "slow" in comparison to the normative group, teachers would need to spend less time in directly instructing these pupils, resulting in a mechanism for more efficient management of the instructional environment.

The purpose of this chapter is to describe the application of three types of cognitive-behavioral therapy interventions in the remediation of academic skills problems. In particular, a case example of the use of self-instructional training for an academic problem in math is presented to illustrate in detail how the technique is applied.

OVERVIEW OF COGNITIVE-BEHAVIORAL THERAPY FOR ACADEMIC PROBLEMS

Self-Instruction

Vygotsky (1962), a developmental psychologist, investigated the importance of the interaction between thought and behavior. Specifically, he studied the role of private speech as a mechanism for bringing behavior under control of an individual. He proposed that this inner, private speech developed progressively in children, beginning with their behavior being under the control of the external environment. The next stage in the development involved talking out loud and bringing behavior under verbal control. In the final stage children verbally regulate their behavior through internal or silent speech.

Influenced by such investigations on the controlling effects of speech and thought on behavior, Meichenbaum and Goodman (1971) designed one of the initial studies using the idea of self-instruction to enhance student performance during independent learning tasks. Their intent was to teach impulsive children to think before they act. Through training in this strategy, children were taught to self-verbalize statements both overtly and covertly in such situations as error-correction, guidance, problem-solving, and reinforcement (Wood, Rosenberg, & Carran, 1993). The basic tenets behind the self-instructional model are to teach students to become more cognizant of the demands of a specific task, which will then lead to an understanding and ability to monitor their use of strategies. The end goal is to enable the students to be in control of their learning (Graham & Wong, 1993). Although many of the early studies in self-instructional training focused on nonacademic tasks, a recent review by Miller and Brewster (1992) reported positive applications of self-instructional training to reading and mathematics skills.

Training in self-instruction consists of several steps and can vary from being very task specific to focusing on more general problem-solving strategies. Initially, the strategy is described and modeled by the trainer. Then the student practices the strategy both overtly and covertly using verbal self-instructions. In the last stage of the training, the child receives feedback from the trainer and is required to self-evaluate. Tied to the correct performance of the strategy may be external contingencies as incentives (Fox & Kendall, 1983).

Studies have found self-instructional training to be effective for students with learning disabilities (LD) as well as those who may be termed "inefficient learners." An inefficient learner, as defined by Swanson (1989), is a student "who either lacks certain strategies or chooses inappropriate ones and/or generally fails to engage in self-monitoring behavior" (p. 4). Specifically, this strategy has been effective across a number of academic areas, including reading comprehension, handwriting, and mathematics. Miller, Giovenco, and Rentiers (1987) taught fourth and fifth graders to use self-instruction to monitor their comprehension performance in reading. They used both below-average and above-average readers, and both groups received either three sessions of training in self-instruction or an equivalent didactic instruction. Their results indicated that both groups performed better after the self-instructional training. Additionally, it was found that both groups were able to generalize the self-instructional training to new reading tasks. On these transfer tasks, the below-average readers reportedly performed at a level that was commensurate with their above-average peers.

Blandford and Lloyd (1987) used self-instructional training to enhance the handwriting performance of two learning disabled elementary school students. In their study, two elementary school-aged boys were taught to use a cue card that included self-evaluation questions emphasizing important aspects of proper handwriting. The students were instructed to read each question and mark in a grid next to the question whether they had followed the step correctly. Contingent reinforcement was not used during baseline or treatment phases. Once the students demonstrated improvement in their handwriting performance, the teacher told them that they no longer needed to use the cards. Data continued to be collected during this time to assess short-term maintenance. Results indicated that the self-instructional training was effective in improving the handwriting performance of both students, and maintenance effects were reported as both students' handwriting was rated above baseline levels when use of the prompt card was discontinued.

Self-instruction has also been used with more severely disabled populations of students. Two institutionalized adolescent males with identified severe behavioral disorders were taught a variety of cognitive-behavioral modification components, including self-instruction, in an attempt to increase their academic performance (M. Miller, S. R. Miller, Wheeler, & Selinger, 1989). Whereas one student experienced difficulty in math, the other had more problems when he encountered a reading curriculum. The first student was taught a self-instruction subtraction technique called Touch Math. This intervention was temporarily successful but was enhanced by the trainers to consist of a more structured, self-instruction package that included a step-by-step checklist of the Touch Math procedure. The student was instructed to monitor his behavior throughout a lesson by placing a check after each step as it was completed. Use of the checklist was faded gradually until the student monitored his behavior without external cues.

The second subject in this investigation was taught a self-instruction sequence for decoding words. This strategy required the student to ask himself three questions when he encountered a word that was unknown. The student first applied this strategy to one method of reading during the initial intervention phase and then was required to apply the strategy to a different type of reading curriculum in the second intervention phase. The purpose of changing the curriculum while maintaining the same strategy was to enhance generalization. Data for both students indicated increased academic performance as a result of the self-instructional training. The data also suggested that the students were able to generalize the use of the strategies to other material (Miller et al., 1989).

The effectiveness of self-instructional training versus didactic instruction was investigated by Graham and Wong (1993). In their study, 45 average readers and 45 poor readers across grades 5 and 6 were randomly assigned to one of three groups: (1) didactic teaching of a strategy, (2) self-instruction, or (3) control (no training). Students in the first two groups learned a mnemonic strategy called 3H (Here, Hidden, and In My Head). These students were taught to think of these three terms when they had to answer text-explicit and text-implicit comprehension questions and figure out where to find the answer. Those students in the self-instruction group also learned three additional questions to ask themselves as they used the 3H strategy. Results of this study indicated that students in both the didactic teaching group and the self-instruction group improved in their reading comprehension performance. Further analysis showed that the self-instructional training was more effective than didactic teaching in enhancing performance and in maintaining comprehension performance.

Although self-instructional training has been found to be effective with these populations across a variety of academic settings, several limitations remain. First, the generalization of this strategy across settings and over time appears limited (Gerber, 1986). In many studies, self-instructional training has resulted in improvements only in the particular tasks or skills to which it has been applied. Given that the underlying premise of self-instructional training is that one is teaching students a method for approaching novel material, it is somewhat disappointing that generalization of the strategy to new material, as well as over time, does not typically occur. Researchers have noted that it is important that self-instructional training incorporate the use of general rather than specific self-instructional training when the procedure is applied. Use of more general instructions has been found to be more likely to result in generalized outcomes (Kendall & Wilcox, 1980; Schleser, Meyers, & Cohen, 1981). Still, the overwhelming research literature suggests that self-instructional training once learned for one content area must be taught in others. In many ways, this is not surprising, given that Stokes and Baer (1977) have long shown that the "train and hope" method of generalization does not usually result in desired outcomes.

Second, some practitioners have expressed concern with the amount of time that is required to train students in the self-instruction strategy, thus questioning the cost-effectiveness of the procedure (Wood et al., 1993). Self-instructional training is usually applied in a one-on-one therapeutic situation. The procedures take time for students to learn and the effort to have children "speak out loud to themselves," a very unnatural act for most children, can often be a difficult barrier to overcome. Unless the outcomes are strong and positive, school personnel may rightfully question the time investment and detraction from the instructional process.

Finally, few studies have investigated the effectiveness of self-instructional training with different populations. Whereas this type of training has been shown to be effective for students with learning problems, this is a rather heterogeneous group of individuals. For example, the term "learning disability" (LD) is not clearly defined, and to promote self-instructional training for all students with LD may be inappropriate. Similarly, for students with learning problems and externalizing behaviors, such as attention-deficit/hyperactivity disorder, such cognitive-behavioral approaches have not resulted in generalization and maintenance of behaviors for clinical populations (Hinshaw, 1992). Before an accurate match between the student's difficulties and the type of training can be determined, the influence of various subject variables (i.e., academic achievement, age, level of knowledge) must be further investigated (Graham & Wong, 1993).

Strategy Training

Although the focus of much of the training in cognitive-behavioral therapy of academic skills has been with self-instruction, a more metacognitive approach to skills training has been emphasized in order to promote generalized problem-solving skills (Shapiro, 1988). "Metacognition" can be defined as the ability to monitor one's current level of understanding and learning. Applying this concept to the use of strategies, "metacognition" refers to a student's ability not only to learn a strategy, but also to be able to discern when that strategy is appropriate for the task which he or she is encountering at the time (Bransford, 1979). It is proposed that many children develop metacognitve skills in a specific developmental pattern. A child is first taught a strategy by a teacher or parent and is presented with opportunities to practice that strategy. As the child progresses through school, other strategies are taught and learned in a similar manner. Eventually the child develops the ability to select and monitor the effectiveness of various strategies based upon the given task. Finally, the child associates positive learning outcomes with the use of strategies, and the cycle continues to perpetuate (Borkowski, Estrada, Milstead, & Hale, 1989).

It has been suggested by some researchers that the difficulties students experience in the educational setting may not be due to their lack of cognitive abilities, but to their inability to apply, monitor, and appraise their use of such specific strategies that facilitate the learning process (deBettencourt, 1987). The breakdown in the application of the strategies may occur in a number of places. The student may not understand the strategy when it is initially presented and may not experience enough practice with the strategy to learn how to generalize its use to new tasks. The student may comprehend the strategy when trained, but may lack the ability to judge its appropriateness across situations. In some cases, students may fail to utilize strategies because of the lack of successful outcomes in academic performance to associate with the use of the strategy (Borkowski et al., 1989).

If students can be taught how to employ particular strategies independently, it is believed that their ability to improve on their academic success will be enhanced. Although the term "strategy training" is broad, there are three main training approaches that have been investigated: (1) Lloyd's Academic Strategy Training, (2) Torgesen's Strategy Training, and (3) Deshler's Learning Strategies Model. These three models all focus on the need for students to be taught systematic methods for approaching tasks. Additionally, each approach was developed primarily for use by students with learning disabilities. Each model, however, differs in the types of techniques that it emphasizes.

In Lloyd's Academic Strategy Training Model (Lloyd, 1980), the strategy involves steps through which students move to solve recurring academic problems. Instruction in the strategy involves training in prerequisite skills before training in the actual sequence of steps. For example, if the goal was to teach a student multiplication of single-digit numbers, the prerequisite skills of addition and carrying of numbers would be reinforced along with understanding and recognition of the multiplication sign. Then, the actual steps to complete a multiplication problem would be defined for the student and teaching of the strategy would involve demonstration, modeling, corrective practice, and reinforcement (deBettencourt, 1987).

Torgesen's (1982) procedures were studied primarily in the laboratory setting. On the assumption that students often have knowledge of these learning strategies but fail to apply them, this approach involves teaching individuals to generalize previously learned strategies to other types of tasks. One method that is recommended is to provide incentives for a student to apply the strategy. Another method suggests following through three levels of direct instruction: (1) instruction in highly specific task strategies, such as completing an addition problem in math; (2) general strategy instruction, such as verbal rehearsal of the problem-solving procedure; and (3) a more generalized training in metacognitive processes, such as self-monitoring and predicting.

Deshler's model (Deshler et al., 1980) focuses on the needs of the adolescent to successfully master the educational curriculum. In this model, the strategy is first taught in isolation and then applied to controlled material. When the student demonstrates mastery of the strategy, he or she then applies the strategy to general classroom material (deBettencourt, 1987). An example of this model is a strategy used to enhance reading comprehension called Multipass. Teaching involves the student learning the steps of the strategy through modeling and verbal rehearsal, and practicing them until they are mastered. Then, the student applies the strategy to selected reading material and is tested to assess its impact on comprehension. Finally, the student is instructed to use the strategy in his or her classroom reading material as performance is continually assessed (Schumaker, Deshler, Alley, Warner, & Denton, 1982).

One of the criticisms of the "strategy training" models is the lack of agreement in the definition of the term. In addition to the three models briefly described earlier, there are many more, each differing from the others in some particular way. This lack of consistency in use of the term may cause confusion when attempts are made to replicate studies, as well as when one recommends "strategy training" as an intervention for a student. As with the self-instruction training, the systematic study of the generalization and maintenance effects of these strategies has been questioned. Finally, the appropriateness of certain strategies may be limited to select groups of students. Because the term "learning disabled" is just as nebulous as strategy training, not all students with LD may benefit from this type of intervention (Schumaker, Deshler, & Ellis, 1986). It appears that there is a strong need for further investigation into the efficacy of both self-instructional and strategy training for students experiencing academic problems (deBettencourt, 1987; Lenz & Hughes, 1990; Shapiro, 1988).

Self-Monitoring

A function that is viewed as invaluable to both individuals and groups is the ability of people to regulate their own behavior (Reid & Harris, 1993). When applied to the educational setting, the ability to self-regulate behavior becomes, to some degree, a survival skill for students. Students who experience academic difficulties are frequently described as being easily distracted, unmotivated, and inattentive. Given the ability of the student to perform the task that is presented, the student's lack of success may be attributed to the inability to self-regulate his or her behavior.

Self-monitoring is a self-regulation strategy that has been found effective in improving attentional behaviors (DiGangi, Maag, & Rutherford, 1991; Hallahan, Lloyd, Kosiewicz, Kauffman, & Graves, 1979; Harris, 1986) as well as academic performance (Harris, 1986; Lalli & Shapiro, 1990). The self-monitoring strategy consists of two components: self-observation and self-evaluation. Using this strategy, a student is trained to respond to an external cue and determine the occurrence or non-occurrence of a specific target behavior (self-observation). The student then records the results of the observation in some predetermined manner (self-recording; Prater, Hogan, & Miller, 1992).

Self-monitoring is believed for several reasons to be a viable intervention for students with learning difficulties. First, as these individuals learn the skills involved in self-monitoring, they can then apply these skills to more advanced types of learning strategies, such as self-management and self-reinforcement. Second, studies suggest that students with learning problems are characterized by behavior deficits shown to be amenable to self-monitoring procedures (Hughes & Boyle, 1991).

Studies supporting the efficacy of self-monitoring strategies for academic problems have been reported. An investigation conducted by Lalli and Shapiro (1990) found that self-monitoring was an effective strategy for teaching sight–word acquisition to elementary school-aged learning-disabled students. Carr and Punzo (1993) taught three male students with behavior disorders/emotional disturbances to self-monitor in three academic areas: reading, mathematics, and spelling. Students made gains in academic accuracy, productivity, and on-task behavior across all subject areas. Self-monitoring of performance was also found to have a positive effect on the spelling achievement and on-task behavior of young adolescents (Reid & Harris, 1993).

The use of this strategy is not without its concerns. In a review by Hughes, Korinek, and Gorman (1991), only a small percentage of studies were found to use self-monitoring in isolation. The other studies reviewed incorporated additional strategies, such as positive reinforcement and token economy, which tends to raise a question as to whether self-monitoring alone is truly an effective strategy. In an attempt to investigate this question, Lalli and Shapiro (1990) studied the effects of self-monitoring alone and in combination with external contingent reward on sight–word acquisition. Students in both conditions improved their sight–word vocabulary. Additionally, these authors found that the introduction of the contingent reward did not enhance the effects found with the self-monitoring in isolation for the majority of the students.

Another question regarding the use of self-monitoring concerns the target behaviors for training. Typically this strategy has been used for such target behaviors as on-task performance and attention to task. Some researchers have suggested that students would perform better if specific academic behaviors were targeted, noting that increases in attention do not automatically lead to improvement on task performance (Snider, 1987). As noted by Reid and Harris (1993) we may be creating well-behaved underachievers if we avoid targeting specific academic behaviors (i.e., productivity and accuracy). In order to investigate this issue, Lloyd, Bateman, Landrum, and Hallahan (1989) found little difference in outcome when either attention or productivity variables were self-monitored. However, a more recent study found differential effects of on-task behavior and academic performance of students' responses depending on whether they were monitoring attention or performance (Reid & Harris, 1993). Maag, Reid, and DiGangi (1993) assessed the effects of self-monitoring on-task behavior, academic productivity, and academic accuracy using a mathematics task. Although all three interventions resulted in improvements, self-monitoring academic productivity or accuracy was generally superior. Taken together, the results of these studies may indicate that there is no "best" method of self-monitoring for all individuals in all settings and with all tasks. Further investigation into the differential effectiveness of the possible alternative variables for monitoring appears warranted.

The issue of social validity is also of concern. Does the use of this strategy result in meaningful outcomes that are worth the time and effort to teach students the strategy? Prater et al. (1992) contend that teaching students a skill that allows them to function more independently in the classroom may help to decrease the resistance that some general-education teachers may have when working with such students in their classrooms. In addition, as these students develop self-regulating behaviors, they can manage their own performance when direct supervision is not available.

Limitations of Cognitive-Behavioral Therapy

There are many methodological shortcomings that can be identified in the present body of literature concerning the application of cognitive-behavioral therapy to academic problems. The research in this area has been criticized for its lack of clarity in the explanation of the methodology used in the various studies. For example, the interventions used in some studies may incorporate treatment packages rather than just self-instructional training or self-monitoring. Unless the specific components of these packages are identified and thoroughly explained, replication of results may be limited (Meador & Ollendick, 1984).

Lack of long-term follow-up data has also been identified as a major limitation in this literature. This appears to be particularly perplexing because cognitive-behavioral therapy was suggested as an alternative treatment to the more transient effects of strict behavioral interventions. The concern expressed by some investigators is that even though a particular intervention is highly successful in one setting or with one specific skill, that intervention may need to be rethought in terms of ongoing curricular demands and the needs of the individual student (Gerber, 1986).

Finally, the amount of structure required to teach a student to utilize self-instructional and self-monitoring strategies may vary. Gerber (1986) speculates that the amount of structure needed is inversely proportional to the cognitive maturity of the prospective learner. Others question the prerequisite skills necessary in order for the student not only to grasp the skill but also to apply it independently in the natural environment (Graham & Wong, 1993).

One of the strongest and most important criticisms of cognitive-behavioral therapy is the lack of data to support its generalization to tasks outside of the specific task used in the training. Most studies find that self-instruction works on the task used during initial instruction but does not generalize without programming the instruction to other stimuli. Those studies that have found generalization have not been replicable (Billings & Wasik, 1985).

Despite its limitations, a sufficiently strong database exists to support the use of cognitive-behavioral therapy for the remediation of academic skills problems. The procedures appear to be applicable across academic domains, including both content and basic skills areas. As such, cognitive-behavioral therapy can be an effective and potentially important technique for use by school personnel with a broad group of students who possess all types of learning needs.

CASE ILLUSTRATION[1]

The case selected to illustrate the use of cognitive-behavioral therapy for an academic skills problem shows the use of self-instruction training in the remediation of a deficit in mathematics. In particular, the student had extensive skills deficits in all academic areas, as well as substantial motivational difficulties. The child selected to illustrate cognitive-behavioral therapy presents with a fairly typical set of problems that include attention-deficit/hyperactivity disorder (ADHD), low self-esteem, poor academic performance, and the presence of performance difficulties.

The assessment of this student also shows the use of curriculum-based assessment, a strategy for evaluating academic skills that focuses on the student's actual performance from the curriculum materials in which the student is being instructed (Shapiro, 1989). Whereas the details of this assessment methodology are far beyond the scope of the present volume, the approach examines both the instructional environment and the student's skills using techniques that are consistent with behavioral assessment. Interested readers are encouraged to read Shapiro (1989), Shinn (1989), Salvia and Hughes (1990), or many of the other excellent resources available that describe the conceptual and methodological aspects of curriculum-based assessment.

The intervention used for this student was based on the procedures described earlier developed by Meichenbaum and Goodman (1971). Essentially, the student was taught a strategy using self-talk to approach the process of learning to regroup (borrow) in subtraction. The self-instruction procedures were gradually faded from overt speaking out loud to covert self-talk.

Background

Ray was a 10-year-old boy enrolled in the fourth grade. He was reported to be having academic difficulties in all areas, as well as significant behavior problems. Recently diagnosed as having ADHD, Ray was taking 10 mg of Ritalin twice per day. Although his teacher reported some improvement in his attention to tasks since beginning the medication, little change in his academic performance had been observed.

Academically, Ray was reported by his teacher as significantly behind in reading, math, and other language-arts subjects. His greatest deficiency, however, was noted to be in all aspects of mathematics. According to his teacher, Ray was functioning about 2 to 3 years behind skills expected for a fourth-grade student.

Ray also had shown significant behavioral and emotional difficulties. Beyond his distractibility, he was reported by his teacher to frequently make negative self-statements and was often rejected by his classmates in social situations. Ray tended to play alone and was not very popular among his peers.

At home, Ray lived with his parents and two stepsisters, ages 14 and 17. Ray's mother had a significant number of pet birds in the home, and Ray was given extensive responsibility for their care and feeding. It was reported that Ray often spoke in school about all the time he spent taking care of the birds when at home.

Initial Assessment

As noted, Ray's academic skills were assessed using procedures consistent with the model of curriculum-based assessment defined by Shapiro (1989). Specifically, the assessment process included (1) structured interviews with both Ray's teacher, Mrs. Rogers, and Ray himself, (2) direct observations of Ray's classroom behavior during academic activities, (3) an examination of Ray's worksheets and other independent seat work produced during academic activities, and (4) direct, curriculum-based assessment of skills in reading, math, spelling, and written expression.

Teacher Interviews

Mrs. Rogers indicated that in reading, Ray had been receiving remedial reading directly from the reading specialist. Whereas the average student in her class was placed in the 3-2 book (second book of third grade) of the Houghton Mifflin Basal Reading Series, Ray was currently struggling in the 2-2 book of the series. Beyond the remedial reading that Ray had been receiving, Mrs. Rogers noted that Ray received an additional 60 minutes of reading in the regular classroom. That time was divided into 30 minutes of independent seat work and 30 minutes of group reading activities. Typical seat work included writing story summaries and other tasks focused on improving reading comprehension. Compared to other students in Ray's reading group (lowest in the class), Ray showed somewhat worse performance than his peers in sight–word recognition and comprehension, and read orally about the same as his peers.

Mathematics was instructed by dividing the class into two groups based on ability. Ray was currently placed and working in the fourth-grade level of the Addison-Wesley Mathematics Series. A total of 60 minutes per day were allotted for math, with approximately 30 minutes of the time spent in instruction to the entire class and the remaining time engaged in independent seat work designed to reinforce the group instruction. Mrs. Rogers reported that the average student in her class was able to multiply three-digit by one-digit numbers with regrouping. By comparison, Ray was reported as having significant difficulties in subtraction and addition skills in which regrouping was required. He was also reported as having significant difficulties in the application of mathematics to measurement, telling time, changing and comparing money, and general numerical problem solving.

Teacher-reported problems were also noted in spelling and written language. In these areas, Ray had consistently shown very poor performance with significant difficulties completing assignments, expressing thoughts, and writing mechanics.

Student Interview

Ray was interviewed about his performance in each subject area. Using a semistructured interview format, Ray indicated that he considered reading his best and easiest subject. Ray did admit that although math was not considered difficult, he was having far more trouble with this subject area than his peers. In general, the interviews with Ray suggested that he seemed to be aware of the problems he was having academically but that his motivational level for improvement was limited.

Direct Observations

Ray was observed for 3 days over 20-minute academic periods of reading, math, and spelling instruction using the State Event Classroom Observation System (SECOS; Saudargas & Zanolli, 1990). In addition, during each observation, a randomly selected peer was observed to provide a classroom normative level for each behavior. The SECOS uses a systematic, time-sampling methodology and reports levels of behavior known to have strong relationships to academic performance. Results of these observations showed that in reading, Ray exhibited levels of on-task behavior as high or higher than peers (over 90% on-task). Indeed, Mrs. Rogers was highly interactive with Ray and showed levels of approval that approached one every 2 minutes. In contrast, Ray's on-task levels were far below his peers during math (70% on-task compared to 100% for peers), with significantly high rates of looking around (20%) and other, nonengaged activities (7%). Similar outcomes to math were evident when he was observed during spelling.

Direct Assessment

In reading, a curriculum-based assessment was conducted to determine Ray's instructional level. The "instructional level" is defined as "the point where material has not yet been completely mastered (mastery level), but also is not too difficult (frustional level)" (Shapiro, 1989, p. 97). Three reading passages taken from the second-, third-, and fourth-grade level books of the Houghton Mifflin Reading Series were read aloud. Additionally, for one of the three passages at each level, a set of questions were asked to screen for comprehension. Results found that Ray was at mastery at the 2-2 level, instructional in the 3-1 and 3-2 levels, and frustrational at the fourth-grade level. Comprehension levels were below the accepted criterion of 80% correct, beginning at the 3-1 level. These results suggested that Ray should be instructed in the 3-1 level of the series, with emphasis on developing understanding and meaning from the material. This was consistent with the teacher's report.

Direct assessment of mathematics was conducted by administering a series of timed 2-minute worksheets, each assessing a specific curriculum objective. Beginning with the addition of three-digit numbers with regrouping from 10's to 100's columns, Ray was assessed in subtraction (two digits with regrouping), as well as multiplication facts. Results revealed that although Ray was at mastery level in addition, he was found to be at frustrational level (less than 10 digits correct per minute) in all subtraction skills. He likewise was frustrational in all multiplication problems. Additionally, an examination of these worksheets found that Ray did not completely understand the algorithm for subtraction. At times he was noted to have subtracted the smaller from the larger number.

The assessment of spelling and written language found Ray to be performing at the fourth-grade instructional level in the material that he was being taught. Although he showed some deficiencies in these areas, the problems did not appear to be severe enough to warrant specifically targeting these areas for remediation.

Diagnosis/Skills Deficit

In general, Ray was found to have significant academic deficiencies, especially in reading and math. Although his performance in reading was certainly not at the level it should have been, he did seem to be making progress deemed acceptable by his teacher. However, in mathematics, Ray showed substantial and significant problems that warranted consideration for special remediation. In particular, his teacher had begun to teach multiplication and division, which required mastery of basic facts in subtraction, as well as an understanding of the regrouping process for subtraction and addition. Clearly, it was imperative that Ray's deficiencies in this area be targeted for remediation.

Course of Treatment/Intervention

In consultation with the teacher, the evaluator decided that Ray needed to relearn the algorithm for regrouping (borrowing), particularly with subtraction. Performance of this skill at an instructional and eventual mastery level, should facilitate other computational objectives currently being taught, such as multidigit multiplication.

To teach subtraction with regrouping, a series of visual and verbal prompts were developed. Specifically, a "cue card" was provided that listed four important instructions, along with a corresponding example (see Figure 16.1).

The cue card was placed on the top of Ray's desk during sessions held three times per week by the teacher. Each session lasted a maximum of

Therapist	Student
1. Self-talks and performs tasks.	Observes.
2. Self-talks.	Performs tasks.
3. Observes student and cues when necessary.	Self-talks aloud and performs tasks.
4. Observes student.	Subvocalizes self-talk and performs tasks.
5. Observes student.	Performs tasks silently.

FIGURE 16.1. Cue card placed on Ray's desk.

20 minutes. Ray was presented with a set of 20 problems involving three-digit minus three-digit subtraction with regrouping. Using the cue card, self-instructional training was implemented. Following the procedure as outlined originally by Meichenbaum and Goodman (1971), the teacher proceeded to follow the steps indicated in Figure 16.2.

The first step in the process requires the student to become comfortable with talking out loud. This is typically done with a task not related to performance on the desired academic task. In Ray's case, he was instructed to complete a "connect-the-dots" puzzle, speaking aloud as he moved from one dot to another. For example, the teacher in the initial session modeled the following:

"What is my problem? I need to connect the dots in order. Let me find number 1. Here it is, so I place my pencil here. Now, holding my pencil on number 1, let me find number 2 with my finger. Good, here it is so I draw a line from number 1 to number 2. Now let me find number 3. How am I doing? I am taking my time and soon I will finish the picture."

This was repeated until the six dots were connected to complete the task.

After the teacher modeled talking out loud, Ray was asked to perform the task while the teacher spoke aloud. Next, Ray was prompted to complete the task himself while he spoke aloud. This process continued until Ray appeared comfortable with speaking aloud as he performed the required task.

The use of self-talk was then implemented with the subtraction regrouping problems. No more than two steps were taught in any single session. As indicated in Figure 16.1, the first step involved having the teacher perform the task as she spoke aloud and Ray watched. After the teacher completed five problems, Ray was prompted to try a problem while the teacher spoke aloud, the second step in the process.

<u>Step 1</u>

Work from right to left

$$
\begin{array}{r}
3 \ | \ 4 \\
- \ | \ 8 \\
\hline
\end{array}
$$

<u>Step 2</u>

Always subtract the bottom
from ther top number.

$$
\begin{array}{r}
3 \ | \ 4 \\
- \ | \ 8 \\
\hline
\end{array}
$$

<u>Step 3</u>

Is the top number smaller than the
bottom number? If so, regroup.

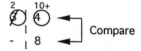

Compare

<u>Step 4</u>

Subtract each column.

$$
\begin{array}{r}
^2\not3 \ | \ ^{14}\not4 \\
- \ | \ 8 \\
\hline
2 \quad 6 \\
\end{array}
$$

FIGURE 16.2. Self-instruction steps for student and therapist.

In the next session, the teacher began at Step 2 (teacher engages in the self-talk while the student performs the task), and then subsequently added Step 3. In this step, Ray used self-talk and performed the task while the teacher simultaneously watched and cued him if he failed to follow the steps to solve the problem or stopped talking aloud.

This step was repeated again in the next several sessions as the teacher began to provide fewer cues and Ray gradually subvocalized the self-talk while performing the task. During the fourth step, Ray was encouraged to show that he was using all the steps on the cue card but was not required always to talk aloud. Finally, over the next few sessions, Ray was encouraged to perform the task silently, talking only to himself.

At the end of each session, Ray was given 2 minutes to do as many three-digit regrouping subtraction problems as he could. Consistent with curriculum-based assessment, the number of digits correct per 2 minutes were recorded on the sheet and placed on a graph by Ray. Number of digits correct has been found to be a more sensitive metric to evaluate student progress than simply the number of problems correct (Shapiro, 1989).

Results of the procedure are shown in Figure 16.3. Ray began at a baseline level of two digits correct per minute. This level is far into the frustrational range for his age. In consultation with the teacher and using known instructional/mastery criterion levels for this type of curriculum material, the evaluator set a goal for Ray to attain 20 digits correct per minute (mastery level) across the 4 weeks of the intervention program. Likewise, it was decided that an acceptable level of performance for Ray would be 10–19 digits correct per minute, which represents an instructional level.

As shown in Figure 16.3, Ray responded extremely well to the intervention. Immediately at the start of the intervention, Ray performed be-

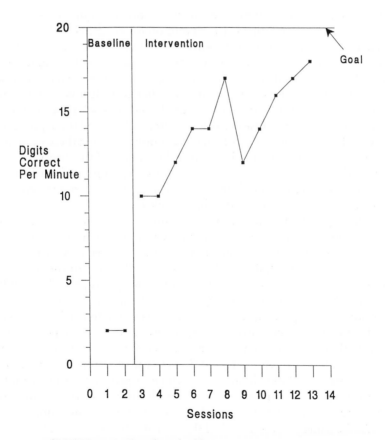

FIGURE 16.3. Results of self-instruction intervention.

tween 10 and 19 digits correct per minute, approaching the goal at the end of the 4-week period.

Ray's teacher expressed extreme satisfaction with his progress and agreed to continue the intervention into the student's future. Ray likewise indicated that he was very happy with his performance and felt proud that his grades in math had improved. Equally important was his teacher's report that Ray was now making many more positive statements (i.e., "This is fun," "This is easy," "I can do it") when faced with challenging math computational problems. His teacher noted that he seemed much more willing to tackle more difficult work and was much better at accepting errors.

DISCUSSION

This case example describes how self-instructional training, just one type of cognitive-behavioral therapy intervention for academic skills, was used to teach an important skill to a student with highly deficient mathematics skills. By using self-instruction, the student was actually taught a technique that could easily be applied to other skills in mathematics besides regrouping in subtraction. For example, when a student is trying to master long division, a similar set of cue cards and self-talk procedure could be applied. Indeed, because the student already has used these procedures successfully in one area of mathematics, simply applying these same strategies to long division would be a natural outcome of the intervention. In a sense, the student has not just learned how to perform subtraction with regrouping but actually has learned a new cognitive skill: how to approach mathematical computations that have multiple steps.

Although the present case was certainly very successful, it is important to recognize that this procedure may not always result in such positive outcomes. Individual students vary in the degree to which they are willing to accept the "talk-out-loud-to-yourself" basis of the procedure. Indeed, some students are highly resistant to using this procedure, and for them it is unwise to persist in trying to apply the self-instruction technique. Additionally, the procedure can be time consuming to teach and requires significant one-on-one instruction. Such instruction may be possible in an individual therapeutic session but not in a classroom with a large number of students. It is strongly suggested that the use of self-instructional training be limited to those situations in which appropriate student motivation for improvement is evident, along with the necessary resources (i.e., an individual therapist) available for effective implementation.

At the same time, it is critical that when self-instructional training is being taught to an individual student, the student's teacher be appraised of what is exactly being taught. As such, the teacher can provide effective opportunities for the student to practice his or her newly learned skills.

In general, the use of cognitive-behavioral therapy for improving academic skills has significant potential for effecting positive outcomes in students. As a procedure based on the prevention of future academic skills problems, these techniques clearly offer an important and potentially valuable resource for school personnel in reducing the presence of troubling academic failure. It is also important for practitioners to be aware of the broad limitations and cautions that have been found in the research. Continued efforts are needed to examine the ways in which cognitive-behavioral therapy can be used to remediate academic skills.

NOTE

1. Many thanks to Maria Jimenez, graduate student in school psychology at Lehigh University, for the use of the case study presented here.

REFERENCES

Billings, D. C., & Wasik, B. H. (1985). Self-instructional training with pre-schoolers: An attempt to replicate. *Journal of Applied Behavior Analysis, 18,* 61–67.

Blanford, B. J., & Lloyd, J. W. (1987). Effects of a self-instructional procedure on handwriting. *Journal of Learning Disabilities, 20,* 342–346.

Borkowski, J. G., Estrada, M. T., Milstead, M., & Hale, C. A. (1989). General problem-solving skills: Relations between metacognition and strategic processing. *Learning Disability Quarterly, 12,* 57–70.

Bransford, J. D. (1979). *Human cognition: Learning, understanding, and remembering.* Belmont, CA: Wadsworth.

Carr, S. C., & Punzo, R. P. (1993). The effects of self-monitoring of academic accuracy and productivity on the performance of students with behavioral disorders. *Behavioral Disorders, 18,* 241–250.

deBettencourt, L. U. (1987). Strategy training: A need for clarification. *Exceptional Children, 54,* 24–30.

Deshler, D. D., Alley, G. R., & Carlson, S. C. (1980). Learning strategies: An approach to mainstreaming secondary students with learning disabilities. *Education Unlimited, 2,* 6–11.

DiGangi, S. A., Maag, J. W., & Rutherford, R. B. (1991). Self-graphing of on-task behavior: Enhancing the reactive effects of self-monitoring on on-task behavior and academic performance. *Learning Disability Quarterly, 14,* 221–230.

Ellis, E. S., & Lenz, B. K. (1990). Techniques for mediating content-area learning: Issues and research. *Focus on Exceptional Children, 22,* 1–16.

Fox, D. E., & Kendall, P. C. (1983). Thinking through academic problems: Application of cognitive-behavior therapy to learning. In T. R. Kratochwill (Ed.), *Advances in school psychology* (Vol. 3, pp. 269–301). Hillsdale, NJ: Erlbaum.

Gerber, M. M. (1986). Cognitive-behavioral training in the curriculum: Time, slow learners, and basic skills. *Focus on Exceptional Children, 18*, 1–12.

Graham, L., & Wong, B. Y. (1993). Comparing two modes of teaching a question-answering strategy for enhancing reading comprehension: Didactic and self-instructional training. *Journal of Learning Disabilities, 26*, 270–279.

Hallahan, D. P., Lloyd, J. W., Kosiewicz, M. M., Kauffman, J. M., & Graves, A. W. (1979). Self-monitoring of attention as a treatment for a learning disabled boy's off-task behavior. *Learning Disability Quarterly, 2*, 24–32.

Harris, K. R. (1986). Self-monitoring of attentional behavior versus self-monitoring of productivity: Effects on on-task behavior and academic response rate among learning disabled children. *Journal of Applied Behavior Analysis, 19*, 417–423.

Hinshaw, S. P. (1992). Academic underachievement, attention deficits, and aggression: Comorbidity and implications for intervention. *Journal of Consulting and Clinical Psychology, 60*, 893–903.

Hughes, C. A., & Boyle, J. R. (1991). Effects of self-monitoring for on-task behavior and task productivity on elementary students with moderate mental retardation. *Education and Treatment of Children, 14*, 96–111.

Hughes, C. A., Korinek, L., & Gorman, J. (1991). Self-management with students with mental retardation in school settings: A research review. *Education and Training in Mental Retardation, 26*, 271–291.

Kendall, P. C., & Wilcox, L. E. (1980). Cognitive behavioral treatment for impulsivity: Concrete versus conceptual trainining in non-self-controlled problem children. *Journal of Consulting and Clinical Psychology, 48*, 80–91.

Lalli, E. P., & Shapiro, E. S. (1990). The effects of self-monitoring and contingent reward on sight word acquisition. *Education and Treatment of Children, 13*, 129–141.

Lenz, B. K., & Hughes, C. A. (1990). A word identification strategy for adolescents with learning disabilities. *Journal of Learning Disabilities, 23*, 149–163.

Lloyd, J. (1980). Academic instruction and cognitive behavior modification: The need for attack strategy training. *Exceptional Education Quarterly, 1*, 53–63.

Lloyd, J. W., Bateman, D. F., Landrum, T. J., & Hallahan, D. P. (1989). Self-recording of attention versus productivity. *Journal of Applied Behavior Analysis, 22*, 315–324.

Maag, J. W., Reid, R., & DiGangi, S. A. (1993). Differential effects of self-monitoring attention, accuracy, and productivity. *Journal of Applied Behavior Analysis, 26*, 329–344.

Meador, A. E., & Ollendick, T. H. (1984). Cognitive behavior therapy with children: An evaluation of its efficacy anf clinical utility. *Child and Family Behavior Therapy, 6*, 25–44.

Meichenbaum, D., & Goodman, J. (1971). Training impulsive children to talk to themselves: A means of developing control. *Journal of Abnormal Psychology, 77*, 115–126.

Miller, G. E., & Brewster, M. E. (1992). Developing self-sufficient learners in reading and mathematics through self-instructional training. In M. Pressley, K. R. Harris, & J. T. Guthrie (Eds.), *Promoting academic competence and literacy in school* (pp. 169–222). New York: Academic Press.

Miller, G. E., Giovenco, A., & Rentiers, K. A. (1987). Fostering comprehension monitoring in below average readers through self-instruction training. *Journal of Reading Behavior, 19,* 379–393.

Miller, M., Miller, S. R., Wheeler, J., & Selinger, J. (1989). Can a single-classroom treatment approach change academic performance and behavioral characteristics in severely behaviorally disordered adolescents: An experimental inquiry. *Behavioral Disorders, 14,* 215–225.

Prater, M. A., Hogan, S., & Miller, S. R. (1992). Using self-monitoring to improve on-task behavior and academic skills of an adolescent with mild handicaps across special and regular education settings. *Education and Treatment of Children, 15,* 43–55.

Reid, R., & Harris, K. R. (1993). Self-monitoring of attention versus self-monitoring of performance: Effects on attention and academic performance. *Exceptional Children, 60,* 29–40.

Salvia, J., & Hughes, C. (1990). *Curriculum based assessment: Testing what is taught.* New York: Macmillan.

Saudargas, R. A., & Zanolli, K. (1990). Momentary time sampling as an estimate of percentage time: A field validation. *Journal of Applied Behavior Analysis, 23,* 533–537.

Schleser, R. S., Meyers, A. W., & Cohen, R. (1981). Generalization of self-instructions: Effects of general versus specific content, active rehearsal, and cognitive level. *Child Development, 52,* 335–340.

Schumaker, J., Deshler, D., Alley, G., Warner, M., & Denton, P. (1982). Multipass: A learning strategy for improving reading comprehension. *Learning Disability Quarterly, 5,* 295–304.

Schumaker, J. B., Deshler, D. D., & Ellis, E. S. (1986). Intervention issues related to the education of LD adolescents. In J. K. Torgesen & B. Y. Wong (Eds.), *Psychological and educational perspectives on learning disabilities* (pp. 329–365). Orlando, FL: Academic Press.

Shapiro, E. S. (1988). Preventing academic failure. *School Psychology Review, 17,* 601–613.

Shapiro, E. S. (1989). *Academic skills problems: Direct assessment and interventions.* New York: Guilford Press.

Shapiro, E. S., & Cole, C. L. (1994). *Behavior change in the classroom: Self-management interventions.* New York: Guilford Press.

Shinn, M. R. (Ed). (1989). *Curriculum-based measurement: Assessing special children.* New York: Guilford Press.

Snider, V. (1987). Use of self-monitoring of attention with LD students: Research and application. *Learning Disability Quarterly, 10,* 139–151.

Stokes, T. F., & Baer, D. M. (1977). An implicit technology of generalization. *Journal of Applied Behavior Analysis, 10,* 349–367.

Swanson, H. L. (1989). Strategy instruction: Overview of principles and procedures for effective use. *Learning Disability Quarterly, 12,* 3–14.

Torgesen, J. K. (1982). The learning disabled child as an active learner: Educational implications. *Topics in Learning and LD, 2,* 45–52.

Vygotsky, L. (1962). *Thought and language.* New York: Wiley.

Wood, D. A., Rosenberg, M. S., & Carran, D. T. (1993). The effects of tape-recorded self-instruction cues on the mathematics performance of students with learning disabilities. *Journal of Learning Disabilities, 26,* 250–258.

17

Play Therapy with a Sexually Abused Child

Susan M. Knell
Christine D. Ruma

C ognitive-behavioral play therapy incorporates cognitive and behavioral interventions within a play therapy paradigm. It uses verbal as well as nonverbal communication and incorporates both cognitive and behavioral interventions. However, cognitive-behavioral play therapy is more than the use of specific techniques. It provides a theoretical framework that is based on cognitive-behavioral principles and integrates those principles in a developmentally sensitive way (Knell, 1993a, 1993b, 1994).

Cognitive-behavioral play therapy is designed specifically for preschool- and school-age children, and emphasizes the child's involvement in treatment by addressing issues of control, mastery, and responsibility for one's own change in behavior. By incorporating attention to cognitive variables in treatment, the child is helped to become an active participant in change (Knell, 1993a). When children identify and modify potentially maladaptive beliefs, for example, they may increase their capacity to experience a sense of personal understanding and empowerment.

The literature on cognitive-behavioral interventions with young children is limited. This may be due, in part, to the belief that such interventions are not applicable with young children. Some researchers have argued that cognitive-behavioral interventions are beyond the cognitive capabilities of young children (e.g., Campbell, 1990). In contrast, Knell (1993a, 1993b, 1994) contends that with minor modifications, the principles of cognitive therapy can be applied to young children. Among the most important differences are that the principles of collaborative empiricism, the reliance on the inductive and Socratic methods, and the use of homework assignments, as delineated by Beck and Emery (1985), do not play a major role in cognitive-behavioral play therapy.

DEVELOPMENTAL ISSUES

Psychotherapy with children and adolescents presents unique challenges not necessarily present with adults. Preschool-age children exhibit certain abilities and limitations, such that principles related to working with school-age children, adolescents, and adults cannot merely be extrapolated to apply to younger children. Among the most critical issues in work with young children in therapy relates to their cognitive functioning. Cognitive issues in child therapy are often obscured by play, which may lead the therapist to focus more on nonverbal rather than verbal communications (Shirk, 1988). Shirk further argues that theoretic underpinnings of therapy may influence the importance paid to cognitive issues. For example, if abreaction, or emotional release, is considered to be the basis of change, then cognitive differences may be ignored as play substitutes for words as a means of therapeutic change. Although these cognitive components take on increasing sophistication as the child gets older, according to Shirk, they nonetheless exist for individuals of all ages.

The work of Piaget (e.g., 1926, 1928, 1930) has influenced much of our thinking about children's cognitive development. For children in the preoperational stage of development (ages 2–7 years) thinking is by definition concrete, illogical, and egocentric. Yet, more recent theorists have suggested that these theories underestimate the child's abilities, and focus on what individuals cannot do, rather than what they can do (e.g., Gelman & Baillargeon, 1983). Even so, there are striking limitations in the preoperational child's thinking, many of which are thought to interfere with the child's ability to benefit from more verbally focused psychotherapies, such as cognitive therapy.

Piagetian principles have been extrapolated by Harter (1977, 1983) and applied to affective spheres. The same cognitive limitations that lead a child to faulty logic and errors in understanding can be adapted to describe the child's understanding of social phenomena, such as social relationships and perspective taking. Because young children can focus on only one of two opposite affective dimensions at a time, their understanding of affective material is often characterized by all-or-nothing thinking. Such phenomena, akin to conservation of affect, greatly influence the way the young child understands experiences and the feelings and emotions elicited by them.

Cognitive therapy with adults assumes that an individual has the cognitive capacity to differentiate between thinking that is rational and irrational, logical and illogical. Although an adult may need help in identifying and labeling such thoughts, once delineated, the individual can understand these inconsistencies. For example, feelings that appear to be all or nothing in nature may certainly be experienced by an adult, but through cognitive therapy, the individual may come to understand the limitations such thinking offers. Such assumptions are not necessarily true with children. In fact, what may appear to be irrational from an adult's perspective may seem quite rational to the young child.

Despite such significant differences in the cognitive abilities of children and adults, cognitive therapies with children and adolescents are receiving increased attention (e.g., Emery, Bedrosian, & Garber, 1983; Kendall, 1991; Wilkes, Belsher, Rush, Frank, & Associates, 1994; Zarb, 1992). However, much of the literature deals with school-age children and adolescents, with little attention paid to preschoolers. Knell (1993a) contends that cognitive therapy can be used with young children, although the treatment must be communicated in indirect ways, such as through play. The therapist must be aware of developmental issues and adapt therapeutic strategies accordingly.

APPLICATIONS OF COGNITIVE-BEHAVIORAL
PLAY THERAPY

In order for young children to benefit from cognitive-behavioral play therapy, interventions need to be presented in a format that is accessible to them. The most common method is modeling, learning that occurs as a function of observing the behavior of others and the consequences of that behavior (Bandura, 1969). Among the characteristics shown to improve the efficacy of modeling is the use of coping models in which the model gradually acquires new skills, as opposed to a mastery model, which presents a confident, flawless performance (Bandura & Menlove, 1968; Meichenbaum, 1971). Utilizing a coping-model approach, modeling in cognitive-behavioral play therapy often involves a puppet or doll that demonstrates acquisition of adaptive coping skills. The model may verbalize problem-solving skills or solutions to particular problems that parallel the difficulties faced by the child. Thus, the child is exposed to a model demonstrating behaviors that the therapist wants the child to learn. Although puppets and dolls are used most frequently to model behaviors, other forms may include drawings, films, and books.

Another commonly used method is that of role playing, in which the puppets (dolls) practice tasks and receive feedback from the therapist. Through role playing, children practice skills with their therapist and receive ongoing feedback regarding their progress. For children who may be too young to benefit from direct role playing, it is possible to use a modeling technique so that dolls or puppets complete the role play, and the child observes and learns from watching the models practice particular skills. For example, children can be taught skills to help deal with any future abuse, with the therapist role playing both an offender and a child who is trying to say "no," get the perpetrator away, and seek help. The child can listen as the therapist has the puppet practice and receive feedback.

GENERALIZATION AND RELAPSE PREVENTION IN COGNITIVE-BEHAVIORAL PLAY THERAPY

One important goal of therapy is for the child to maintain adaptive behaviors after the treatment has ended and generalize these behaviors to the natural environment. It is important for the therapist to incorporate efforts to promote and facilitate generalization into treatment, rather than assuming that it will occur naturally (Meichenbaum, 1977). It may be necessary to deal directly with issues of generalization through using real-life situations in modeling and role plays, involving significant adults in the child's life in the treatment, teaching self-management skills, and continuing even past the initial acquisition of skills to ensure that adequate learning occurs.

Therapy should also be geared toward helping the child and family prevent relapse. The primary way this is done is by preparing the parent and child not only for what to expect, but also for what to do when certain things happen. By doing so, high-risk situations that present a threat to the child's sense of control can be identified. It is important to "inoculate" individuals against failure through preparation, in part to avoid "panic" when there are roadblocks (e.g., Marlatt & Gordon, 1985; Meichenbaum, 1985). For example, a child and family can be taught to use previously learned skills if a particular stressful event occurs, or if specific symptoms or problems recur.

IMPACT OF SEXUAL ABUSE ON CHILDREN

Victims of sexual abuse are often left with distorted perceptions and beliefs about both the incident and themselves. Finkelhor and Browne (1986) have identified four traumagenic dynamics (trauma-causing factors) related to sexual abuse, that provide a framework for conceptualizing children's reactions to the abuse. These factors are traumatic sexualization, betrayal, powerlessness, and stigmatization. Within this framework, one may identify the primary ways in which a child has been affected by maltreatment and direct treatment specifically to these areas.

Porter, Blick, and Sgroi (1982) identified 10 impact issues common to victims of child sexual abuse:

1. "Damaged goods" syndrome
2. Guilt
3. Fear
4. Depression
5. Low self-esteem and poor social skills
6. Repressed anger and hostility
7. Impaired ability to trust
8. Blurred role boundaries and role confusion
9. Pseudomaturity and failure to accomplish developmental tasks
10. Problems of self-mastery and control

The first 5 issues are thought to be present for all victims; the last 5 are considered to be specific to incest victims.

Both of these models describe common outcomes of child sexual abuse, based on the child's cognitions and beliefs regarding the sexual behavior. Another critical factor related to a child's response to the sexual abuse is the attribution of blame for the event. Although it may appear that children who do not blame themselves for the abuse have the healthier belief, it has been suggested that this mode of thinking is related to a sense of helplessness (Shapiro, 1989). Similarly, Janoff-Bulman (1979) distinguished between behavioral self-blame and characterological self-blame. The former involves attribution to a particular behavior or mistake; the latter, attribution to enduring personal qualities. Studies suggest that individuals who have behavioral rather than characterological self-blame tend to have better adjustment, perhaps because they believe they can avoid further victimization by changing their behavior (Janoff-Bulman, 1979; Major, Mueller, & Hildebrandt, 1985).

A young child's beliefs are clearly influenced by many factors, including those of the parents. In the case of sexual abuse, parental response to the child's disclosure of abuse is critical in shaping the child's cognitions and beliefs about the abuse. A parent who reacts with blame, horror, or anger toward the child gives a different message than one who responds with support for the child (Friedrich, 1990).

Although there may be common sequelae of abuse, the impact may manifest itself differently in each child. Frequent symptoms of very young children include sleep disturbances, regression in toileting and other skills, expressions of anger and fear, and sexualized behaviors (Beitchman, Zucker, Hood, da Costa, & Akman, 1991; Browne & Finkelhor, 1986; Finkelhor, 1990; Kendall-Tackett, Williams, & Finkelhor, 1993). Additionally, several factors are commonly believed to affect the severity of the child's reaction to sexual abuse. A less severe reaction may be the result of factors such as shorter duration and less frequent sexual contact, less intrusive sexual acts, the absence of force or threat of force, and the perpetrator being an individual other than the child's parent (Browne & Finkelhor, 1986). Better adjustment is also predicted for a child with good coping skills and maternal support upon disclosure (Kendall-Tackett et al., 1993). The latter findings with regard to maternal support uphold the notion that positive parental response may be a critical factor in better outcome.

PSYCHOTHERAPY WITH SEXUALLY ABUSED CHILDREN

The literature regarding treatment for sexually abused children generally recommends some combination of individual, group, and/or family treatment. The role of family therapy in the treatment of sexually abused children has generated much controversy among therapists. Two camps have evolved: The first focuses on restoring victims to mental health and protecting them from further abuse; and the second sees family issues as critical in conceptualizing and treating the abused child (Friedrich, 1990). Despite differences regarding whether family treatment should be part of a comprehensive treatment plan, there is little argument that family issues are often pertinent, regardless of whether the abuse is intra- or extrafamilial. Even when individual psychotherapy is indicated, work with the family is often included and, according to Friedrich (1990), should have well-articulated goals.

In regard to individual treatment, much of the literature relates to the treatment of incest victims and overlooks the needs of children maltreated by a known and trusted, although not biologically related, perpetrator. Additionally, although much treatment literature is focused on older school-age and adolescent victims of sexual abuse, less has been written about treating preschool-age children. Ruma (1993) has provided one of the few specific treatment approaches for the preschool-age victim.

Traditional play therapy has been adapted for use with children who have been sexually abused, although the focus of these approaches is often on the relationship between child and therapist (e.g., Gil, 1991; Walker & Bolkovatz, 1988). Gil captures the essence of this approach in her belief that "there is an attempt to demonstrate to the child through therapeutic intervention the potentially rewarding nature of human interaction. . . . If given a nurturing, safe environment, the child will inevitably gravitate toward the reparative experience" (pp. 51–52).

The importance of a positive therapeutic relationship, possibly reparative in nature, is stressed in much of the literature on psychotherapy with sexually abused children (e.g., Friedrich, 1990; Gil, 1991). However, recent literature highlights the importance of a more directive, structured approach to working with sexually abused individuals (e.g., Friedrich, 1990). One logical intervention is through cognitive-behavioral therapy which, by definition, is structured, directive, and goal oriented.

COGNITIVE-BEHAVIORAL PLAY THERAPY WITH SEXUALLY ABUSED CHILDREN

Recent literature has documented the use of cognitive-behavioral therapy with sexually abused children (Deblinger, McCleer, & Henry, 1990; Ruma, 1993). Cognitive-behavioral play therapy is directive, yet allows the child to develop a sense of control within the structure set by the therapist. This is advantageous, because many sexually abused children avoid matters related to the abuse, perhaps in an effort to avoid the anxiety and negative feelings associated with their maltreatment experiences. However, the structure of cognitive-behavioral play therapy allows the child to maintain a sense of trust and control, which is a central issue in the treatment of most sexually abused children (Sgroi, 1982). The experience of sexual abuse often is a betrayal of the child's relationship with the perpetrator (assuming that the maltreater is not a stranger). Because their trust has been betrayed, sexually abused children often test the therapeutic relationship in ways that youth with other problems do not. For example, sexually abused children may behave provocatively toward their therapists to see if the therapist will harm them. Additionally, control is taken away from the child. Furthermore, many molested children have difficulty expressing negative feelings. Incestuous families are often typified by their lack of expression of feelings (Friedrich, 1990; Sgroi, 1982). Cognitive-behavioral play therapy provides a framework within which they may express a range of emotions.

A variety of treatment techniques are utilized in cognitive-behavioral play therapy with sexually abused children. Given the limited cognitive abilities of young children and the anxiety that sexual abuse may arouse, play provides sexually molested children a means to express their thoughts and feelings. Some of the most important treatment techniques in cognitive-behavioral play therapy with sexually abused children are bibliotherapy, drawings, art, and puppet and doll play.

Bibliotherapy

Bibliotherapy is commonly used with sexually abused children. There are a number of benefits of reading stories to children about sexual abuse. First, hearing a story about another child who was sexually abused helps children understand that they are not the only ones who have been maltreated. Second, it allows them to see that they are not alone in their feelings, particularly in regard to feelings about the perpetrator. Through modeling, a child may see how others learn to cope with conflicting feelings, such as both love and fear of the perpetrator, particularly if he or she was a known and trusted individual in the child's life. Third, the stories help the child to see that others have learned to gain control over similar situations. This is useful, for example, when the child is reluctant to disclose specific aspects of the abuse. Finally, stories may provide a means of desensitizing the child to the anxiety related to the abuse, and therefore help him or her begin to deal with feelings about the experience.

The therapist will want to select or adapt a story so that some of the variables are similar to that of the child's experience (e.g., relationship to or gender of the perpetrator). However, bibliotherapy stories are usually purposefully vague in many respects (e.g., type of sexual touching not clearly specified). Consequently, these stories are not likely to color a child's recall of the actual abuse. The stories focus on the more similar aspects of abuse, such as confused feelings and thoughts, and the positive results of disclosure.

In addition to stories that directly address sexual abuse situations, therapists often rely on more indirect stories. One example, *Once Upon a Time: Therapeutic Stories* (Davis, 1988) is a collection of short stories that uses metaphors to address issues of abuse. These stories may be particularly useful for children who are too anxious to listen to stories that directly discuss abusive situations. Finally, even when a metaphorical approach is too anxiety provoking, stories may be read in a child's presence but not directly to the child (e.g., reading a story to a puppet with the child in the room).

Drawings/Art

Self-created picture books may be used to help children disclose their own personal history of abuse (L. Hartman-Makovec, personal communication, March 1990). Children are encouraged to tell their story of abuse in small steps through their drawings. They begin with the least threatening aspect of the abuse, and as they are able to cope with their anxiety, they gradually portray more threatening aspects of the maltreatment. By drawing the abuse experience, the child can disclose through art what happened.

Through their pictures, children may express their cognitive distortions about the abuse in ways that they could not in words. For example, children frequently exaggerate the difference in size between the perpetrator and themselves, making the perpetrator much larger and or themselves much smaller than reality. Children may also leave out features and/or extremities when they draw themselves or depict the perpetrator in a grotesque way by exaggerating body or facial features. The therapist can then identify and help the child correct these distortions. As the pictures portray more threatening material, the therapist can help desensitize the child to the details related to the abuse.

Other Art Media

Another medium that is useful with young children who have been sexually abused is play with clay. This activity can be structured so that the child depicts different aspects of the abuse through the clay. Some children feel a sense of control when modeling clay figures depicting themselves as bigger than the perpetrator. Others may feel a sense of mastery and control by destroying a clay model of the perpetrator or saying things to the model that they could not say to the actual person. As with other modalities, the therapist can address distorted beliefs through the child's clay representations.

Puppet and Doll Play

Puppets, dolls, or other figures can be used in cognitive-behavioral play therapy in several different ways. The therapist can structure play scenarios around the specific issues with which the child is struggling (e.g., mistrust, sadness). First, if the child cannot tolerate the anxiety that might be evoked by structured play around the abuse, the play scenarios might involve "another child," similar to the child being treated, but with a different name. Second, a sequence similar to the drawing technique can be used, and is particularly helpful for children who have difficulty expressing themselves through art. With either of these techniques, the therapist can correct the child's distortions by modeling corrective thoughts or experiences via the dolls or puppets. In addition, children can practice, or the therapist can model, prevention skills through doll or puppet play.

CASE REPORT

Background Information

Julie is a 5-year-old girl who was referred for therapy due to allegations of sexual abuse. She was seen in cognitive-behavioral play therapy for a total of 13 sessions over a 3½ month period. This section gives a brief history of Julie, a description of her presenting features, and a discussion of the course of her therapy.

Julie is the middle of three children living with both biological parents. Her parents are professionals who live in a middle class neighborhood. Prior to the disclosure of sexual abuse, the family, including Julie, was not experiencing any unusual stresses or difficulties. Julie had made a good adjustment to the beginning of kindergarten several months before the onset of therapy.

Julie's disclosure of sexual abuse was prompted by her mother's questioning her after some suspicious behavior by an adult neighborhood male. Upon questioning, Julie disclosed that Mike had "pee-peed" and "touched her" that day. She also disclosed that on a previous occasion, he had shown her his "privates" and told her it was a squirt gun. The first incident had occurred in a bathroom; the second incident, upstairs, while her family was elsewhere in the house. Upon hearing this, the parents contacted the Child Protective Services and filed criminal charges against the neighbor, Mike.

Approximately 6 weeks after the disclosure, the parents sought therapy for Julie. Since the incidents of sexual abuse and subsequent disclosure and investigation, Julie had begun displaying several symptoms. Julie had become concerned about the need to urinate and consequently felt the need to go to the bathroom frequently; however, she was afraid to go into the bathroom alone. She also became fearful of going to school because of the possible need to use the rest room while at school or on the school bus. Finally, Julie became afraid of being alone on one floor of the house while other family members were on another level.

Initial Assessment

At the first appointment, Julie's mother was interviewed, providing a history of the abuse as she understood it, as well as a complete developmental history of Julie. Julie's parents were concerned about Julie's current symptoms, as well as the effect the abuse might have on their daughter in the future. They had taken Julie to see another therapist for one or two sessions prior to this, but had discontinued that therapy due to dissatisfaction with the therapist's availability. The mother also completed the Child Behavior Checklist (CBCL; Achenbach, 1991). Figure 17.1 contains the initial CBCL profile. Although there were no clinically significant ele-

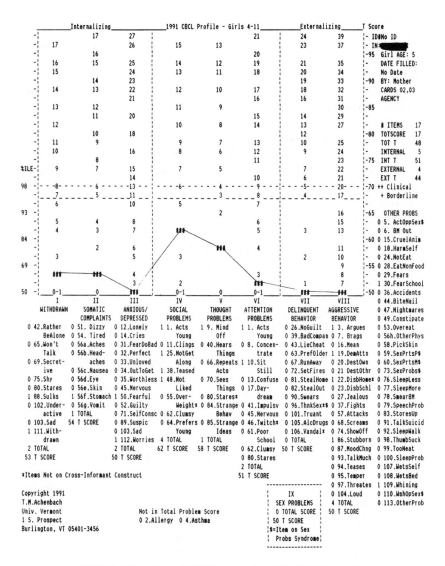

FIGURE 17.1. Initial CBCL completed by Julie's mother.

vations, and none of the scores were exceptionally high, there were several significant items that were endorsed as being somewhat or sometimes true. These items included Withdrawn, Fearful, Acts Young, Can't Get Mind Off Certain Thoughts, and Fears School. The scale of Social Problems was at the 87th percentile and that of Thought Problems was at the 80th percentile. All other scores were at the 63rd percentile or lower.

Case Conceptualization

At the time Julie was referred, she had already disclosed information about the abuse to her mother. According to Julie's statements, the maltreatment had occurred only two times, had been committed by a non-family member, and did not include penetration or violence. Her family believed her disclosure and supported her. Additionally, they were not experiencing any other stressors that might have been significant factors in treatment.

Julie's symptoms concerning a need to urinate and fear of being separated from family members in the house seemed to be related to the context in which she had been abused. Although neither incident occurred in Julie's home, the anxiety and fear caused by the trauma of being maltreated generalized to her own home. The fear of using the bathroom was likely related to being touched in her genital area by the perpetrator, as well as the fact that one incident of abuse occurred in a bathroom. Her fears related to using the bathroom generalized to school as well. It is significant that although the incident of abuse in the bathroom had occurred at least several weeks prior to disclosure, the symptoms did not manifest themselves until after she disclosed the abuse to her parents. This would suggest that the disclosure served as a trigger for these memories. Similarly, her fear of separation from her family manifested itself after disclosure. It seems that once she was aware that it was "safe" to tell her parents what had happened, and that the perpetrator could do no further harm, Julie clung to her parents in an effort to be totally safe.

These factors contributed to a diagnostic impression of a child who had been negatively affected by the experience of being sexually abused, but who was not severely traumatized by it. The therapist's perception was that Julie's prognosis was positive. Given Julie's age, play therapy was chosen as the primary treatment modality. Her family was included in treatment, particularly in an effort to help them deal with the effects of the abuse and to know how best to help Julie, but it did not appear that family psychotherapy was indicated. Specific play activities were selected based on Julie's interests, ability to use them as a means of communication, and their usefulness in meeting the main treatment goals of encouraging disclosure, correcting maladaptive cognitions about the abuse, and decreasing symptomatology.

Course of Treatment

Although Julie was not included in the first session, she was seen at each subsequent appointment. Either one or both of Julie's parents were also seen for at least a small portion of each session to discuss her progress and to answer any questions they had. On two separate occasions, the entire family was included in a session. Several different play modalities were employed, including bibliotherapy, drawing techniques, puppet play, and clay modeling. Because there was a criminal case in process against the alleged perpetrator, the therapist was especially mindful of being nonleading regarding the abuse experiences while still directing the course of therapy.

The following is a summary of each of the remaining 12 play therapy sessions after the initial assessment appointment.

Session 1

After some brief introductory work, the therapist questioned Julie as to her understanding of the reason for therapy. Julie quickly stated that she was there to talk about what Mike had done to her. Following a discussion of the purpose of meeting, the therapist read "The Hidden Boxes" (Davis, 1988). This is a story about a princess who was given a box, but told that she must not let anyone know about it. The more the princess kept this secret, the more upset she became. When the princess finally told an adult about her secret, she felt a great sense of relief. Julie then said she felt sad when she thought of Mike. She also said that since she told her mom about the abuse it had helped her feel better.

Sessions 2 through 6

The primary task during these five sessions was to make a book of drawings about what had happened with Mike (see Figure 17.2, Pictures a–i).

Because Julie was initially very anxious to disclose the abuse, she jumped directly to drawing the abuse after completing the first picture of the home where the abuse occurred. After Julie drew each picture, she dictated the story to the therapist. The first three pictures (Pictures a, b, and c) were done during the second session and depict the first incident of abuse. During the week after drawing the first three pictures, her parents reported that Julie had become more fearful of using the bathroom alone. Although this increase in symptoms persisted for a brief time, it appeared to be an appropriate and expected reaction to her recalling in therapy this incident of abuse.

The next three drawings (Pictures d, e, and f), done during the third session, depict the second incident of abuse. After each picture and story was completed, the therapist would simply ask Julie to draw what happened next. Pictures d, e, and f are essentially the same and do not disclose any abuse, simply the setting where it occurred. Each time Julie was asked to draw what happened next, she simply repeated what she had just drawn and said. It appeared that she was uncomfortable with describing the remainder of the incidents.

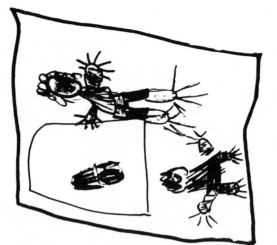

FIGURE 17.2c. "I came in. He stared at me and stuck his private out. I ran out the door. Mike said nothing."

FIGURE 17.2b. "Mike was in the bathroom. The door was closed. I knocked on the door and he said, 'come in.'"

FIGURE 17.2a. "Mathew's house. It was a great big birthday party for Mathew."

FIGURE 17.2e. "First I was down there and I got mad. Then I punched the punching bag and I got really angry because Mike was still down there."

FIGURE 17.2d. "I was going downstairs to punch the punching bag. Mike was still down there."

FIGURE 17.2g. "I got real mad. I wished I could punch him in the belly. Mike was really mean. Mike stuck his private out. It looked really scary."

FIGURE 17.2f. "He came back downstairs and I got real mad. I said, 'Mike get out of here.' He stayed there."

FIGURE 17.2h. "Mike stuck out his private and she [Julie] was real scared."

FIGURE 17.2i. [No caption.]

383

The final three pictures (Pictures g, h, and i) were drawn during each of the three subsequent appointments. Each week Julie was reluctant to continue working on her picture book, which resulted in the pace of drawing being decreased. After reviewing the previous drawings, Julie was again asked to draw what had happened next. She again drew the same picture as the previous three and did not want to tell the story. At this point, the therapist introduced the use of puppets. Julie's puppet then told the therapist's puppet the story to go with the picture. It was with this technique that Julie disclosed that "Mike had shown her his privates."

The fifth session was very similar, in that Julie again drew the same picture and did not want to tell the story. This time Julie used the puppet to say that she was afraid to tell the story for fear that Mike might hurt her. The therapist's puppet attempted to correct this distortion, but Julie was still unable to go further. (Later, in Session 7, Julie disclosed that Mike had threatened her and told her not to tell anyone about what they were doing.) In the sixth session, before starting work on Julie's book, the therapist read her the story of "Taffy and the Invisible Magic Bandage" (Davis, 1988). This story is about a dog who has a fear of talking about a secret, but finds that when she does, her fears do not come true, and she feels much better. Julie's mother was given a copy of this story to take home and read to her daughter.

After reading the story, Julie proceeded to draw a similar picture to the previous ones but resisted attempts at telling the story that went with it. It was clear at this point that Julie was not willing to go any further with telling her story. During the three previous sessions and this one, Julie had repeatedly become anxious and stopped her disclosure at the same point. In Julie's initial disclosure to her mother, and then later in therapy, she reported that this was when Mike had touched her in her genital area. It appeared that this aspect of the abuse was more anxiety provoking than the rest.

Session 7

The focus of this session was for Julie to share her story with her family. The purpose of this is to further desensitize the child and family about the abuse and to dispel any secrets that might be held by the family. Julie showed her family each of the pictures that she had drawn while the therapist read the story. When the story was over and Julie's mother asked her about the rest of the abuse that she had originally disclosed, Julie said that she did not know what words to use to tell about it. However, Julie was willing to act it out with puppets, asking her father to play the puppet of the perpetrator. By whispering to her father, Julie was finally able to disclose the rest of the abuse. Julie disclosed that in addition to exposing himself to her, Mike had also touched her in her genital area and threatened her not to tell. It seems significant that Julie was able to disclose this most threatening aspect with her family present and her father playing the role of the perpetrator. Julie appeared to feel safe and protected in this family setting.

Session 8

Julie had not presented any significant distortions related to sexual abuse through her drawings; however, it seemed that such distortions might exist in her thinking. To further assess this, the therapist and Julie engaged in puppet play involving incidents of sexual abuse between adult and child puppets. During the puppet play, Julie consistently stated that it was not the child's fault. She displayed no sense of damage to the child and repeatedly said that the child should tell an adult because she would feel better.

Session 9

Due to scheduling problems, there was approximately a 3-week gap between Sessions 8 and 9. The parents reported that during this time, Julie had begun having nightmares as frequently as four to five times per week. When Julie was asked to draw a picture of one of her nightmares, she drew a picture of a girl who was scared. The therapist then asked Julie to draw another picture depicting a good ending to her nightmare. She drew a picture of herself yelling for her "huge" dad, and her dad coming for her.

Session 10

The parents reported no further nightmares during the past week. They also reported that for several weeks Julie had not been displaying any symptoms related to use of the bathroom or fear of being in a room alone. Based on the decrease in symptoms, the lack of any apparent distorted perceptions related to the abuse, and Julie's ability to disclose, we began to plan for termination.

During the play therapy portion of this session, Julie requested to play with modeling clay. The therapist allowed this, suggesting that Julie make a figure of Mike. Julie quickly agreed and also made a figure of herself. The figure of herself was proportionately smaller than that of Mike. The therapist stood the two figures up face to face and asked Julie what she would like to say to Mike. Julie began laughing at Mike and said that she wanted him to go to jail because he was bad. She repeated different variations of this several times, seeming to fully enjoy herself when laughing at Mike. She eventually punched the figure of Mike, knocked him over and smashed him. This play sequence allowed Julie the opportunity to feel in control of Mike and express her feelings to him. This was especially important to do through play because the perpetrator was not admitting to the offenses or receiving any treatment, and thus Julie would not have an opportunity to confront him in person.

Session 11

This session was scheduled to be the last one before termination. The therapist and Julie discussed the reasons for termination and their feelings related to this event. In preparation for termination, a decision was made with Julie and her family to mark the end of treatment with a "party," in order to help Julie anticipate the end of therapy as a positive event. Together they planned a termination "party" that, at Julie's request, would include her whole family. Julie felt that she was ready to end therapy. She stated that she had come here to talk about Mike so that it didn't make her feel so bad. She also said that she used to think about Mike all the time, but now she only thinks about him "a little." In order to better assess the change in Julie's thoughts and feelings related to Mike, the therapist drew a measuring line from 0 to 100 on a chalkboard. The therapist asked Julie to mark on the line how strongly she felt "mad," "sad," or "scared" when she thought about Mike, both before therapy and now. For mad, Julie marked 100 for both, before and now. For sad, she marked 100 before and 0 now. For scared, she marked 7 before and 0 now. Julie then included "happy" to this list and rated 0 for both before and now.

Although Julie seemed quite certain of her ability to talk to her family if she were ever exposed to sexual abuse again, the therapist engaged her in a puppet play to practice and reinforce this skill. In this play, the therapist's puppet (Gramps) attempted to trick Julie's puppet (Jimmy) into sexual touching. Despite several attempts at threats and manipulations, Jimmy went immediately and told his mother. Although Jimmy's mother did not believe him immediately, he insisted and the mother finally responded appropriately. Julie then put on the police puppet and arrested Gramps and put him in jail. Next, Julie sent a therapist puppet to the jail to talk to Gramps. The therapist (played by Julie) told Gramps that he should apologize to Jimmy, and said that he would "get better." Through this play, not only did Julie practice her disclosure skills, she again showed that she understood that responsibility for the abuse rested with the adult, not the child, and that it is possible to be abused but learn to "get better."

Termination

Since Julie's mother had completed the initial CBCL, she was asked to complete one at termination (see Figure 17.3). This time, all of the scales were within the normal range. The significant items mentioned previously all had decreased from 1 to 0.

```
           Internalizing          1991 CBCL Profile - Girls 4-11          Externalizing      T Score
                17      27                           21      24      39    - ID
      17        26            15      13             23      37    - IN:
                16                            20                          -95  Girl AGE: 5
      16        15      25     14      12     19      21      35    -      DATE FILLED:
      15        24     13      11     18      20      34    -            01/25/94
                14     23                     19      33    -90  BY: Mother
      14        13     22     12      10     17      18      32    -      CARDS 02,03
                21                     16      16      31    -      AGENCY
      13        12            11      9              15      14      30    -85
                11     20                     15      14      29    -
      12               10      8             14      13      27    -      # ITEMS     8
                10     18                     12            -80  TOTSCORE    8
      11        9            9      7     13      10      25    -      TOT T      40
      10               16     8      6     12      9      24    -      INTERNAL    1
                8                     11            23    -75  INT T      39
 %ILE-    9     7     15     7      5             7      22    -      EXTERNAL    3
                14                     10            6      21    -      EXT T      42
 98  --8----   6 --13--  --6-----4----9--   -5----20---  -70  ++ Clinical
      7____     5 ____11__   ____3____8___  4____17___   -    + Borderline
      6                10     5             7                          -
 93  -      2                            16    -65  OTHER PROBS
      5      4      8                     6      15    -      0 5. ActOppSex$
      4      3      7     4             5      3      13    -      0 6. BM Out
 84  -                                          -60  0 15.CruelAnim
            2      6            1      4             11    -      0 18.HarmSelf
      3                5     3                     2      10    -      0 24.NotEat
 69  -                                          9    -55  0 28.EatNonFood
      2      1      4                     3             8    -      0 29.Fears
                3            ###           2      1      7    -      0 30.FearSchool
 50  -  ###      ###     ###     0-1     ###     ###     ###     ###    -50  0 36.Accidents
        I        II      III     IV      V       VI      VII     VIII         0 44.BiteNail
     WITHDRAWN SOMATIC  ANXIOUS/ SOCIAL  THOUGHT ATTENTION DELINQUENT AGGRESSIVE  0 47.Nightmares
              COMPLAINTS DEPRESSED PROBLEMS PROBLEMS PROBLEMS BEHAVIOR  BEHAVIOR  0 49.Constipate
```

I WITHDRAWN	II SOMATIC COMPLAINTS	III ANXIOUS/ DEPRESSED	IV SOCIAL PROBLEMS	V THOUGHT PROBLEMS	VI ATTENTION PROBLEMS	VII DELINQUENT BEHAVIOR	VIII AGGRESSIVE BEHAVIOR	
0 42.Rather BeAlone	0 51.Dizzy	0 12.Lonely	0 1. Acts Young	0 9. Mind Off	0 1. Acts Young	0 26.NoGuilt	1 3. Argues	0 53.Overeat
0 65.Won't Talk	0 54.Tired	0 14.Cries	0 11.Clings	0 40.Hears Things	0 8. Concentrate	0 39.BadCompan	0 7. Brags	0 56h.OtherPhys
0 69.Secretive	0 56a.Aches	0 31.FearDoBad	1 25.NotGet Along	0 66.Repeats Acts	0 10.Sit Still	0 43.LieCheat	0 16.Mean	0 58.PickSkin
0 75.Shy	0 56b.Headaches	0 32.Perfect	1 38.Teased	0 70.Sees Things	0 13.Confuse	0 63.PrefOlder	0 19.DemAttn	0 59.SexPrtsP$
0 80.Stares	0 56c.Nausea	0 33.Unloved	0 48.Not Liked	0 80.Stares±	1 17.Day-dream	0 67.RunAway	0 20.DestOwn	0 60.SexPrtsM$
0 88.Sulks	0 56d.Eye	0 34.OutToGet	0 55.Over-Weight±	0 84.Strange Behav	0 41.Impulsv	0 72.SetFires	0 21.DestOthr	0 76.SleepLess
0 102.Underactive	0 56e.Skin	0 35.Worthless	0 62.Clumsy	0 85.Strange Ideas	0 46.Twitch±	0 81.StealHome	0 22.DisbHome±	0 77.SleepMore
0 103.Sad	0 56f.Stomach	0 45.Nervous	0 64.Prefers Young	0 TOTAL	0 61.Poor School	0 82.StealOut	0 23.DisbSchl	0 78.SmearBM
0 111.Withdrawn	0 56g.Vomit	0 50.Fearful	2 TOTAL	50 T SCORE	0 62.Clumsy	0 90.Swears	0 27.Jealous	0 79.SpeechProb
0 TOTAL	0 TOTAL	0 52.Guilty	52 T SCORE		0 80.Stares	0 96.ThnkSex±$	0 37.Fights	0 91.TalkSuicid
50 T SCORE	50 T SCORE	1 71.SelfConsc			1 TOTAL	0 101.Truant	0 57.Attacks	0 92.SleepWalk
		0 89.Suspic			50 T SCORE	0 105.AlcDrugs	0 68.Screams	1 86.ThumbSuck
		0 103.Sad				0 106.Vandal±	0 74.ShowOff	0 73.SexProbs$
		0 112.Worries				0 TOTAL	1 86.Stubborn	0 87.MoodChng
		1 TOTAL				50 T SCORE	0 87.MoodChng	0 93.TalkMuch
		50 T SCORE					0 93.TalkMuch	1 94.Teases
							1 94.Teases	0 95.Temper
							0 95.Temper	0 97.Threaten
							0 97.Threaten	0 104.Loud
							0 104.Loud	1 109.Whining
							1 109.Whining	0 110.WshOpSex$
							3 TOTAL	0 113.OtherProb
							50 T SCORE	

±Items Not on Cross-Informant Construct

```
Copyright 1991
T.M.Achenbach
Univ. Vermont                    Not in Total Problem Score
1 S. Prospect                    0 2.Allergy  0 4.Asthma
Burlington, VT 05401-3456
```

```
-------------------
|      IX         |
| SEX PROBLEMS    |
| 0 TOTAL SCORE   |
| 50 T SCORE      |
|$=Item on Sex    |
| Probs Syndrome  |
-------------------
```

FIGURE 17.3. Termination CBCL completed by Julie's mother.

Session 12

Before starting the termination "party," the therapist met with Julie's parents to discuss issues related to termination. The parents were given information regarding "normal" child sexual behavior in order to help them react appropriately to any sexual play that Julie may engage in. The potential recurrence of symptomatology related to the sexual abuse at various developmental milestones was also discussed. The family was encouraged to continue to be open to discuss abuse-related issues with all of their children whenever the opportunity arose.

The therapist met briefly with Julie to again discuss feelings related to termination. However, Julie was so excited about the "party" that she was only able to focus on termination-related issues for a very limited amount of time. The entire family then joined in the "party."

Follow-Up

Follow-up was obtained from the mother 8 months after the termination of treatment. At that time, she reported that Julie was continuing to do well. The mother did not report any further concerns regarding Julie's emotional or behavioral functioning. Julie's mother also completed a CBCL 8 months after termination (see Figure 17.4). In comparing this profile with the initial CBCL, it should be noted that it was also a nonclinical profile, with all scales at the 50th percentile, with the exception of Anxious/Depressed scale, which was at the 55th percentile. The scales of Social Problems and Thought Problems, which had been elevated at the initial assessment, were now at the 50th percentile. As was true with the termination CBCL, each of the positively endorsed significant items on the initial CBCL had again decreased from 1 to 0.

DISCUSSION

The present case provides an example of the successful use of cognitive-behavioral play therapy with a sexually abused child. There are a wide range of ways in which children are sexually molested, and similarly, the range of emotional and behavioral sequelae of the abuse will differ for each child. It is important that we not consider the act of sexual abuse as a distinct entity, or consider all sexually abused children as necessarily manifesting the same reactions to the maltreatment. If sexual abuse and its effect on a child can be thought of along a continuum in regard to severity, duration, and other aspects of the maltreatment, then Julie might be considered to fall at the less severe end of the continuum. Her mal-

1991 CBCL Profile - Girls 4-11

	Internalizing				Externalizing		T Score
	17	27	15	13	21	24 39	-ID■
17		26				23 37	-IN:■
	16				20		-95 Girl AGE: 6
16	15	25	14	12	19	21 35	- DATE FILLED:
15		24	13	11	18	20 34	- 08/31/94
	14	23			19		-90 BY: Missing
14	13	22	12	10	17	18 32	- CARDS 02,03
		21			16	16 31	- AGENCY 01
13	12		11	9		30	-85
	11	20			15	14 29	-
12			10	8	14	13 27	- # ITEMS 9
	10	18				12	-80 TOTSCORE 9
11	9		9	7	13	10 25	- TOT T 41
10		16	8	6	12	9 24	-
	8				11	23	-75 INT T 48
%ILE- 9	7	15	7	5		7 22	- EXTERNAL 1
		14			10	6 21	- EXT T 37
98 -8- - - - 6 - - - 13 - -	- - 6- - - - 4 - - - 9 - - -	-5- - - 20- - -	-70 Clinical
7 5 11	3 8 17	- + Borderline
6	10	5	7		-
93	2	16	-65 OTHER PROBS
5 4 8	6	15	- 0 5. ActOppSex$
4 3 7	4 5	3 13	- 0 6. BM Out
84		-60 0 15.CruelAnim
2 6	1 4	11	- 0 18.HarmSelf
	5	2 10	- 0 24.NotEat
3	3	9	-55 0 28.EatNonFood
69			- 1 29.Fears
2 1 4	3	8	- 0 30.FearSchool
###	2 2 1 7	-50 0 36.Accidents
50 ### ### 0-2	### ### ### ### ###	- 0 44.BiteNail

I WITHDRAWN	II SOMATIC COMPLAINTS	III ANXIOUS/DEPRESSED	IV SOCIAL PROBLEMS	V THOUGHT PROBLEMS	VI ATTENTION PROBLEMS	VII DELINQUENT BEHAVIOR	VIII AGGRESSIVE BEHAVIOR	OTHER PROBS
0 42.Rather BeAlone	0 51. Dizzy	0 12.Lonely	0 1. Acts Young	0 9. Mind Off	0 1. Acts Young	0 26.NoGuilt	1 3. Argues	0 47.Nightmares
0 65.Won't Talk	0 54. Tired	0 14.Cries	0 11.Clings	0 40.Hears Things	0 8. Concen-trate	0 39.BadCompan	0 7. Brags	0 49.Constipate
0 69.Secret-ive	0 56a.Aches	0 31.FearDoBad	0 25.NotGet Along	0 66.Repeats Acts	0 10.Sit Still	0 43.LieCheat	0 16.Mean	0 53.Overeat
0 75.Shy	0 56b.Head-aches	1 32.Perfect	1 38.Teased	0 70.Sees Things	1 17.Day-dream	0 63.PrefOlder	0 19.DemAttn	0 56h.OtherPhys
0 80.Stares	0 56c.Nausea	0 33.Unloved	0 48.Not Liked	0 80.Stares*	0 41.Impulsv	0 67.RunAway	0 20.DestOwn	0 59.SexPrtsP$
1 88.Sulks	0 56d.Eye	0 34.OutToGet	0 55.Over-Weight*	0 84.Strange Behav	0 45.Nervous	0 72.SetFires	0 21 DestOthr	0 60.SexPrtsM$
0 102.Under-active	0 56e.Skin	0 35.Worthless	0 62.Clumsy	0 85.Strange Ideas	0 46.Twitch*	0 81.StealHome	0 22.DisbHome*	0 73.SexProbs$
0 103.Sad	0 56f.Stomach	0 45.Nervous	0 64.Prefers Young	0 TOTAL	0 61.Poor School	0 82.StealOut	0 23.DisbSchl	0 77.SleepMore
0 111.With-drawn	0 56g.Vomit	0 50.Fearful	1 TOTAL	50 T SCORE	0 62.Clumsy	0 90.Swears	0 27.Jealous	0 78.SmearBM
1 TOTAL	0 TOTAL	0 52.Guilty	50 T SCORE		0 80.Stares	0 96.ThnkSex*$	0 37.Fights	0 79.SpeechProb
50 T SCORE	50 T SCORE	1 71.SelfConsc			1 TOTAL	0 101.Truant	0 57.Attacks	0 83.StoresUp
		0 89.Suspic			50 T SCORE	0 105.AlcDrugs	0 68.Screams	0 91.TalkSuicid
		0 103.Sad				0 106.Vandal*	0 74.ShowOff	0 92.SleepWalk
		1 112.Worries				0 TOTAL	0 86.Stubborn	0 98.ThumbSuck
		3 TOTAL				50 T SCORE	0 87.MoodChng	0 99.TooNeat
		52 T SCORE					0 93.TalkMuch	0 100.SleepProb
							0 94.Teases	0 107.WetsSelf
							0 95.Temper	0 108.WetsBed
							0 97.Threaten	1 109.Whining
							0 104.Loud	0 110.WshOpSex$
							0 TOTAL	0 113.OtherProb
							50 T SCORE	

*Items Not on Cross-Informant Construct

Not in Total Problem Score
0 2.Allergy 0 4.Asthma

IX SEX PROBLEMS
0 TOTAL SCORE
50 T SCORE
$=Item on Sex Probs Syndrome

FIGURE 17.4 Follow-up CBCL completed by Julie's mother.

treatment was not incestuous, although her neighbor was a known and trusted individual; the abuse occurred two times, rather than frequently; no penetration had occurred, although she was fondled by the perpetrator; and her parents believed her as soon as she told them what happened. Consequently, she presented with relatively few symptoms compared with many sexually abused children (e.g., encopresis, sexual acting out). Treatment of Julie's nightmares, fear of the bathroom, and fear of being alone was relatively brief, although successful. Julie and her family appeared to have been functioning well prior to the neighbor's abuse of Julie. Because of this, and the fact that attention was paid to her disclosure relatively soon after the abuse, these symptoms may not have had a chance to become more serious, and thus difficult to treat.

For cognitive-behavioral play therapy to be effective, it must provide structured, goal-directed activities, as well as allow time for the child to bring spontaneous material to the session. By allowing the child the opportunity for unstructured play, he or she may convey information that might not arise if sessions are entirely structured and therapist directed. An example from the present case occurred when Julie wished to play with the clay. The therapist permitted her to do this, but at some point focused Julie's play by requesting that she make a clay figure of the perpetrator. Through her clay representations of herself and the perpetrator, Julie conveyed angry feelings at the perpetrator, along with her perception that he had deprived her of any control. The play structured by the therapist allowed Julie to express her feelings and gather a sense of control.

Our experience suggests that cognitive-behavioral play therapy is effective with a wide range of sexually abused children (Ruma, 1993). One cannot necessarily generalize Julie's treatment to work with children who have suffered more extensive abuse. It is most likely that the treatment itself would not differ; however, the length of time in treatment might be significantly increased for a child who had been multiply abused over a long period of time. Other issues may influence both the type and duration of treatment. For example, a child whose disclosure is not believed by his or her parents will likely bring additional issues of mistrust to therapy that will need to be addressed in treatment. Similarly, abuse by a family member may present additional problems, often related to the division of family loyalties, which add other issues to be addressed in treatment.

A wide range of techniques and approaches can be incorporated into cognitive-behavioral play therapy. The approaches utilized most successfully with sexually abused children include bibliotherapy, drawings, art, and puppet play. With Julie, all of these approaches were used to desensitize her to feelings associated with the abuse, give her the courage to disclose details of the abuse, show how others learn to cope with their feelings, help to identify and correct maladaptive distortions about the abuse, and reinstate a sense of control over her life. Although they were not used this way with Julie, in some cases, drawings and bibliotherapy are also used to convey to an abused child that other children are similarly maltreated and experience similar feelings, as well as to teach prevention skills.

In using cognitive-behavioral play therapy, one must be flexible and able to change modalities as needed. For instance, when it was clear that Julie was not able to tell the story of abuse on her own, puppets were incorporated into the drawing techniques. Similarly, puppet play was introduced into the first family session for the same reason. When using cognitive-behavioral play therapy with sexually abused children, the therapist needs to estimate the child's readiness to disclose the details of the abuse through the drawing technique. If the therapist finds that the child is not yet able to tolerate this level of anxiety, it will be necessary to first introduce less threatening modalities. Whether or not a perpetrator overtly threatens a child not to disclose what has happened, there is often a covert or perceived threat that makes disclosure, especially for very young children, difficult.

One important goal is to help the child generalize learned behaviors to the natural environment from the therapeutic setting, as well as to maintain adaptive behaviors learned after the treatment has ended. The therapist must incorporate these goals into treatment, rather than assuming they will occur naturally. In the present case, generalization and response prevention were incorporated in a number of ways, including teaching and reinforcement of self-protection skills and puppet play to teach Julie the skills should she need to disclose any future abuse. Additionally, the parents were provided guidelines for what to expect in regard to normal sexual development, so that they could be aware of any problems that might arise in the future. Finally, open communication and discussion were modeled for the family and encouraged in an effort to prevent future problems. One final aspect of importance in cognitive-behavioral play therapy with sexually abused children is for the therapist to handle termination in a way that does not contribute to the child's potential difficulties with trust and feelings of abandonment. It is often helpful to hold a celebration to mark the child's achievements at the termination of therapy. This occasion can be used to reinforce the child's sense of self-control, as well as to help him or her see what has been accomplished through his or her own efforts in treatment.

REFERENCES

Achenbach, T. M. (1991). *Manual for the Child Behavior Checklist 4–18 and 1991 Profile*. Burlington: University of Vermont, Department of Psychiatry.

Bandura, A.(1969). *Principles of behavior modification*. New York: Holt, Rinehart & Winston.

Bandura, A., & Menlove, F. L. (1968). Factors determining vicarious extinction of avoidance behavior through symbolic modeling. *Journal of Personality and Social Psychology, 8*, 99–108.

Beck, A. T., & Emery, G. (1985). *Anxiety disorders and phobias: A cognitive perspective*. New York: Basic Books.

Beitchman, J. H., Zucker, K. J., Hood, J. E., da Costa, G. A., & Akman, D. (1991). A review of the short-term effects of child sexual abuse. *Child Abuse and Neglect, 15*, 537–556.

Browne, A., & Finkelhor, D. (1986). Initial and long-term effects: A review of the research. In D. Finkelhor, S. Araji, L. Baron, A. Browne, S. D. Peters, & G. E. Wyatt (Eds.), *A sourcebook on child sexual abuse* (pp. 143–179). Beverly Hills, CA: Sage.

Campbell, S. (1990). *Behavior problems in preschool children.* New York: Guilford Press.

Davis, N. (1988). *Once upon a time: Therapeutic stories.* Oxon Hill, MD: Nancy Davis.

Deblinger, E., McCleer, S. V., & Henry, D. (1990). Cognitive behavioral treatment for sexually abused children suffering post-traumatic stress: Preliminary findings. *American Academy of Child and Adolescent Psychiatry, 29,* 747–752.

Emery, G., Bedrosian, R., & Garber, J. (1983). Cognitive therapy with depressed children and adolescents. In D. P. Cantwell & G. A. Carlson (Eds.), *Affective disorders in childhood and adolescence—An update* (pp. 445 -471). New York: Spectrum.

Finkelhor, D. (1990). Early and long-term effects of child sexual abuse: An update. *Professional Psychology: Research and Practice, 21,* 325–330.

Finkelhor, D., & Browne, A. (1986). Initial and long-term effects: A conceptual framework. In D. Finkelhor, S. Araji, L. Baron, A. Browne, S. D. Peters, & G. E. Wyatt (Eds.), *A sourcebook of child sexual abuse* (pp. 180–198). Beverly Hills, CA: Sage.

Friedrich, W. N. (1990). *Psychotherapy of sexually abused children and their families.* New York: Norton.

Gelman, R., & Baillargeon, R. (1983). A review of some Piagetian concepts. In J. H. Flavell & E. M. Markman (Eds.), *Handbook of child psychology: Vol. 3. Cognitive development* (pp. 167–230). New York: Wiley.

Gil, E. (1991). *The healing power of play.* New York: Guilford Press.

Harter, S. (1977). A cognitive-developmental approach to children's expression of conflicting feelings and a technique to facilitate such expression in play therapy. *Journal of Consulting and Clinical Psychology, 45,* 417–432.

Harter, S. (1983). Cognitive-developmental considerations in the conduct of play therapy. In C. Schaefer & K. J. O'Connor (Eds.), *Handbook of play therapy* (pp. 95–127). New York: Wiley.

Janoff-Bulman, R. (1979). Characterological versus behavioral self-blame: Inquiries into depression and rape. *Journal of Personality and Social Psychology, 37,* 1798–1809.

Kendall, P. C. (1991). *Child and adolescent therapy.* New York: Guilford Press.

Kendall-Tackett, K. A., Williams, L. M., & Finkelhor, D. (1993). Impact of sexual abuse on children: A review and synthesis of recent empirical studies. *Psychological Bulletin, 113,* 164–180.

Knell, S. M. (1993a). *Cognitive-behavioral play therapy.* Hillsdale, NJ: Jason Aronson.

Knell, S. M. (1993b). To show and not tell: Cognitive-behavioral play therapy. In T. Kottman & C. Schaefer (Eds), *Play therapy in action* (pp. 169–208). Hillsdale, NJ: Jason Aronson.

Knell, S. M. (1994). Cognitive-behavioral play therapy. In K. O'Connor &

C. Schaefer (Eds.), *Handbook of play therapy* (Vol. 2, pp. 111–142). New York: Wiley.

Major, B., Mueller, P., & Hildebrandt, K. (1985). Attributions, expectations, and coping with abortion. *Journal of Personality and Social Psychology, 48,* 585–599.

Marlatt, G. A., & Gordon, J. R. (Eds.). (1985). *Relapse prevention: Maintenance strategies in the treatment of addictive behaviors.* New York: Guilford Press.

Meichenbaum, D. (1971). Examination of model characteristics in reducing avoidance behavior. *Journal of Personality and Social Psychology, 17,* 298–307.

Meichenbaum, D. (1977). *Cognitive-behavior modification: An integrative approach.* New York: Plenum Press.

Meichenbaum, D. (1985). *Stress inoculation training.* New York: Pergamon Press.

Piaget, J. (1926). *The language and thought of the child.* London: Routledge & Kegan Paul.

Piaget, J. (1928). *Judgment and reasoning in the child.* London: Routledge & Kegan Paul.

Piaget, J. (1930). *The child's conception of physical causality.* New York: Harcourt, Brace & World.

Porter, F. S., Blick, L. C., & Sgroi, S. M. (1982). Treatment of the sexually abused child. In S. M. Sgroi (Ed.), *Handbook of clinical intervention in child sexual abuse* (pp. 109–146). Lexington, KY: Lexington Books.

Ruma, C. (1993). Cognitive-behavioral play therapy with sexually abused children. In S. M. Knell (Ed.), *Cognitive-behavioral play therapy* (pp. 199–230). Hillsdale, NJ: Jason Aronson.

Sgroi, S. (1982). *Handbook of clinical intervention in child sexual abuse.* Lexington, KY: Lexington Books.

Shapiro, J. P. (1989). Self-blame versus helplessness in sexually abused children: An attributional analysis with treatment recommendations. *Journal of Social and Clinical Psychology, 8,* 442–455

Shirk, S. R. (1988). Introduction: A cognitive-developmental perspective on child psychotherapy. In S. R. Shirk (Ed.), *Cognitive development and child psychotherapy* (pp. 1–16). New York: Plenum Press.

Walker, L. E., & Bolkovatz, M. S. (1988). Play therapy with children who have experienced sexual assault. In L. Walker (Ed.), *Handbook of sexual abuse of children* (pp. 249–269). New York: Springer.

Wilkes, T. C. R., Belsher, G., Rush, A. J., Frank, E., & Associates. (1994). *Cognitive therapy for depressed adolescents.* New York: Guilford Press.

Zarb, J. (1992). *Cognitive-behavioral assessment and therapy with adolescents.* New York: Brunner/Mazel.

18

Treatment of a High-Functioning Adolescent with Autism

A Cognitive-Behavioral Approach

Catherine Lord

Formal cognitive-behavioral methods have typically not been a major form of treatment of autism. However, several of the tenets of cognitive-behavioral therapy are very similar to principles typically used in interventions with individuals with autism. One important concept is that what seem like irrational acts often make sense when one understands the meaning of particular actions to the person who is carrying them out. Thus, an autistic boy may have a tantrum during large group activities because this results in his having "time-out" in a quiet room, which he finds less overstimulating. An autistic girl may slap her own face when asked to move from snack time to speech therapy because she does not understand where she is going or why she is being taken away from food. An adolescent with autism may recite commercials as a way of using his or her limited spontaneous language to participate in a conversation. In each case, the particular behavior has to be interpreted in terms of the context in which it occurs and the role it serves for the child. This assumption is the basis for a number of communication interventions for autism (Carr, 1977). The implication for *treatment* is that when autistic children or adults engage in unusual behaviors, these behaviors may be attempts at communicating intentions that they do not know how to express in other ways (Schopler & Reichler, 1971). These behaviors may be changed by providing alternative ways of communicating, such as gesture or sign language, or by addressing the situation(s) that maintain them.

Cognitive-behavioral theories often are based on the assumption that clients possess the ability to think and act in ways appropriate for the situation, but because of their understanding or expectations in the situation, they do otherwise. The focus is on teaching cognitive skills or on rectifying cognitive processes (Spence, 1994). This assumption is not necessarily appropriate for autism. Autistic children and adults often do, in fact, lack very basic social behaviors typically seen in normally developing infants (Lord, 1991). For example, deficits in the use of referential looking, responsive vocalization, or the linking of speech and socially directed facial expressions are defining characteristics of autism across chronological age and development. Thus, the problem for the client is not just one of selecting an appropriate behavior on the basis of a reasonable understanding of the situation, but also of having access to the behavior in the first place. Teaching an autistic child not to grab objects from others will be most effective if he or she has an alternative method for obtaining objects.

In addition, a number of theories contend that the primary deficit in autism, or at least in autism without mental handicap, has to do with differences in specific aspects of thinking, such as metarepresentation and "theory of mind" (Baron-Cohen, Leslie, & Frith, 1985). These theories focus on difficulties autistic individuals have understanding what other people know. For example, autistic children have difficulty in understanding that someone has a false belief about a situation, such as not realizing that a friend had to leave unexpectedly (Baron-Cohen, Tager-Flusberg, & Cohen, 1993). It has also been suggested that autism reflects a specific deficit in metarepresentation, that is, the ability to think about thinking or about other forms of representation (Leslie, 1987). This deficit affects play and pretending as well as other aspects of cognitive development. A child who does not realize that not everyone has the same knowledge he or she does or thinks in the same way he or she does is at a definite disadvantage socially.

If such deficits represent the essence of autism, use of "standard" cognitive techniques that require self-evaluation and reflection may be problematic (Kanfer, 1975; Stark, 1990); hence, the need to be clinically flexible and developmentally sensitive. Many individuals with autism also lack the language skills typically required for careful assessment of cognitive schemas (Kazdin, Colbus, & Rodgers, 1986). Several researchers question the appropriateness of cognitive treatment for children under 12 or 13 years of age, a developmental and language level reached by few adolescents with autism.

Within these limitations, the following case study illustrates ways in which a modified form of cognitive-behavioral treatment was employed to help an adolescent with autism reduce obsessive behaviors and cope with frustration. The assumption underlying the methods employed was that helping the client to label his own feelings and thoughts and to communicate these thoughts and feelings to others would reduce difficult behaviors and anxieties. The intervention was in accord with cognitive-behavioral approaches, including self-monitoring, affective education, cognitive restructuring, and self-instruction training. In addition, the goal of replacing maladaptive thoughts with more positive, goal-oriented cognitions, is similar to more traditional cognitive-behavioral therapies carried out with other populations.

CASE ILLUSTRATION

History

A 19-year-old young man with autism, whom we will call "Jeremy," was diagnosed with autism when he was 4½ years old. At that time, he was independently judged to meet criteria of the third edition of the *Diagnostic and Statistical Manual of Mental Disorders* (DSM-III; American Psychiatric Association, 1980) by several child psychiatrists and clinical psychologists. His score on the Childhood Autism Rating Scale (CARS; Schopler, Reichler, & Renner, 1988) was 34 (30 is generally used as the cutoff for autism). He also currently met ICD-10/DSM-IV draft (American Psychiatric Association, 1994) diagnostic criteria on the basis of the Autism Diagnostic Interview (Le Couteur et al., 1989)

Jeremy had a history of very delayed language development. At age 5, he communicated primarily through repetitions of stereotyped phrases, many of them learned from television. He seldom used speech in a socially directed manner. As a young child, he had taught himself to read and to type and enjoyed typing phrases from commercials (although not always things that he had actually seen spelled out), when given access to a typewriter.

Jeremy had a history of a significant discrepancies in his verbal and nonverbal abilities. By age 19, his language was fluent but very repetitive. Typically, he scored higher on expressive than on receptive language scales. Although his test scores varied over the years, he generally received verbal/IQ scores between 50 and 60, with performance scores varying from 80 to 113, depending on whether the test was timed and the degree to which the test focused on visual–spatial matching or conceptual material (such as the Raven's Progressive Matrices or the Leiter International Performance Scale, on which he scored in the average to above-average range) versus more social material, such as in the Picture Arrangement subtest of the Wechsler Intelligence Scale for Children—Revised (on which he consistently scored more than two standard deviations below the mean; Wechsler, 1974).

Jeremy lived with his parents, who were in their mid- to late 40s, and an older brother, Ted, who was in his early 20s. Ted also showed many autistic behaviors but had never received a formal diagnosis of autism. Ted had graduated from high school, but had many difficulties during his last few years of school. He had never found employment and had a history of substance abuse, that, by parental report, was under control at the time of this intervention. Ted was currently attending a local junior college and had minimal interactions with any of his family members, although he lived at home. Their parents were well-educated, gentle people who had remained remarkably cheerful in their dealings with professionals after years of challenges in seeking services for their two boys. They had received family therapy and counseling intermittently over the years but were often uncomfortable asking for help or discussing difficulties. The father was frequently out of town as part of his job. This was a source of distress for Jeremy's mother, who worked part time at a nearby hospital but sometimes felt overwhelmed by her responsibilities.

At the time of the referral, Jeremy was in a categorical class for autistic adolescents in a special public school for handicapped children. One teacher and two full-time assistants worked in the classroom with six students. Jeremy had been in the same class for nearly 6 years, with few changes in classmates. He had had the same teacher for the last 3 years. Jeremy had been in a noncategorical preschool program and in an elementary class for mentally handicapped children. He was then placed in special classrooms for autistic children, most of which were in special schools. In Jeremy's current placement, he was by far the most verbal and highest functioning student. Another student, with whom Jeremy had gone to school, had graduated the previous summer. This changed the makeup of the class so that the majority of students were now nonverbal.

Jeremy had a history of obsessional behavior, beginning when he was about 13 years old. He also had a history of violent behavior at home, particularly toward his mother. The precipitant for the referral was an increase in the severity and frequency of this behavior at home. Violent behavior was also beginning to occur at school, directed only to his main teacher. In addition, there had been an increase in rituals and compulsive behaviors, particularly at home, but also at school, including a fear of things happening twice, the need to walk in certain patterns and touch certain walls and furniture, and an expressed desire to type lists and recite cartoons. These actions were phenomenologically similar to behaviors seen among children with obsessive–compulsive disorder without autism. Jeremy had also recently begun to hit himself on the head at home and at school, and to destroy objects at home occasionally, such as throwing a computer through a window. Such behaviors had been seen in the past (since about age 13), but had been relatively rare. All of these difficulties (except throwing objects) occurred frequently throughout the day.

In the current assessment, it was sometimes possible to identify the precipitant of Jeremy's aggressive, violent behavior, and sometimes not. The most common, identifiable precipitant was his need to avoid doing something twice. For example, if Jeremy was trying to get his pants on and did not get his foot in the pant leg correctly the first time, he would rip the pants off his body and scream because he did not want to have to do it twice. If he got into a car and his mother had to turn the key twice in the ignition, Jeremy would scream, have a tantrum, and hit her. For this reason, his family began the custom of never turning the ignition off when Jeremy was present, so that there was no possibility that they would turn the key twice. When Jeremy was upset, he shouted statements such as "I'm stupid!" "My head is going crazy!" "My brain doesn't work right!"

Another of Jeremy's compulsive behaviors was to recite cartoons. He insisted that his mother answer him in certain ways, playing the part of cartoon characters. If she did not do this, Jeremy would badger her, begin to hit himself and, occasionally, hit her until she did so. Consequently, Jeremy's mother generally answered him in whatever manner he wanted.

Interventions

For over a year, Jeremy had been attending a social group for autistic adolescents and adults on a weekly basis through a clinic for individuals with developmental disorders. During the social group, a card system called "Checks for Cokes" was instituted, so that for every 15 minutes that Jeremy did "well" (i.e., did not act inappropriately), he could give himself a check. Jeremy carried this card in his shirt pocket and knew to give the card to one of the group leaders on a regular basis. As shown in Figure 18.1, when Jeremy had earned four checks, he could engage in 5 minutes of "silly talk" alone in the bathroom or in a separate room. If he received five checks without needing "silly talk," he was then allowed to purchase a soft drink from a vending machine. This system was instituted because of Jeremy's frequent demands that others answer his questions and enact cartoons, as well as frequently making negative statements about himself. The system was quite effective. Although Jeremy's behavior still ranged from being very agitated during the social group to being more or less calm, this method reduced the episodes of violence and silly talk to almost zero on almost all occasions. However, it should be noted that there were two group meetings (out of 20 over a 6-month period), during which Jeremy became so agitated that he needed to be removed from the group. He was allowed to sit by himself or talk to one of the leaders (which was seen as a neutral consequence) for the remainder of the time.

```
┌─────────────────────────────────────────┐
│            Checks for Cokes             │
│                                         │
│  ✓     = No silly talk                  │
│        No hitting or throwing           │
│                                         │
│           7:00–7:15 ✓                   │
│           7:15–7:30 ✓                   │
│           7:30–7:45                     │
│           7:45–8:00 ✓                   │
│           8:00–8:15                     │
│           8:15–8:30 ✓                   │
│                                         │
│        4 ✓s  = 5 minutes of silly talk  │
│        5 ✓s  = coke                     │
└─────────────────────────────────────────┘
```

FIGURE 18.1. Jeremy's "Checks for Cokes" card.

A separate cognitive-behavioral program was instituted at school. As shown in Table 18.1, lists of inappropriate behaviors were posted in various parts of the classroom, so that they were visible to Jeremy and to the teachers at all times. On this list were included not only the behaviors that Jeremy was not to do (which included hitting [self or others], throwing things, or shouting), but also alternative behaviors in which he could engage, including lying on a mat and hitting a pillow. As described in other programs (Graziano, Mooney, Huber, & Ignasiak, 1979; Grossman & Hughes, 1992), a variety of techniques was employed. Jeremy was given training in relaxation techniques and given access to a tape recorder and his own relaxation tape (Cautela & Groden, 1978).

Jeremy was given a card on which had been drawn a small thermometer. As shown in Figure 18.2, pasted on the thermometer was a red strip

TABLE 18.1. Jeremy's Choices

Do not:	Do:
Hit self or others	Hit pillow
Throw	Use thermometer
Shout	Lie on the mat
Use silly talk	Use relaxation tape

that Jeremy could move up and down to indicate his frustration level. Jeremy was taught to identify his frustration level by moving the red strip down to indicate calm, to intermediate positions that were labeled "Doing All Right" and "Feeling Worried," and to an end point labeled "Out of Control." Jeremy was prompted to use the thermometer every 15 minutes to identify how he felt. If Jeremy indicated that he was in the highest position, then alternative behaviors to whatever he was doing were suggested. If Jeremy identified himself as "Feeling Worried," then he was encouraged to carry out simple relaxation exercises involving breathing techniques and to visualize the check system. Jeremy was encouraged to look at his list, imagine a card full of checks, and to say to himself, "I'm getting worried, but I can do it." If the thermometer moved beyond this level, Jeremy was encouraged to complete whatever task he was working on (often the teacher was present and was able to reduce the task in some way so he could complete it quite rapidly) and to proceed to the mat, where he could lie down in the corner of the room and either hit the pillow or put it over his head. Lying on a mat is somewhat unusual behavior for a 6-foot tall, 19-year-old; however, Jeremy chose that position as the best way of limiting stimulation and getting control of himself. It was felt by the teachers that this position was helpful, because they were more easily

FIGURE 18.2. Jeremy's thermometer.

able to contain him if he wanted to jump up and destroy something or hurt someone.

Various other cognitive-behavioral techniques were used. For example, on the advice of a cognitive-behavioral therapist, his mother attempted to have Jeremy sit in the car, listening to his favorite music with earphones, while she repeatedly tried to start the car and failed. This technique of exposure with habituation and response prevention is often effective with anxiety disorders. However, in this case, Jeremy became extremely violent, attempted to hit his mother, leaped out of the car, and ran off before anyone could catch him. A passerby who witnessed Jeremy hitting his mother called the police. A police officer arrived, who was able to restrain Jeremy, but the incident was very upsetting, particularly for his mother.

We also attempted to determine what Jeremy thought would happen if something such as the turning of the car ignition did happen twice. However, Jeremy did not understand such questions presented orally or in writing. He typically answered in terms of what he would do (become upset, hit someone, become angry, turn red), rather than what he thought he was avoiding by preventing things from happening twice.

Jeremy also had trials of a range of medications including lithium, Haldol, chlorpromazine, Orap, and fluoxetine. Field trials of fluoxetine resulted in some minimizing of his agitation and increased his ability to focus on tasks, but this effect was not maintained after the initial 6-week period, and he became increasingly agitated and uncomfortable.

Summary and Conclusions

Overall, the combined intervention of using a card to monitor Jeremy's levels of arousal and access various privileges, as well as to provide a visible indicator of state and a written reminder of rules, was moderately effective. Aggressive behaviors shown by Jeremy during the first 2 months of the school year were reduced, with weeks during which there were no incidents (with two notable exceptions), until February of the following year. However, in February, Jeremy's violent behavior began to increase at home and then at school. At that time, Jeremy was gradually weaned from lithium, which he had been placed on after fluoxetine, because it was felt that the medication was having no lasting effect. He was eventually suspended from school because of violent behavior toward his teacher. He had also become aggressive with other students. The school recommended inpatient treatment, but it was not possible to find an inpatient program experienced with autism that would accept Jeremy and with which his parents felt comfortable. Local community-based group homes all had long waiting lists and were not able to take Jeremy because of his need for intense supervision and the possible danger to staff and other clients. He remained at home throughout the school year and the summer. Much of his aggression decreased, as did his obsessive behaviors. However, his parents felt they were not in a position to control his behavior. They continued to avoid occasions when something would happen twice. They also regularly participated in his cartoon enactments and some of his other obsessions. They used the card (Checks for Cokes) when they went places that Jeremy enjoyed, (i.e., McDonald's) and used the thermometer in situations that were likely to be difficult (e.g., a new restaurant, church). They were pleased with the information and control these interventions gave them.

CONCLUSIONS

This case study describes the ways in which focused, cognitive-behavioral interventions can be employed in treating patients with autism. Although these interventions were moderately effective, much was left to be desired. Various cognitive-behavioral strategies are appropriate for use with clients with autism, including self-monitoring and self-evaluation; providing a self-observation, relaxation training; and the use of visible indices to reflect thoughts and feelings. On the other hand, this case also represents the limitations of these techniques, particularly when dealing with adolescents and adults who are aggressive or violent, situations in which the stakes are too high to allow placement of an individual in a deliberately upsetting situation to be tested. Had more appropriate support services been available, that is, either inpatient placement or round-the-clock home-based behavior technicians, it is not clear whether more could have been done to use the cognitive methods delineated. At one point, for example, a home-based therapist worked with Jeremy's mother on a daily basis to arrange positive activities for him after school. The goal was to provide Jeremy with some other sources of pleasure than his obsessions. This was successful for a brief period of time, but was very taxing for Jeremy's parents. It was terminated when they felt they had learned as much as they could and wanted to attempt to carry out the program on their own.

Jeremy's parents were desperate for help, but were unable to carry out several of the interventions. For example, they could not use the card with checks or the lists at home, although they could use them when they went out. In part, this was because Jeremy's father was often out of town and his mother felt powerless to deal with Jeremy's physical assaults. Jeremy's family did not feel able to modify their behavior at this time, and could not accept the possibility of his living out-of-state (which would have been necessary in order to find an appropriate inpatient program). Home-based support was not available with sufficient intensity, nor was staff with sufficient experience available on a regular basis to be very useful. These limitations highlight the importance of treating or examining behavior in its social context, and of designing interventions that can be implemented with the resources available. As for the situation of many other young people with severe behavioral difficulties, questions continue not only as to what should be done, but also as to who can and will do it.

Altogether, cognitive-behavioral methods have potential as methods of dealing with behavioral difficulties of autistic children and adults. However, given the pervasiveness and the severity of the disorder that we call autism, and also given the extent of cognitive and language handicaps experienced by most individuals with autism, it seems important to be realistic about the goals for interventions and the need for other methods and appropriate support services.

REFERENCES

American Psychiatric Association. (1980). *Diagnostic and statistical manual of mental disorders* (3rd ed.). Washington, DC: Author.

American Psychiatric Association. (1994). *Diagnostic and statistical manual of mental disorders* (4th ed.). Washington, DC: Author.

Baron-Cohen, S., Leslie, A. M., & Frith, U. (1985). Does the autistic child have a "theory of mind"? *Cognition, 21,* 37–46.

Baron-Cohen, S., Tager-Flusberg, H., & Cohen, D. (1993). *Understanding other minds: Perspectives from autism.* Oxford: Oxford University Press.

Carr, E. (1977). The motivation of self-injurious behavior: A review of some hypotheses. *Psychological Bulletin, 84,* 800–816.

Cautela, J., & Groden, J. (1978). *Relaxation.* Champaign, IL: Research Press.

Graziano, A. M., Mooney, K. C., Huber, C., & Ignasiak, D. (1979). Self control instruction for children's fear reduction. *Journal of Behavior Therapy and Experimental Psychiatry, 10,* 221–227.

Grossman, P. B., & Hughes, J. N. (1992). Self control interventions with internalizing disorders: A review and analysis. *School Psychology Review, 21,* 229–245.

Kanfer, F. H. (1975). Self management methods. In F. H. Kanfer & A. P. Goldstein (Eds.), *Helping people change* (pp. 309–355). New York: Pergamon Press.

Kazdin, A. E., Colbus, D., & Rodgers, A. (1986). Assessment of depression and diagnosis of depressive disorder among psychiatrically disturbed children. *Journal of Abnormal Child Psychology, 14*(4), 499–515.

Kendall, P. C., & Chansky, T. E. (1991). Considering cognition in anxiety disordered youth. *Journal of Anxiety Disorders, 5,* 167–185.

Le Couteur, A., Rutter M., Lord, C., Rios, P., Robertson, S., Holdgrafer, M., & McLennan, J. D. (1989). Autism Diagnostic Interview: A semi-structured interview for parents and caregivers of autistic persons. *Journal of Autism and Developmental Disorders, 19*, 363–387.

Leiter, R. (1979). *Leiter International Performance Scale: Instructional manual.* Wood Dale, IL: Stoelting.

Leslie, A. M. (1987). Pretense and representation: The origins of "theory of mind." *Psychological Review, 94*, 412–426.

Lord, C. (1991). A cognitive-behavioral model for the treatment of social-communicative deficits in adolescents with autism. In R. J. McMahon & R. D. Peters (Eds.), *Behavior disorders of adolescence* (pp. 155–174). New York: Plenum Press.

Raven, J. C. (1956). *Guide to using the Coloured Progressive Matrices.* London: H. K. Lewis.

Schopler, E., & Reichler, R. J. (1971). Developmental therapy by parents with their own autistic child. In M. Rutter (Ed.), *Infantile autism: Concepts, characteristics and treatment* (pp. 206–227). London: Churchill.

Schopler, E., Reichler, R. J., & Renner, B. R. (1988). *The Childhood Autism Rating Scale (CARS).* Los Angeles: Western Psychological Services.

Spence, S. H. (1994). Practitioner review: Cognitive therapy with children and adolescents: From theory to practice. *Journal of Child Psychology and Psychiatry, 35*, 1191–1228.

Stark, R. (1990). *Childhood depression: School-based intervention.* New York: Guilford Press.

Venter, A., Lord, C., & Schopler, E. (1992). A follow-up study of high-functioning autistic children. *Journal of Child Psychology and Psychiatry, 33*, 489–507.

Wechsler, D. (1974). *Manual for the Wechsler Intelligence Scale for Children—Revised.* San Antonio, TX: Psychological Corporation.

19

Concluding Comments

Mark A. Reinecke
Frank M. Dattilio
Arthur Freeman

During our initial discussion about the development of this text, we toyed with the title "Comprehensive Casebook of Cognitive Therapy with Children." After further consideration, however, we decided to drop this title because it would be difficult to produce a text that would adequately meet the criteria for "comprehensive." The field of cognitive-behavioral therapy with children is relatively young, the utility of many of the interventions described have not yet been tested empirically, and evidence for the generalizability and stability of therapeutic gains made by children who have received cognitive therapy is limited. Moreover, the processes mediating behavioral and emotional change during psychotherapy with children are not well understood. As such, an attempt to develop a "comprehensive" text would be premature. Rather, it was our intention to address selected topics that would be interesting and useful, but at the same time, unique to other texts of this caliber. Because we were somewhat limited as to space, we selected chapters that reflected issues frequently encountered by mental health professionals as well as topics that would appeal to a range of readers. There are, no doubt, many important topics that were not included in the text. Cognitive therapy has been employed, for example, in crisis intervention with teenagers and families, pediatric psychology, inpatient treatment of young children, pain management, and infant psychiatry. Similarly, issues of race, ethnicity, gender, and social class may be important in the development of effective treatment programs, and deserve careful consideration.

It was our aim to maintain a developmental focus, to base interventions on a sound understanding of the empirical literature, and to emphasize the interaction of cognitive, affective, behavioral, social, and environmental factors in children's adjustment and development. During recent years, a great deal of attention has been directed toward understanding cognitive concomitants of behavioral and emotional problems experienced by children. At the same time, a number of investigators have described an array of social, environmental, and interpersonal factors associated with adjustment problems during childhood. Unfortunately, these literatures have developed independently and there have been few attempts to develop integrated models for understanding the etiology of childhood psychopathology. In clinical practice, however, one must attend to the full range of factors—both cognitive and interpersonal—that may be contributing to or maintaining a child's difficulties. It is in this spirit that our contributors incorporated an understanding of each of these variables into their treatment programs.

As the 21st century approaches, it is our belief that cognitive-behavioral therapies will continue to be an intervention of choice for clinical practitioners. This is supported by the current goals of managed care, and by patients' desires for brief, problem-oriented treatment. Research suggests that cognitive therapy can be effective for treating a range of behavioral and emotional problems experienced by adults. The utility of cognitive therapy with children, although not yet demonstrated, remains promising. With this in mind, we hope that the readers will benefit from our efforts, as well as the efforts of our contributors.

Index